SCRUPULOUS
THOROUGH
FEARLESS

——— The ———
CPIB Story

SCRUPULOUS THOROUGH FEARLESS

—— The ——
CPIB Story

Clement Liew

Published by

World Scientific Publishing Co. Pte. Ltd.
5 Toh Tuck Link, Singapore 596224
USA office: 27 Warren Street, Suite 401-402, Hackensack, NJ 07601
UK office: 57 Shelton Street, Covent Garden, London WC2H 9HE

National Library Board, Singapore Cataloguing in Publication Data
Name(s): Liew, Clement.
Title: Scrupulous, thorough, fearless : the CPIB story / Clement Liew.
Description: Singapore : World Scientific Publishing Co. Pte. Ltd., [2022]
Identifier(s): ISBN 978-981-12-6271-5 (hardback) | 978-981-12-6723-9 (paperback) |
    978-981-12-6724-6 (Ebook for individuals) | 978-981-12-6725-3 (Ebook for institutions)
Subject(s): LCSH: Singapore. Corrupt Practices Investigation Bureau--History. |
    Corruption investigation--Singapore--History.
Classification: DDC 363.259323095957--dc23

British Library Cataloguing-in-Publication Data
A catalogue record for this book is available from the British Library.

Copyright © 2023 by Corrupt Practices Investigation Bureau

All rights reserved.

For any available supplementary material, please visit
https://www.worldscientific.com/worldscibooks/10.1142/13035#t=suppl

World Scientific team:
Chua Hong Koon, Yolande Koh, Ng Chin Choon, Nicole Ong, Lai Ann

Printed in Singapore

Foreword

Lee Hsien Loong
Prime Minister of Singapore

Singapore is recognised as one of the least corrupt countries in the world today. Being clean and incorrupt has become ingrained into our system and culture. But Singapore did not start off like this. During colonial days, corruption was widespread. This would have made it difficult for our young nation-state to address pressing issues of the day, including poverty, unemployment, housing shortage, poor public health and a stagnant economy.

Our founding leaders decided that building a clean and incorrupt Singapore was of utmost priority. When the PAP won the elections in 1959 and took their oath of office, they wore white shirts and trousers, symbolising their determination to keep the Government clean and incorruptible. This set the tone and standard which successive PAP governments have continued to reinforce and uphold.

We have spared no effort, nor anyone, in ensuring a clean and honest system in Singapore. We enacted the Prevention of Corruption Act, with a wide scope covering both public and private sectors, which put the burden of proof on the accused to show that he acquired his wealth legally.

But having tough laws was just one half of the equation. The laws also had to be vigorously enforced. We thus made the Corrupt Practices Investigation Bureau (CPIB) strictly independent, fully backed with funding and resources. We instituted checks and balances to "guard the guardians", to make sure that no one—not even the Prime Minister—is above scrutiny.

The late Mr Lee Kuan Yew commented that a key factor of Singapore's effective anti-corruption strategy is having a CPIB that is "Scrupulous, Thorough and Fearless" — the apt title of this commemorative book. It chronicles the Bureau's journey over the decades and tells the story of its struggles and fights against the evil of corruption. Indeed, CPIB has played an instrumental role in keeping Singapore corruption-free. On behalf of all Singaporeans, I thank the generations of CPIB officers for carrying out their mission fearlessly, resolutely, and relentlessly.

This book reminds us never to become complacent in our fight against corruption, and always to uphold the highest standards of honesty and integrity. Singapore's success depends on keeping our nation and society clean and non-corrupt. We must all do our part in this vital endeavour. We must never tolerate corruption.

I congratulate the CPIB on its 70th anniversary, and wish it every success for the years ahead.

Message

Goh Chok Tong
Emeritus Senior Minister

A fish rots from the head downwards, according to an ancient saying. Applied to modern institutions, it means that if its leadership is incompetent, the organisation will weaken. Applied to a country, it means that the country will decay if its leaders are corrupt.

Singapore must thank Mr Lee Kuan Yew and his Old Guard colleagues for placing integrity and competence at the heart of good governance. Without these two attributes, imagine where Singapore, a small, geographically disadvantaged country, might be today, and whether Singaporeans could hold their heads high anywhere in the world.

Singapore's success did not happen by chance but by the choices our founding generation of leaders made and the examples they set. They were determined to eradicate a corrupt way of life. They put in place strong laws, ensured an independent judiciary, cleaned up the public service and built up CPIB to enforce the laws against corruption resolutely.

More importantly, the values of integrity and incorruptibility are now ingrained in our society. All political leaders since independence have held them as absolute values. So too must future generations of leaders and Singaporeans.

CPIB is a central organisation that keeps Singapore clean. It must be free from political interference. In 1991, soon after I became Prime Minister, I introduced amendments to the Constitution of Singapore to have an elected President and to safeguard the appointment of the Director of CPIB.

The Prime Minister's choice of the Director is subject to the President's approval when hitherto it was not. The Constitution empowers the Director to go directly to the President should the Prime Minister stop him from investigating any individual under suspicion of corruption. This means that CPIB can investigate anyone, without political influence, favour or fear of reprisals.

Singapore must always uphold the highest standards of competence, integrity, and good governance. The dedicated men and women of the CPIB have worked tirelessly to fight corruption since 1952. Continue with your good work. Your success helps to prevent the Singapore Merlion from rotting.

Congratulations on your 70th anniversary, CPIB! Well done.

Preface

Denis Tang
Director Corrupt Practices Investigation Bureau

CPIB has been an integral part of our nation's legacy and heritage in the fight against corruption. This book is written in recognition of the sacrifices, the courage and the perseverance by generations of CPIB officers who have contributed in immense ways to ensure that all corruption cases are investigated fairly and thoroughly. Once called *The Incorruptibles*, they left no stones unturned as they sought justice and truth. They have put duty above self. Our pioneer Directors and officers have laid a solid foundation and paved the way for us to carry out our work professionally and efficiently. While they remain mostly unnamed in this book, their stories of guts and tenacity were demonstrated throughout the chapters. Most of the breakthroughs in the cases would not have been possible without them.

CPIB is not on its own. We would not have been able to fulfill our mission without the strong political will, the tough anti-corruption laws and penalties, and a constant vigilance against corruption by the citizenry. Our youths are our future and I hope they ensure that the seeds of anti-corruption are always rooted in our society. It is with this intent, that this history book is co-created with a group of students from the Yale-NUS College.

My heartfelt gratitude goes to officers past and present for being standfast and steadfast, and their family members for their staunch support all these years, and to our community partners who have worked conscientiously with us.

As CPIB commemorates its 70th year of existence, we recount the arduous anti-corruption journey to reach the current high standard. Our tenacity of purpose and commitment to fight corruption have left an indelible mark in the Bureau's history and legacy. CPIB is determined to uphold our duty and mission faithfully, to keep Singapore, our home which we hold dear, corruption-free and the best place to fulfill our aspirations and dreams.

Acknowledgements

Clare Tan
Senior Deputy Director (Planning, Research, Corporate Relations), CPIB
Lead, CPIB History Project Team

It has been a 3-year journey researching and writing this book, which would not have been possible without the invaluable assistance and numerous contributions from a number of people and institutions.

Professor Tan Tai Yong (who is the consultant for this book) and the students of Yale-NUS College, Nur Hazeem, Frances Pek, Joshua Tee and Tavis Tan, who co-created this publication with the CPIB History Project Team (Fong Bao Xian, Nuramira Ahmad, Chua Mei Xuan, Lee Choon Khiang, Ong Seng Hock, Ashley Santa Maria and Hairul Siddeeq). Their tireless efforts and strong commitment together with the writer, Clement Liew, have been instrumental in the successful completion of this book.

Oral history interviews with former CPIB Directors, retired and serving officers, as well as media editors have enriched the content of this book. A word of heartfelt thanks too to many other CPIB officers who have contributed their precious time and effort in the race to complete the book.

The National Archives of Singapore, the National Museum of Singapore, the Parliament of Singapore, the Singapore Police Force, the Singapore Land Authority, SPH Media Limited, the United Kingdom National Archives and the British Library must be acknowledged for their contributions to the publication as well.

Finally, Director CPIB Denis Tang and the Leadership Group warrant a very special mention for believing that only a history book can capture the rich heritage and legacy of the CPIB, and for giving the Project Team their utmost support and affirmation.

Contents

Foreword v
Message vii
Preface ix
Acknowledgements xi
Introduction xv

Part One: Legacy 1819–1945 1

Chapter One: Corruption & the Law in the Nineteenth Century 3
Chapter Two: Corrupt Practices & Punishment in Early Colonial Singapore 6
Chapter Three: From the Early Twentieth Century 29
Chapter Four: Syonan Days 41

Part Two: Laborious Birth 1945–1953 61

Chapter Five: Liberation, Rehabilitation & Challenges 63
Chapter Six: Corruption & Legislation 78
Chapter Seven: Anti-Corruption Branch 91
Chapter Eight: Prelude & Postlude 100
Chapter Nine: Opium Heist 105
Chapter Ten: Special Investigation Team 121
Chapter Eleven: Establishment 127

Part Three: Long & Winding Road 1953–1959 151

Chapter Twelve: On a Proper Footing 153

Chapter Thirteen: Constable at the Helm, on the Eve of Change ... 171
Chapter Fourteen: Stormy Seas & Rugged Road ... 188
Chapter Fifteen: PAP's Philosophy & Measures Against Corruption ... 211

Part Four: Nation-Building Journey 1959–1989 ... 237

Chapter Sixteen: Beginning with the Cleaning Up ... 240
Chapter Seventeen: Tackling the Culture of Corruption ... 258
Chapter Eighteen: Vanguard! ... 282
Chapter Nineteen: Headwinds ... 295
Chapter Twenty: For Home & Country ... 311

Part Five: Vigilance & Readiness 1989–2010 ... 337

Chapter Twenty-One: Trends & Measures Towards the New Millennium ... 340
Chapter Twenty-Two: Being Ready ... 363
Chapter Twenty-Three: Standards, Capabilities & Engagements ... 375
Chapter Twenty-Four: In Retrospect ... 380

Part Six: Metamorphosis & Roots 2010–2022 ... 389

Chapter Twenty-Five: Challenges in a Changing Time & Climate ... 392
Chapter Twenty-Six: Metamorphosis ... 409
Chapter Twenty-Seven: Planting for the Future ... 428

Afterword: Reflections from Our Youths ... 441

Introduction

The story of the CPIB is intertwined with the story of Singapore's journey as a nation. This narrative starts in the colonial times, as there is a need to know and understand our past before our present and future journey can be better appreciated. This is one of the more important contributions of this book; it provides a richer contextualisation of the place of the Bureau in the national discourse surrounding change and nation-building. In tracing the origins of the social values of Singapore's colonial society by walking through the years of the nineteenth century into the twentieth century, one can examine the forces of corruption as well as change that created the status quo when the Bureau came into being in the 1950s. The overarching question in this narrative journey is the very nature of corruption in Singapore society. Few in the country today still remember the wild days when a gift or token of appreciation was not only customary, but even expected by those who served the public. This was also not a time when the people of the land frowned upon such practices.

In pre-war colonial times, most people in Singapore were immigrants and sojourners with little or no resources. While the wealthy mercantile community had the means to pay a little to accelerate essential and desired services, the not so well-off found themselves parting with much-needed earnings or savings to land jobs or secure spaces or licences to ply their wares or sell cooked food. Often, in those early days, the health inspectors or street constables wielded great authority to make or break any individual. All that was needed was a little *kopi* money for the enforcement officer to turn a blind eye or to just move on. Under such conditions, the street-smart survivalist quickly learnt the way to get by. This was essentially how tolerance for petty corruption became entrenched in the colonial days.

▶ Scrupulous, Thorough, Fearless

Besides, most of the domiciled people of the land, up till the early 1950s, were not highly educated. Many were even illiterate. They needed to work in order to have enough to eat, pay rent and send money home to the land of their origins. Singapore was their home in their sojourn, but certainly not their homeland on which they could grow roots. So, the norms and practices which helped everyone get by simply persisted till Singapore's nation-building journey commenced.

Besides the general poverty that fuelled wants, there were vices whose perpetrators were only too willing to pay any sum to escape detection or detention because the pay-off for their trades had been far more lucrative than the losses suffered on account of the bribes. In the nineteenth century, while the government revenue farms, which included liquor and opium, mainly controlled the corruption which could have been associated with these vices, it was gaming, or gambling, which had become the big-money vice that was the main corruptor of police peons and constables, the main public officers of the day. Of course, when the Chinese triads were pervasive in the mid-1800s, not only did the vices they controlled become syndicated, they even created a system of bribery of public officers. This resulted in a more serious problem after the Straits Settlements was detached from British India and became a Crown Colony from 1867 to 1870. With its own legislature and executive branch of government, there were more laws, rules and regulations, a regular law court, and many more government departments. Naturally, instances of bribery of government officers, other than police constables, also increased. By the 1920s, when the British Government and military started investing heavily in infrastructural works, bribery associated with the island's developmental work started becoming a source of corruption. Amongst these were conspiracies to circumvent the government's tender system. Basically, there was no official mind or political will to bring about change from above.

With all the privation and shortages during the years of the Japanese Occupation, corrupt practices in Singapore would reach a new peak. People just had to do what was necessary to survive, including dealing with the black market to get whatever was needed; many of these items were either stolen or pilfered from government stores. The subsequent liberation did little to alleviate the corruption problem. As shortages, inflation and unemployment continued, so did the range of corrupt activities. This was the socio-economic situation when the British Empire started decolonialising, and many colonies, including Singapore, were undergoing constitutional development. Local leaders quickly learnt that to build a nation on a solid foundation, enforcement and laws were not enough; the promulgation of the 1937 Prevention of Corruption Ordinance and the establishment of the Anti-Corruption Branch in 1940 saw almost no change in the state of affairs. The nation had to be forged with new attitudes, and a set of core values based on an ethos of a clean society and government. There was a need for a strong government with the political will to see through changes, and for good men to helm the government.

Although the CPIB was created as a result of a law enforcement situation, its development was shaped by the socio-political conditions of the milieu. While the government needed to instil the necessary values required to forge the Singapore nation and polity, the Bureau became an arm of the state that neutralised the corrosive effects corruption had on Singapore's society and economy. The Bureau maintained constant vigilance and fought corruption on a warpath till the mid-1980s when its labour started reaping positive results. By this time, Singapore was fast becoming known as a corruption-free state, and there were fewer public officers taken to task for corrupt acts. This was partly due to the emergence of a public service with an ethos that rejected corruption, and mainly because the Singapore Government had created a mostly graft-free society by the 1990s. By this time, many of its cases were from the private sector. These had to be dealt with resolutely. Unlike many other nations which only tackle public sector corruption, the Singapore Government considers corruption in the private sector as equally damaging to Singapore's reputation as a clean place with a level playing field for businesses and investments. In this light, even with a largely incorruptible and efficient Public Service, the work of the Bureau was still far from done. Entering the new millennium, the Bureau found itself having to keep up with the changing trends of the day, including modern day technological advances that made corruption in the private sector even more complex and challenging. One aspect of this challenge is the evolving transnational nature of corruption in the twenty-first century. The Bureau met this challenge by building bridges with other anti-corruption agencies across the globe.

Today, the CPIB has joined the national effort to work together with the citizenry and prepare itself for the future. Enforcement can only do so much. Transformation and changes achieved must be sustained and translated into the effective and resolute fight against corruption.

Part One

Legacy
1819–1945

The history of corrupt practices in Singapore, and the prosecution of such acts, can be traced to the early days of British colonial rule. Starting out as an outpost of the British East India Company, the island was essentially subjected to the directives of the Company and laws of British India, and these would have been consistent with British laws. At the same time, the Singapore settlement also adhered to the instructions and regulations formulated by Stamford Raffles,[1] a right he possessed as the Lieutenant-Governor of British Bencoolen. From 1826, when Singapore became part of the Straits Settlements, it also adhered to the policies and regulations of the Penang Presidency,[2] the administrative capital of the settlements. On the ground, administratively, the Straits Settlements as a whole also subscribed to a laissez-faire policy for the most part of the first half of the nineteenth century. That is, communal headmen were given certain authority to manage their own people, especially when it came to the maintenance of law and order. This came to be known as the British system of Indirect Rule. On the whole, there was no well-defined legal system in the Straits Settlements during the early decades of British Singapore. Nevertheless, there were still acts and activities considered illegal and corrupt for which the administration applied disciplinary measures or prosecution.

It was only after 1867 when the Straits Settlements was made a Crown Colony and had its own governor and legislative body that the Straits' first locally formulated laws criminalising corruption were written. Before this, corrupt acts involving public (and Company) officials took the form of petty corruption like the acceptance of bribes at the workplace. Large-scale or more serious forms of corruption mainly surfaced from the early twentieth century when robust economic development and large-scale infrastructural development (spending) saw the massive circulation of money and wealth throughout Malaya. While keen competition fuelled corrupt practices amongst businesses fighting for a share of the profit pie, the pursuit of this wealth also saw the emergence of ways and means to defeat government regulations standing in the way of (illegal) money-making opportunities. It was in this context that the first ordinance specifically crafted for the prevention of corruption was introduced in 1937. It was following this that the Anti-Corruption Branch was formed as a sub-branch of the Criminal Investigation Department (CID) in 1941.

Corruption became more widespread during the difficult years of the Japanese Occupation when shortages were the order of the day and hyperinflation had made money more and more useless by the day. One had to "trade" or offer "gifts" to secure necessities. The situation became even more acute after liberation when the shortages persisted and wages were low. It was in this socio-economic context that syndicates arose to circumvent government regulations controlling currency exchange, food and essentials by smuggling and other means. While many turned to offering "gifts" to officials to secure what they needed, others resorted to quick means of moneymaking, namely dealing in narcotics and other contrabands as well as through illegal gambling activities. By 1950, it felt that the level of corruption amongst government officers had reached an intolerable state, and more had to be done to address the problem.

Chapter One

Corruption & the Law in the Nineteenth Century

"It is a truth universally acknowledged, that a man in possession of substantive public authority, must be in want of a bribe."[3] It was perhaps truer that people who had the means and a vested interest were also in search of ways and means to ensure their opportunities for gain were guaranteed. Either way, the act of corruption has always been about the misuse of "authority for private gain",[4] and not simply about the erosion of moral values or even ethics. In the nineteenth century, the opportunity for corrupt practices by officials had been abundant since the very raison d'être for the East India Company's (EIC) presence in the East was the management of Britain's eastern trade and accumulation of wealth that was associated with it. As the Crown Agent for Britain's eastern trade from the seventeenth to the eighteenth centuries, the EIC was also responsible for the administration of all British commercial and political affairs in India and all her eastern colonies.[5] As such, EIC officials who controlled and enforced the Company's monopolies and commercial opportunities in this trade became central figures in the Company's commercial and financial affairs. Yet, the EIC had allowed their traders (ship captains and senior officers) to conduct their own private trades while they were on the Company's payroll.[6] This opened the door for systemic "corruption" within the EIC; company officials often placed their personal commercial interests above the Company's, which essentially made them competitors with their own employer. This "corruption" arising from private trades by Company men was so pervasive that it ultimately undermined the Company's bottom line. The EIC eventually banned private trades by Company servants.[7] It should also be noted that allowing Company officials to engage in private commerce fostered animosity among government officers in the colonies and bred "political" as well as commercial corruption.

When Singapore was made a British Factory (trading post) in early 1819,[8] the island was not exactly terra nullius as it was a small village of a few hundred residents, headed by their chief, the Temenggong of a greatly diminished Johore Sultanate, spread along the banks of the Singapore River. Together with Sultan Hussein Mohamed Shah (Tengku Long), whom Stamford Raffles recognised as the rightful sovereign of the Sultanate, both Malay Chiefs wielded de jure authority over Singapore. The EIC, however, exercised de facto control within the Factory boundary of Singapore. Cession of the whole island to the British would only occur in 1824 following the Anglo-Dutch Treaty. From this time till 1826–1827, when the settlement received its first Charter of Justice, there was no regular or formal legal system. The adoption of this Charter followed the creation of the Straits Settlements in 1826,[9] which saw Singapore, Malacca and Penang merged into a single administrative polity,[10] with Penang becoming its capital. Singapore was then subjected to the laws of Penang, enshrined in its First Charter of Justice which had already been in operation since 1807. However, at the same time, the Straits British communities also practised a laissez-faire policy which adhered to a system of Indirect Rule where settlers were placed under the control of their own chiefs. In early 1823, Raffles also added to the legal complexities afflicting Singapore when he inked the colony's "first" laws which he simply called "Singapore Regulations" of 1823.[11] And when he left Singapore in mid-1823, the island was placed under the supervision and laws of the Bengal Presidency. From this point till 1826, John Crawfurd, the colony's second Resident, followed Indian laws for the administration of justice.[12] When the Straits Settlements' own Charter arrived in 1827, it became the new law of the land.[13] As such, Singapore's judicial heritage in its foundation years could be best described as a hotchpotch tapestry of laws, regulations and legal precedents.[14] This was not an ideal situation to deter criminal acts like corrupt practices.[15]

The first overt mention of "corruption" in EIC–Indian legislation was made in the 1856 Police Act, Act XIII of 1856, which added bite to the fight against criminal acts in general across all Indian territories, including the Straits Settlements. In this Act, "bribery" was highlighted, and explicitly described, as a dismissible or prosecutable act.[16] The next legislative development as far as the war on corrupt practices was concerned could only occur after 1867, the year the Straits Settlements was made a direct Crown Colony of Britain following its Transfer from Indian oversight to the Colonial Office in London.[17] It was only after this "constitutional" development that the Straits Settlements would possess their own legislative body that could formulate laws locally, although British laws and government regulations would still apply. It was in 1871 that the Straits Settlements Legislative Council promulgated Ordinance IV of 1871, the Straits Settlements Penal Code.[18]

Chapter Two

Corrupt Practices & Punishment in Early Colonial Singapore

Instances of corrupt practices amongst East India Company (EIC) officials and employees had already been prevalent since the days when William Farquhar and Stamford Raffles were still involved in Singapore. Basically, the misuse of "authority for private gain" had manifested in various forms and ways.[19] These corrupt practices included the acceptance of bribes to subvert or defeat government policies and regulations such as helping persons to circumvent government monopolies, and licensing farms that included the control of opium retail, gambling and alcohol. There were also instances of receiving payments for perjury (corrupt perjury).[20] In particular, it was in the area of illegal gambling (gaming) and sales of opium and arrack (spirits) that corruption had been most extensive, mainly involving the local police. Farquhar had discovered in the latter part of 1819 that the increase in Singapore's population led to increased instances of "underhand monopolies" in the local retailing of items for which the EIC had placed regulatory controls. Apparently, in the absence of strong government control, locals had organised their own syndicates to manage these vices. And over time, these organised groups had jostled for control and monopoly. In light of this, in November 1819, Farquhar sought Raffles' approval to impose controls on the sale of these items in order to "suppress private disputes" as well as reap the benefits of such a measure. This was an important initiative for Farquhar as the Singapore Factory, having been a free port, had collected no revenue from the island's thriving commerce.

As such, up till this time, Farquhar's administration had no independent income.[21] The licensing of the retail of arrack and prepared opium, and for the right to operate gaming tables (shops), were collectively called licence farm or revenue farm.[22] Farquhar commenced Singapore's first revenue farm at the start of 1820. Gambling in the Chinese town, at this time situated at Boat Quay, on the southern banks of the Singapore River, was placed under the *Kapitan Cina* (Captain China) who taxed each gaming shop monthly to defray the cost of street cleaning and maintenance of the kampong.[23] The control of prepared opium and arrack sales followed later.[24] From this point, the revenue farms system would become the most important source of income for the local government for the rest of the century.

Gaming and Corruption

Although the importance of the licence farms to local government revenue had been more than clearly demonstrated during the months of Raffles' town rebuilding in 1822–1823, they formed the seed money used to kick-start works and compensation for resumption and redevelopment efforts.[25] Nevertheless, the Lieutenant-Governor waited till the revenue farm monies in the Singapore coffers were depleted during his town planning and rebuilding period before ending the gaming farm.[26] Of course, before the ban on gaming could become enshrined in regulation, Farquhar wrote to Raffles in April 1823 informing him that he had restarted the gambling farm. His argument was that prohibition of gaming would lead to the Chinese secretly operating the gaming tables themselves, and this would pave the way for "all means of bribery or corruption" of the Police. Farquhar suggested allowing the Chinese *towkays* (business owners) to operate the system. The government could impose fines when rules were broken and this would deter the gambling Chinese from resorting to illegal activities.[27] Raffles disagreed. He was of the conviction that gambling, in any form, licensed or illegal, would "always be a source of temptation and corruption" for the Police. He cited Penang's experience abolishing their gaming farm in 1810.[28] Hence, despite Farquhar's restoration of the gaming farm, Raffles issued Regulation IV in May 1823, outlawing gaming. However, after Raffles' departure from Singapore in mid-1823, John Crawfurd repealed all of Raffles' regulations, including the regulation against gambling.[29] Nevertheless, the revived farm was once again abolished in 1829 after Singapore became part of the Straits Settlements during the Penang Presidency, this time permanently.[30] Yet, by this time, illegal gaming had become extensive across the island,[31] and correspondingly, more instances of corruption amongst government officers.[32]

By the early 1830s, illegal gaming houses flourished in Singapore, and with this development, the extensive bribery of police peons who protected them. It was difficult to put an end to the illegal gaming houses because they did not operate from established shops like the former gaming houses of the gambling farm, but in residential houses.[33] Nevertheless, illegal gaming had been so rampant that it became common from 1832 for police peons to be found guilty and indicted for receiving bribes.[34] By 1833, there were numerous gaming houses across the island, and it was estimated that just along Church Street (today Waterloo Street) there were about 20 gaming houses. Most of these private gaming houses were "apparently under the protection of the subordinates of the Police" (peons).[35] This was no secret, and it was well-known even outside of the Straits.[36] By the 1840s, with little improvement on the state of affairs, and the EIC authorities and the local government showing little will to stem the problem, civil society debated on whether the gaming farm should be restored since the situation seemed no different from the days of the farm. The only difference after the ending of the gaming farm was that the government was now deprived of a valuable source of revenue. They blamed the unchecked gambling on the island for "the general corruption of the Police". The gaming syndicates had substantial means with which they were able to purchase police "connivance at their practice of secret gambling".[37] Although several constables had already been dismissed by the early 1840s for permitting gambling shops to operate within their jurisdictions, it was public knowledge that a large part of the police Jemadars' (commissioned officers of the Indian Army) and peons' wages included large amounts acquired from their connection with gambling dens, and the income they secured from "the normal extortions of ignorant and timid natives".[38]

> **Corruption of Men**
>
> "The vice of gambling favours corruption of manners... The excess of this vice has caused even the overthrow of empires. It leads to conspiracies and creates conspirators. Men overwhelmed with debt, borne down with the weight of misfortune which the negligence or prodigality has engendered, are always ready to obey the orders of any bold chieftain who might attempt a decisive stroke, even against the highest ruler in a state."
>
> *Straits Times 16 Sep 1845*

Police Gaming Conspiracy

The first instance of organised corruption involving government officers had been exposed in Singapore in the nineteenth century, ironically occurring after a much celebrated "police reform". In response to the poor state of affairs in Singapore in the early 1840s, the mercantile community of Singapore gathered at a Public Meeting on 10 February 1843 to discuss the state of crime and policing on the island. The assembly raised nine resolutions which they presented to the government. At the same time, the Singapore Chamber of Commerce recommended the ideal strength of the island's Police Establishment.[39] The Supreme Government (Bengal) responded and acceded in August 1843 when it sanctioned the increase of the Singapore police strength from 116 to 150, and Jemadars, Duffadars (non-commissioned officers of the Indian Army) and three additional European constables to a total of six. The salaries of the constables were also doubled from 75 to 150 rupees per month, and there was to be a new post of Deputy Superintendent of Police who was remunerated 400 rupees monthly.[40] A month later, the government appointed Thomas Dunman, an assistant in the Agency House of Messrs Martin, Dyce & Co., to the position of Deputy Superintendent of Police as well as Deputy Magistrate.[41] Interestingly, Dunman had no prior law enforcement experience and had not been in Singapore for long, arriving only in 1840. Nevertheless, he was appointed Deputy Superintendent upon employment in September 1843, and he was expected to forge a "more efficient system of police". However, he spent more time performing his duty as magistrate in his first few years in the service than in his police duties.[42] The structure of the Police Establishment hardly changed with the 1843 reforms. The Resident Councillor was still the "Commissioner", while Dunman was made functionally in charge of the daily operations; fundamentally, the main improvement from 1843 was the increased strength to the police force.[43]

The day of reckoning for the "corrupted" came in 1845, when the local government confronted, for the first time, the long festering organised corruption within the Police Establishment following public complaints and civil society action. Although everyone knew that the Police on the ground had avoided the gambling dens, which civil society called "houses of infamy", the Police had consistently claimed that it was not avoidance (dereliction and cowardice) but insufficient manpower that prevented enforcement action. They asserted that the way the Singapore houses were built provided multiple routes of egress for gamblers when raids were carried out. Then, the house of cards held up by deception collapsed in mid-1845 when an "overseer" of a gambling den reported to the authorities that she had been cheated by her employer — Telligoviden, who was also the Head Jemadar of the peons (native police)![44] Investigations into the case opened a window as to how the gaming shopowners had operated with impunity up till the 1840s.[45] While some den operators had the Police in their pockets, others had no choice but to cooperate with the Police who extorted them. Either way, they had "protection". In fact, all the "brawls, murders, robberies" around the gambling dens were also "carried out under the eye of the Police, undetected (blind eye) and unsuppressed". Interestingly, it was also amongst these houses of vice that Telligoviden and his underlings (peons) also maintained their own gambling house offering Chinese games of chance.[46] Such was the shock and embarrassment to the Establishment that the Police held a parade to dismiss the head of the native police in full view of the magistrates, the Deputy Superintendent and the rank and file within the Force. Following this demonstration that left an "impression" on all peace officers (another name for constables in the 19th century), a letter from the Governor warning them against fostering relationships with gambling houses was also read out.[47] The parade ended with the Police proclaiming Telligoviden's dismissal "at the corner of every street of the Town by sound of gong".[48]

Although the extent of the gaming enterprise had been common knowledge in the 1840s, the Establishment appeared to have been genuinely shocked by the level of involvement of its own peons in this affair. Civil society was less sympathetic. The public had known that the "illegality of gaming shops" had provided the police peons the perfect "opportunity for extortion", and the receipt of "hush" monies grew into a regular protection racket.[49] Hence, they felt that Telligoviden's public shaming had fallen short of what was truly due — he was only "suspended but not hanged".[50] Besides, civil society believed that they, and not the Police Establishment, were responsible for exposing the "evil practice" of gambling, and had Telligoviden "dragged before the bar of public justice". They also demanded that the Police continued the suppression of gaming and the associated corruption, as Telligoviden's "accomplices" were still in the wind, and there were still 145 gaming shops in operation, "unvisited and unheeded by the Police" in September 1845.[51] The public were also aware that constables and peons had been explicitly instructed not to enter these "receptacles of murderers and robbers". In this connection, the magistrates also desired to know who had issued that order.[52] Although the law of the land had clearly made public gaming illegal, the Chinese were given permission by the Police to gamble openly for two weeks during their Chinese New Year festivities. The

▶ Legacy

Singapore magistrates opined that it was ultra vires of the Police to grant this suspension of provisions of the law, albeit temporarily, and especially when no magistrates had been consulted.[53]

British authorities had known that the abolition of the government-controlled gaming farm had resulted in the proliferation of illegal gaming dens. However, the view of the Establishment was that the "bribery system" involving the island's police peons was not solely due to the enticements of the gambling houses but the low wages they were paid.[54] By the start of 1846, when most of the low wage police were already "in the regular pay of the keepers of the gambling shops", there were close to 200 gaming shops in Town at this time.[55] The revenue farms, gaming or otherwise, were not ipso facto the causes of police corruption, but simply conduits for their illicit practices by poorly paid peace officers. As a case in point, in 1846, the government found that the Police handling the sirih farm had been corrupt as well.[56] Hence, while the local government of the EIC regime was unwilling to raise wages (and expenditure) or augment the police force any further, it also did not place great emphasis in routing the illegal gaming establishments, and enforcement took the normal course of routine policing work. Unfortunately, this meant that corrupt practices amongst police personnel were not actively sieved out but handled when complaints were made. As no concrete action had been taken other than a dismissal parade, within a month after Telligoviden had been dispatched, the Establishment experienced a second shockwave with an exposure that was far more serious than the Jemadar's treachery.

In October–November 1845, Singapore was hit by another aftershock that utterly compromised the reputation of the entire Police Establishment. This time, the extent of corruption amongst European constables was busted wide open when a Chinese gambling den owner set out to expose the duplicity of constable Charles Cashim and his band of corrupt men. It was in 1843, the year of the police "reform" that Cashim and his merry men organised a system of "collection" from the gaming houses around Kampong Glam and Tanjong Rhu. Operating from the Kampong Glam

Police Station, they collected hush money from the den owners to allow the illicit gambling to continue unchecked. The constables appointed a collector to visit the gaming shops to collect the gaming "taxes" which differed from shop to shop. The average collected was $20 per month and the shopowners had no choice but to pay this "subscription" or close shop. It was around the last quarter of 1845 that one of these den operators complained to the Magistracy that Cashim was operating this extortion racket when he encountered difficulties paying his $20 subscription. He put up some goods as security but the constables still demanded cash. Fearing for his own safety, he reported the matter to the local magistrate in the hope of getting some "protection". Before taking this step, "in order to obtain the requisite proof, he borrowed the necessary sum, paid the tax, and received back his goods, all in presence of witnesses. He then made his complaint to the Magistrate." Cashim was swiftly dismissed, and then arrested. He was out on a bail of $1,000, and awaited trial which was slated for early 1846.[57] By April 1846, Cashim was convicted for receiving bribes to connive with the gaming bosses in order to allow them to operate with impunity. In this instance, the judiciary did not allow the Police to "cheat the hangman" by way of summary dismissal. After all, the irony was not lost on the administration that the constables' racket began in 1843, the year of the police reform. Cashim was not given the same leniency of dismissal which Telligoviden had enjoyed. He was sentenced to 18 months' imprisonment, fined $1,000, and if he could not pay, he would be further imprisoned till the fine was paid.

It was during Cashim's trial that even more details regarding the modus operandi of the corrupt cops came to light. Maintaining his innocence, he asserted that all the other constables had received bribes for the past three years, each receiving $20 monthly from the gambling shops.[58] In response to this damning accusation, the constables witnessing the session in the gallery remonstrated that they were innocent and that it was their superiors who gave the order "not to interfere with the gaming shops" and to allow open gaming during the Chinese New Year period. When the Magistrate

▶ Legacy

Group of Chinese gamblers in a gambling den, 1880s.
Source: Courtesy of National Archives of Singapore.

demanded to see the order, they claimed it was given verbally. So, the Magistrate summoned Dunman, the Deputy Superintendent of Police, to ascertain if there had been such an order. Dunman confirmed it. He declared that it was his predecessor, Major James Low, who had issued the order. Dunman explained that he believed this arrangement started when Low tried to motivate his policemen to do their duty suppressing the gaming shops. In order to counteract the effects of bribery by the den keepers, the police on the ground were promised half the money they found on the tables during raids. However, when they proceeded with the plan, it was found that the constables and peons had been overly focused on the gaming shops and neglected their other duties entirely. So, the arrangement was annulled and the order was given to stay away from the gaming shops. By early 1846, the number of gaming shops in Singapore had increased to

191. At this point, Dunman believed that the Police had inadequate means, and therefore little could be done to effectively suppress the large number of gambling houses, and instances of bribery of police could not be absolutely prevented.[59]

One can only imagine the considerable consternation the Magistrate, the Grand Jurymen and civil society felt when they realised the depth of defeatism afflicting the Police Establishment as far as corruption in the Force was concerned. It was one thing to discover the Cashim scandal so soon after the Telligoviden affair, but quite another to hear the Deputy Superintendent's admission that little could be done about the state of affairs in the 1840s. So, civil society, in conjunction with the judiciary, did something about it.

The People and Our First Good Men

There was a great deal of reluctance in the mid-nineteenth century to tackle most acts of organised crimes head-on unless they directly threatened British colonial rule. Even then, policies and actions were reactive rather than preventive. The EIC was, after all, a commercial body that did not relish expending significant resources unnecessarily. The whole philosophy of Indirect Rule had been based on the maintenance of an administration on the cheap; to use local leaders as collaborators in the colonial enterprise.[60] In this context, the EIC administration in Singapore did not maintain a substantial police force for the most part of the nineteenth century, and even those within the force were by and large lowly educated peons led by a handful of native Jemadars and untrained European officers. As a case in point, Dunman himself was not a professionally trained police officer. As such, while it was not unexpected that the Police Establishment as a whole had been lacking in some areas, the disenchantment of the general public in Singapore, having witnessed one scandal after another, was also expected. It was soon after Cashim's conviction in April 1846 that the Straits Settlements Recorder (Judge)

▶ Legacy

Pasir Panjang Road, Singapore, near the junction with Clementi Road, with the police station on the left, 1900s. A police peon is on patrol in a rural district.
Source: Courtesy of National Archives of Singapore.

called for immediate action to rid the island of the gambling dens and all their corrupting effects.[61] One good man answered the call — constable Alfred Simonides.[62]

From April 1846 to most of 1848, Simonides led a band of uncorrupted peons and crippled most of the gambling operations within Town, and with them, the source of the funds used for corrupting police on the island. They were our first good men. They answered the call of the few good folks of colonial Singapore. They were resolute. In less than a month after they started raiding the Town's illegal gaming shops, most of the dens which had operated openly when they had constables' and peons' protection had mostly disappeared from sight.[63] By the end of 1846, these good men had permanently shut 111 gambling dens in Town,[64] while the rest remained underground. Beyond doubt, Simonides and his peons enjoyed unmitigated success essentially because they did not accept bribes to close an eye nor did they extort the perpetrators of the gaming and corrupt conspiracies that severely afflicted the Force hitherto this time. And of course, some level of bravery was also demonstrated on the job. In November 1846, Simonides took his police party beyond the Town's boundary in pursuit of the gaming operators who took their business out of municipal lines. In the 1840s, the jungles of the interior had almost no police presence and had been the domain of the Chinese secret societies, hence fraught with danger. In one such operation at the outskirts of Town, a new constable aiding Simonides' raiding party, John Newby, was hurt in the line of duty.[65] Nevertheless, this did not deter Simonides from surveying and penetrating deeper into the interior of the island from July 1847 in search of the gaming dens which relocated there from Town.[66] By mid-1848, although there were still no police stations in the interior, Simonides and his peons were still able to make their way across the island (north) to arrest more members of the gambling syndicate.[67]

Simonides' success in dealing with illegal gaming, from 1846–1848, demonstrated that it was not impossible to tackle illegal gaming and the associated corrupt activities. It was a wonder just how one good man's conviction could change the course of law and order environment, albeit in just a few short years.[68] For his efforts in crushing the gaming houses, which also contributed to mitigating corruption amongst peace officers, the Resident Councillor, Recorder (Judge-Magistrate) and Grand Jurors (magistrates) presented constable Simonides with a gold medal in early 1847. He was also given six silver medals to award the peons whom he considered most deserving.[69] Yet, the public acknowledgement of the good work done by these good men was not ipso facto the end of corruption or public gaming in Singapore. There were still corrupt practices occurring even during the height of Simonides' anti-gaming drive,[70] and it was not easy to successfully prosecute gaming operators.[71] The "rewards" for these men were in fact the "high note" of the public statement the Singapore community had been voicing for years—they detested the ambivalent demeanour of the Colonial and Police Establishments in dealing with matters of law and order, and their security, within the colony. Unfortunately, the colonial administration did not take kindly to public criticism of the police force levelled by civil society and the magistracy, and this sparked a judicial-constitutional crisis in Singapore (and the Straits Settlements) in 1847.

Judicial Crisis, 1847

The progress of fighting the illegal gambling racket, which was also behind the corrupting of police personnel, hit a "speed-bump" in 1847 when the governing Council of India, on 19 February, promulgated the India Act No. III of 1847 — an Act to provide for the Appointment of Constables and Peace Officers at the Settlements in the Straits.[72] The Act effectively limited the ability of the Straits Settlements judiciary and grand jurymen from continuing their agitation and directing police action, independent of the Police Establishment.[73] Although the Act seemed innocuous, from the name it was given, it was the response of the Governor of the Straits Settlements, Lieutenant Colonel William John Butterworth (August 1843– March 1855), to the open criticism from the Singapore Grand Jurors and Recorder.[74] In April 1846, the magistrates even instructed Dunman to formulate a set of Rules and Regulations for the Police to use as a guide, months after these gentlemen directed Simonides to start his crusade.[75] The magistrates' directives that launched the anti-gaming and anti-corruption drive were seen by the Governor as an affront to administration. What everyone did not realise, till Dunman adhered to the magistrates' instruction to formulate the Police's first Rules and Regulations, and Simonides set out to clean up the streets, was that the Straits Settlements Second Charter had actually given the Judiciary the responsibility to instruct the Police.[76] And the Recorder was within his rights to allow the Grand Jurors to address police inefficiency in their presentments.[77] Clearly, there was discordance between the interpretation and operation of the Council of India Act No. XII of 1839 (Municipal Act – EIC Regulation) and the Second Charter of Justice (1827, Royal Charter). Hence, Butterworth crafted the new "ordinance" to plug the constitutional loophole that allowed the Judiciary to have a say over functions of peace officers.

Irrespective of the objective of the new Act, it threatened to reverse all that had been achieved in 1846 against illegal gaming and the ability of this big-money industry to corrupt officials. Before its promulgation, a draft of the Act was published in the local papers in mid-October 1846.[78] The Singapore public was alarmed, and they wasted no time to express their opinion of the draft Act.[79] It was not so much about who could "appoint" peace officers in the colony or whether the judiciary could direct the police force, but whether the local community had a right to voice their dissatisfaction and shape changes which had a direct impact on them. In a last-ditch effort to forestall the introduction of the Act, they submitted a memorial directly to the Governor-General of India in November 1846.[80] Yet, the Governor pressed on, and the bill for the new law, Act III of 1847, was passed by the governing Council of India in February 1847. Within months of the Act being put into operation, a judicial crisis ensued when a large number of Grand Jurors (who were also Justices of Peace) in Singapore and Penang resigned from their positions.[81] The Singapore community then planned and submitted a petition to the British Parliament to repeal the Act.[82] Against this backdrop, Dunman's submitted Rules and Regulations for the Police was put on the shelf, temporarily.

Interestingly, the more overt and immediate impact of Act III of 1847 had been a "comical" one. Within days of its implementation, "every house of Church Street" (gambling dens) openly invited passers-by to enter. Then, the farcical twist; so many repressed Chinese had rushed to partake in their favourite pastime that in a spate of mad gambling, many lost so much that they became financially ruined. Many of them left Singapore for Sydney to labour as coolies.[83] At this point, when the big-money corruptors returned, many fell into poverty from their own "moral" corruption. Although Simonides was still on the job and the prosecution of illegal gamers continued, Simonides' "anti-gambling task force" was no longer backed by the judiciary or enjoyed public support.

Also, there were fundamental shifts in the law and order condition heading towards the 1850s that necessitated Butterworth accepting significant changes to the status quo of the Police Establishment. The new threats, and source of corruption, came in the form of the Chinese secret societies, the largest of which was the famed *Thian Ti Huey* (Heaven and Earth Society). It was not till the 1850s that they moved beyond outright banditry, piracy and plundering to operating vices in the Straits Settlements. Naturally, as the new big-money syndicate, the *hueys* became the new source of corruption for the officialdom.[84] Of course, having been the most dangerous and violent organisation of the day, peace officers might just turn a blind eye to their activities so as not to be "whacked" or made to disappear.

So, what of those few good men? Simonides continued to do well right up till 1848. In fact, Simonides became the exemplar of the good constable the colony had been desiring for so long. In mid-1847, he published the colony's first police "training manual", *The Constables' Guide, or a Collection of the Principal Laws Regarding Peace Officers*.[85] Up till this time, constables and peons in the Straits Settlements were untrained policemen. And with Dunman's set of Police Rules and Regulations stuck in limbo, the Police had no codified standards, or code of conduct, which they could follow. In early 1848, Simonides was temporarily raised to the post of Deputy Superintendent of Police, covering Dunman who himself became a temporary Superintendent.[86] However, this was as far as Simonides would go in his career in the police force.[87] In April 1849, he was declared insolvent. While it was not a secret that he had become a constable in 1844 when the hotel he owned at Boat Quay went under,[88] few had known that the debacle left him a debtor. Under threat of prosecution and incarceration, he borrowed more money at high interest to service his original debts. By 1848, Simonides could no longer sustain his payments and one of his creditors brought him to court.[89] He lost everything he had during the proceedings and was forced to leave the job.[90] The irony of Simonides' tragic ending as a constable was that it was the indisputable testimony that he was not corrupt, and clearly, he had never resorted to extortion or abuse of his authority for illicit gains throughout his short police career to bail him out of his predicament. Had he done so, he would not have become bankrupt. Simonides also continued his crusade against the illegal gambling dens during his bankruptcy trial till his resignation.[91]

Of Law and Order

The immediate years following the promulgation of India Act No. III of 1847 saw a weakening of the collaborative form of colonial administration. This in turn affected the ability of the British administration in Singapore to maintain law and order, as well as to combat corruption within the local Police Establishment. Dunman had yet to implement his set of Police Rules and Regulations, and the Police were so badly paid "that the only recruits were unemployed men in desperate financial straits, many of them stranded sailors who became policemen as a temporary stopgap occupation". In Dunman's view, "an underpaid, overworked force had no inducement to court danger with possible injury or death. It was more profitable for policemen to accept bribes from gambling house keepers and more prudent to keep away from violence." Dunman fought to have better "calibre" peace officers,[92] a need which the Grand Jurors also echoed till they were silenced in 1847. So, the corruption continued, and the gambling dens returned each time after Simonides closed them down. In 1848, two European constables were dismissed from the Force for receiving bribes involving the gambling houses.[93] By early 1849, when Simonides left the job, illegal gambling was once again conducted openly in parts of Town, sometimes with police peons standing at the gaming tables or nearby.[94]

The new law of 1847 essentially did little to resolve the impasse that existed between the Charter of Justice and the Municipal Act (1839). The Judiciary and the public in Singapore still had legal rights granted to them

▶ Legacy

in the Royal Charter; Act XII of 1839 was not designed to work alongside the Charter. Accordingly, the Governor amended the 1839 Municipal Act with a new ordinance, Act IX of 1848, to provide additional sources of funding for the Municipal and Police Establishments.[95] This Act clearly placed the oversight of the Police under the Municipal Committee. Hence, the police force was to be entirely funded and directed by the local municipality while the magistracy would oversee the application of the law. It was at this juncture that the Municipal Committee implemented the rules for the police force,[96] identical to the set of Rules and Regulations articulated by the Grand Jurors. These rules encompassed issues like the quality and qualification of the policemen, promotions, remuneration, uniform, discipline and more. Most importantly, the new Police Rules and Regulations also specified dismissal in cases of misconduct, including corruption.[97]

While Act IX of 1848 somewhat resolved the impasse between the executive and judiciary, and provided the opportunity to improve the efficiency of the police force, the EIC's austerity measures of the day which saw a reduction of police wages in 1848 effectively ended this endeavour.[98] It hampered the recruitment of better men for the Force; it also created the conditions where poorly paid constables remained susceptible to corrupt practices. In consequence, there was still no real impetus to weed out corruption and few corrupt officers had been taken to task and dismissed going into the 1850s.[99] In fact, the government of the day was more focused on changing the laws to align with Indian Laws. As a case in point, in March 1850, Straits Settlements' Criminal Law (India Act XIV of 1850) was passed to align the Straits Settlements' system with Calcutta's. Then the Prevention of Gambling Act (India Act XXXIV of 1852) was passed in September 1852.[100] Although these legislations represented progress, no significant improvements were actually made. The big-money syndicates of the time still had the resources to corrupt officials.

Singapore's first Police Act (India Act XIII of 1856) was introduced just before the EIC's governance of India ended. It was the first specific legislation dealing with crime and punishment before Singapore's first Penal Code was promulgated. The Police Act was basically an Indian legislation that the EIC administration applied to the Straits Settlements in an effort to standardise the laws for all Indian territories.[101] Under this Act, police pay was near doubled in the hope of defeating inefficiencies and corruption in the Force. It also created the post of Commissioner of Police to oversee the police force.[102] While Act IX of 1848 placed the entire Police Establishment under the Municipality, the Police Act reduced the role of the Municipality in police matters to just payments.[103] The Police Act also marked a significant milestone as far as legislation against corruption was concerned; it made the acceptance of a bribe a criminal act in its own right. With the 1849 Police Rules and Regulations, corrupt practices fell under the general reference of "misconduct" which was only a dismissible offence.[104] The 1856 Police Act listed "bribery" as a main criminal act described in its own section,[105] and guilty persons were charged using this Act in the immediate period after it went into operation.[106]

However, by the early 1860s, illegal gambling was still pervasive across Singapore. Local government was certain that "a part of the Police" had been "cognisant" of it, estimating that a total of $3,000 in bribe money had been paid to the police monthly. Clearly, enacting legislation alone was not the solution to battling corruption. In an 1879 Police Commission of Enquiry, it noted that "the inspectors of police were not, as a body, men on whose fidelity and capacity reliance could be placed". Most of them joined the Force "not by merit, but by circumstance". It was hard to attract men with low pay. "Corruption was believed to exist amongst them to a greater extent than was provable in a Court of Law." The Chief Justice noted that "bribery and corruption were rife" amongst the native police as "they were hopelessly over-worked, getting about four hours' rest at a time, with the result that they were always going to sleep on their beat...".[107]

The first law promulgated locally to deal with corruption in the public

Ordinance No. IV. of 1871

THE PENAL CODE.

CHAPTER IX.

Of Offences by, or relating to, Public Servants.

Public servant taking a gratification other than legal remuneration in respect of an official act	161
Taking a gratification, in order, by corrupt or illegal means, to influence a public servant	162
Taking a gratification for the exercise of personal influence with a public servant	163
Punishment for abetment by public servant of the offences above defined	164
Public servant obtaining any valuable thing without consideration, from person concerned in any proceeding or business transacted by such public servant	165
Persons offering gratification	165A
Public servant disobeying a direction of the law, with intent to cause injury to any person	166

Taking a gratification in order, by corrupt or illegal means, to influence a public servant.

162. Whoever accepts or obtains, or agrees to accept or attempts to obtain, from any person, for himself or for any other person, any gratification whatever, as a motive or reward for inducing, by corrupt or illegal means, any public servant to do or to forbear to do any official act, or in the exercise of the official functions of such public servant to show favor or disfavor to any person, or to render or attempt to render any service or disservice to any person with the Government, or with any member of the Legislature, or with any Lieutenant-Governor, or with any public servant, as such, shall be punished with imprisonment of either description for a term which may extend to three years, or with fine, or with both.

Taking a gratification, for the exercise of personal influence with a public servant.

163. Whoever accepts or obtains, or agrees to accept or attempts to obtain, from any person, for himself or for any other person, any gratification whatever, as a motive or reward for inducing, by the exercise of personal influence, any public servant to do or to forbear to do any official act, or in the exercise of the official functions of such public servant to show favor or disfavor to any person, or to render or attempt to render any service or disservice to any person with the Government, or with any member of the Legislature, or with any Lieutenant-Governor, or with any public servant, as such, shall be punished with simple imprisonment for a term which may extend to one year, or with fine, or with both.

service was the Straits Settlement's Penal Code of 1871 (evolved from Penal Code of 1870 and Amendment of 1871). In the Straits Settlements Legislative Council Ordinance IV of 1871, Chapter IX specified that any public servant who "accepts or solicit bribes" shall be punished.[108] As far as locally written legislation was concerned, it was in the 1871 Penal Code that "corruption" was specifically defined as an illegal act, although the first legislation enacted solely as an anti-corruption law was only introduced just before WWII.[109]

Bureaucracy and Corrupting Public Servants

When the Singapore public agitated for the "Transfer" of the Straits Settlements from EIC control to direct Colonial Office oversight, it was thought that Singapore would be spared the official neglect from an overarching authority and a new regime might finally provide the attention the colony needed to progress unimpeded. When the EIC Government dissolved in 1858, that wish did not materialise. Instead, the Straits Settlements remained under the Indian Government, which was by this time directly under the Crown. The Straits communities then pushed to have their settlements be made a Crown Colony. This was achieved in 1867, and from then, the Straits Settlements could form its own Legislative Council to formulate and enact laws, as well as to have its own Executive Council to administer and govern the colony without deference to the Government in India. As a part of the transition into a self-governing Crown Colony, the Straits Settlements saw an expansion of its government departments, services and responsibilities.[110]

Naturally, there were more local regulations, licensing and statutory requirements, and all these involved inspections and payment of fees and fines. It was therefore not surprising that from the 1870s, there were more cases of corrupt practices amongst public servants other than the Police. The licensing departments, in particular, had been greatly affected by corruption. In 1870, and then again in 1875, corruption among the staff

▶ Legacy

of the Registry of Hackney Carriages led to strikes by the carriage owners and riders.[111] Even the police court was not spared of corrupt officials.[112] The press had remarked that a system of "black-mailing" in Court was occurring under the noses of the magistrates;[113] after court peons in the police court were caught extorting 25 cents from people attending Court, for which they were sentenced to three months in prison, it was found that the clerks and interpreters in the Court were all levying their own "little fines" as well.[114]

The enlargement of the Straits Settlements bureaucracy in the post-Transfer years also saw corrupt practices spread across government bodies, including the "traditional" native peons and European constables. When the hackney strike occurred again in 1875, the Legislative Council noted that many in the police force had been corrupt not only in their dealings with "hack owners and syces" but also "in their dealings with the native population" generally.[115] However, it is perhaps truer that all public servants who wielded "authority" were open to taking advantage of helpless "natives".[116]

Greed and immoral nature were not the only building blocks of a corrupt society. Fundamentally, in colonial times, the corruption that flowed through the corridors of government offices had been fuelled by low pay, and the police force had been the biggest official body afflicted by this condition; poor wages bred corruption and had been the main obstacle to attracting better people into the police force. And since the *hueys* had the means to corrupt, many in the Force were either in the *hueys* or in cahoots with them.[117] By the 1870s, it was increasingly believed that raising police pay would resolve all these issues; better pay could induce "better candidates" to join the force and then "bad apples" could be replaced.[118] However, the corruption franchise had extended to almost all branches of government that had direct dealings with the public (civil service wide) and not just within the Police. Hence, while increasing wages within the police force might mitigate some of the problems of the day, it would not have changed anything as far as the general corrupt bureaucracy

> ### Bribing Public Servants
>
> "Evidently, the Police, and all others in authority, are alive to the fact that giving and receiving bribes by public servants are getting too common in the Colony. Prosecutions are being made right and left..."
>
> Mid-Day Herald and Daily 2 Nov 1897

was concerned.

At this time, the prosecution of corrupt officials had not been given great priority. Of the 1,229 cases of crime and serious rule-breaking by police personnel in 1886, only 105 ended in dismissal from the force, and of these, only five had been involved in corruption.[119] In the context of the pervasive corruption of the police force at that time, the low rate of dismissal for bribery underscored just how anti-corruption enforcement measures had been lacking in the latter half of the nineteenth century.

By the end of the nineteenth century, the general social environment within the Straits Settlements had not improved despite the Transfer and the promulgation of legislation locally to deal with the problems within the Straits. In fact, bribery in the Straits was said to have had reached a "fearful" level.[120] Up until the end of the century, illegal gaming houses were still a source of corrupting influence on the Police, and the *hueys* had become the overarching controllers of illegal gambling and most other vices in the Straits, and therefore the source of the big-money corrupting public servants.[121] As a case in point, in the mid-1880s, the bigger *hueys* had rebranded themselves as *kongsi* (companies) and became far more organised than before. Several of these *kongsi* banded together and started a "joint" bribery system. Gambling houses paid a subscription to a central pool from which the *kongsi* used to bribe the Police in order to avoid detention. They started a bribery fund! The *kongsi* also employed informers who provided advance warning of arriving police and helped obstruct, or delayed, the Police from executing their warrants.[122] In the scheme of things, the "not as efficient" police force of the day could not deter the "better organised" gaming-bribery syndicate. The increase in petty corruption within bureaucracy during this period, involving "tea money" and the "squeeze", only exacerbated the bad situation in the Straits.[123]

The police court at South Bridge Road, Singapore, 1900s.
Source: Courtesy of National Archives of Singapore.

Chapter Three

From the Early Twentieth Century

Municipal Scandal

The biggest case of corruption uncovered after the turn of the century was the 1909–1910 Municipal Scandal — the corruption of the municipal government itself! Until this time, most cases prosecuted were mainly petty cases involving lower-rank police or public servants who extorted and took bribes.[124] On 15 September 1909, the Governor appointed an independent commission of enquiry, the Municipal Enquiry Commission, to look into and report on the matter.[125] The corruption within the Singapore municipality was so scandalous that it was known from London to Shanghai.[126] The British Parliament (House of Commons) had, in fact, called for an independent enquiry into the Singapore affair.[127] The Commission of Enquiry revealed that amongst the irregularities of the Straits Settlements municipality, mainly in Singapore, involved questionable assessments of houses (rates), secret commissions given by contractors to municipal staff, sanitation inspectors and peons, and procurement of pipes and meters without tender, fake tenders, accepting gifts from suppliers and more.[128] It was also the Commission's opinion that "inefficiency in the principal encouraged corruption and crime among the Governor's subordinates".[129]

There were little remedial measures following the Municipal Scandal affair except for fines, dismissal and forced retirement, partly because most of the guilty parties had been Englishmen or high officials who could not be publicly named.[130] Large European firms like United Engineers were also implicated.[131] But more importantly, the nature of the corrupt acts involved run-of-the-mill special commissions, gifts, bribes, special considerations, preferences, absence of proper tenders and more.[132] The Municipal Enquiry Commission also found that a "few of the municipal officials were in receipt of bribes from the local engineering firms who had formed a ring to pool profits…"[133] It was also discovered that the President of the Municipal Council had been so detached from the operations of the municipality that abuses were allowed to occur. While the culprits were made to give up or return their gains, the whole affair was by and large "glossed over". Nevertheless, as a token response, the local government ended the elected representative system of the municipality in 1913.[134] The public view of the affair was that it was whitewashed. As a result, when the government attempted to introduce an income tax in the Straits in 1910, the general public opposed the measure, asserting that the establishment of such a facility (a department to collect income tax) would only create another platform for corrupt officials to solicit bribes.[135]

Infrastructural Works, Money and Corruption

Up till the 1910s, there were not many large-scale government projects which brought in large amounts of monies.[136] From the 1920s to 1930s, substantial development schemes were started in Singapore: urban renewal of Chinatown in the 1920s–1930s; Singapore Improvement Trust housing in the 1920s–1930s; administrative infrastructure like the new General Post Office (Fullerton) in the 1920s; Municipal Building (City Hall) in the 1920s; the new Court House (High Court) in the 1930s; and defence works across the island, including the Naval Base, in the 1930s. The Kallang Airport was also started and completed in the 1930s, and was part of the larger seafront reclamations across Singapore; the Kallang Basin Reclamation and Beach Road Reclamation Schemes (Raffles Reclamation Ground) were both started in the 1930s.[137] All these works made local contracting trade most lucrative. It was in this "money environment" that more serious cases of graft and "conspiracies" occurred.[138]

Large amounts of development monies flowed into the colony, and almost all contractors engaged to carry out these works were Chinese businesses which in one way or another were involved in offering or paying "gifts" to smoothen transactions. Eventually, there arose a fear that corruption within the "construction" industry would damage the commercial and economic confidence in the colony. This concern became even more critical after the Great Depression (1929–1932) when the economic progress of the Straits Settlements had been fragile and had to be protected from any erosion of confidence. Hence, the 1937 Prevention of Corruption Ordinance was promulgated. It was stated clearly in the Ordinance that corruption had to be suppressed in consideration of commercial interests, beside public morality.[139] It was at this juncture that

Contractors' Rule, Government's Rue

"It was said the other day in the House of Commons that Singapore is the kingdom of heaven for contractors… it is more correct to say that it is such a kingdom not so much for contractors as for the underlings in various government departments.

As a rule, a contractor has to tender for a work at a price which is about 50 per cent above actual cost, because he will have to bribe separately several subordinate officers in the department.

If he does not gratify them, difficulties, one after another, will be placed in his way and cannot possibly get over them successfully.

Sometimes, middlemen who already enjoy the confidence of these unscrupulous men, tender, but their figure necessarily would be about ten or fifteen per cent higher than that of a contractor who actually does the work. The party who really lose is, therefore, the government."

Malaya Tribune 25 Oct 1924

▶ Legacy

the war in Europe started and the spectre of war extending into Asia became real. The British Military Establishment took over the running of things in 1939 to prevent foreign exchange assets and other resources passing through the trade and commerce of the colonies from falling into enemy's hands, especially strategic resources. And these included the sale and procurement of building materials. Hence, the military imposed Emergency Regulations in 1939 to control such supplies, among other things.[140]

The Captain Charles Loveday Affair[141]

It was common in the pre-war years to hear government officers or police saying matter-of-factly, *"makan coffee lima puloh sen"* (50 cents coffee money) just to provide a service which they ought to have given as part of their responsibility.[142] Still, regardless of how they had become a norm in everyday life, these petty illegal gratifications, up till 1900, had played second fiddle to the *huey*-controlled big-money rackets — gambling and other vices. This situation started changing in the early twentieth century when government officers handled more money than the gaming syndicates. In the 1930s, Singapore island was a hub of building activities, mainly military and defence works. By this time, contracts, awarded through tender, came under the purview of the Chief Surveyor of Works in the Chief Engineers Office. With war just over the horizon, all strategic resources, including building materials and building works, came under control regulations. It was also the responsibility of the officer overseeing building regulations to tender out and award works. In 1939, this officer was Captain Charles Loveday of the Royal Engineers. He decided who was to be invited to tender for works.[143]

Prior to Loveday's ring of "participating" contractors and suppliers, an acquaintance of his who had great influence over local contractors, Soh Hun Swee, told him of another ring of contractors. They had organised themselves into a loose grouping which cooperated in tenders so as to avoid a price war amongst themselves. It was a small circle of three contractor-suppliers.[144] Started in 1938, members of this ring agreed amongst themselves that if more than one in the group participated in the same tender, they would all tender "at a gross profit of 15%". The successful tenderer would give the other, or others, up to 2.5% of the price they tendered and won.[145] Soh had known of this arrangement and brought it to Loveday. The Captain, however, was unimpressed by the margins that could be gotten from this ring. So, he proposed a new ring with new arrangements which was to be composed of "new blood" of a wider grouping of contractors who could also offer more money.

In June 1939, Loveday started his new ring with Soh as partner, and they pulled in Robert Scott Macmillan in July to form the core of their grouping. While Soh was a building materials "salesman" in the employ of Guthrie and Co. Ltd.,[146] Macmillan was a director of Standard Engineering Co. Ltd., and the Malayan Wire Mesh and Fencing Co. Ltd. When Macmillan arrived at Singapore in 1937, he also started the Sino-British Engineering Corporation (Malaya) Ltd., which dealt in tiles, steel and building materials. He was the firm's Managing Director.[147] Interestingly, Soh was "listed" as a Director of Sino-British Engineering when the ring was started.[148] Loveday basically, in his capacity as the officer overseeing the Chief Engineers Office, leveraged the government's list of approved vendors and implemented an invitation to tender system instead of having open bids. He then created grouping bands based on contract values for contractors on the list — $50,000, $100,000, $150,000, and up to $500,000. Loveday then, through Soh and Macmillan, discreetly spread the word amongst contractors and suppliers that they could be placed on the list by joining their ring. The "membership fee" was dependent on the quantum of the fees they paid. While $500 got one onto the $50,000 value list, $5,000 placed a member on the $500,000 works value listing.[149] Those in their respective value bands were invited to tender for works projected at their value levels, together with other non-ring contractors. The member invited to tender would then "mark-up" the value of his bid by 10%. He was required to

▶ Legacy

put half of the mark-up value into a pool to be shared by all the members of his band, and the remaining 5% was paid when he was awarded the tender. In this way, in the ring, even if other participating members had not been "invited" to bid for a job, all members would still get a cut. The tenderer, aside from paying the 10% forward, did not have to dip into his main tender sum to pay the collective since this was covered by his "mark-up". Hence, it was only the government which lost out. It was Soh and Macmillan who managed all money matters in this arrangement, with Soh handling the Chinese contractors. As for Loveday, he took half of every 10% mark-up, and the balance was shared equally amongst the rest in the ring.[150]

The problem with this arrangement was that anyone could pay their way into the list, even people not familiar with construction works.[151] This was the real "treachery" of the Loveday affair. He had appointed companies with no experience in building works to build defence installations for the island. When the structures erected by his co-conspirators started crumbling, the ring's shoddy works were discovered, and these included substandard bricks and concrete works that crumbled upon touch.[152] As these could not be hidden, he co-opted his staff to collaborate in the inspection of completed works as well. In this instance, their criminal conspiracy did not just threaten to harm the confidence in the colony's businesses, it also compromised the strategic defence facilities and structures built. Loveday also allowed members of his ring to procure Japanese building materials when such purchases from Japan had been banned as such transactions would have channelled to the Japanese much needed foreign exchange resources,[153] and these could have been used to support the Japanese war effort.

The Loveday conspiracy fell apart in March 1940 when Soh was arrested for attempting to bribe Lieutenant Frederick Norman Croft, Surveyor of Works, Royal Engineers.[154] As Loveday was on home leave, he instructed Croft to liaise with Soh when he visited their office at Fort Canning for matters involving a tender. Croft was not part of the ring, so he did not expect anything out of the normal should take place. Soh, on the other hand, was unaware of the situation on Loveday's side. He simply assumed that Croft was a subordinate of Loveday's, and that Croft would be handling Loveday's affair during his absence. So, he offered Croft $10,000 and the choice of a motorcar which he could choose from a dealership at Orchard Road.[155] Croft reported the matter to his superiors and the Police, as Soh was a civilian. Together with the Police, a trap was set for Soh when he returned to Croft with the money. As the standard of proof needed in corruption cases had been high, a hidden microphone was also employed to tap their conversation.[156] Soh, whom the authorities described as the English-speaking Hokkien, was arrested and charged in March 1940, under the 1937 Prevention of Corruption Ordinance, Section 3b and 4, for corruptly giving $10,000 to Croft. The case was handled by Assistant Superintendent of Police (ASP) EV Fowler of the Detective Branch.[157] However, fortunately for Soh, he was quickly acquitted on a technicality — Croft had been instructed by a superior to "take" money from a Chinese contractor. This meant that Soh's actions were not unsolicited.[158]

With his partners in crime now on the "side of the law", it was no surprise that it was only a matter of time that Loveday was eventually discovered, caught, court-marshalled and sent into hard labour. But the damage was done... including substandard defence works on the eve of war.[159] Loveday's treachery had a greater impact than the 1910 Municipal Scandal as far as public harm and future anti-corruption policies and initiatives were concerned.[160] Yet, despite the seeming "checkmate", since the prosecutor in his Court Martial had basically used the civilian members of the first and second rings as witnesses to prosecute Loveday,[161] as things eventually panned out, Loveday was able to avoid prosecution in two-thirds of all the charges he faced. Although the Straits Settlements 1937 Prevention of Corruption Ordinance was already in operation, Loveday was charged under English law for defrauding the British War Office through conspiracy.[162]

▶ Legacy

Yet, it was still not an easy task to find Loveday guilty on all charges despite the fact that Soh produced $106,000 worth of bearer bonds and $44,000 cash that he held for Loveday.[163] These bonds certainly exposed his intent. They were "unregistered" and "no records exist that list the owners' names".[164] However, the strength of evidence alone was not sufficient to successfully convict Loveday on all charges.[165] Ultimately, Loveday was only found guilty on eight out of 25 charges, and sentenced to four-and-a-half years' of "penal servitude" (hard labour) for "defrauding the War Department" and "corruptly obtaining" a total of $169,000 for "assisting building contractors to obtain work from the War Department".[166]

In 1941, a year after the Loveday case, the Anti-Corruption Branch (ACB) was established within the Criminal Investigation Department (CID). Although the case had been prosecuted through court martial under Emergency Regulations, and not in the civil court,[167] news of the affair had been so shocking to the public that it was widely covered in contemporary news circles. The affair had left such an indelible mark in the Establishment's memory that it was still referred to as a lesson to be learnt when the government started reforming its processes and procedures in the post-war years.[168] In this light, the 1909–1910 Municipal Scandal paled in comparison with the Loveday case. One immediate result of the affair was that it led local authorities, including the War Department, to review the way they had conducted tenders and handled contracts… on the eve of war! It was realised that dangers lurked when the entire process of procurement had been centred on one department head. There was also no standard system for awarding contracts: contracting parties did not have to prove that they were professionals in the same area of works or supply that they were tendering. This explains why there had been shoddy works or substandard materials used. A second or third layer of contractors and suppliers receiving a much smaller cut of the awarded amount were usually used.

It was during the Loveday case that the subject of income tax arose once more. When it was first mooted in the 1910s, it was a matter of prudence and preparation for the eventual loss of opium (excise) revenue.[169] By the 1930s, contribution to the government income from opium revenue had already shrunk to an all-time low. The need for an income tax regime had become even more critical. Unfortunately, the Loveday affair launched another torpedo into the endeavour, for a second time. Resistance to the government's second attempt at tax and revenue reforms echoed the same charge: an Income Tax Department would only be another channel for corrupt officials to line their pockets. The lack of trust in government once again defeated a most necessary measure. As with the failure of the Straits Government to introduce income tax in 1910, the Loveday affair also sunk efforts to implement this tax regime in 1940.

While the prosecution of Loveday had been considered a major success in fighting corruption, it was also a source of humiliation for the British military and Government. The fact that the case reverberated beyond Singapore's liberation and had formed part of the post-war lesson on the need to combat corruption effectively attests to this. The lesson learnt was that laws could only apply punitive measures. It was also necessary to implement preventive measures in administrative procedures that obstructed corrupt tendencies.

One Good Man

During the Loveday trial, Soh Hun Swee, a co-conspirator, was asked if there were any contractors who did not receive anything from the ring. He replied, "Yes, Wee Cheng Soon. He didn't receive anything from the ring and didn't want any money from the ring. He didn't know about the ring."

Malaya Tribune 10 Aug 1940
Straits Times 10 Aug 1940

▶ Legacy

Vaux's Sword & Wisdom

FG Vaux, Counsel for Prosecution in Loveday's Trial:
"He organised system of **wholesale corruption** for his own benefit"

Singapore Free Press 7 Aug 1940

"To a dishonest person the opportunities of **corrupt practices were unlimited**"

Malaya Tribune 7 Aug 1940

"Conspiracy was an offence under **Common Law** of England and had been defined as consisting of the agreement of two or more persons to do an unlawful act or to do an unlawful act by unlawful means"

Straits Times 7 Aug 1940

"The Prevention of Corruption Act had been on the Statute Book in England since 1906… could only find in the law books, three cases of prosecution under this Act since that year, and it was only after the passing of an amending act, namely the Act of 1916, that convictions were obtained… by this section,… the general rule that a person is innocent until he is proved guilty was **turned completely upside down**, and money was presumed to be corruptly obtained until it was proved to the contrary…. **The payment of money is presumed to be corrupt payment until the accused establishes that it is not.**"

Straits Times 7 Aug 1940

Anti-Corruption Measures

Most early cases of corruption were "petty" infringements committed by lower rank public officers; stealing a little from here and there, "squeezing" a few common folks they were supposed to serve, turning a blind eye to law breakers, after some monetary inducements. The largest cases involving this class of corruption were mainly collusions between several of these officers which was generally considered "conspiracies" in contemporary sources. Of course, there were also European officers and officials who brought disrepute at a much higher level, but such cases were less common, or less commonly discovered. The more serious threats had come from the big-money *hueys*, *kongsi*, the gambling syndicates and other vices, but by the 1930s, the convergence of all these corrupting forces and their collusion with corrupt government officers had threatened to further destabilise the socio-economic environment within the Straits Settlements. The much-needed response came in November–December 1937 when the first anti-corruption legislation was enacted by the passing of the Prevention of Corruption Ordinance. After this Ordinance was enacted, corruption acts charged under this ordinance were considered "seizable offences".[170]

The Prevention of Corruption Ordinance No. 41 of 1937 made bribery and secret commissions in public or private business punishable by the law. It was based mainly upon contemporary English statutes. The provisions of the Ordinance had taken reference from similar English, Australian and Indian (British) laws.[171] Besides the provisions for imprisonment and fines, the critical feature of the 1937 Prevention of Corruption Ordinance was the presumption of corruption clause. Derived from the 1916 British Prevention of Corruption Act, this provision would have given the Police the perfect weapon against corruption. Yet, corruption remained rife because legislation alone could not fight the corruption battle. Good men with strong will were still needed to implement the law.[172] It took time for the authorities to use this legal instrument in corruption cases. Soh, who was arrested in March 1940, was only the second corruptor to be charged under the 1937 Act.[173] The charge was decided by Fowler, head of the Detective Branch. And even then, Soh was ultimately let off when charges against him were dismissed on the grounds that Croft had received instructions from his superiors to receive bribes from Soh, and so, he was not entirely culpable.[174] Nevertheless, the ordinance was still considered useful as it allowed Fowler to hold Soh in detention for months while the investigation into Loveday had been ongoing.[175] In any case, following Soh's case, the 1937 Prevention of Corruption Ordinance was used in prosecution at least half a dozen more times before the end of 1941, when the Battle of Malaya had already started.

Singapore's first anti-corruption body was finally created in March 1941. By the following month, the new ACB, within the CID, was already receiving public information about corrupt cases. But for the most part of the remainder of 1941, the ACB had only one staff — its first head, Fowler.[176] This certainly explains the modest application of the 1937 Prevention of Corruption Ordinance till the end of 1941. Together, the establishment and introduction of the ACB (of one man) and the Prevention of Corruption Ordinance had represented a significant milestone in the battle against corrupt practices in Singapore. It was not only about the numbers arrested or prosecuted, but also about the lessons learnt and the legal and administrative processes already completed. In promulgating the 1937 Ordinance, it was already stated during the reading of the Bill in the Legislature that the government did not expect the Ordinance to eradicate corruption, but only to give the government another weapon to do so. It should also be noted that the main purpose of the 1937 Ordinance was to complement the provisions provided in Chapter 9 of the Penal Code.[177]

Chapter Four

Syonan Days

The level of corrupt practices reached an unprecedented peak during the years of the Japanese Occupation. In fact, it became more of the social norm; shortages of everything, from food to medicine, created the condition for the populace to find any way and means to acquire what was needed.[178] Beyond the regular rations and whatever the people could grow themselves, the main source of their supply was the black market. The reality of the day was that "it was impossible to do business without heavily bribing Japanese officials", and no one could get service in the government or municipality without greasing somebody's palm.[179] At a time when the Japanese controlled all imports and transportation, notwithstanding smuggling, all black market supplies would have been from Japanese-controlled sources. That is, these goods were more than likely "corruptly" taken from government stores or warehouses, or extorted from desperate persons.

While it has always been generally true that corruption in any society, within any regime and at any time, would have had a destabilising effect in society, the fact of the matter was that it was also the Japanese's Achilles' heel during the Occupation period. It was well known during the Occupation years that the Japanese military police had been the most corrupt amongst the Occupation troops,[180] and it was serendipitous that this included Japanese soldiers performing guard duties. They provided some leeway for people interned in camps to bribe their captors to leave the compound to buy food.[181] Guerrilla fighters in the Malayan jungles

▶ Legacy

were also able to survive in hiding because they were able to bribe villagers and others for food and shelter.[182]

Also, the Japanese Military Administration (JMA), after the atrocities of the Sook Ching massacre,[183] was actually focused on restoring law and order across Malaya. So, generally, this meant that most things were ignored or tolerated as long as peace was not disturbed and Japanese rule was not threatened. Under these conditions, some level of corruption became a constant in Malayan society. It was noted that gambling dens had thrived in the Malay States. These were operated by prominent men and protected by native police.[184] And generally, crimes involving extortion and corruption had remained unreported.[185] Nevertheless, occasionally, the JMA would intervene when collaborators they empowered to help keep order had themselves overstepped their authority. In mid-1945, when the JMA received complaints that members of Malacca's *Jikeidan* (Peace Preservation Corps) had been corrupt and had taken bribes, the JMA came down hard on them.[186] In March 1943, the JMA introduced the Maintenance of Public Peace and Order Law which generally covered all legal matters, including corruption. It was from this point that a number of corruption cases were brought to court and charged under this Law. Interestingly, the range of punishments permissible under this "ordinance" included hard labour on one end and the death sentence on the other. In May 1945, the JMA charged detective Chong Kit Cheong for illegal gratification totalling $19,500 which he extorted from 20 people in Kuala Lumpur from January to March 1945. Chong was a collaborator whom the JMA made a detective of police in March 1942. The trial judge thanked him for his service and collaboration over the years but lamented that he had abused his authority by illegally arresting civilians and extorting from them money for personal use. His actions had undermined public confidence in the police department. With that, the death sentence was passed under Article 6, Section 1 of the 2603 (1943) Maintenance of Public Peace and Order Law. He was executed as an example to the others in the Police.[187] Chong was likely the first police officer and the first person convicted for corruption to be executed.

The Japanese were also the first to use the issue of corruption in Malaya as a political tool or platform for political mileage. In late 1942, as part of their "hearts and minds" strategy, the local Japanese press started editorialising the evilness of the British regime which was afflicted by bribery and corruption.[188] By 1944, almost two years after Syonan days started, the rhetoric of the propaganda shifted from "we are better because the British were corrupt", to "we must fight corruption together". In the context of food and general shortages becoming more acute by this time, it was felt that something had to be done to stop hoarding and to prevent anyone cornering the market, like the black marketeers. In a new editorial on local corruption, the need for an anti-corruption body was even articulated: "An organisation should be set up to prevent any possibility of corruption, because graft will nullify the best of intentions underlying the scheme to guarantee food for everybody. Corruption and co-prosperity cannot exist together, and since our aim is the latter, the former must be eradicated at all cost."[189] At the same time, community leaders were also roped in to echo the regime's efforts to fight bribery and corruption.[190]

Corrupt practices during the Japanese Occupation had been blamed for the poor and corrupt environment in post-war Singapore. While it is certain the British Straits Settlements had its fair share of petty corruption as well as big-money bribery led by organised syndicates, the degenerated "morals" of the war years had been altogether a very different creature. While the conspiracy of the Loveday types had not been possible during the Occupation, gaming and other vices continued to thrive. This legacy of corruption, born out of war, affected everyone in the post-war years. President SR Nathan, who was a young man during the Syonan years, saw how wartime "corruption and social disintegration contributed to the difficulties well into the post-war era".[191] The lessons learnt on how to get by, to survive, or to get ahead, had been street lessons for the young and old. There is an account of how Abraham Joshua, a prisoner at Sime Road

▶ Legacy

camp, escaped from the camp twice to steal Straits currency from the home of another internee in order to buy Klim condensed milk for his child who could not take the infant powder issued in the camp. When the war ended, the theft was discovered and Abraham was charged for theft.[192] Was it wrong to steal? Yes. Had he any other options? Yes. Did he bribe the guards? Probably yes. Would he do it again? Probably yes. What compounded his tragedy was that he did not manage to purchase enough milk for his child even after all the walls and obstacles he had to negotiate. The $400 Straits currency he stole had to be exchanged for banana money which the shops selling tinned milk accepted. A dishonest trader took advantage of his plight and put the "squeeze" on by setting the exchange rate at six Straits dollars to one banana note. He got $66 banana notes in return. And this was a time of hyperinflation.

While Abraham might not return to those ways after liberation, the youth who lived through Syonan days had been socialised in a certain way of life, just like Oliver Twist and his band of brothers. In the late 1940s and 1950s, there was significant consensus on the ground that it was the experiences of the Occupation years that fostered the lax attitude towards petty corruption in the post-war years,[193] especially among those who grew up during the Occupation years. Hence, by the early 1950s, when Singapore's pioneering leaders were trying to forge a nation, general corruption and the general acceptance of corrupt practices like *kopi* money or betting with illegal bookies, or even giving little offerings to speed up day-to-day transactions, had been deep-seated issues all political leaders had to address.

The general war-time corruption issue also affected the police force of the day. It was the Police that spearheaded anti-corruption effects in the pre-war years. However, the Police Establishment had other legacy issues to deal with as well. On the eve of the Japanese invasion of Singapore, the strength of the police force in Singapore was "4,173 officers and men, and a clerical staff of 171... The majority of the rank and file then were largely Malays from Malacca, Negri Sembilan and Penang."[194] Many of them remained at their post during the Occupation years. By and large, most of the Force had no higher than primary school education. They were also not spared from the general corrupting influences of the war years. All these issues formed the backdrop for the establishment of the Corrupt Practices Investigation Bureau in 1952.

Endnotes

[1] In 1819, Stamford Raffles gave his instructions on the administration of the Singapore station to William Farquhar, Singapore's first British Resident (administrator). It was in late 1822 that Raffles penned Singapore's first locally written Regulations (laws). See Clement Liew, "Town Planning and Building in Early Colonial Singapore, 1819–1839: Sir Stamford Raffles and the Collaborative Development of a Colonial Port City", PhD Dissertation, Nanyang Technological University, National Institute of Education, 2010, pp.28–40, 119–24.

[2] The Straits Settlements comprised Singapore, Malacca and Penang. Malacca came under British rule from 1824 when Bencoolen was given to the Dutch in exchange for Malacca under the terms of the 1824 Anglo-Dutch Treaty. In 1826, with the formation of the Straits Settlements, Penang was made the capital of the new polity. At the same time, this new polity was raised to the level of an Indian Presidency; this meant that it could have its own governor and promulgate its own laws and regulations. The other Indian Presidencies at this time were Bengal, Madras and Bombay.

[3] Adapted from the first line of Jane Austen's *Pride and Prejudice*: "It is a truth universally acknowledged, that a single man in possession of a good fortune, must be in want of a wife." The irony is that the truth is quite the opposite.

[4] *Anticorruption in Transition: A Contribution to the Policy Debate* (Washington, D.C: The World Bank, September 2000), p.4.

[5] Basically, officials of the East India Company (EIC) had formed the Government of India till the mid-nineteenth century. The EIC had termed all British settlements, trading posts and colonies east of the Indian Ocean as eastern settlements, and these included Singapore and Hong Kong, even though Hong Kong was administered directly by the British Admiralty after the 1839–42 Opium War. It should be noted, within the context of the EIC's establishment, Stamford Raffles' substantial rank was "Senior Trader", even though he was the Lieutenant-Governor of Java, then of Bencoolen. Nigel Barley called Raffles a "colonial trader". See Nigel Barley, *The Duke of Puddledock: In the Footsteps of Stamford Raffles* (UK: Monsoon Books, 2010).

[6] PJ Marshall, "The Bengal Commercial Society of 1775: Private British Trade in the Warren Hastings Period", *Bulletin of the Institute of Historical Research*, Vol. 42, No. 106 (Nov 1969): 173. In the EIC, "private trading by individuals coexisted with official trade of the company". As venturing into the East to trade had entailed much hardship and risk, the EIC allowed its employees to undertake private trade as an incentive to join the Company.

[7] Margot Finn and Kate Smith (eds.), *East India Company at Home, 1757–1857* (London: UCL Press, 2018), pp.7, 88, 97, 319, 372–373. It was in the latter half of the eighteenth century when the accumulation of wealth from private trade and political corruption by EIC officials reached its peak. Private trade at this time earned EIC ship captains 10 times their normal salary. Their gain was proportional to the Company's loss. Essentially, private trade became a form of regulated corruption and had become the root of corrupt practices in the eastern colonies. See CH Philips, *The East India Company 1784–1834* (Manchester: Manchester University Press, 1940), p.23. It was partly because of "endemic corruption" that the EIC was "gradually deprived of its commercial monopoly and political control". See https://www.britannica.com/story/5-fast-facts-about-the-east-india-company.

[8] Raffles secured the right to establish an EIC "Factory" on the island of Singapore. A "Factory" in this case refers to a "trading establishment at a foreign port or mart". See Henry Yule and AC Burnell, *The Concise Hobson-Jobson, The Anglo-Indian Dictionary* (UK: Wordsworth Reference, 1996), p.346.

[9] *Malaya Law Review*, Vol. 11, No. 1 (1969): 96.

[10] See https://heinonline.org/HOL/LandingPage?handle=hein.journals/sjls11&div=12&id=&page=; Under the 1825 British Parliamentary Act 6, George IV, c85, s21, the Residencies of "Singapore and Malacca" were "annexed to Penang as one Presidency". Farquhar had relinquished British control over Malacca in 1818. The town was returned to British rule in 1824 following the terms of the Anglo-Dutch Treaty of that year which exchanged British Bencoolen for Dutch Malacca.

[11] Straits Settlements Records L17, 58–63, 28 Jan 1823; https://www.singaporelawwatch.sg/

About-Singapore-Law/Overview/ch-01-the-singapore-legal-system.

[12] These laws were contained in the EIC's own Charter, the East India Company Act 1813, also known as the Charter Act 1813, within sections XXXIII-XL. The provisions of this Act/Charter provided the EIC with the privilege of monopoly over many matters in India and her colonies. For full content of Act of Parliament 1813, 53 George III. Cap.155, see *The Bengal and Agra Annual Guide and Gazetteer for 1842*, Vol I (Calcutta: William Rushton and Co., 1842), pp.99–141. Also see Charles Burton Buckley, *An Anecdotal History of Old Times in Singapore* (Singapore: Fraser & Neave, 1902, p.197.

[13] *Singapore Chronicle* 5 Sep 1827. Proclamation: The Straits Settlement would receive its Royal Letters of Patent for its Court of Judicature, on the 7th year of King George's the IV reign. Also see Charles Burton Buckley, *An Anecdotal History of Old Times in Singapore*, p.197.

[14] Up till the end of the Penang Presidency in 1830, Singapore had experienced the discretionary application of various laws and regulations observed within the Straits Settlements. While the general laws of Britain applied, EIC and Indian laws and regulations were also observed by local administrators. The local Residents also observed the principles of Indirect Rule which gave indigenous leadership some leeway to apply their own "system" of justice within their own communities. The system of Indirect Rule had been enshrined within the treaties signed with the Malay rulers of Singapore in 1819. Terms of the agreement provided for the formation of a *Rooma Bechara*, a ruling council or assembly, that brought together all the heads of communities, the Malay Rulers and the British authority, to preside over administrative and judicial issues. See Charles Burton Buckley, *An Anecdotal History of Old Times in Singapore*, pp.58–9. In 1829, when Tan Che Sang, an important local headman in early Singapore, was called upon to give testimony on behalf of the Chinese in Court, instead of swearing on the Bible to speak the truth, he swore to speak truthfully "by cutting off a cock's head" in Court. See *The Asiatic Journal and Monthly Register for British India and its Dependencies*, IV (Jan–Apr 1831): 86–7.

[15] While the use of community leadership as an adjunct to colonial administration had lasted into the first half of the nineteenth century, no one knows exactly when this system of Company and "frontier justice" ended in early Singapore. Scholars have suggested that the "justice [was dispensed] through the headmen", would have been "officially terminated" with the introduction of the Second Charter. Suffice it to say, up till this time, corrupt practices amongst locals and officials would not have raised too many eyebrows. See Clement Liew, "*Ordo ab Chao* at the Far End of India: Chinese Settlers and Their Colonial Masters", *Journal of Asian History*,Vol. 50, No. 1 (2016): 161–62. *Ordo Ab Chao* is Latin for "order out of chaos"; Wong Choon San, *A Gallery of Chinese Kapitans* (Singapore: Ministry of Culture, 1963), p.28.

[16] Legislative Council of India, Act No. XIII of 1856, Section XIII, assented by Governor General, 13 Jun 1856. The 1856 Police Act was more relevant to the battle against corruption than the Third Charter of Justice that was introduced a year earlier in August 1855.

[17] The British Government ended the right of the EIC to administer India following the 1857–58 Indian Rebellion. This effectively abolished the EIC Indian Government. Following the promulgation of the Government of India Act, 1858, the EIC was "nationalised" and the Government took over all of the Company's possessions and assets in India. See Ben Johnson, "*The East India Company and its role in ruling India*", https://www.historic-uk.com/HistoryUK/HistoryofEngland/The-East-India-Company/. Following this, India became a Crown Colony of Britain and was administered directly by the British Government. In this context, the Straits Settlements became sub-colonies of the British India Colony. That is, India retained oversight of the Straits Settlements from 1858. It was a situation that the Straits communities considered no better than when they were under EIC rule. So, they continued their agitation for a "Transfer".

[18] The 1856 Police Act was an Indian legislation that included the Straits Settlements. Although the 1871 Ordinance was not the first instance corruption had been outlawed here, it was the first locally written legislation on the matter and it considered local contexts and conditions.

Penal Code 1871 (Ordinance IV of 1871), Chapter IX, Sections 161‑171 (gratification and abetment), cover corrupt offences by public servants; Sections 109, 116 (abetment) covers bribery by anyone (including bribers). See John Augustus Harwood, *The Acts and Ordinances of the Legislative Council of the Straits Settlements, From 1st April 1867 to 1st June 1886*, Vol 1 (London: Eyre and Spottiswoode, 1886), pp.360–64, 373–375; *Straits Times Overland Journal* 9 Sep 1871.

[19] These include the failure to perform their duty to provide services, or withholding services in order to solicit reward, or taking action to abet in order to be rewarded or for gain.

[20] Matthew Bacon, Sir Henry Gwilliam & Charles Edward Dodd, *A New Abridgment of the Law with Large Additions and Corrections*, Vol 7 (Philadelphia: Thomas Davis, 1846), pp.433–34.

[21] Revenue collected from farming out these consumables could then be used to finance the monthly payments to the Sultan and Temenggong as well as to give government an income, a part of which could be used to fund policing within the settlement. See Straits Settlements Records L10, 192–93, 2 Nov 1819.

[22] The use of "farm" meant letting out, or farming out.

[23] Chinese headman.

[24] Straits Settlements Records L10, 367–372, 5 May 1820. Farquhar had to first resolve the standing practice in the settlement. At this point, residents wishing to retail opium on the island had to first seek permission from the Malay Chiefs.

[25] Justine Crump, "The Perils of Play: Eighteenth-century Ideas about Gambling", Unpublished Seminar Paper, Centre for History and Economics, University of Cambridge, 2004, pp.1–28. Raffles still continuously questioned the need to maintain the gaming farm, since gambling was considered immoral in early Victorian society.

[26] Clement Liew, "Town Planning and Building in Early Colonial Singapore, 1819–1839: Sir Stamford Raffles and the Collaborative Development of a Colonial Port City", PhD Dissertation, Nanyang Technological University, National Institute of Education, 2010, p.138. Between January to June 1823, Raffles wrote his famed Singapore Regulations — in all, six Regulations were promulgated. It was Regulation IV (May 1823) that permanently banned gambling on the island. Raffles had closed the gaming farm prior to the formulation of the regulation. See Straits Settlements Records L17, 58–63, 28 Jan 1823; Sophia Raffles, *Memoir of the life and public services of Sir Thomas Stamford Raffles* (Singapore: Oxford University Press, 1991), pp.39–62. Raffles had proclaimed in Regulation IV that "the practice of gaming [was] highly destructive to the morals and happiness of the people".

[27] Straits Settlements Records L15, 27, 16 Apr 1823; L14, 27–29, 16 Apr 1823, Farquhar, Resident Singapore, to LN Hull, Acting Secretary to Lieutenant Governor (Fort Marlborough).

[28] Straits Settlements Records L19, 164, Jul 1823. From then gambling continued illegally. And despite resolute action and large fines, gaming continued unabated. In 1820, the Penang Government discovered that almost the entire police force of the island, "European constables and native police", had taken large bribes and conspired with the gaming syndicates to circumvent the laws against gaming.

[29] *Singapore Chronicle* 27 Dec 1832.

[30] When Singapore became part of the Straits Settlements from 1826, it was subjected to Penang's Presidency's First Charter of Justice. Soon after, the Presidency received its Second Charter, which provided the Colony with its first professional judge (Recorder) in 1827. Part of this system of justice was the creation of the Grand Jury for each settlement. These juries were composed of leading members of each respective settlement. They were empowered to inquire and recommend policies to the Straits Settlements Governor or the Recorder. It was the Grand Jury presentments against gaming houses to the Recorder in 1828–1829 that ended this revenue farm. See *Singapore Chronicle* 19 Jul 1832, quoting the Memorandum of Government Fullerton, 18 May 1829, published in the *Asiatic Journal* of February 1832. *Singapore Chronicle* 26 Feb, 29 Apr, 2 Jul 1829.

[31] It was noted that by early 1828, cock fighting, which was part of the gaming farm, could be

found in all the Straits Settlements. Penang was the first settlement that banned this game which was "one of the brutal amusements of civilised life". Malacca and Singapore followed suit in the same year. See *Singapore Chronicle* 17 Jan 1828. In early 1829, the Singapore Grand Jury made a presentment to the government desiring an end to the licensing of "Public Gaming Houses". The magistrates felt that the licensing of this vice would not "lessen" gambling in Singapore but only "increase" it. See *Singapore Chronicle* 26 Feb, 29 Apr, 2 Jul 1829.

[32] The Singapore Resident noted in 1929 that the court had noticed that "native" police, court interpreters and swearers had demonstrated "propensity" for being corrupted, and this was linked to their salary levels. See Straits Settlements Records A62, 17, 7 Oct 1829. Minutes by Resident Councillor K Murchison. It was also around this time that instances of witnesses were found guilty of perjury in court (corrupt perjury). In one instance, the testimony of an Indian witness differed from a previous testimony given. It was proven that he had been "wilful and corrupt". *Singapore Chronicle* 4 Dec 1828.

[33] *Singapore Chronicle* 10 Mar 1831.

[34] Home Department Public, 30 Oct 1832 No. 15 — Letter from R Ibbetson, Governor of Prince of Wales Island, Singapore and Malacca, to HT Prinsep, Secretary to the Government of Bengal, 12 Aug 1832–30 Oct 1832, in National Archives of India. The police peons were probably prosecuted under the provisions of the Second Charter.

[35] *Singapore Chronicle* 16 May 1833.

[36] *Singapore Chronicle* 30 May 1834. The *Madras Gazette*, on 22 February 1834, jested about the Singapore Police having been "over-anxious" about their "regularly paid bribes from the gambling shops", although they acknowledged the low pay the peons were receiving.

[37] *Singapore Free Press* 31 Mar 1836. At this time, it was well-known that the Police were "notoriously corrupt" and were deeply involved in gaming; police constables and peons tended to use "their illicit gains" to gamble at the places they were protecting.

[38] *Singapore Free Press* 26 Sep 1844.

[39] *Singapore Free Press* 16 Feb 1843; CB Buckley, *An Anecdotal History of Old Times in Singapore*, p.386.

[40] *Singapore Free Press* 24 Aug 1843.

[41] *Singapore Free Press* 28 Sep 1843; CB Buckley, *An Anecdotal History of Old Times in Singapore*, p.386. Till July 1843, Dunman was still engaged in the import and export activities of the firm. See *Singapore Free Press* 6 Jul 1843.

[42] *Singapore Free Press* 5 Oct 1843; CB Buckley, *An Anecdotal History of Old Times in Singapore*, pp.394–95.

[43] *Singapore Free Press* 5 Oct 1843; *Straits Times* 23 Sep, 3 Oct, 4 Nov 1845.

[44] Every *Phoa* gaming shop had an attractive female employed, and most of the time they were also the overseers of the shop. Telligoviden himself operated such a *Phoa* and had one of such women employed. It was his shop overseer who lodged a complaint against him; he took her jewellery — a gold pin valued at $180, a gold tobacco box worth $98 and a gold head ornament worth $22. Telligoviden also owed her $150 for overseeing the gaming shop between 8 January and 8 April 1845, at $50 per month. The total Telligoviden owed and took from her amounted to $378. See *Straits Times* 16 Sep 1845.

[45] Aside from operating from rented premises, which provided distance between the den operators and their shops, which also limited losses in case of raids, each gaming shop was also maintained by an "overseer" employed by the operators. See *Singapore Free Press* 1 Oct 1846, 7 Jan 1847; *Straits Times* 16 Sep 1845.

[46] There were three Chinese games which the gambling shops offered: *Wha-way* (36 cards, drawing the same card wins 3 times the bet, house commission 3% of winnings), *Phoa* (spinning a box of 4 sides, red and white sides and two plain, red wins 3 times the bet, house commission 10% of winnings) and *Koon Sho Choa* (12 cards in a box, bets placed on a board printed with images of the cards, drawn card wins 10 times the bet). *Phoa* was the most popular of the three. People can be found playing this game in almost every street. The game was so popular that the gambling shops were often

called *Phoa* shops. See *Straits Times* 16 Sep 1845.

[47] *Singapore Free Press* 2 Oct 1845.

[48] *Straits Times* 16 Sep, 3 Oct 1845.

[49] *Singapore Free Press* 2 Oct 1845.

[50] *Straits Times* 16 Sep 1845.

[51] *Straits Times* 16 Sep, 3 Oct 1845.

[52] *Straits Times* 16 Sep, 3 Oct 1845.

[53] *Singapore Free Press* 2 Oct 1845.

[54] *Singapore Free Press* 14 Mar 1844, 24 Aug 1849.

[55] CB Buckley, *An Anecdotal History of Old Times in Singapore*, p.448; *Singapore Free Press* 7 May 1846.

[56] *Straits Times* 1 May 1846. The Malays chewed sirih (betel) leaves habitually.

[57] *Singapore Free Press* 13 Nov 1845.

[58] *Singapore Free Press* 7 May 1846; *Straits Times* 9 May 1846: CB Buckley, *An Anecdotal History of Old Times in Singapore*, pp.446–48. Cashim claimed that he was charged by another guilty bribe-taking constable, and the charge against him was false. See *Singapore Free Press* 14 May 1846.

[59] *Singapore Free Press* 7 May 1846; *Straits Times* 9 May 1846: CB Buckley, *An Anecdotal History of Old Times in Singapore*, pp.446–48.

[60] But this arrangement was clearly an abject failure in as far as the maintenance of law and order was concerned. Communal leaders did not wield absolute authority over their countrymen as their influence had been based more on affluence and not mandate. Besides, even within a single dialectal community, leadership had been varied, and this leadership was not political in nature. In fact, more often than not, communal leaders tended to be partial towards their own clansmen.

[61] *Singapore Free Press* 21 May 1846.

[62] There is very little historical information on Alfred Simonides. It appears that he had arrived in Singapore sometime in 1843. In that year, he became proprietor of a boarding house called Marine Hotel, situated along Boat Quay, along the Singapore River (No. 20 Boat Quay). See *Singapore Free Press* 21 Sep, 5 Oct 1843.

[63] *Singapore Free Press* 21 May 1846.

[64] *Singapore Free Press* 29 Apr 1847; Walter Makepeace, Gilbert Edward Brooke & Roland Bradell, *One Hundred Years of Singapore: Being Some Account of the Capital of the Straits Settlements From its Foundation by Sir Stamford Raffles on the 6th February 1819 to the 6th February 1919* (London: Murray, 1921), p.257. Simonides' exploits became stuff of legends about bravery and ingenuity, and his stories spread as far as India. Simonides and his peons were able to detain more than a dozen gamers in each raid. He took on the dens of the famed gaming district of Church Street (see *Straits Times* 22 Aug 1846) and conducted operations that resembled commando raids. One such example was his raid on a den at Kampong Malacca in October–November 1846. In the 1840s, Kampong Malacca was still an "islet" in the middle of the Singapore River. It was only accessible via a narrow bridge made of small planks. The gambling den sat on a wooden platform held up by wooden poles (stilts) above the waterline. Surrounded by water, no one could surprise this gambling den without the spotters seeing them approach. So, Simonides got some of his peons to disguise themselves as fishermen on sampans to move in and close off access to the kampong, while others approached the islet by swimming up to the den and scaling the poles. Simonides assailed the compound from all sides. This became one of the rare raids where the den boss failed to escape. Details of this raid were reported in the Calcutta press. See *Singapore Free Press* 7 Oct 1847; *Straits Times* 18 Nov 1846.

[65] *Straits Times* 14 Nov 1846. In November 1847, Simonides detained a number of the Singapore Sultan's followers and scions for cockfighting (gaming) near the Sultan's premises at Kampong Glam. Regular peons would not have been so daring. In all, 10 persons were charged in court and fined $2 each. See *Singapore Free Press* 25 Nov 1847.

[66] Some months earlier, at midnight, on 30 April 1846, some 200 Chinese secret society men from deep in the jungle descended on and sacked the family house of the magistrate's clerk, Thomas Hewetson, on Mount Elizabeth, situated at the end of Orchard Road, near Tanglin. The brigands plundered for an hour, trapping and threatening

the family who held the invaders at bay with just one musket, and the Police never came. See *Singapore Free Press* 2 Apr 1846 (Hewetson), 29 Jul 1847 (Survey); *Singapore Free Press*; *Straits Times* 1 May 1846; CB Buckley, *An Anecdotal History of Old Times in Singapore*, p.445.

[67] In March 1848, Simonides' party was able to make their way into the northern part of the island (9 miles) to effect the arrest of town gamblers who eluded the Police. When they were making their way back to Town, a gathering of about 200 Chinese attacked the party in an attempt to free their compatriots. The peons had to continuously fire volleys at them to hold them back. See *Straits Times* 11 Mar 1848. By May 1848, Simonides went far beyond any local constable had gone in pursuit of his suspects.

[68] Interestingly, Simonides' anti-gambling operations also impacted the general revenue generation in Singapore, even though gaming had not been part of the licensing farm system. As all the dens had operated from rented properties, the shutting of more than 100 gambling houses had also deprived the property owners of rental income. The average monthly rental rate of each house during this period was about $20–$30. Following the clampdown, these houses became deserted, and the owners found it hard to rent them out even at half the prevailing rates. At the same time, businesses in Town also suffered great losses as there were far fewer "consumers" in the streets: shopkeepers had depended on gambier and pepper coolies from the interior visiting Town in large numbers to gamble. Here, they would also spend their income on general items sold in the shops. Following the anti-gambling raids that curtailed their gaming activities, they stopped going into Town. In fact, many gaming shops shifted into the interior where they could operate with impunity. See *Singapore Free Press* 1 Oct 1846, 7 Jan 1847. The mini economic downturn in Town truly attests to the impact of Simonides' work which greatly reduced illicit money circulating in Town.

[69] *Singapore Free Press* 21 Jan, 29 Apr 1847 (Quoting report from T Church, Resident Councillor, Singapore, 17 January 1847), 3 May 1847. Walter Makepeace, *One Hundred Years of Singapore*, p.257. It was felt that Simonides and his peons deserved public commendation as they had achieved the "impossible". The Police Establishment had earlier claimed that "the evil of the gambling shop" was "impossible to prevent". The gold medal was worth $80, that is, 80 silver dollars.

[70] In mid-1846, an opium revenue farmer instructed (bribed) the police peons attached to his farm to plant illicit opium on a rival merchant, Ang Ah, who had just been awarded the rights to operate the opium farm in Johore. The opium and spirits farmers of Singapore had been losing $100 per day per farm on account of the Johore farms. The peons assaulted Ang Ah and dragged him to the opium farmer's office. Fortunately, another merchant, Frommurze Sorabjee, saw the commotion and demanded the peon to send Ang Ah to the Superintendent of Police and Magistrate. Charges against him were immediately dismissed. Ang Ah then took the peons to court and was awarded $65 for their assault. See *Singapore Free Press* 4 Jul 1846; *Straits Times* 4 Jul 1846: CB Buckley, *An Anecdotal History of Old Times in Singapore*, p.430.

[71] *Singapore Free Press* 29 Apr 1847; *Straits Times* 18 Jul 1846.

[72] Council of India Act, No. III of 1847, 19 February 1847. The Act was sent to the Straits on 17 March 1847 and it was published in full the very next day. See *Singapore Free Press* 18 Mar 1847.

[73] Stated in the Act: "from and after the 19th day of March 1847, no Constable or Subordinate Peace Officer or other person appointed to perform duties of police shall be appointed by the said Court at their General and Quarter Sessions or otherwise" — Section I, Council of India Act, No. III of 1847, 19 February 1847. That is, police or peace officers can only be appointed by the government body that pays them. Therefore, they do not take instructions from the Court.

[74] In the Grand Jury session on 27 April 1846, attended by both the Recorder and the Governor, the Jurors blamed "the inefficient state of the Police" for the high instances of crime in Singapore. There had been many attacks and kidnapping of persons by the Chinese secret societies. The Governor, however, felt that the

▶ Legacy

Grand Jury's presentment contained certain "unbecoming" expressions, and he rebuked them on almost every point See *Singapore Free Press* 30 Apr 1846. The Indian press took great interest in the polemic between the Governor of the Straits Settlements and the people of Singapore. They noted that serious "differences" arose following the Grand Jury's presentation (*Spectator* — Madras, 4 Jun 1846), and the Governor's objection to their description of the local police as "disgraceful" (*Atlas* — Calcutta, 5 Jun 1846). Other papers noting the issue included the *Madras Crescent* 9 Jun 1846 and *Calcutta Star*. See *Singapore Free Press* 16, 23 Jul 1846.

[75] *Singapore Free Press* 14 May 1846. For the Regulations in full, see *Singapore Free Press* 16 Nov 1849. This occurred during the Grand Jury session on 27 April 1846. It was in this session that the Judiciary asserted its right to appoint Dunman the Superintendent of Police (from Deputy) and to have him concentrate on police matters rather than magistrate duties. Dunman was to submit his Rules and Regulations to the magistrates for their feedback. The government objected to magistrates' intrusion into the executive sphere, citing India Act No. XII of 1839 (Municipal Act) as having superseded the Charter of Justice (Second) in as far as oversight of police matters was concerned. The magistrates disagreed, and pointed out correctly that the 1839 Act made no mention on the appointment or management of the Police. See *Singapore Free Press* 14 May 1846. In any case, Dunman's formulated Rules and Regulations was indeed circulated to the magistrates for consideration. See *Singapore Free Press* 22 Oct 1846.

[76] *Straits Times* 17 Oct 1846. The new Act was crafted to correct this anomaly.

[77] *Singapore Free Press* 30 Apr 1846. In fact, months before a draft of the new Act was published, the Grand Jurors formulated a set of instructions as a guidance for the local police. In July 1846, CH Caldwell, Senior Court Clerk, announced that a copy of these "instructions" was ready. See *Straits Times* 18 Jul 1846. Earlier in February 1846, the Penang community had already drafted their own new police regulations Act which they submitted to their magistrates for feedback. See *Singapore Free Press* 26 Feb 1846.

[78] The governor had already submitted the Bill for the new Act to the governing Council of India on 12 September 1846, a month before publishing it in the local press. See *Singapore Free Press* 15 Oct 1846.

[79] The Singapore community shared their feelings about the "stupid" draft Police Act in the press. On 10 November 1846, they held a Public Meeting to express their "hurt" over the matter. See *Singapore Free Press* 5, 12 Nov 1846.

[80] *Singapore Free Press* 26 Nov, 3 Dec 1846. This course of action was taken after the Governor rejected a petition the Justices of Peace submitted to him in October 1846. See *Singapore Free Press* 25 Mar 1847.

[81] *Singapore Free Press* 25 Mar, 6 Apr, 17 Jun 1847, 14 Jun 1849. Also see CB Buckley, *An Anecdotal History of Old Times in Singapore*, pp.465–66.

[82] *Singapore Free Press* 27 May, 10 Jun 1847. The petition was signed by 215 people. John Crawfurd presented the case at the House of Commons and made a similar address to the House of Lords. Also see CB Buckley, *An Anecdotal History of Old Times in Singapore*, pp.465–66. The Singapore Justices of Peace pointed out that the Supreme Government in India promulgated the Act "without seeing results" achieved in the year (Simonides), and as a case in point of the ineffectiveness of the Police was demonstrated when the police leadership ordered their men not to interfere with gambling houses and allowed gambling during Chinese New Year. The Governor's point was contained in his reply to the Justices of Peace in Correspondence no. 46, gen no. 223 of 1847, 27 March 1847.

[83] *Singapore Free Press* 29 Apr 1847.

[84] The Chinese secret societies had become a significant force in Singapore. Many of them had been rebels who fled China fighting the Manchus. They had deep resources which they used readily for bribery and corruption to "defeat the course of justice". See *Singapore Free Press* 6 Oct 1849. The most poignant example of how the *hueys* "defeated the course of justice" with their

big money occurred in late 1849 to early 1850 when constable Gliddon led his team to Boo Koo Kangkar to close down the gaming operations there. This was at the end of Bukit Timah Road where the travellers crossing the interior of the island would come to take a boat down the Kranji River to Johore. By this time, everyone knew that the village of the district, Sungei Kranji Village (today, at the junction of Mandai and Woodlands Road), had been a significant gambling district by 1849, probably due to Simonides' actions in 1846–1847 that pushed most of the gaming shops out of Town and into the interior. See *Singapore Free Press* 7, 14 Jun 1850. By the 1850s, the independent den operators had given way to highly organised Chinese secret societies which had the muscle to control multiple vice rackets. They became the new corruptors in the Straits Settlements, while the Police Establishment of the Straits remained unchanged, unimproved, unprepared and still under-resourced.

[85] *Singapore Free Press* 8 Jul 1847.

[86] *Straits Times* 25 Mar 1848; *Singapore Free Press* 8 Jun, 30 Nov 1848.

[87] When the opportunity surfaced for his permanent appointment in that position, he was shunned because he was about to be made an insolvent and was "not in favour with higher powers." See *Singapore Free Press* 30 Nov 1848.

[88] Simonides was the proprietor of Marine Hotel in 1843. See *Singapore Free Press* 21 Sep, 5 Oct 1843.

[89] The creditor who took Simonides to Insolvency Court was China Tomby Maupilly. In 1844, he gave Simonides a loan for which he charged up to 10% interest. By 1848, when the Police suffered a pay reduction, he could no longer keep up with payments. When the official assignee seized his properties, only $18 had been monetised. At that point, his pay was 125 rupees monthly (about $30). As he had a family of five children and a wife to support, he declared he would be seeking a "more lucrative" job in order to clear his debts. See *Straits Times* 21 Mar 1849. As for China Tomby, he had been incarcerated in Penang for larceny and as an insolvent debtor since 1844, presumably after he gave Simonides a loan. When he completed his jail time in 1848, he applied to be relieved from his insolvent debt. Following his release, he brought Simonides to court to recover his loan. See *Singapore Free Press* 27 Jun 1844, 15 Mar 1849. Simonides' trial was set for March 1849. See *Singapore Free Press* 30 Nov 1848.

[90] Simonides' assets were disposed of in a public auction. All his possessions were sold, including his insurance policy which was worth 5,000 rupees (to take over his policy). See *Straits Times* 23 Nov 1848. At this point, the loan outstanding to China Tomby was $2,500. See *Singapore Free Press* 7 Apr 1849.

[91] Up till mid-1848, Simonides and his peons were still raiding illegal gambling dens in Town and in the rural districts, and prosecuting the culprits in court. See *Straits Times* 26 Aug 1848. By early 1849, Simonides was the Head Constable. See *Singapore Free Press* 29 Mar 1849.

[92] CM Turnbull, *A History of Singapore 1819-1988* (2nd ed. Singapore: Oxford University Press, 1989), pp.57-58; *Straits Times* 9 May 1846.

[93] *Straits Times* 14 Oct 1848.

[94] *Singapore Free Press* 5 Apr 1849. Of course, there were other constables who had done their job to pursue illegal gambling cases after Simonides' departure, but none had been as successful, and Simonides was the first to lead the charge soon after the Cashim affair placed doubts on the other constables. There were other raids that led to the prosecution of dozens of gamblers and gaming-house bosses in each case (separate raids carried out by Constable MacDonnell, Head Jamadar Armogam, Head Jemedar Alie Khan, Inspector Shea, Jemedar Koss Gunny and Head Constable Borthwick). See *Singapore Free Press* 12 Oct 1849, 22 Mar, 4, 14 Jun, 7, 12 Jul 1850.

[95] "Council of India, Act No. IX of 1848: an Act to repeal Acts No XII of 1839 and XII of 1840, and to raise funds for Police and Municipal purposes for Straits Settlements by levying an assessment upon rents, produce and income derived from buildings and lands within the settlement, and by taxing carriages, wagons, carts, horses...." See *Straits Times* 13 May 1848.

[96] Passed by the Municipal Committee on 29 October 1849.

[97] *Singapore Free Press* 16 Nov 1849. Letter from Municipal Committee to Resident Councillor no.67, 25 Oct 1849. And the appended set of rules for the organisation of the police force. Also see *Singapore Free Press* 5 May 1854. Municipal Committee meeting on 26 April 1854: Rules and Regulations for the Guidance of the Police Force of Singapore was passed by the Municipal Committee on 29 October 1849.

[98] *Singapore Free Press* 27 Jul, 3 Aug 1849.

[99] *Straits Times* 6 Feb 1855.

[100] India Act XXXIV of 1852, the Gambling Act, was passed on 10 September 1952.

[101] Bill/Act for regulating the Police of Calcutta, Madras and Bombay, and the Settlements of Prince of Wales' Island, Singapore, and Malacca. See *Singapore Free Press* 8 Nov 1855.

[102] Thomas Dunman remained the Deputy Superintendent of Police till late 1850 when he became the Acting Superintendent. He was then appointed Superintendent in early 1851. By 1855, Dunman was spending more time as the Sitting Magistrate (Police Magistrate), and by mid-1856, he was also made the Assistant Resident Councillor. By this time, it was only known that the new Police Act had been passed by the Governor General and would be put into operation at the start of 1857, and Dunman may not be in charge of the Police by this time. From October 1856, Dunman served in the Municipal Council (before the Act was passed, the municipality was just a committee) as a member. He was still the Sitting Magistrate at this time. See *Singapore Free Press* 27 Jul 1849, 11 Jan, 22 Oct 1850,14 Feb, 12 Dec 1851, 16 Aug 1855, 8 Apr, 29 May, 2 Oct, 4 Dec 1856. In November 1856, the government announced that Henry Somerset Mackenzie would be appointed Resident Councillor as well as Singapore's first Commissioner of Police. Arthur Wahab was to be the Deputy Commissioner. By virtue of being the Resident Councillor, Mackenzie was also a judge. See *Singapore Free Press* 27 Nov, 8, 11 Dec 1856, 4, 8 Jan 1857. In May 1857, it was decided that Mackenzie should not hold the post of Commissioner of Police and the Resident Councillor concurrently. So, Mackenzie resigned from his police post and Dunman was appointed the Commissioner of Police in his place. See *Singapore Free Press* 7 May, 14 May, 18 Jun, 23 Jul 1857.

[103] *Straits Times* 4 Nov 1856, 2 Jul 1859; *Singapore Free Press* 7 Aug 1856, 5 Sep 1863. In April 1854, the Police Establishment was 260 strong. See *Straits Times* 2 May 1854. The Supreme Government in India had claimed that the Police in the Straits had been corrupt when the Force was placed under the purview of the Municipality, and that the local Police Establishment was not a professional force.

[104] *Singapore Free Press* 16 Nov 1849.

[105] In Indian Act XIII of 1856, Section XIII states that officers asking for or accepting bribes, unauthorised rewards, or omitting to do official duty could be fine or imprisoned. In Section XXVIII, those engaged in embezzlement or breach of trust may be imprisoned. All rules, regulations and ordinances relating to the Police were repealed when the new Police Act came into operation at the beginning of 1857. See *Singapore Free Press* 8 Nov 1855.

[106] *Straits Times* 4 Nov 1856, 2 Jul 1859; *Singapore Free Press* 7 Aug 1856, 5 Sep 1863.

[107] Walter Makepeace, *One Hundred Years of Singapore*, Vol. 1, pp.250-51. Sir William Robinson appointed a Police Commission of Enquiry in 1878 to examine the organisation of the Police and to look into its inefficiency. The Commission's report, published in early January 1879, noted that the Police were inadequately paid and that the Chinese were known for their free-handed offering of bribes, mainly because "this was how things were with officials in their home country". See *Singapore Daily Times* 4 Jan, 27 Oct, 22 Nov 1879; *Straits Times Overland Journal* 10 Sep, 31 Oct 1879.

[108] The current Singapore Penal Code – Chapter IX, still deals with corrupt acts: "Public servant taking a gratification, other than legal remuneration, in respect of an official act", Sections 161-65.

[109] Corrupt practices covered under the original 1870 Penal Code included: Dishonest misappropriation or conversion of moveable property under Section 403 (Chapters IV & V of Penal Code); Dishonestly receiving and

retaining stolen property under Section 411; and Assisting in the concealment, disposing of and making away with stolen property under Section 411–414, 424 (Chapters XXXII & XXXIII). See *Straits Settlements Government Gazette* (SSGG) 3 Jun 1870, pp.190, 198; 1 Jul 1870, p.316. In short, the Penal Code contained the first anti-corruption laws that specifically considered the position of the Straits communities. In Penal Code 1871 (Ordinance IV of 1871), Chapter IX, Sections 161–171 (gratification and abetment), cover corrupt offences by public servants; Sections 109, 116 (abetment) covers bribery by anyone (including bribers). See John Augustus Harwood, *The Acts and Ordinances of the Legislative Council of the Straits Settlements, From 1st April 1867 to 1st June 1886: Together with Certain Acts of Parliament, Orders of Her Majesty in Council, Letters Patent, and Indian Acts in Force in the Colony of the Straits Settlements*, Vol 1 (London: Eyre and Spottiswoode, 1886), pp.360–64, 373–75.

[110] Among the new government departments which were created after the Transfer were the Chinese Protectorate and the Auditor General's Department. The total wage bill of the Straits Settlements Government was around $433,000 in 1868. In 1873, it was $530,000. See *Straits Times Overland Journal* 7 Nov 1872.

[111] In the first incident, the strikers' complaint against Kristnasamy, the Registry Assistant, for bribery and extortion landed him in court. The magistrate dismissed the bribery charges because the man only took "one bottle of gin and 50 cents". See *Straits Times* 5 Feb, 26 Mar 1870. In the 1875 strike, 120 carriage owners and syces (carriage drivers) complained to the Governor that they had been "squeezed" and ill-treated. They provided details of the infraction, and the identity of the police inspector and native Sergeant Major involved. So, the Governor appointed a committee to enquire into the matter. See *Straits Observer* 17 Sep 1875; *Straits Times* 23 Oct 1875. Hackney carriages were horse-drawn carriages that plied the streets of Singapore in the nineteenth century. They were the "taxis" of the early days, and they had to have licences (government fees) to operate.

[112] In 1897 the Chief Clerk BBJ Rozells of the police court and Court's Head Peon, Baboo, were arrested for taking bribes from the Chinese men who were in court bailing out others. The charges against Baboo were withdrawn later. See *Singapore Free Press* 1 Dec 1897; *Singapore Free Press* (Weekly) 7 Dec 1897, 25 Jan 1898, 5 Jan 1899; *Mid-Day Herald and Daily* 2 Nov 1897, 16 Apr 1898.

[113] *Mid-Day Herald and Daily* 2 Nov 1897.

[114] *Straits Independent and Penang Chronicle* 3 Aug 1892. In response to the situation, senior police officer WA Cuscaden, declared that "a system of bribery existed in connections with bails" in the court. If anyone was kept waiting till some small offering is given, they should go to him directly. See *Straits Times* 29 Jul 1898.

[115] *Straits Times* 23 Oct 1875.

[116] In February 1873, W Stewart of the Public Works Department was charged for corruption in the awarding of a government contract. Stewart's bail was set at $3,000. After he was charged, the press noted that "bribery and corruption amongst government servants" was on the increase. See *Straits Times Overland Journal* 27 Feb 1873. In October 1889, a Chinese interpreter at the Registry of Deeds was dismissed for "misconduct". See *Straits Times Weekly Issue* 15 Oct 1889. In September 1891, two staff from the Suppression of Rabies Department were sentenced to four to six weeks' for extorting a bribe from a Chinese woman. After they demanded 75 cents from the woman, she went to the Police who then gave her some marked money to give the two men. See *Singapore Free Press* (Weekly) 22 Sep 1891. In 1897 and 1899, a municipal market keeper and a sanitation inspector, both Europeans, were prosecuted for receiving bribes from market stall owners. *Straits Times* 26 Nov 1897, 23 Aug 1899; *Singapore Free Press* 23 Aug 1899; *Singapore Free Press* (Weekly) 24 Aug 1899.

[117] *Straits Times Overland Journal* 7 Oct 1871.

[118] *Straits Times Overland Journal* 7 Oct 1871. During a debate in the Legislative Council on 13 June 1872, one legislator declared that it was "impossible to put an end to bribery entirely", but some good might come with increasing wages or applying the whip. See *Straits Times Overland Journal* 29 Jun 1872.

▶ Legacy

[119] *Straits Times Weekly Issue* 25 Apr 1887; *Straits Times* 13, 22 Apr 1887.

[120] *Straits Independent and Penang Chronicle* 15 May 1889.

[121] *Straits Observer* 15 Nov 1876. In the 1870s, even with the establishment of the Chinese Protectorate and promulgation of Ordinances (Peace Preservation Act of 1867, Dangerous Societies Suppression Ordinance, Act XIX of 1869, Amendments 1870, 1872, and 1877) to check the Chinese secret societies, the *hueys* had still sufficient power and resources to bribe.

[122] *Straits Times Weekly Issue* 13 Dec 1886; *Straits Times* 8 Dec 1886. The increasing threat from the *hueys* led the government to amend the laws regulating secret societies. This led to the promulgation of the Straits Settlements Ordinance 1 of 1889, Societies Ordinance.

[123] *Straits Times Weekly Issue* 13 Dec 1886; *Straits Times* 8, 10 Dec 1886. Straits Settlements Governor Frederick Aloysius Weld responded to the urgency of the threat and crisis stemming from the *hueys* by appointing a Commission on Public Gaming and Lotteries (8 April to 26 June 1886) to review the situation (which included links with the *hueys*) and recommend remedial action and to see if further legislation was needed. The Commission completed its report in December 1886. The Gambling Commission identified several Chinese games, *Wah Whoey* (*Wha-way*), *Tuah*, *Poh* (*Phoa*) and *Chap Jee Kee*, as having been the sources of *huey* briberies.

[124] *Singapore Free Press* (Weekly) 26 Aug 1909; *Straits Times* 18 Mar, 25 Oct 1910, *Malay Tribune* 5 Feb 1914.

[125] *Singapore Free Press* (Weekly) 26 Aug 1909; *Weekly Sun* 26 Nov 1910.

[126] *Straits Times* 25 Oct 1910.

[127] *Weekly Sun* 26 Nov, 26 Dec 1910; *Straits Times* 21 Nov 1910. Members of the House also recommended abolishing the representative system.

[128] *Singapore Free Press* (Weekly) 29 Dec 1910; *Straits Times* 23 Sep, 25 Oct 1910, 15 Feb 1911; "Straits Settlements (Municipal Administration)", House of Commons Sessions, Volume 25: 4 May 1911, column 583.

[129] *Singapore Free Press* 1 Sep 1911.

[130] Of the two senior municipal staff found to have committed wrongdoing, one had resigned and left Singapore while the other was retired when the municipality was reorganised. See "Straits Settlements (Municipal Administration)", House of Commons Sessions, Volume 25: 4 May 1911, col. 583; "Straits Settlements (Maladministration)", House of Commons Sessions, Volume 26: 1 June 1911, col. 1,347. The governor had informed members of the House of Commons in early 1911 that he had planned for the "complete revision of the (1887) Municipal Ordinance".

[131] *Straits Times* 23 Sep 1910.

[132] *Straits Times* 23 Sep 1910.

[133] *Singapore Free Press* 14 Oct 1910. The gravest acts in this affair was perhaps the destruction of the merchant's ledger books that would have shown details of monies transferred to officials. There was, however, no major contract works involved and no significant collusion between the officials.

[134] *Straits Times* 15 Feb 1911. In the 1889 municipal elections, a new arrangement applied — based on the Straits Settlements Municipal Ordinance of 1887. The electorate, in this instance, voted based on electoral wards. So, they voted for their representatives. This representative system was officially abolished in 1913. Prior to 1899, the electors simply voted for local representatives in the commission as a collective. The new Municipal Ordinance, No. VIII of 1913, came into operation on 1 June 1913. See *Straits Times* 31 May 1913. Under the authority of Section 6 of new ordinance, the government nominated commissioners for Malacca, Penang and Singapore. See *Straits Echo* 4 Jun 1913; *Weekly Sun* 7 Jun 1913; Supplement to the *SSGG* No.75, 2 Oct 1914, p.18; The new ordinance had additional sections specifying how contracts (financial limits) had to be managed, and requirements for tender in municipal processes. See *SSGG* 18 Oct 1912, pp.1635, 1640–44.

[135] By 1909–1910, the Straits Government was already fully aware that the days of depending on revenue collected from the opium farms (excise) would soon come to an end. More than

a decade later, the Government would establish the Opium Revenue Replacement Fund to prepare for this eventuality. However, in 1910, the solution conceived to prepare the Straits communities for the eventual loss of revenue was for the implementation of an income tax. The Singapore government had hoped that funds collected from an income tax could aid the Harbour development efforts (Tanjong Pagar Dock). See *Singapore Free Press* (Weekly) 11 Dec 1910.

[136] *Malaya Tribune* 5 Feb 1914.

[137] Lim Tin Seng, "Land and Sand: Singapore's Reclamation Story", *Biblioasia*, Vol. 13, No. 1 (Apr–Jun 2017): 18–19.

[138] In 1920, a contractor offered a bribe to a Municipal engineer to give a better variation price for the extra works he was already undertaking at Wallich Street, Chinatown. See *Malaya Tribune* 5 Aug 1920; *The Singapore Free Press* 6 Aug 1920; *Straits Times* 9 Jun 1920. In early 1924, a number of public complaints aired in the pages of the press over beat cops asking for coffee money from contractors. See *Straits Times* 23, 27 Feb, 5 Mar 1924. In 1937, a Chinese contractor engaged in municipal works gave a police inspector a bribe to let pass his rental of squatter housing on his property illegally — to see them as illegal squatters. See *Morning Tribune* 6 Aug 1937; *Malaya Tribune* 6 Aug 1937. In 1939, a contractor offered a constable a bribe to unauthorise people through a gate at the Naval Base. See *Singapore Free Press* 31 May, 6 June 1939; *Malaya Tribune* 8 Jun 1939; *Straits Times* 6 Jun 1939

[139] Prevention of Corruption Ordinance, 1937. Straits Settlements Ordinance No. 41 of 1937.

[140] *Singapore Free Press* 1 Sep 1939; *Morning Tribune* 12 May, 28 Aug 1939; *Malaya Tribune* 28 Aug 1939; *Straits Times* 28 Aug, 1 Sep 1939; *Sunday Tribune* 27 Aug 1939.

[141] The Loveday Affair was full of twists and turns as well as technicalities that played out in military court and over the press for more than two weeks.

[142] *Straits Times* 23 Feb 1924.

[143] *Straits Times* 10 Aug 1940. As such, Loveday was well placed to manipulate the system by setting up a scheme of preferred vendors and contractors.

[144] *Singapore Free Press* 27 Jul 1937; *Malaya Tribune* 10 Aug 1940. One of the key members was a major brick supplier.

[145] *Straits Times* 21 Aug 1940; *Morning Tribune* 21 Aug 1940. There were hints that other Chinese contractors had occasionally participated in this ring, but nothing was ever confirmed since that ring had ended when the Loveday endeavour started. The first ring was only discovered by the military when Loveday's circle of complicity was exposed in 1940, and they realised it was the second ring they had apprehended.

[146] *Malaya Tribune* 20 Aug 1940.

[147] *Singapore Free Press* 23 Aug 1940.

[148] *Singapore Free Press* 23 Aug 1940. It was a possibility that the new ring had used Sino-British Engineering in their ring activities to move monies around for payments and collections. However, this was not conclusively proven during the trial.

[149] *Malaya Tribune* 10 Aug 1940. During his trial, Loveday admitted that he had received up to $5,000 for favourable consideration by a contractor even before he formed his rings. See *Malaya Tribune* 20 Aug 1940.

[150] *Singapore Free Press* 22 Aug 1940; *Straits Times* 21 Aug 1940. Members (contractors) of the Loveday ring included Gammon (Malaya) Ltd., Fogden Brisbane & Co. Ltd., United Engineers Ltd., AG Dobb & Co., Lye Huat & Co., Woh Hup and other Chinese companies. See *Singapore Free Press* 21 Aug 1940. An example of the ring's selected tender and sharing system was Woh Hup's award to build married soldiers' quarters at Nee Soon Village. When Woh Hup was invited to bid, it deposited 5% of the tendered sum, $400,000, into the ring's pool. Upon award, they deposited the last 5%.

[151] *Singapore Free Press* 28 Aug 1940. Herbert Fancott, director and secretary of Gammon (Malaya) Ltd, declared that a "large number of works which had been given to Chinese contractors, who did not have qualified civil

engineering staffs, made the European contractors sit up and take notice".

[152] *Malaya Tribune* 14, 20 Aug 1940; *Straits Times* 20 Aug 1940.

[153] *Malaya Tribune* 10 Aug 1940.

[154] *Malaya Tribune* 10 Aug 1940.

[155] *Straits Times* 10 Aug 1940.

[156] *Morning Tribune* 27 Aug 1940; *Singapore Free Press* 8 Aug 1940.

[157] *Singapore Free Press* 25 Apr 1940; *Straits Times* 25 Apr 1940. In this instance, Soh Hun Swee became the first in the Straits to have been charged under the provisions of Singapore's (Straits Settlements') first anti-corruption Ordinance.

[158] *Straits Times* 10 Aug 1940; *Malaya Tribune* 9 Aug 1940.

[159] *Straits Times* 10 Aug 1940. The defence works included barracks, bunkers, machine posts and hospital facilities.

[160] *Singapore Free Press* 14 Aug 1940; *Straits Times* 22 Aug 1940.

[161] *Straits Times* 10 Aug 1940; *Malaya Tribune* 9 Aug 1940. The Chinese merchants involved became prosecution witnesses.

[162] *Parliament of the United Kingdom of Great Britain and Ireland Prevention of Corruption Act of 1906* (6 Edw.7 c.34 or 1906 Edward VII, Chapter 34), https://assets.publishing.service.gov.uk/government/uploads/system/uploads/attachment_data/file/260777/4759.pd. The Act was amended in the Prevention of Corruption Act 1916 (6 & 7 Geo.5, c.64) which provided the tool of presumption of guilt till proven innocent.

[163] *Singapore Free Press* 7 Aug 1940.

[164] "Whoever physically holds the paper on which the bond is issued is the presumed owner, giving them a greater measure of anonymity than more common bond offerings", see https://www.investopedia.com/articles/bonds/08/bearer-bond.asp.

[165] *Singapore Free Press* 23 Aug 1940; *Straits Times* 3 Sep 1940; *Morning Tribune* 5 Jul 1941.

Accepting the statements provided by Loveday's accomplices had been problematic as these were uncorroborated and these witnesses were all also "trying to save their skins".

[166] *Singapore Free Press* 5 Sep 1940; *Malaya Tribune* 8 Oct 1940. For details of all 25 charges, see *Straits Times* 6 Aug 1940. As for the civilian members of the ring, the government removed 13 firms which were involved from the list of approved contractors while retaining a handful that provided strategic services. The true quantum of monies transacted through the Loveday ring was astonishing and difficult to estimate. For the list of cheques issued, see *Straits Times* 8 Aug 1940. Not included are the monies which Loveday and Soh Hun Swee, Woh Hup and several other Chinese and European firms, and parties outside of Singapore, collected. The final figure should be two times more than the total above, since Loveday himself alone received half of all the takings.

[167] *Malaya Tribune* 6 Aug, 8 Oct 1940.

[168] *Straits Times* 5 Jan, 4 Dec 1947; *Malaya Tribune* 25 Nov 1949.

[169] The solution was to establish an Opium Revenue Replacement Fund using a percentage of current opium revenue. It was envisaged that the fund, after reaping gains from long-term investments, would provide future revenue when the opium farm was eventually abolished.

[170] *The Laws of the Straits Settlements* (Edition 1926), Vol III, (London: Waterlow & Sons, 1926), p.339. Contained in Penal Code Section 162, "Shall not arrest without warrant". "The crux of the issue lies in the distinction made between seizable and non-seizable offences under the law."

[171] *Annual Report on the Social and Economic Progress of the People of the Straits Settlements, 1937*, Colonial Reports, Annual No. 1863, p.74. The English statutes that the 1937 Act had taken reference from were the 1906 and 1916 British Prevention of Corruption Ordinances; Also see *SSGG* Extraordinary, Vol. LXXII, No. 88 (19 October 1937): 3092.

[172] *Singapore Free Press* 14 Feb, 8 Mar 1940; *Straits Times* 14 Feb, 8 Mar 1940. In fact, although a little late, the 1937 ordinance was in fact put to test in September 1939, when Tan

Teow Lin, salesman for Sime Darby and Co. was charged under this ordinance for corruptly pocketing illegal commissions from the sale of 300 bags of flour. Tan Teow Lin basically took advantage of shops which were desperate for limited produce at a time of war. The war in Europe had started and many items which were placed under Emergency Regulations had been controlled. In September 1939, when Yong Chin Foh of Chop Tong Hin approached Sime Darby and Co. for a consignment of flour, Tan Teow Lin offered Yong Chin Foh the flour at a premium of an additional 45 cents per bag. They wanted 300 bags. This meant that Tan Teow Lin had solicited a total of $135. The threat was simple and direct — if Chop Tong Hin refused to "cooperate", Tan Teow Lin would just sell the flour to another buyer. Yong Chin Foh complained to the authorities and Tan Teow Lin was apprehended and charged under the 1937 Ordinance, the first in the Straits to have been given this honour. In March 1940, he was fined $1,350, or 4 months' "rigorous imprisonment", if he could not pay.

[173] *Singapore Free Press* 25 Apr 1940; *Straits Times* 25 Apr 1940.

[174] *Straits Times* 22 May 1940.

[175] ASP EV Fowler was able to repeatedly postpone Soh Hun Swee's multiple applications for bail from March through May 1940 on the grounds that he needed time to prepare for the trial. During this time, Fowler even made the argument that Soh Hun Swee had committed a "very serious and grave offence", and besides, the crime he was charged for was "a non-bailable offence". See *Straits Times* 12 Mar 1940. Hence, Soh Hun Swee's attempts to get bail were all rejected, till Fowler finally recommended a $25,000 quantum. See *Malaya Tribune* 9 May 1940; *Straits Times* 19 Mar, 3 Apr 1940.

[176] *Singapore Free Press* 2 Apr 1941; *Straits Times* 2 Apr, 28 Jun 1941.

[177] SSGG Supplement, No. 92, 26 November 1937, Legislative Council Proceedings 15 October 1937, p.120.

[178] *Singapore Free Press* 23 Feb 1950. JDM Smith, Acting Colonial Secretary shared his thoughts during a session of the Legislative Assembly in 1950: There was "considerable corruption in Singapore at present in the ranks of the servants of the public and throughout the rest of community". He was of the opinion that it was an aftermath of the Japanese Occupation when people had "to descend to very devious methods to secure their livelihood. After liberation, the shortage of commodities and certain controls had made the people more corrupt".

[179] *Straits Times* 14 Feb 1950.

[180] *Straits Times* 12 Jan 1946.

[181] *Sunday Tribune* 19 Jan 1947. The military police at Sime Road Camp was infamously corrupt.

[182] *Straits Times* 7 Oct 1945.

[183] The Japanese purged many Chinese during the first days of the Occupation.

[184] *Syonan Shimbun* 13 Oct 1942.

[185] *Syonan Shimbun* 21 Jun 1945.

[186] *Syonan Shimbun* 1 Jun 1945.

[187] *Syonan Shimbun* 31 May 1945. No other cases of corruption tried in court during the Occupation period had ended with a death sentence. The only other death sentence given to a non-murder case was that of a violent robbery gang's ring leader. See *Syonan Shimbun* 13 Jul 1943.

[188] *Syonan Shimbun* 9 Oct 1942.

[189] *Syonan Shimbun* 11 Jul 1944.

[190] *Syonan Shimbun* 1 Jun 1945.

[191] SR Nathan, *An Unexpected Journey: Path to the Presidency* (Singapore: Editions Didier Millet, 2011), p.115. SR Nathan was President of Singapore from 1999 to 2011.

[192] *Straits Times* 21 Dec 1946.

[193] Legacy of Corruption, *Malaya Tribune* 3 Dec 1945.

[194] Hashim bin Haji Ahmad, DSP, "History of the Singapore Police Force — The Early Days", in *Singapore Police Magazine*, Sep 1968, p. 4.

Part Two

Laborious Birth
1945–1953

When the war ended, the people of Singapore had expected that their lives would improve and the normalcy of pre-war years would return. However, the disruptions that war had caused and the deterioration of social order during the Occupation years led to the continuation of socio-economic difficulties as well as the creation of new problems for the island. In fact, the problem of corruption reached levels not experienced even in pre-war years. Persistent shortages, continued rationing, widespread poverty, extensive dislocation of peoples, lack of proper housing and the erosion of law and order had all exacerbated the circumstances that made corrupt practices even more pervasive after liberation. A critical source of the problem was the poor quality of the police force at this time. The peace officers of the post-war Police Establishment were essentially members of the pre-war Straits Settlements Police Force who were also a part of the Japanese Police Establishment during the Occupation years, when many of them had been openly corrupt. Similarly, the general population had for several years adopted various means and practices to get by during Syonan days, and they continued to do so after liberation. These habits could not be easily unlearnt, especially when extreme conditions persisted after the war. Although there was already an anti-corruption department within the Police Establishment at this time, by the early 1950s, corruption had become so rampant that more significant measures had to be taken. That

▶ Laborious Birth

critical push came in 1952 when a special team of government officers were brought in to investigate a case of police corruption so egregious that special men were chosen to investigate the Police Establishment itself. It was the few good men of this special team who formed the core of the CPIB.

The CPIB was born at a most critical point in Singapore's history. The British Empire was in the throes of decolonisation and Singapore had started its constitutional journey in forging a nation. Central to the success of this endeavour was the creation of stable government institutions which the people could trust and support. In this context, the general corruption of government officers in the post-war years was essentially destabilising and had threatened the very fabric of nation-building.

Chapter Five

Liberation, Rehabilitation & Challenges

British rule returned to Singapore and Malaya with the establishment of the British Military Administration (BMA) which administered the peninsula from September 1945 to April 1946. However, the end of war did not see the end of general shortages of everything. Control of food and essentials returned, and once again, people had to depend on ration cards to get their everyday needs. When the BMA declared the Japanese banana notes useless soon after liberation, they did so before they could fully circulate the new Malayan Dollars, and this left people with no physical currency to buy anything for a short period of time.[1]

All they had in cash and savings were banana money. Of course, it did not help that most people lost most of their pre-war savings, assets and wealth during the Occupation. The entire situation was exacerbated by the late arrival of adequate supplies in Singapore for more than a year after liberation. Initially, the BMA had to distribute free sugar and rice.[2] And when an adequate supply of new Malayan currency was in circulation, hyperinflation returned as there was again more money then there were supplies. These issues, including the shortage of housing, jobs and much more, took years to resolve, providing the impetus for the black market and petty corruption to return, or in reality to continue.

The pre-war Singapore–Malaya political and governing landscape was also completely altered after liberation; as early as in 1943, the British War

Cabinet had already planned for the creation of the Malayan Union (MU) in post-war Malaya to include all Malay States and polities of the Malayan Peninsula with Singapore as the sole remaining Crown Colony.[3] This essentially dissolved the Straits Settlements, with Penang and Malacca joining the Union. After the BMA's tenure ended and civilian oversight returned, Singapore had to reconstitute many institutions, including its municipality and legislature. The Singapore government had almost no income at this point and its coffers were also greatly depleted, notwithstanding Malacca and Penang taking their share of the Straits Settlements treasury to the new MU. Besides, most of the remaining reserves were in Sterling which was an impediment when the United States (US) Dollar became the central currency in the new post-war economic order.[4] Under these circumstances, funding, administration, recovery and development had been an unprecedented challenge.

Socio-Economic Challenges

Liberation marked the end of Japanese military rule, but it did not herald the return to normalcy, and certainly not an instant end to the problems of the day. By late August 1945,[5] even before the return of the British Forces on 4 September,[6] the Japanese military had already pulled back from public spaces and the civilian police assumed control. For several months, even after the restoration of British rule, large- and small-scale looting occurred almost on a daily basis.[7] Basically, it took time for the BMA to bring in supplies, and in the interim, the shortage of everything, including basic food items, pushed many to "grab" what they could, creating to some extent a chaotic situation for the BMA.[8] While rationing provided necessities, there were many other items which were scarce and not rationed such as clothing, medicines, stationery and more. Even for rationed goods, these were sold or distributed at subsistence level. Most people had to barter for all their needs or give up precious belongings like jewellery for that purpose, just as they did during the Occupation. The source of these non-rationed supplies was essentially concentrated in the black markets which held enormous supplies of army rations and medical supplies brought to Singapore by the returning Allied Forces. Many arriving servicemen and women turned to the black markets where they sold their allocations at low prices, or bartered for local cloths which they paid for at high prices and sold for even higher prices and profits when they returned home.[9] In this "corrupt" environment, those who controlled the distribution of food and other essentials became important officials who could impact the welfare of any family or make or break businesses. These were the very government officers who were exposed to bribery and other corrupt acts during the immediate post-war years.

It should also be noted that for the most part of the BMA period, military and Red Cross supplies (for ex-internees and prisoners of war [POWs]) could be seen everywhere, openly displayed for sale along roads at "ridiculous prices" from Town to Bukit Timah Road.[10] Most of these army and Red Cross stores had been stolen by corrupt troops, servants and civilians working in camps. They either sold or bartered their illegally gotten goods for a quick buck and these ultimately became black market supplies.[11] However, such pilfering was not just a matter of corruption or theft. The reality was perhaps more enigmatic. Food rations aside, the black market was also the place where individuals acquired scarce medical supplies. In November 1945, when there was no guarantee that anyone could find penicillin even in public clinics, one could still secure a bottle of this limited commodity for $15 at the black market.[12] This was well beyond the means of most of the working class as most menial labourers only earned between $0.80 and $1 a day at this time.[13] Under such conditions, when most people had to make do without some essentials, a simple infection could become life-threatening for some.[14]

Pervasive shortages saw the escalation of prices of everyday items, and this was the main cause of hardship for the general population for years after liberation. By the end of September 1945, when general wages were less than pre-war levels, hawker prices had risen by two to three

▶ Laborious Birth

times pre-Occupation prices, and the retail prices of essentials like rice, sugar and salt rose by three to five times.[15] While the price controls were promulgated by this time, for instance with fish and vegetables, the BMA's Food Department did not have sufficient manpower to enforce price control regulations,[16] at least not till years later. As a result, by the end of September 1945, just weeks after the return of the British, food prices skyrocketed, rising daily; rice rose from 10 cents a kati to 35 cents, tomatoes, from 15 cents to 96 cents, yam from five cents to 10 cents, long beans from eight cents to 25 cents, cucumber from six cents to 50 cents and bean sprouts from three cents to 35 cents.[17] And it got worse month to month.[18] Urgent action was required. For those without means, their situation was desperate. In consequence, large-scale looting and corrupt practices, especially amongst government employees, continued throughout the BMA period, undoubtedly fuelled by the combined impact of general shortages and high prices. Hence, it was suggested that the BMA should supplement its own labourers' pay with a temporary "post-war allowance".[19]

In early November 1945, Major General Ralph Hone, the BMA's Chief Civil Affairs Officer for Malaya, set up a Cost of Living (COL), Wages Inquiry Committee to look into the socio-economic conditions of the working population in Malaya and to recommend ways to improve the situation.[20] Led by CJ Pyke, the Economic Adviser to the Malayan Union Government, the COL committee released its interim findings that allowed the BMA to take further steps to confront the problem of high prices and rampant black-marketeering.

First, although essentials had already been "rationed" or controlled since liberation,[21] the ration card system for food collection was only implemented at the end of December 1945 to ensure fair distribution and to check abuses.[22] At the same time, the BMA also started providing all its employees cheap meals on a cooperative basis to combat the high cost of living.[23] When the COL committee submitted its full and final report to the restored civilian governments of Singapore and the Malayan Union by the end of June 1946, it recommended that public servants receive a special monthly relief (COL allowance) of $10, and "10% of their basic pay in 1941, up to a maximum of $35".[24] The Pyke Committee also recommended the continuation of price controls and the setting up of government shops to control the distribution of food in order to squeeze out black marketeers. Besides restoring basic needs and socio-economic stability, it was envisaged that any effort to alleviate the day-to-day difficulties of public servants would also lessen their need for illegal gratification, and in this way, the black markets might be kept at bay by depriving them of a significant supply of illicit goods.

When the BMA period ended, the civilian Singapore government simply continued and expanded the earlier relief measures of the Pyke Committee; the BMA's scheme providing cheap staff meals was expanded to include any needy persons or labourers who needed such a facility,[25] while wages were raised and the COL allowance was made a permanent feature for all government employees.[26] However, even though basic wages and allowances were continuously adjusted upwards in less than a year,[27] the general renumeration still fell short of expectations, and was certainly still insufficient to meet the rising cost of living.[28] As such, it is not surprising that, since liberation, corrupt practices amongst government officers and the black market activities continued unabated into the 1950s.

Restoration of Civilian Administration

Even though a lot had been achieved during the BMA period, serious progress towards the recovery and rebuilding of Singapore's war-damaged landscape and economy could only be considered after the restoration of its civilian administration. The military had been in charge, and civilian management, though planned, had to wait for the BMA to restore law and order, all governing institutions as well as the provision of basic necessities. It was during the BMA phase that the communal leaders of Singapore realised that the Straits Settlements as a polity was no longer in existence. By the time of the BMA's handover of authority to civilian rule in April 1946, Singapore would stand alone as a Crown Colony as Malacca and Penang had become part of the MU. This meant that whatever little remained of the pre-war Straits Settlements coffers (reserves), held safely in Britain during the war, were to be redistributed among the three settlements.

In short, Singapore awoke to a whole new reality upon liberation. For the first time since 1826, it had to navigate on its own and confront all the issues and difficulties in rebuilding the island's socio-political, economic and law and order infrastructure. The economy was in shambles, and the government needed to find new revenue streams as there was no more income coming from the pre-war opium revenue farm.[29] Furthermore, Great Britain implemented currency controls on all its colonies to secure the much needed US Dollar to service its war debts.[30] This effectively limited Singapore's ability to accumulate foreign exchange which the colony needed to purchase essentials, and building and industrial resources.[31]

As soon as the BMA handed over authority to the Singapore and MU civilian administrations in April 1946, both governments realised that there was no greater need at that time for the introduction of income tax (personal and company taxes) to supplement government income. The lessons the Straits Settlements learnt from its abortive pre-war attempts (1909–1910, 1939–1940) to introduce the income tax was not lost to the post-war governments. The earlier initiatives were defeated by public perception and belief that corruption amongst government officers would turn the income tax into their personal money tap. Basically, by the late 1940s, the general public still had little trust and confidence in the government. Just as in the pre-war years, they feared that a new taxation department would only provide another avenue for corrupt officials to solicit money. Hence, while the government ramped up its fight against corruption in order to build confidence and trust in the government,[32] it implemented the income tax in 1947–1948 without waiting for the situation to improve first. However, this did not mean that the matter was fait accompli and the government could move on. In fact, it was now even more imperative that measures against corrupt practices had to be ramped up as there was no certainty that the new tax system would be permanent and that it would not be derailed by the lack of public support. The Singapore and MU governments faced a new challenge in 1948 when leftist agitation and a communist insurgency precipitated the Malayan Emergency. All it took to stir unrest was to convince segments of the population that the government was oppressive and corrupt. The difficult conditions of the post-war years also provided the "ripe" conditions for leftist agitators to exploit. At this time, American observers noted that "malnutrition and disease spawned outbreaks of crime and violence. Communist-led strikes caused long work stoppages in public transport, public services, at the docks and at many private firms. The strikers were largely successful in gaining the higher wages needed by the workers to meet rising food prices."[33]

In order to establish socio-economic stability, more had to be done to restore proper government services, law and order and government revenue streams. However, to achieve these objectives, it was necessary to hire new civil servants, and more of them, especially within the Police. The government, of course, did not have sufficient means to do so during the recovery years. Even the implementation of income tax in 1948 helped little as the first contributions would only be collected in 1949. As such, the poor socio-economic conditions persisted throughout the latter part of the 1940s. War and Occupation had basically created more issues than physical damage, dislocation,[34] loss of lives and property. Basic housing, schools, municipal, health and all other facilities also required funds for rehabilitation and further development.[35] On the social front, the new demographic realities also placed a great strain on limited government resources. There were thousands of overaged children who had not attended school during the Occupation years, and the post-war baby boom

▶ Laborious Birth

Mobile Rationing Unit at Nee Soon, 1949.
Source: Ministry of Information and the Arts Collection, courtesy of National Archives of Singapore.

A mother with baby securely bound to mother's back by a cloth pick-a-back and a child in tow holding a ration card at a Chinese provision store, 1950.
Source: The Straits Times © *SPH Media Limited. Permission required for reproduction.*

Street scene, Singapore, weeks after liberation. 1945.
Source: Courtesy of National Archives of Singapore.

further exacerbated the problem. While the urgency and rush to restore old schools and build new ones had been a significant burden on the government's coffers, the general illiteracy had a greater impact on Singapore extending into the 1950s. In 1947, there were 163,000 children of primary school age, and 78,000 teens who were of post-primary education age. By 1949, only 110,000 of the former and 8,300 of the latter were in school. And a large number of those in primary schools were in old-style vernacular school that only taught basic literacy.[36]

In short, a third of the children did not receive schooling, and they would remain uneducated till they reached adulthood. Also, just over 10% of the teens of the island were attending post-primary education, and that small catchment would be the main source from which the island could draw for its educated workforce going into the 1950s. As far as the Police and Civil Service were concerned, the problem of low education and low pay in the service would not be eradicated within the 1950s.

Graphic "Waiting to Land" by Peng, *The Straits Times*, 10 October 1953, p.10.
Source: The Straits Times © *SPH Media Limited. Permission required for reproduction.*

While inefficiency and corrupt practices continued among government officers, it was also not easy to replace them with new and better staff. As far as the post-war police force was concerned, it was constituted by the officers of the old Straits Settlements Police Force. Many of them were just 14 years of age when they joined the Force before the Occupation. While this did not necessarily mean they were bad men, it explained why it was so difficult to tackle the large-scale syndicated criminal activities and their corrupting ways in the 1940s and 1950s. A more effective police force was needed to deal with criminal enterprises which were becoming increasingly sophisticated.[37]

Restoration of Police Infrastructure

The restoration of law and order was of greatest importance before rehabilitation of the island could commence. Hence, the reconstitution of the police force had been of the utmost importance. However, there was the need to first purge collaborators and policemen who were overtly corrupt during the Occupation, and to retrain those remaining in the Force.[38] The process of purging in Singapore and the MU started almost immediately with the return of the British; it was not that the Japanese Military Authority simply retained the incumbent Straits Settlements Police Force as the island's civilian Police Establishment, but that a great many within the Establishment "had thrown in their lot with the Japanese", becoming collaborators and not just mere functionaries.[39] In Singapore, there were also about 400 police officers who were appointed during the Occupation. They were summarily dismissed by the BMA, together with a smaller number of collaborators from the original Force.[40] Retraining was also planned, but the Police Depot (Police Training School) at Thomson Road was in such a state that much had to be done to restore the facility. As such, the retraining of all 1,200 police personnel at Singapore needed to be done 100 at a time. The month-long refresher course started on 1 October 1945, and the British Parachute Brigade was in charge of the training course.[41] There were no new police recruits during the time of the BMA. Returning the Police Establishment to strength after the war had not been an easy task. Yet, the responsibility for combating corrupt practices, when civilian rule returned, was squarely in the hands of the much-weakened police force.

Rebuilding the police infrastructure in the post-war period had been a colossal task. While traitors had to be purged, the old had to be retrained and there were few suitably educated locals to be recruited. The government was also lacking the financial resources to undertake most rehabilitation needs.[42] Although the government already introduced income tax in December 1947 (first collection in 1949), collecting enough funds to underwrite all government needs would take some time. The collection for the first assessment year fell short of projections. By this time, the government had lost most of its pre-war revenue streams, including its entrepot trade which remained disrupted for years after liberation. Britain had also imposed exchange controls which hampered recovery and rebuilding processes.[43] Fortunately, the Singapore government still had one option to augment the Police Establishment. The Police Commissioner reactivated the Police Volunteer Reserves (PVR), which was called the Special Constabulary (SC) when it was reconstituted in September 1945.[44] It was about a fortnight after liberation when a call was made to the pre-war police volunteers to gather and to reconstitute the Force.[45] On 26 September 1945, a small force of about 100 pre-war volunteers had regrouped, registered and continued their police duties guarding strategic places. Their main function was to relieve the regular police from such tasks and allow them to concentrate on their "prevention and detection duties".[46] Headed by a former PVR officer, Major Wee Kah Kiat, the SC was headquartered at the Central Police Station from September 1945.[47] By October, the Special Constables were assigned to where they were needed most — guarding the BMA's godowns and other facilities from being looted.[48] And, as it was to be expected, blackmarketeers and others caught by the Special Constables for breaking into and stealing from warehouses were also detained for attempting to bribe them.[49] Even though the SC had been outside the main Police Establishment when it was restarted during the BMA period, it grew into an integral part of Singapore's law and order community by the time civil rule returned.[50] And fortunately, although a small Force, there were enough good men in the SC to make a difference.

Amongst the more notable anti-corruption actions involving the SC in its early years was the interdiction of several smuggling cases involving corrupt regular policemen. The first case involved Criminal Investigation Department (CID) Detective Busu bin Mohd Shah who found out that a colleague, Detective Ahmad bin Haji Nasir, and constable Khamis bin Hassan from the Kandang Kerbau Police Station, were conspiring with a Chinese *towkay* (black marketeer) to raid and rob the government's Base Ordinance Depot at Kim Seng Road. Busu kept a watch on the depot and on his colleagues. On 30 April 1946, after Busu received credible

▶ Laborious Birth

information that the raid was imminent, he rushed to the Havelock Road Police Station for help. He returned to the depot in a taxi with two Special Constables, Osman bin Shaari and Goh Cheng Siew. However, as they approached the depot, the raid had already taken place, and the culprits in a lorry and a taxi were making their escape. Busu and the Special Constables intercepted the vehicles. Ahmad was in the taxi while Khamis was in the lorry. At this point, Ahmad pleaded with Busu for help. He declared that the goods belonged to Inspector Che Osman, another CID officer. He then offered Busu and the Special Constables a $1,000 bribe. When Busu and the constables did not "play ball", all of them drove to CID Headquarters, including the lorry containing 30 bales of textile. Ahmad had believed that he had colleagues back at the office who would help out in this situation, and Busu would be "taught a lesson".[51] As things turned out, Ahmad and Khamis were arrested and given 18 months' jail time, while the lorry driver received nine months. As for Busu and the Special Constables, they were commended by the Magistrate for their honesty and integrity.[52]

Following closely behind the Base Ordinance Depot heist was the Siglap smuggling case which saw corrupt policemen drawing a revolver on Special Constables who tried to stop them. On 9 June 1946, SC Inspector Lee Cheng Teen and other Special Constables, while patrolling along Siglap Road, came upon Police Detective Yong Kok Liong and constables A Arumugam and Jantar bin Chien in a lorry with six labourers at the beach. They were in possession of 4,200 katis of rice in 25 bags. They had no permit to possess the rice nor permission to move it.[53] The police party was obviously smuggling the controlled essential staple, and they resisted arrest. It was during the melee that Yong unholstered his revolver and pointed it at Lee. The three police officers were convicted and sent to prison.[54]

There was no question that there were good men in the SC, and its reconstitution had been timely for the police force. Nevertheless, it remained a very small outfit until the Malayan Emergency (June 1948) when 200 more officers were recruited to support the Force's guarding and escorting duties.[55] One reason for the lack of development of this auxiliary Force was that it was composed of paid regulars and the government was still not in a position to expend significant resources even for the main Police Establishment in the latter part of the 1940s. Instead, about a year after the SC had been restarted, the Singapore government established the Volunteer Special Constabulary (VSC). As a volunteer unit, the officers of the VSC were not salaried. Thus, the volunteer constables cost the Police Establishment little to maintain. Functionally, the VSC filled an important gap; while the SC supported the police force and guarded facilities in the day, the volunteers mainly performed night duties in four-hour mobile or foot patrols in their own business or residential districts. Essentially, the VSC scheme was designed for residents to help protect their own districts, together with regular police, at a time when "looting, housebreaking, theft and burglary" were rampant. They had no special uniform and wore only an armband with letters "SC (V)" in white.[56] When the Emergency started, the armed SCs and VSCs were in demand by businesses who preferred them over their own *jaga* or security guards.[57] It was also less likely that any of the volunteers would have been involved in corrupt practices since they were deployed with other regulars for several hours of patrols, and they were guarding their own districts, businesses and residences.

Chapter Six

Corruption & Legislation

Transition and Legislation

All things considered, confronting corruption was not a top priority during the British Military Administration (BMA) period. The Americans observed that, "the military administration was far from a panacea for all Singapore's ills. The BMA had its share of corrupt officials who helped collaborators and profiteers of the Japanese Occupation to continue to prosper. As a result of the inefficiency and mismanagement of the rice distribution, the BMA was cynically known as the 'Black Market Administration'. However, by April 1946, when military rule was ended, the BMA had managed to restore gas, water and electric services to above their pre-war capacity."[58] Although strides had been made during the BMA period, there were still mountains to climb before any semblance of normalcy and socio-economic progress could be restored. Communal and business leaders in Singapore continued to rally for more to be done throughout the BMA period.

In November 1945, the Colonial Office set up the Singapore Advisory Council (SAC) composed of 17 civilian members to work with the BMA in preparation for the eventual return to civilian rule and for the rehabilitation of Singapore.[59] However, they also functioned like the legislators of the pre-war years, bringing up critical issues of the day during council sessions for the government's deliberation. Key members of the SAC, like Tan Chin Tuan (1908–2005) and Dr Chen Su Lan (1885–1972), were noted for their support for more measures against corruption in the government. Tan also reminded the government that the public servants employed by the government after liberation had been the same people who worked for the corrupt Japanese regime. He reminded government department heads to be vigilant. As for Chen, he argued that the purge of the police force should be continued. During the Occupation, they were behind the "extortion, bribery, blackmail, torture and murders". He pointed out that the public resented the retention of corrupt officers.[60] Chen also vigorously raised the issue of setting up an anti-corruption body for Singapore. The pre-war Anti-Corruption Branch of the Criminal Investigation Department (CID) had yet to be re-established at this time. A month later, in December 1945, the BMA announced that they had already restarted the Branch,[61] albeit as a token force at this time. During the SAC's third session in January 1946, the SAC unanimously articulated its support for the new "anti-corruption department", noting that it should be manned by special officers, and promising that "no mercy to be shown for those found guilty of corruption", high or low ranked. Of course, the SAC also realised that no anti-corruption efforts could succeed without public cooperation.[62] However, despite these positive steps forward, more was only possible after the BMA relinquished control and the island's civilian government restored from 1 April 1946.

Basically, in order to pass suitable laws to battle widespread corruption, Singapore had to first restore its legislative body, and this would take time to materialise. Fortuitously, the British Government provided a stopgap solution when the BMA's tenure ended: the SAC was allowed to continue to function, empowered to fill that "legislative" gap to approve local laws till polls could be called to elect new lawmakers.[63] Singapore's first Legislative Council was installed two years later in April 1948. In the meantime, Bills for new laws were presented to the SAC, and this included the amendments to the 1937 Prevention of Corruption Ordinance. It was realised very soon after liberation that the extent and nature of corruption in society and amongst public servants that the pre-war Ordinance needed amending to enable the government to better deal with the new realities.

▶ Laborious Birth

The original law, "the Prevention of Corruption Ordinance, 1937 (No. 41 of 1937), makes punishable bribery and secret commissions in public or private business". It was based mainly on corresponding English statutes. A critical feature of this Ordinance was the presumption of corruption clause, which applied to bribery cases involving public officers or public bodies. While in general terms, the 1937 Ordinance provided the government and judiciary sufficient powers to deal with corrupt practices, the authorities realised that the realities of the post-war era required more "bite" and greater specificity in the language and scope of this law. Hence, the 1937 Prevention of Corruption Ordinance was amended in two Bills tabled before the SAC in early September 1946[64]: the Prevention of Corruption (Amendment) Ordinance, 1946 and the Evidence Ordinance (Special Provisions), 1945.

The first Bill, which amended the 1937 Ordinance, allowed the Police to arrest, search and investigate offenders for corrupt offences.[65] Corruption offences were initially non-arrestable because of a legal technicality. Under the Criminal Procedure Code, an offence other than those in the Penal Code is non-arrestable unless it is punishable with imprisonment for three years or more. The Prevention of Corruption Ordinance (Amendment) of 1946 therefore increased the maximum imprisonment term for a corruption offence from two years to three years, which consequently allowed police officers to arrest a person suspected of having committed such offence.[66]

As for the second Bill, Evidence Ordinance (Special Provision) 1945, it provided a new rule of evidence which allowed the courts, when trying corruption cases, to take into consideration as a relevant fact that the accused was in possession of assets for which he could not provide a satisfactory account.[67]

Besides legislative reforms, the fight against corruption on the judicial front was given an added boost in 1947 with the creation of the fourth Criminal District Court, designated the Corruption Court. One of the major obstacles to the speedy prosecution of corruption cases was the congestion of the Singapore courts.[68] The creation of a court dedicated to corruption cases was a significant milestone for the island's anti-corruption drive. While other courtrooms also handled corruption cases, the fourth ensured that priority was given to corruption cases. However, new measures such as this required funding. The MU and Singapore governments had little option but to push through the implementation of income tax by the late 1940s.

Legislative reforms and judiciary developments undoubtedly provided the necessary tools for the administration to tackle corruption within the government service. However, to permanently eradicate runaway corruption in the city, there was still a need for the government to establish a more professional and honest Civil Service. This could never be achieved quickly or resolutely without the requisite financial and human resources. There was also a need for the total rehabilitation of Singapore's socio-economic infrastructure in the late 1940s; the creation of jobs, restoration of the economy, improvement in the hiring of suitable policemen, better pay for civil servants, especially the Police, and more. All these were long-term processes which would take time to reap results. However, in the meantime, improving enforcement measures was necessary. The re-establishment of the Anti-Corruption Branch (ACB) and the eventual creation of the CPIB were the next necessary steps in the journey forward.

Corruption in the New Regime

The transition from military to civilian administration did not make the battle against crime, specifically corruption, any easier. The BMA had started the process of purging public servants and policemen who had collaborated with the Japanese as well as those whom they could prove were corrupt and had engaged in extortion and blackmail during the Occupation. After the BMA's handover, as corruption was still rife across the island, the civilian government felt that there were a number of "black sheep" who were still in the Police and government service who needed to be weeded out.[69] One critical facet of this problem was the continued shortages that afflicted every community on the island throughout the latter part of the 1940s. Unemployment was widespread, prices of staples continued to be high and rehabilitation and development had been unequal across the island. In 1947, Singapore suffered two setbacks; weekly rice rations per head fell to an all-time low and quality of the rice distributed to the population had also been of the poorest quality.[70] Under such conditions, it was observed, "malnutrition and disease spawned outbreaks of crime and violence",[71] and this included all kinds of corrupt practices. Although numerous arrests had already been made during the BMA period of persons trying to bribe sentries of food and supply depots as well as those guarding train stations (smuggling supplies),[72] the poor socio-economic conditions simply sustained even more instances of corruption, and much of these had been associated with black market rackets.[73]

Corruption had also assumed a political dimension in the post-war years. The end of war ushered in an era where the sojourning immigrants of Malaya were becoming rooted settlers. Faced with shortages, privation and unemployment, these settlers did not remain silent about their plight, and political parties of the day were quick to exploit this discontent by articulating their support for the masses' demand for change. The socialist movement, in particular, had been most vocal about workers' welfare and rights, and against corruption in government.[74] Hence, they supported most labour actions which mainly took the form of industrial strikes (work stoppages).[75] One particular strike by the busmen of the Singapore Traction Company (STC) in 1947 was sparked when a couple of bus conductors with the company were caught cheating on the collection of fares. They were to be prosecuted but their union viewed it as just another "whacking" of the small men on the street by the government. The stoppage of the STC services practically paralysed city transport. In the ensuing negotiations, the government and the STC were forced to take the strikers and their union to court where the union's secretary provided a definition of corrupt acts and what constituted a "squeeze".[76] While no party had declared cheating a little on the collection of fares was considered a wrongful act, the labour's representatives were quick to point out that the busmen were pushed into a corner by the "greedy" bosses of company management who underpaid them and forced them to work under harsh conditions. Of course, the standard management response was that they could not pay more as the company had been losing money on account of their corrupt practices. Whichever had been the case, the social unrest created and their narrative that the government was corrupt had threatened the successful implementation of the much-needed income tax.[77]

> ### A Cancer
>
> Bribery and corruption, together, is "a cancer which might grow and destroy the whole body... like Caesar's wife, officials must be above suspicion, and lack of confidence, in this respect, strikes at the whole foundation of good government."
>
> Justice Gordon-Smith
> *Malaya Tribune* 1 Jun 1949

Post-War Corruption Modus Operandi

Before World War II (WWII), corruption amongst public officers was seen by the man on the street as simply a fact of life; mostly involving small *kopi* or tea monies to get or get away with things. Only criminal or gaming syndicates were engaged in big-money gratifications, and most of these cases involved corrupt policemen. Of course, the Loveday episode involving contractors and large-scale defence infrastructural works was an unprecedented exception. Then the war changed everything, and the corruption franchise became widespread. In the late 1940s and early 1950s, there was significant consensus on the ground that it was the experiences of the Occupation years that fostered the lax

▶ Laborious Birth

attitude towards petty corruption in the post-war years.[78] The most common corrupt practices in the post-war recovery period included a range of activities:

Looting and Black-Marketeering

While general looting in the immediate post-war years had been mostly associated with people who had little and were desperate for food and other essentials, such looting would also pilfer anything which could be monetised. Looters had moved in large groups numbering from 50 to hundreds. Amongst the first items to be picked were the thousands of abandoned cars and equipment the Japanese left along the streets when surrender approached. In exchange for money, most of the lifted goods eventually ended up on the black market. These goods included supplies taken from government stores, or had been corruptly taken from these stores by people guarding them, or by people who bribed the sentries who guarded the depots and godowns to turn a blind eye. Big firms with an abundance of goods on site, like Messrs Borneo Motor Co. Ltd., were also a favourite target of looters and victims of corrupt guards.[79]

Extortion and Squeezing

Although being "squeezed" and extorted were not new in the corruption circle, these practices became more prevalent after the war when everyone, including public servants, took home low wages and the control of essentials lay in their hands. It was still common for "squeezing" and extortion to occur throughout the 1950s. While "squeezing" mainly involved petty amounts, and the guilty parties often claimed they had been driven to such practices due to dire circumstances, as in the case of the 1947 STC strikers, such corruption was considered to have been the most harmful in the day. When "squeezing" became a norm of the time, the whole social environment would seem to be corrupt. As for extortion, this was usually perpetrated by officials with power of leverage; policemen or inspectors of controlled items threatening the ignorant or guilty with jail, extensive fines or termination of licences if they did not receive some form of gratification for letting them off the hook. Instances of employing leverage included the typical traffic offences, raids on unlicensed retailers, on those who flouted price or currency controls as well as those caught gambling illegally. Perhaps the most egregious acts in this class of corruption were the extortion of honest businesses or truly ignorant individuals. In one of the more publicised cases of extortion by policemen, Detective Wong Lai Hooi was convicted and sentenced to three months' rigorous imprisonment for extorting $60 from Teh Tiang Hong, a second-hand goods dealer. In early 1946, Wong visited Teh's shop at Tanjong Pagar and accused the dealer of selling motor-car tyres illegally as he had no licence to do so. However, the detective offered to update (endorse) the dealer's licence for him, but demanded $60 for travelling expenses. Teh reported the matter to the Police.[80]

In a separate case in 1946 which also involved a second-hand goods dealership, a detective attached to the Second-hand Dealers' Licence Department, Tan Teck Hian, was reported to have extorted a dealership at Geylang Road. Instead of forking out the $400 the detective wanted, the dealer reported the matter to the ACB, which then set a trap for the detective with some marked notes. Hence, when Assistant Superintendent of Police (ASP) Patrick J Shannon of the ACB sent two officers to raid the detective's office where they found the money in his possession, Tan's explanation that the cash was saved up during the Occupation years held no weight. He was sentenced to six weeks of rigorous imprisonment for possession of the money, and six months for extortion.[81] Basically, officials who wielded enforcement powers and licensing functions had more opportunities and had been more amenable to corrupt practices.[82] It should also be noted that those who paid the extorted sums without reporting the offence were also liable to be charged for corruption.[83]

> **Tea Money and High Prices**
>
> "Tea money is not confined to housing. Many businessmen report that before they can buy goods, tea money has to be paid to wholesalers' clerks who otherwise give preference to others more willing to pay bribes because they are themselves proposing to black market the good.... Singapore people are much too backward in helping the authorities to force prices down. It is no good the people crying out loud that wages are too low and cost of living allowance inadequate if they are not prepared to support the authorities in fighting racketeers."
>
> EV Fowler, Deputy Commissioner of Police, CID
> *Singapore Free Press* 11 Jul 1946

Bribery and Tea Money

These were the most common forms of corrupt acts during, before and after the war. Interestingly, what we come to know as *"kopi* money" was once also called "tea money", obviously due to the influence of the colonial society and of the English press. However, the Malays at this time seemed to have preferred the term *"kopi* money".[84] The main difference after WWII was the extent and pervasiveness of petty corrupt acts. While it was generally agreed that the Occupation years created the conditions for widespread corruption and the lax attitude towards the matter in the post-war period,[85] it was also not disputed that the difficult socio-economic conditions of the day had also played a critical part in fostering the situation.

In terms of corrupt practices, tea money or *kopi* money was perhaps the smallest act of corruption in the world of bribery. Normally, the small sums of *kopi* money are passed on to clerks or guards, mostly voluntarily, to "lubricate" a transaction, or as a gesture of "appreciation". The amounts given tended to range between $1 and $50. Of course, sometimes such bribes came in the form of small *makan* or beverage, and sometimes literally tea or coffee.[86] Tea money could also be demanded, but in this instance, the infringement crosses over to the realm of extortion.[87] In the first few years after liberation, it was common for matters concerning food supply to involve small bribes: issuance of ration cards,[88] food prices inspections,[89] being in possession of food and other essentials without the requisite permit[90] and more. It was also common to find tea monies offered to lower-ranked government officers like clerks and court officials who controlled access or issuance of permits, licences and even identity cards.[91] Perhaps, as an intended deterrent,[92] the penalty imposed for offering *kopi* money was always much more than the fine for the original offence.[93]

Then there were the outright bribes to avoid arrest or prosecution. Such cases normally involved larger bribes, although not necessarily so. The lines are blurred between outright bribery and the offering of *kopi* money, but the former often involved an attempt to get away with a criminal act or to gain criminal access while the latter was usually a means to smoothen transactions. Attempts to get around a traffic offence or fines would normally be considered outright bribery even though the bribe amount could be small. To avoid arrest for fighting, theft and even looting, the wrongdoers often resorted to bribery.[94] Of course, there were no lack of examples of huge bribes in post-war Singapore, and these were not necessarily linked to the big-money vices of the day. Often, they involved large-scale thefts,[95] attempts to circumvent imports and exports control measures,[96] currency exchange controls, entry controls,[97] serious crimes,[98] large-scale betting rackets[99] and even more.

Singapore's biggest corruption case in the post-war period occurred in 1946–1947 when a web of corruption was uncovered involving a number of wealthy merchants of the colony and the most senior officers of the Food Control Inspectorate: Chief Inspectors James McPherson and Claude William Roberts. Both men, who were police inspectors attached to the Food Control Office, received bribes from multiple individuals who sought to trade in foodstuff in Singapore bypassing food control

▶ Laborious Birth

regulations. Between May and June 1947, eight Chinese merchants paid McPherson thousands of dollars each for his assistance. In total, $26,800 had been offered to McPherson. The ACB dealt with the case under ASP PS Gordon, and the businessmen were charged under the Prevention of Corruption Ordinance (Section 3b, Ordinance 41 of 1937). However, for some strange reason, McPherson was allowed to return to Britain on medical leave when the case was still pending. He eventually became uncontactable and never returned. This left the prosecution with no key witnesses to examine or to prosecute. At this juncture, the Colonial Office intervened, declaring that McPherson would be allowed to "retire" and all the confiscated bribe monies would be treated as "unclaimed property" which the Police retained. As for the eight, they were all acquitted under the circumstances.[100]

As for Roberts, his corruption trial started a year earlier in a separate case. He was approached by several Chinese *towkays* on 28 August 1946 seeking his help to bring in 140 bags of rice from Siam illegally. Roberts was to arrange safe passage for the railway trucks carrying 24 tons of rice. The train with the rice arrived in the evening of 7 September 1946, and someone promptly delivered a cheque of $1,500 to Roberts the same evening.[101] The rice was to be loaded onto three lorries and brought into Town the next morning. Before leaving the train yard, both Roberts and McPherson personally inspected the rice truck. ASP PJ Shannon of the ACB was informed of the affair almost immediately when the train arrived.[102] Roberts was caught and allowed out on bail. His trial was slated for 1947. In the end, only one Chinese merchant was charged but in this case, he was also acquitted due to the lack of proof. Hence, Roberts was not charged.[103]

However, in June 1947, before his first corruption case had been settled, he again conspired with another *towkay,* Koh Teng Huang, to import 198 bags of white Rangoon rice (27,583 katis). Apparently, it was McPherson who "found" the rice in Koh's premises at Boat Quay, but Roberts released the bags of rice after seizing them. However, both Roberts and McPherson were complicit in the affair; while Roberts instructed the food control guards at Koh's premises to leave, McPherson skilfully avoided being caught red-handed. It was Food Controller J Hamer who reported the matter to the Police and set the trap for Roberts. Roberts was charged under Section 109 of the Penal Code and Section 5 and Section 17(i) of Food Control Proclamation No. 10 of 1945. While McPherson got away because he was on leave, Roberts was fined $500 for abetting Koh, and Koh was fined only $75.[104] Both Roberts and McPherson were linked to several other corrupt cases throughout 1947.[105] This was truly a difficult and embarrassing time for the Food Control Department, and broadly speaking, for the government as well.

Big-Money and Organised Crime

The pre-war big-money spinner, *Chap Ji Kee* ("Twelve Cards" in Hokkien), made a reappearance in the late 1940s. And once again, police officers were caught taking bribes from this syndicate. However, *Chap Ji Kee*'s impact on the corruption scene was only to become a serious problem in the 1950s.[106]

Widespread Corruption

"The success of the Anti-Corruption Branch is in direct proportion to the measure of support which it is receiving from the public.

There are unscrupulous men in Singapore today who, with the experience gained during the Japanese Occupation, are acquiring material goods without the least concern for moral standard.

Those men often have in their payroll those who could assist them in attaining their object.

And who could help them? The man in charge of the stores, the lorry driver who conveys the goods... the policeman who looks the other way while the goods are being loaded up, the price control inspector who is somewhere else when the sale is on, the custom official who passes the goods as non-dutiable and on through a long list of persons who might stand in the way of a successful deal.

Again, unnecessary delays and obstacles have often been placed in the way of those who apply for certain permits for trading purposes and the situation is made even more difficult when applicants do not speak the English language. But these difficulties are removed or 'taken care of by someone within if applicants are able to contact the "right source"'. Usually through a third party who makes all the necessary 'arrangements' and likewise receives a 'a form of thanks for his service'.

The common practice of having to offer 'tea money' for premises, rooms, favours and more to landlords or their agents is classified under the corruption category and such matters should be reported immediately."

Police Spokesmen
Malaya Tribune 12 May 1947

Chapter Seven

Anti-Corruption Branch

The Anti-Corruption Branch (ACB), established in 1941, was restarted in December 1945. It had oversight of the responsibilities provided under the Straits Settlements Prevention of Corruption Ordinance No.14 of 1937 (Amendment 1946). As a police institution, the ACB was staffed by police personnel and it ultimately reported to the Police Commissioner.

Re-Establishment and the Establishment

Within a month or two after liberation, the need for an anti-corruption body was already greatly felt.[107] When members of the Singapore Advisory Council (SAC) like Tan Chin Tuan and Chen Su Lan raised the matter within the council, the Police Commissioner revealed in early December 1945 that a unit had already been formed.[108] It restarted with the appointment of an officer within the CID to oversee corruption cases. However, there is almost no information on the progress of this unit for the next few months, or who was in charge, but it is certain that little had been achieved in the first half of 1946.[109] It is certain though that Assistant Superintendent of Police (ASP) PJ Shannon of the CID had been the officer-in-charge of the ACB by June–July 1946, but he was also involved in CID's other operations at the same time.[110] Nevertheless, Shannon had the ACB fully operational by July–August 1946, starting with a raid on the food control centre at Victoria School where people went to renew their ration cards.[111]

It was around this time when the ACB became highly active that the two Bills to strengthen anti-corruption measures were introduced and passed: the Prevention of Corruption Ordinance (Amendment), 1946 and the Evidence (Special Provisions) Ordinance, 1946.[112] By September 1946, the ACB had another weapon in its arsenal when an additional district court was created to deal with corruption cases.[113] This became the fourth Criminal District Court, designated the Corruption Court. It was only after these developments that Shannon brought his first 16 cases to trial in September–October 1946.[114] Amongst the September 1946 cases brought to trial by the ACB included extortion bids by a police detective, a constable accepting a bribe not to apprehend persons on armed charges and corruption in departments issuing ration cards.[115] In March 1947, Shannon prosecuted a CID detective for extortion.[116] He would leave the ACB soon after this,[117] and was replaced by ASP SP Gordon. The ACB now had a European officer-in-charge and two Asiatic officers.[118] By this time, the ACB was already well established within the CID, and its office was situated within the Empress Place Secretariat Building.[119] The unit's strength grew quickly by mid-1947. In late May 1947, the ACB had 10 investigators under Gordon and the unit reported directly to the Chief of the CID, RCB Wiltshire. The Chief was resolute in his war against corruption, declaring a new anti-corruption drive.[120] Wiltshire revealed his plans: he would detain all corrupt officials. It was common knowledge that corruption existed amongst the ranks of the Police, Customs, Food Controller, Price Inspectors and others. Wiltshire added that "there were only two types of corruption — the payer of 'graft' money and the receiver. Without information by the payer, practically no headway could be made."[121]

Battle Lines

Securing the food distribution system from the exploitation of corrupt officials was given priority by the ACB. Difficulties in getting essentials like food had the potential to become flashpoints that created discontent, encouraging looting or even insurgency, especially during the Malayan Emergency. Yet, from 1946 to the early 1950s, despite the continuous prosecution of corrupt officials in the Food Control Department, the Police had failed to stop such offences. The situation at the Victoria School Rationing Office was particularly bad. It was revealed in Court that people who queued at the centre to renew their ration cards had been pushed back day after day until some "remuneration" had been given. Shannon, who raided the school on 27 July 1946, found 70–80 people waiting there. When asked who had given money, and why, one Chinese woman revealed that she did so because she had seen others do it. Another said that he placed $4 on top of his ration card which was on the desk of the clerk because he saw others do it. The most poignant account came from a Chinese lady, Kok Ah Moi, who had queued from four in the morning till the office closed and yet could not get her card renewed. Then people told her that she had to give some money, and she did this by placing $3 on her card that was on the clerk's table.[122] Yet, despite the prosecution of the clerks involved in this affair, the ACB was never able to eradicate these corrupt practices. In 1949, the ACB even arrested food control clerks who had issued unauthorised ration cards for cash — a card for one cost $22, while a card for two persons cost $55.[123] Of course, the Food Control Department had actively terminated guilty employees to remove bad hats. In 1946 and 1947, almost 200 staff were terminated. From thence, the CID screened all new hires in the department.[124] Yet, the problem persisted in the 1940s and 1950s.

Other commonly recurring forms of corrupt practices which the ACB dealt with through the latter half of the 1940s included those related to vehicle licensing, allocation of housing by the Singapore Improvement Trust (SIT), traffic offences, illegal hawking, and more.[125] Amongst these, those involving extortion had been the most egregious which the ACB had to handle. They normally involved government officers abusing their authority by exploiting those who had already committed a crime or offence, sometimes unknowingly, and who were desperate to get out of their predicament. In such cases, threats were commonly used and sums transacted high. Corrupt police officers and food control inspectors were the main perpetrators in these offences. In one case in early 1947, a CID detective, Ng Pui, instead of arresting a gambling organiser, Ho Chok Pung, demanded $120 from the man. However, when Ho offered only $90, Ng demanded $30 weekly. Pushed to a corner, Ho reported the detective to the ACB. Shannon handled this case.[126] In another case in early September 1946, three food control inspectors, during a raid, found five bags of rice in Chop Kwong Joo Seng which the shop had no permit to hold. The inspectors threatened prosecution if there was no enticement to do otherwise. So, the shop gave in and handed the inspectors $1,500. Shannon was informed of this act of extortion in November 1946. When he called in the store's manager for a statement, Shannon was shown an entry in the store's ledger. It read, in Chinese characters — "$1,500 — rice elder brother extortion (rice *dai khor* extortion — extortion paid to big brother of rice control) on 20 September 1946".[127]

Perhaps, for the ACB, the most egregious corruption case had been the one which involved their very own, Lim Tian Hong (alias *Ti Tah*).

Immigration arrivals going through the Immigration Department, 1958.
Source: Ministry of Information and the Arts Collection, courtesy of National Archives of Singapore.

Renewing and applying for new driving licences at Traffic Police Branch, 1952.
Source: Ministry of Information and the Arts Collection, courtesy of National Archives of Singapore.

Workers registering for employment at the Labour Department, 1950.
Source: Ministry of Information and the Arts Collection, courtesy of National Archives of Singapore.

This self-styled "agent" of the unit was actually just an informant. However, he abused his connections with the ACB by going around, from 1948 to 1949, to extort from multiple individuals, for which he was charged up to a dozen times.[128]

Staying Relevant

There was a sense that the corrupt situation in post-war Singapore had been well beyond any police, any government or even its British colonial master's ability to resolve. Though Wiltshire's 1947 "anti-corruption drive" against "get-rich-quick" employees of government had been more than just rhetoric,[129] it required resources and appropriate men to see it to fruition. Of course, as the Police continuously pointed out, the public must play their part to help, but the problem was more deep-seated than that. Until the shortages and controls had been eliminated, there would always be some desperate persons whom dishonest officials would take advantage of. The rehabilitation of the police force had to also include a significant expansion of the Establishment. Could a handful of men in the ACB effectively tackle a widespread social ill which had become ubiquitous across the island? And the problem also afflicted its own "parent department", the CID itself. Serendipitously, in 1947–1948, just when the government was considering increasing the staff strength of the ACB, the Malayan Emergency started. Plans for augmenting the unit were torpedoed by the urgent need to commit resources to battle the Leftist insurgency. This drained the police force of senior officers as they were placed in new counter-insurgency roles.[130] The matter was revisited once again more than a year later in 1949. Post-war recovery efforts, and the economic lifeline of the British Commonwealth as a whole, had been dependent on the collective's ability to secure United States Dollars (USD). Most strategic resources at this time had to be paid for in USD (the Bretton Woods Agreement),[131] and Britain, which held most of its colonies' gold reserves that had to be used to purchase USDs, had depleted the reserves to such an extent in 1949 that the pound sterling had to be devalued. Thus, exchange controls were put in place to pool the necessary USDs and save the Empire's remaining reserves. In Singapore, however, this effort was compromised by corruption and bribery. Hence, despite limited resources, the government renewed its anti-corruption efforts and plans were made to expand the ACB once more.[132]

At this point, very senior officers assumed oversight of the ACB: the unit was placed under the purview of the Deputy Commissioner of Police (DCP), CID.[133] In late 1948, the DCP was EV Fowler. One of his first anti-corruption salvos came in the form of his "Rewards for Reports" programme. The ACB would pay money for actionable information against corrupt practices.[134] At this point, there were still many cases of corruption involving food ration cards. This had been a critical issue in the relationship between the government and the general population in the immediate post-war period. Many officials involved simply took advantage of the situation; they were slow in issuing the cards, so the people offered tea money to speed things up. Those involved in the allocation of SIT flats also waited to see who had tendered more *kopi* money before processing their applications. As for the SIT situation, discontent in housing matters also created a serious problem on the ground for the government, and the ACB had to ramp up its anti-corruption measures in this area as well. Going into the 1950s, it would appear that the ACB would continue to remain busy, but resolve little as well. Nevertheless, the police force carried out the ACB's planned expansion. In 1950, the unit was relocated from Empress Place to its own premises at Low Hill Road.[135] This shift was part of the ramping up of anti-corruption efforts that started in 1949.[136]

By the end of 1949, the police force reported that it had investigated 290 cases in that year. Of the 105 persons charged in Court, 71 obtained convictions and a number of cases were still ongoing by 1950. While some action had been taken against police offenders, a great number

▶ Laborious Birth

were against conductors of the Singapore Traction Company for misappropriation of fares.[137] In retrospect, the ACB's efforts in 1949, though considerable for less than a dozen men, were considered ineffectual in the larger scheme of things.[138] In fact, some in the public had labelled the ACB the "silent service" for its lack of presence and success.[139]

In early 1950, when the government announced that it was committing more funds to the ACB, it also announced plans for setting up an anti-corruption advisory committee.[140] At the same time, the government launched a full-scale enquiry into corruption within the police force in May 1950. As a result, 17 out of 26 detectives of the Beach Road Division were dismissed. They were given one month's notice. They were all implicated in the corruption involving gambling syndicates. One Non-Commissioned Officer detective was also detained, while the rest who remained in the Force were transferred to other areas. An investigation into this police division was started by the ACB after public complaints.[141]

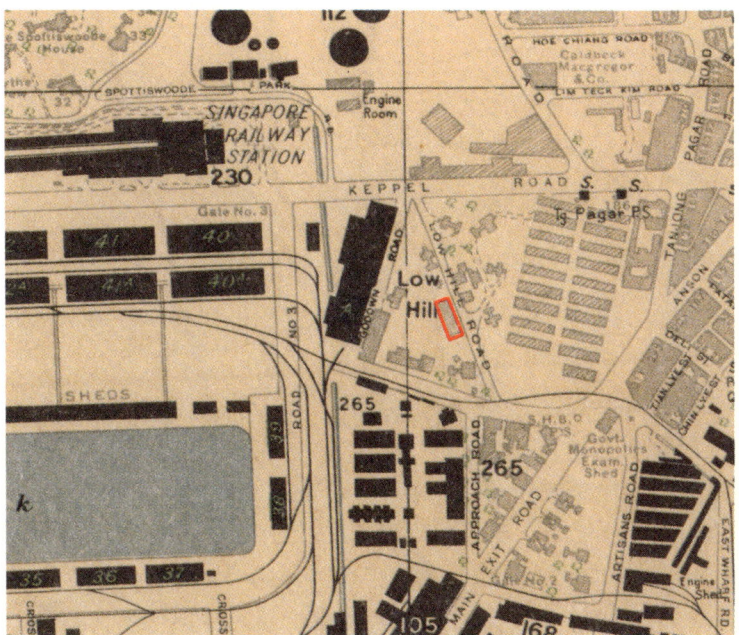

Low Hill Road, 1945.
Source: National Library of Singapore.

Chapter Eight

Prelude & Postlude

Brewing Storm

In 1951, the Police Commissioner was aware that corruption within the police force was worse than previous years. In fact, the problem of corruption in the Force had eroded public trust so much that the threat to derailing progress was not only clear and present, it was near as well. The case of the police detectives complicit in the October 1951 case of hijacking 1,800 pounds of opium worth $400,000, better known as the Ponggol Opium Heist, underscored the large extent of other cases of corruption at the inspector and detective levels since the handover from the British Military Administration (BMA).[142] It was in 1951 that corrupt Police and Civil Service cases hit home close to the heart. In January 1951, the Criminal Investigation Department (CID) arrested a clerk from within the Municipal Treasury Department (Accounts) for corruption. In September 1951, CID detectives forcibly detained a goldsmith just outside the Treasury (Empress Place) and forced him into their vehicle where they robbed him of his gold bars at gunpoint when the vehicle neared the CID Headquarters at Robinson Road.[143] Presumably, they went to work after robbing him! At around the same time, a Volunteer Special Constable was also arrested for conspiring with a police inspector to extort $4,000 from a Chinese grocer. The grocer was told that his brother would be arrested under Emergency Regulations if he refused.[144] In October 1951, the police constable assigned to the CID was charged and sent to prison for stealing belongings of a woman who had surrendered her belongings at the CID charge-room.¹⁴⁵ Could law enforcement officers still be trusted? It was also in 1951 that Legislative assemblymen pressed for more action against corrupt policemen. Legislators like Elizabeth Choy (war heroine) had fought for the right of government to check bank accounts of policemen. Political pressure was growing to keep corrupt police officers in check. However, the new anti-corruption ordinance that planned to address this did not materialise.¹⁴⁶

Going into the 1950s, the other public servants who commanded little public trust were the corrupt housing officials assigning Singapore Improvement Trust (SIT) flats. It had become well-known that bribes had to be given to expedite the allocation of flats. Many SIT flat applicants who submitted applications in 1946–1947 were still waiting their turn in 1951. Then, the 1951 housing scandal hit. In the middle of the year, the SIT issued a mass eviction order to 66–70 flat tenants on grounds that they had improperly leased those flats from the Trust. In reality, they had all given bribes to SIT officials to secure their units and these officials falsified details in their application forms to help them secure their flats. This mass eviction notice shocked the island with such force that the Chinese Chamber of Commerce as well as legislators were calling for the government to intervene by launching an official inquiry to uncover the extent of corruption in the SIT that led to this affair.¹⁴⁷ This was not done and members of the public questioned why the government had been moving in "slow motion" on deciding a course of action.¹⁴⁸ At the end of April 1952, Elizabeth Choy, as a legislator, called on the government to set up a commission of inquiry to investigate corruption in the SIT; since the Police had failed to get to the bottom of the matter, the government should, she proclaimed.¹⁴⁹ The problem with the affair was that almost none of the affected tenants were willing to provide information concerning whom they dealt with when purchasing their flats,¹⁵⁰ and the Trust's management also could not track down the origins of this corrupt affair.¹⁵¹ In the end, only two tenants provided information, and one of them was charged in the police court for engaging in bribery.¹⁵²

In the meantime, despite the scandal still brewing unresolved over two years, corrupt practices continued in the Trust, and other SIT flat allocation clerks were charged in Court for corruption.[153] In one of these cases, Loh Boon Piah received a total of $1,400 from four men from February 1950 to help them get flats. The first briber, Liew Kai Kwan, had referred three other men to Loh, who then helped them falsify details in their application forms to pave the way for their purchase. However, during Loh's trial by jury, he was acquitted for the "abetment of forgery of a letter".[154] This case, as with the case of the mass eviction, underscored just how difficult proving corruption could be when "victims" or co-conspirators did not cooperate. But most importantly, public servants, government departments, and ultimately, the government, were all tainted by such corrupt practices, and this fostered greater social discontent.

Between the Public and the Police

"Bribery is one danger to good relations between the Police and the public.... There is no reason to believe that, comparatively speaking, there is more corruption in the Singapore Police than in other police force, although there is more money in Singapore than in many other places. But, there are always two parties to a case of bribery. The public that persists in such corrupt practices is in danger of getting finally the type of police it deserves."

RE Foulger, Commissioner of Police
Straits Times 26 Oct 1949

Last Ditch Reforms

Following the December 1950 Maria Hertogh riot (11–13 December 1950), it was felt that the Police Establishment was in need of reforms as the whole affair exposed not only the inherent fault lines in the Force but also the great need for better educated policemen.[155] In fact, before the month of the riot, the CID itself was reorganised and calls rang out for the reshuffle of the entire police force.[156] This started in 1951 with the replacement of the Commissioner of Police with a new officer, John P Pennefather, who was brought in specifically to reorganise the Force. Commissioner Pennefather arrived in February 1951. By April, when he announced his plans to reorganise the Force, he started with streamlining the Establishment to make it more efficient, including its hierarchy by merging the two Deputy Commissioner positions into one.[157] By August 1951, Pennefather declared that his police force was now ready to face any emergency, unlike the debacle in December 1950.[158] A factor that weakened the Force was low pay and low morale. Pennefather fixed this by establishing a new Police Pay Code that raised the wages of all police officers.[159]

Then the day came in December 1951, when the Police announced a total reorganisation of the Force in 1952.[160] The earlier CID reorganisation had only augmented the "special" branches within the CID. It did not fundamentally impact the Anti-Corruption Branch (ACB). The 1952 Police reorganisation saw a significant increase in police manpower, especially within the detective services, which meant that the police force was finally able to bring in sufficient new blood to replace old.[161] This ultimately paved the way for the eventual reforming of the main police body. Following the structural changes and the 1952 reorganisation, the "special branches" in the CID were given more resources to succeed. They included the Vice Squad, which also attempted to stop trafficking of women; the Narcotics Branch, which made sense in the post-war period with the elimination of the government opium excise farm; the Gambling Suppression Branch and the Anti-Triads Branch. Back in January 1951, the Narcotics Branch did not even have proper accommodation and had very few staff.[162]

Part of the 1952 reforms was the revision of police pay, a process which Pennefather started in late 1951 with the creation of the Police Pay Code. Low wages had been the main issue that fuelled police corruption. This followed debates in the Singapore Legislative Council where the Police Pay

▶ Laborious Birth

Committee Report was deliberated.[163] As a case in point, the overstretched government had actually been paying policemen allowances in the form of extra rations instead of money.[164] Pay was finally increased in October 1952. In early 1952, political pressure mounted once again for real changes in the police force to combat corruption when City Councillors (former Municipality) like Lim Yew Hock and CJ Paglar advocated that the government form a committee composed of government officers and leading citizens to look into complaints about corruption in the government. Such an initiative would "arouse public confidence" as the public had been slow to cooperate in giving information.[165] This was essentially a call for civilian oversight of the Police in the prevention of corruption efforts by the CID, which itself was filled with corrupt individuals. In fact, just before departing Singapore in February 1952, Pennefather himself suggested that an anti-corruption body separate from the Police should be created. He was, however, careful to phrase his recommendation in terms of the Establishment not having enough police officers to be assigned to this work.[166] In fact, the situation was so critical that a few months earlier, the ACB's new officer-in-charge Supt. CW Byrde[167] remarked that corruption in Singapore was "alarming". It was only days into the job that he had to handle a case of extortion involving a policeman.[168]

The fact of the matter was that all efforts by the ACB and even by the top men of the police force had not even put a dent in the state of corruption on the island. The police reforms were perhaps the last opportunity for the Police to make some headway in their anti-corruption efforts, and this might have saved the ACB from closure. However, it was one reform too late.[169] The level of corruption in the land had reached a level that only extraordinary actions could possibly turn the tide. At stake, in the 1950s, was the "nation" itself. Constitutional developments had started the island on its journey towards being its own nation state. And this was when the big-money corruption returned to Singapore, threatening to compromise all the state apparatus as well as the politicians and future leaders of the land.

Chapter Nine

Opium Heist

The CPIB was established towards the end of September 1952. But the first few men who became the founding members of the Bureau were already working together in May that year as part of a Special Investigation Team put together by the Colonial Secretary to investigate a heinous crime. It was from this group of special men that the CPIB's founding philosophy, work and ethos took form.

And it all started with an opium heist, at a time when the big-money corruptors made a return to Singapore. Several Criminal Investigation Department (CID) officers decided to surreptitiously plan a hidden play-within-a-play, to hijack a shipment of opium from men who were robbing their own boss of the loot, and to set up these men to take the rap for the ultimate heist when they were only involved in the original smuggling and the botched first heist. This was robbery par excellence. They made the world a stage. And playing a part in the cast was David Marshall, the lawyer of most of the men being set up by the CID officers, and soon to be the first Chief Minister of Singapore.

Double-Cross at Ponggol[170]

At around midnight on 26 October 1951, six Chinese men were arrested for smuggling opium for Tan Yong Siah, their alleged boss. According to the arresting officers, Tan had instructed Lim Hock Chiow to hire a tongkang (bumboat) to ferry some men to Mersing on the East Coast of

Johore. There they would meet up with some men on a ship who would load 70 tins containing opium onto the tongkang. The total weight of the load was 1,800 lbs (816.5 kg) that had a street value of $400,000.

Upon returning to Singapore, they headed for Ponggol, where the tongkang was inspected by two Malay customs officers who "discovered" nothing. After that, they loaded their cargo onto a waiting lorry which they parked at the jetty (Ponggol Road) for the night. Their plan was to bring the cargo into Town in the morning. However, after all the men left,[171] and Lim was alone at the tongkang, one of the six men, Lee Peng Chong, who was in the tongkang, returned and claimed that government men were following him, so he drove the lorry away. The lorry was later found at Changi, abandoned and empty. The affair was portrayed as a betrayal of Tan by his own men. The CID arrested and charged all the men involved.[172] Meanwhile, all the stolen opium (just under a ton) was nowhere to be found.

Explosive Trial

It was only during their trial in early March 1952 that the defence lawyers exposed the fact that the accounts of the witnesses provided by the Police were full of inconsistencies.[173] The lawyers, tracing the origins of the used and abandoned lorry, discovered that the accounts book of a petrol kiosk at Raffles Quay had been tampered with. Details in the book would show the movement of the lorry. It was from this point that the whole affair unravelled. The prosecutor and defence lawyers peeled the layers of falsehood and conspiracies placed before them by the arresting officers. They unwittingly discovered that the whole affair could have been conceived and orchestrated by CID Detective Goh Ah Pek and his superior Acting Assistant Superintendent of Police (ASP) Koh Lian Wah, Hokkien Sub-Branch of the CID: suspicion was cast on Lee Keng Lin, a businessman who owned the lorry. He was not informed of the loss of his lorry until 28 October 1951, when he was told where his lorry was parked. When asked, his clerk admitted that the accounts book of the petrol kiosk was altered. The conspirators had tried to make it seem that the boss, Tan, was Lee's customer. But Lee declared that did not know the man. At the same time, Tan declared that he also did not know Lim, the one he supposedly instructed to hire and sail the tongkang to Mersing and back, and that he did not go to Ponggol at all. Tan then claimed that his initial statement to the CID had been coerced. Of course, up till this point, all of them could be lying.

However, the CID detectives involved also put together witnesses to give evidence that the smugglers had been together at a hotel (lodging house) in Geylang on the night of 26 October 1951, presumably after they left Ponggol. Chong Choon Moi, the hotel manager, initially testified that he recognised several of the men (the six men), and they had pistols and handcuffs. On this point, Marshall quickly pointed out that Chong had declared earlier that he did not recognise any of them. The CID detectives had also presented two men, Lim Keng Boon and Ong Choon Pow, claiming that they were part of the original gang, but had now become prosecution witnesses. As it turned out, Ong was the taxi driver who drove the lorry from Ponggol to Changi. After cross-examination by the defence lawyers, he admitted that he had not met any of the accused at the Geylang hotel, and that he was taught what to say by the CID in his earlier declarations. He also revealed that he had no choice but to make false statements about being instructed by Lim Peng Koi, one of the six, to drive the lorry. The detectives had threatened to assault him, just as they did with Lim, right before his eyes. When asked why he did not report the matter, Ong revealed that the detectives had put him in lockup for three weeks after his first contact with them.

At this point, Goh declared that in November 1951, Lim had in November 1951 offered $50,000 to ASP Cheah Teng Cheok of the CID for not charging him. Lim, in response, made a statutory declaration at the High Court that it was the ASP who demanded the money. At this juncture, almost everyone at the trial was likely in deep confusion and consternation.

▶ Laborious Birth

The Court dismissed the charges and the six were released (discharged, not amounting to acquittal). A cloud of suspicion had been cast over the CID. The opium was still missing. The matter was handed over to the Acting Commissioner of Police, NG Morris, who duly cleared Cheah and Wah of any wrongdoing by the third week of March 1952. Clearly, there was no honour among thieves.

Enter Four Good Men

Within a fortnight after the trial ended, a Special Investigation Team was assembled in April 1952 to look into the whole affair as well as the general situation of corruption in the police force. They were the first of the few Good Men who would eventually form the CPIB. The whole affair was not just about an opium heist, or even smuggling. What the detectives did had undermined the law enforcement and justice system of the colony. They did this during the Malayan Emergency, and also when the police force was undergoing reforms. Such public scandals could potentially impact the government's anti-corruption efforts as well as turn the people against the Establishment.

It was serendipitous that the whole Opium Heist affair occurred when two important men helmed the government: Colonial Secretary Wilfred Lawson Blythe (June 1950 to July 1953) and Governor Sir John Fearns Nicoll (April 1952 to June 1955). While the former was anxious to tackle corruption in his police force, the latter, who arrived soon after the Special Investigation Team was formed,[174] was not encumbered by legacy issues. While Blythe ordered the Good Men to assemble, Nicoll supported and shielded the Team till they could formally establish their unit as an independent government body tackling corrupt practices. The Colonial Secretary was so upset by the discovery of the plot in March 1952 that he formed a team which operated outside of the main police force. So, four men quietly gathered to clandestinely investigate the Ponggol Opium Heist. The Anti-Corruption Branch, as a CID department, could not be trusted to investigate their own department. The Colonial Secretary needed to ascertain just how far rot in the Police had penetrated, the extent of the conspiracy and whether these police officers were in cahoots with the big-money syndicates.

This Team included Richard Middleton-Smith, a senior official in the Malayan Civil Service posted to the Singapore Labour Department; Richard Byrne Corridon, a Special Branch officer and ASP Brian N Finch, from the police court. Later, they were joined by ASP Ho Kah Shoon of the Special Branch. They submitted their investigation report to the Colonial Secretary in May. Interestingly, the Team was still working full-time in their original departments while they gathered several hours a day to investigate and write the report on their own time. They had expected to return to their main job after completing their task in May 1952, but the Governor and Colonial Secretary retained them to form the nucleus of the intended unit to replace the ACB of the CID. It seemed that Blythe had decided to adopt Pennefather's suggestion before he left in February 1952 that the colony's anti-corruption body should be independent of the Police Establishment.

The Team regrouped in April 1952, and continued their work at a ground floor room in the Labour Department Building, where they had been meeting since going after the original opium smugglers. They moved into their permanent office at the High Court in the first week of June 1952 after the Public Works Department (PWD) completed renovation works that carved out a corner of the building for the new unit. The Team, however, had no furniture or equipment of their own in their new office. What they had was taken from the Special Branch first. Although they could have an establishment of 12 staff to start, most of the posts were not filled as the ACB was only dismantled in July 1952 and the new Team "assumed" the ACB's responsibilities. This Team answered directly to the Colonial Secretary and Governor, as well as to the Attorney-General of Singapore.

While each member of the Team had specialised skills and were seniors in their fields, they gathered because they had demonstrated a great degree of integrity in the public service. It is important to note that they had formed the core of the anti-corruption service by mid-1952, but this unit had not been named until late September or early October 1952. In the meantime, the unit continued to be described as the Special Investigation Team. From April to May 1952, they were located at the Labour Department, and from June to September 1952, when they moved into the second floor of the Supreme Court, the unit remained unnamed. At this time, most people just assumed the Team would succeed the CID's ACB.

The Team Members

Ho Kah Shoon — Ho joined the Special Branch as a translator in 1936. After liberation, during the time of the British Military Administration, Ho was a key man in the reorganisation of the Malayan Security Service (MSS), the predecessor of the post-war Singapore and Malaysian Special Branch. Ho was then appointed Assistant Local Security Officer before his secondment to the police force as an Inspector. For his part in setting up the MSS, he was awarded the Colonial Service Medal in 1950. Ho then joined the Special Investigation Team on a part-time basis in May 1952. He remained with the unit up till early 1953 when he returned to the Special Branch. He was promoted to ASP sometime after that, and by 1956, he was promoted once again to Deputy Superintendent of Police (DSP), presumably after completing a special 10-month police course in Britain. In 1959, at the tail-end of the Malayanisation movement in Singapore–Malaya,[175] Ho was promoted to Superintendent of Police. As Ho had hailed from Borneo, after his retirement in September 1961, he was recruited by the Chinese Section of the Sarawak Special Branch with the rank of DSP.[176]

Brian N Finch — Before he joined the Special Investigation Team, he was already an ASP. He was attached to the Kandang Kerbau Police Station dealing with general crimes in the district. In August 1951, he gained some popularity when the press posted a picture of him helping an injured lady when a Royal Air Force Hornet (warplane) crashed along East Coast Road.

Its petrol tank and ammunition exploded. Finch was then a Cadet ASP. By November 1951, ASP Finch was posted to the police court where he prosecuted a variety of cases, among which were bribery and criminal breach of trust cases. He then joined the Special Investigation Team sometime in April 1952, also on a part-time basis, and stayed on to form the CPIB. Like Ho, he remained till early 1953. After returning to the police court, among the cases Finch handled included one that involved a Police Inspector of the Traffic Police, Accident and Investigation Section. The inspector took a $50 bribe from a Chinese man who tried to escape prosecution for negligent driving and failing to report the incident within 24 hours. Finch was the investigating officer. After returning from England in 1955, where he went on leave, Finch was posted to the Special Branch where he was eventually reunited with Corridon after the latter completed his tenure in 1956 as CPIB's third Director. This was when both men were involved in a famous raid on the Singapore Factory and Shop Workers' Union (Leftist) when shots were fired during a riot at the Union's premises to save a surrounded officer. At this point, Finch was an Acting DSP. By early 1957, Finch left Singapore permanently as part of the Malayanisation process.[177] Both Ho and Finch had been important members of the Team as they brought their specialised skills. Ho had Special Branch investigative and language skills, while Finch assessed and pursued the successful prosecution of cases.[178]

The Report and Outcome

When the Report on the heist and corruption situation in Singapore was submitted, the Governor and Colonial Secretary were quite determined to close the ACB and found a new independent unit led by a civilian. The Report had been crucial for the government's plan to move forward as the island was generally scandalised by the audacity of the corrupt police officers involved, especially when the police force itself had been undergoing massive reforms in that year to fix inadequacies.[179] The

Governor still had to handle public perception of the affair — it was, after all, played out horrendously in the pages of the press in March 1952. Hence, the administration decided not to follow up on the report overtly so as to protect the image of the Force. As such, what the public knew was that the three CID officers implicated in the Ponggol Opium Heist, Goh, Cheah and Koh, were not found guilty and they went on with their career in the CID battling gangsters and secret societies.[180] Then, at the beginning of July 1952, news was leaked that a Chinese police officer and several detectives had been suspended and an investigation was ongoing. No details were given.[181] Of course, the Acting Commissioner of Police DK Broadhurst (Morris was on leave in England at this time) was swift to deny that any detective had been suspended on suspicion of corruption, although he confirmed one Chinese officer had been suspended for some other matter.[182]

Then, in October 1952, when the establishment of the CPIB had been announced, the Governor finally revealed to the public that the nucleus of the Bureau had been formed by members of a special team appointed to investigate a serious opium smuggling case, for which it enjoyed some measure of success.[183] The Colonial Secretary then "closed" the case in late October 1952 when he declared that the CPIB's recent opium smuggling investigation uncovered other fields of corruption (police conspiracy) but the key person involved had committed suicide.[184]

The contents of the much-awaited Special Investigation Team Report, which also covered much of its own progress,[185] however, provided quite another story:

The Team started work on 21 April 1952, in a room at the Labour Department. They continued meeting there till 17 May when offices in the Supreme Court rooms No. 98–105 on the second floor were ready. Entry to the offices was from High Street.

Initially, the Team read the police investigation papers on the robbery and police internal reports on the investigation, including one to the Commissioner. They also read the notes on the evidence found during the

Police's preliminary enquiry laid before the Police Magistrate. The Team also recorded more statements from RCS Bush, defence lawyer of Lim Peng Koi, one of the six smugglers, of Cheah's alleged involvement in illegal bookmaking and gold smuggling activities on top of the opium case. Three customs officers were also interviewed. It was discovered that they were involved in the initial smuggling case, but the police investigation papers did not reveal this. And, after obtaining a dossier on the opium importer (Tan Ah Choy, father of Tan Yong Siah) from the Comptroller of Customs, the Team discovered that a consignment of opium seized by the Johore Customs in November 1951 had actually been part of the loot lost in the October 1951 heist at Ponggol.

Throughout the investigation, Middleton-Smith was still concurrently handling work at the Labour Department, while Corridon was also still engaged in work regarding the Malayan Communist Party. So, he only devoted three hours on site with the Team daily, while Middleton-Smith committed six hours. Although the Attorney-General had permitted them to work with the Team full-time, Middleton-Smith felt that it was better to relinquish present duties gradually rather than to have a sudden break. The Team had also engaged a confidential stenographer to assist in their work, and Ho joined the Team on 15 May 1952. Then, on 17 May, they moved to their new office at the Supreme Court. Two more staff were hired after this move.

The Team then decided that the best chance they had to discover evidence of bribes paid to the Police was to interrogate Tan Ah Choy and his son, Tan Yong Siah, the original opium importers. So, the Team obtained warrants for arrest and detention under the Banishment Order and held both father and son for interrogation. Before arresting them, the Team had been following them to discover what properties they owned in the hope that raids by customs officers to their houses would uncover evidence to prove that they had engaged in bribery. The Team suspected both father and son had bribed the CID officers before they were double-crossed. However, raids on multiple properties owned by Tan Yong Siah in June

▶ Laborious Birth

1952 discovered nothing.

At the same time, Bush was interviewed again as he had claimed that Tan Yong Siah's life was in danger, and alleged that Cheah had been sending $1,000 a month through the Maxwell Road Post Office to his mother in Penang since 1947. So, the Team visited the Kuala Lumpur Post Office (HQ) to secure money order records of the transactions. However, the Post Office only retained two years of records. It was found that Cheah had only remitted a total of $2,800 in those two years.

The Team kept both detainees in isolation after their arrest so that they could not bribe anyone. Tan Yong Siah was detained at the Special Branch Holding Centre Lock Up. Corridon and Finch took turns to guard him 24 hours daily while Ho spent several hours daily to record statements which implicated ASP Ee Sim Mong and ASP Chan Joo Chua, both officers in the Attorney-General's Office. While he gave information on other opium importers, Tan Yong Siah maintained that he did not bribe the CID officers, Cheah and Koh.

The Report identified large-scale corruption in Singapore as having its roots in opium and gold smuggling, as well as gambling. The Team was keen to embrace the opium problem as part of their scope of duties. On 23 May 1952, they met with the Colonial Secretary and gave their opinion that corruption could not be eliminated without first eliminating the big-time opium dealers. The Team had uncovered information regarding protection money being paid to the Police, including to members of the ACB in connection to *Chap Ji Kee* (a form of illegal gambling). And with regard to the Opium Heist case, the Team had received information that Cheah had acquired, through his mother, a great deal of land in Penang. Ho was credited with having done much work on the ground that unearthed a significant amount of information for the Team. The Report concluded with a number of recommendations and updates: The case against ASP Ee was strong enough to warrant disciplinary action. It had been ascertained that Chan, when he was in the Attorney-General's Office, had knowledge of the Opium Heist at its early stages, but did not inform his superiors.

The Team was certain that Koh had been complicit in the Opium Heist, and action ought to be taken against him, but they had yet to discover indisputable evidence against the others. As for the father-and-son pair, Tan Ah Choy and Tan Yong Siah, the Team was in the process of preparing their Banishment Order.

View of the Singapore River with the bumboats in the foreground and with the Empress Place and the Victoria Memorial Hall in the background, 1954.
Source: Ministry of Information and the Arts Collection, courtesy of National Archives of Singapore.

▶ Laborious Birth

Three customs officers weighing opium seized at Clifford Pier on 24 December, 1953.
Source: The Straits Times © *SPH Media Limited. Permission required for reproduction.*

Governor John Fearns Nicoll inspecting the guard of honour during laying of foundation stone for Red Cross Home for Handicapped Children at Tanah Merah Besar, 8 July 1952.
Source: Ministry of Information and the Arts Collection, courtesy of National Archives of Singapore.

Chief Secretary, Mr Wilfred Lawson Blythe visits government printing office, 21 September 1950.
Source: Ministry of Information and the Arts Collection, courtesy of National Archives of Singapore.

 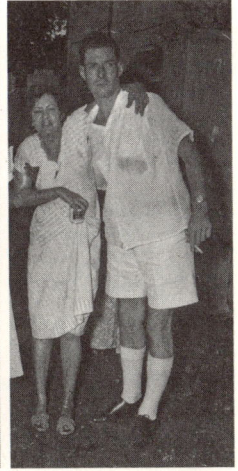

(left): Mr Ho Kah Shoon, Inspector of the Malayan Security Police, was awarded the colonial police medal, 2 January 1950.
Source: The Straits Times © SPH Media Limited. Permission required for reproduction.

(right): Mrs Emma Nepos who was injured on the legs, being helped to an ambulance by Mr BN Finch, ASP, *The Straits Times*, 11 August 1951, p.1.
Source: The Straits Times © SPH Media Limited. Permission required for reproduction.

Yang di-Pertuan Negara Tun Yusof Ishak presenting the Pingat Jasa Gemilang (Meritorious Service Medal) to Director of the CPIB, Superintendent of Police Richard Byrne Corridon, during National Day Awards Investiture Ceremony at Istana Negara, 2 March 1964.
Source: Ministry of Information and the Arts Collection, courtesy of National Archives of Singapore.

Ministry of Labour, 1957.
Source: Ministry of Information and the Arts Collection, courtesy of National Archives of Singapore.

Staff discussion at the Labour Department, 1950.
Source: Ministry of Information and the Arts Collection, courtesy of National Archives of Singapore.

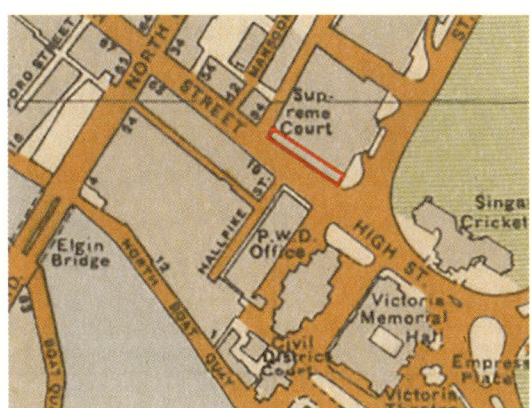

Location of the Special Investigation Team's High Court Office, 1952.
Source: Courtesy of the Survey Department, Singapore.

Supreme Court Building. The CPIB's Office (1952–1960) was on level two of this side of the building.
Source: Courtesy of National Archives of Singapore. Photograph taken by Wong Ken Foo.

Chapter Ten

Special Investigation Team

First Homes

The first meeting place of the Special Investigation Team, unsurprisingly, was a ground floor room in the building housing the colony's Labour Department. Though he was team leader of the Special Investigation Team, Richard Middleton-Smith was also the Assistant Commissioner of Labour; the assignment with the Team was only on a temporary basis. It was fortuitous that the Team's first home would be where the boss had his main office. Middleton-Smith would have had no problem finding a space for his team in this building. The Team operated from this Havelock Road site from April to May 1952.[186] The building itself has a rich history. It was formerly the Chinese Protectorate, an institution responsible for the welfare of all Chinese immigrants; labourers, women and children. It was also responsible for the pre-war Po Leung Kuk, the Society for the Protection of Women and Children. It was also the responsibility of the Chinese Protector to manage the dealings with Chinese secret societies in the latter half of the nineteenth century. Naturally, the Department of Social Welfare also relocated into this building in 1953.

When the Special Investigation Team was already in the process of submitting its Interim Report and preparing to draft the final version, the renovation of the second level of the Supreme Court was completed. Clearly, the Colonial Secretary had no plans to allow them to return to their old jobs. When they moved into their new premises, they had little or almost no assets, not even furniture. These were the humble beginnings for the men who would bear the responsibility of fighting corruption amongst government officers. What they needed, at this point, they were able to solicit from the Special Branch, the department where two of its four founding members had come from.

The office occupied by the Team was the original offices of the Registry of Trade Marks. The Registrar had kindly agreed to move elsewhere in the building because he did not require a space that could make up three offices. It was within this office that the unit would become the CPIB. Middleton-Smith would declare that locating the Bureau at the Supreme Court provided it an important psychological importance in the minds of the public.[187]

Closure of the Anti-Corruption Branch, Legacy Issues

When the Special Investigation Team was formed, very few people knew it existed, and even fewer knew of its real functions. The contractors renovating its new premises at the Court House probably did not know for whom or for what the space was to be used. After all, the unit still had no official name. It was not on any government directory nor did it have a telephone number to contact nor a PO Box to receive mail. In fact, its four members were still officially doing their "day job". And certainly, no one would have guessed that the new unit would be an anti-corruption body, since the Anti-Corruption Branch (ACB) was still in operation.

When the Opium Heist court debacle occurred in March 1952, the ACB pre-empted the government's reaction by announcing that it had submitted its own recommendations in its Corruption Report for further anti-corruption measures to the Commissioner of Police.[188] The Commissioner then promptly forwarded it to the Attorney-General's Office for endorsement.[189] The Report recommended that a separate unit be created, separate from the police force. This unit was to have more staff than the present ACB. It was also proposed to amend the present Prevention of Corruption Ordinance to give wider powers to police officers above ranks of ASP to investigate bank and post office accounts of persons they were investigating, and to use such findings in Court. And, perhaps to show that the Police were driving this reform effort, they revealed to the press in early April 1952 that they were awaiting the government's response to the recommendations in their Report.[190] At the same time, the Police also took the opportunity to publicly air that they needed more manpower: the ACB was authorised to have 16 officers, but they were presently understaffed with only 12 men — one ASP, two inspectors and nine detectives. Three ACB detectives were dismissed during the previous months and it was difficult finding suitable replacements. Hence, they were requesting for a manpower increase in their Establishment for 1953.[191] By this time, the Special Investigation Team was already being formed and would submit their report within a month. The ACB did not know at this junction that the writing was on the wall.

At the end of April 1952, the ACB presented a surprise, or a fait accompli, when they had launched a major investigation into the corruption of the Singapore Improvement Trust (SIT). They had already questioned more than 100 people, 65 of whom were tenants, and most of them had provided statements that they had allegedly given money (bribes) for their flats. Investigations were still ongoing.[192] While this enormous anti-corruption drive appears to have demonstrated the effectiveness of the ACB, it was actually a "re-run" of its 1951 effort which was also positioned as a successful operation that weeded out corruption in the SIT. It was in July 1951 that the SIT started working with the ACB to fine-tune its flat allocation system to "nip any attempt at graft at the very start".[193] This measure was taken in response to a surge in public complaints that the SIT was corrupt. Many who had submitted applications for SIT flats were told in 1951 that the Trust had no records of their applications. Yet, there were some "lucky" ones who got their flats almost immediately between 1946 and 1948. Also, those who applied in 1949 and 1950 got their flats immediately.[194] So, the ACB requested that anyone who sent applications for flats between 1947 and 1949, including those who got no reply from

▶ Laborious Birth

the Board, to contact them. The ACB also published a list of names of applicants whom they wanted to interview.[195] Was not the incessant corruption in the SIT already resolutely dealt with in 1951? In any case, the Police had made it clear that they could, and would, continue to handle corruption in the SIT.

It was not until June 1952, when the Special Investigation Team moved into the Supreme Court, that the existence and nature of this new unit could not be hidden any further. Up until this time, the Police did not know that their ACB's March 1952 Report had not been accepted. Although a new unit independent of the Police Establishment had been formed, it had no relationship with the ACB. In fact, when the government's spokesman announced in May 1952 that a special team had been set up, the details were vague, only stating that the staff were to be "government officers from the Colonial Secretariat", and that it was going to be linked to the ACB, but it would employ different tactics.[196] Although the impending closure of the ACB in July was announced in June, and the Special Team would take over, the new unit still had no name till Middleton-Smith's September 1952 proposals were adopted. Even then, the new unit had no budget to operate.

The ACB closed in July 1952, and the Special Investigation Team assumed its responsibilities, albeit still an unnamed entity. This transition from the ACB to the Special Team was not a simple reconstitution or reforming of an anti-corruption body. It was a paradigm shift that took the steering wheel from a uniformed Force and handed it to civilian oversight. It was a statement that there was a problem in the police force. And the Force had every right to retort, and to remind everyone that they had been "reorganised". During the 1950s police reforms, it was explained that the bulk of the police contingent, just some years before, was still composed of the old pre-war Straits Settlements Police Force, and they had been "corrupted" or made inefficient during the Japanese Occupation. Both Detective Goh Ah Pek and ASP Cheah Teng Cheok, and many others, had been part of this pre-war institution.[197] Understandably, the Governor at

■ 124

this time found himself having to use velvet gloves instead of a bat when handling his law enforcers. It was within this socio-political condition that the CPIB was born.

The fact that three out of four members of the founding team were still policemen, meant that the Commissioner of Police would continue to wield influence over CPIB's police staff members. In fact, Commissioner NG Morris, in public announcements, would occasionally state that he would "instruct" the CPIB to look into certain matters. It should be appreciated that all matters concerning law enforcement, including anti-corruption efforts, had been up till 1952 the sole responsibility of the Police. It was certainly difficult to define an enforcement unit which was connected to the Police and yet independent of the Establishment at the same time. When a government spokesman announced to the press in May 1952 that a Special Team had been set up to investigate corruption among government officers, it was declared that the new unit would be separate from the Police, and was composed of government officers from the Colonial Secretariat, a "concept" not easily understood, perhaps even to the Police themselves. Furthermore, even till the end of 1952, Morris was still unwilling to completely relinquish the Police's anti-corruption portfolio, at least in public eyes. He publicly announced in December 1952 that even though the CPIB had started operations, the Police were still waging war against corruption. Morris asserted that the Police did not simply relax after the creation of the new anti-corruption body, but had remained vigilant, and were working with the CPIB. When the Police received information relating to corruption, it was passed to the CPIB for action. He also shared that the Police worked in close liaison with the CPIB. In this announcement, he declared that battling corruption was still the Police's business and "it will always be so, to fight corruption within our ranks or among the public".[198]

Public housing built by the SIT in the mid-1940s:
Five-storey blocks of flats at Tiong Bahru Road, 1940s.
Source: Ministry of Culture Collection, courtesy of National Archives of Singapore.

Photograph of a family in a newly completed SIT house, 1953.
Source: Ministry of Information and the Arts Collection, courtesy of National Archives of Singapore.

Chapter Eleven

Establishment

CPIB, Arise!

One could say that the CPIB was born in the shadows, without fanfare and arose rather slowly. One issue was that the Good Men from the Special Investigation Team had treaded carefully before July 1952 as the Anti-Corruption Branch (ACB) was still in operation. There was also no government gazette announcing its formation or describing its functions. The Team was formed following an executive order to only four men. As such, it arose clandestinely from the offices of four men who belonged to an organisation which they themselves could not name, at least till end September 1952. Even the Governor and Colonial Secretary had little idea of the scope of work and nature of its establishment till the Special Team leader, Richard Middleton-Smith, a civilian, submitted his "Establishment and Estimates, Organisation and Leadership" plans to the Governor for endorsement because he needed approval for the new unit's budget estimates.[199] This document was submitted during a meeting between Middleton-Smith and the Governor in September 1952; succeeding leaders of the CPIB had come to call it the CPIB's "Charter". The new name of this Bureau was first proposed and explained within Middleton-Smith's bureau paper. Interestingly, the Bureau was born on the day its name was approved.

The formal name of the CPIB only started appearing in public sources from the second week of October 1952. It is likely that Middleton-Smith's proposals were accepted and adopted by the end of September 1952 and

▶ Laborious Birth

the unit was formally constituted between that time and by the first week of October 1952.[200] Regardless, it is clear that the Bureau was established by pulling together members of the Police Establishment and a senior member of the Malayan Civil Service (MCS) which had earlier been tasked to investigate a case of police corruption. It was this Team that morphed into the CPIB. The Bureau was officially outside the Force, and headed by a senior MCS staff. However, because its core members were still police officers, the Bureau was not entirely independent of the police force as far as staff matters were concerned. Nevertheless, the Bureau operated under the authority provisioned in the Straits Settlements Prevention of Corruption Ordinance no.14 of 1937 (Amendment 1946) and the Penal Code. This remained as status quo till 1960 when a new ordinance was introduced which replaced the 1937 law.

Still, mystery surrounded the CPIB in early October 1952. The public was told on 14 October 1952 that the unit's Director, Middleton-Smith, an officer of the MCS, would only answer to the Governor and the Colonial Secretary. Furthermore, the unit worked "in secret rooms on the second floor of the Supreme Court", cut off from the rest of the building. There was only a single pathway to the office and the door was always closed and guarded. There was also "no sign at the door to show that it leads to the Bureau".[201] Up until 21 October 1952, the Colonial Secretary had said nothing more about the unit other than that he would give a statement soon.[202] In short, the new unit only swung into action publicly towards the last two months of 1952.

Middleton-Smith's CPIB "Charter"

The CPIB was born without an originating Ordinance or any gazetted statement of purpose and scope. This left Middleton-Smith's "Establishment and Estimates, Organisation and Leadership" document the only guiding light for the CPIB when it was operationalised. RB Corridon would later call the document CPIB's Charter.[203] Although the Bureau was created to succeed the work of the Criminal Investigation Department's (CID) ACB, it was not a matter of a direct transfer of work scope and responsibilities, working files and unit assets, funds and processes, or even staff and informants. The new unit started with just an empty office space. The CID did not transfer or leave the new unit anything from the ACB to the CPIB.[204] In any case, the new unit was not a constituent of the police force. Hence, Middleton-Smith had to scope and position the CPIB's work, structure, mission and goals from bottom up. The unit therefore had to define its own work and concerns.

Middleton-Smith's Proposal[205]

Critical Point

The Special Investigation Team was assembled with an executive order. All four original members served in this "task force" while they were still members of their respective government establishments — one senior MCS officer (civilian) and three officers of the police force (uniformed service). This was a legacy which was to continue with the creation of the new unit: the civilian officer and uniformed officers would have to be seconded to the unit (task and work), but they remained members of their parent departments.

Legal-Legislative Basis

"Investigation and prosecution in court of cases involving illegal gratification" under the Prevention of Corruption Ordinance No.14 of 1937 and the Penal Code.

Main Objectives and Tasks

"To seek out, identify and bring to justice the large-scale corrupters". These "corruptors" included the "organisers" of opium and gold smuggling, those who organise gambling activities and others engaging in illegal activities involving large sums of monies. Why these groups? It was because "their money seeps through all grades of government and their power inspires fear". That is, they had the resources to corrupt anyone in the government, and the power to coerce all of them. Hence, the new unit had to smash their rackets and system of "protection money". The new organisation had to be "compact, highly trusted and specialised".

Core Work

Research (Investigation). This was to be carried out by a senior civilian investigator who, "preferably", should be someone who had banking or commercial experience, and a Chinese, because most of the criminal organisations at this time were Chinese syndicates. The senior civilian investigator would need support from a couple of registry assistants who could maintain accurate records, and they should know the Chinese language as documents and material on the Chinese syndicates would be in their vernacular. The unit should also employ "propaganda", the promotion of cause and public messaging. This strategy for anti-corruption work had shown results in Malaya, and this could be done through Radio Malaya, the mass media of the day.

Staffing and Security

The new unit should, as far as possible, recruit staff directly and not have seconded public servants. Direct recruitment of civilian investigators was much preferred to police detectives. They should have a special warrant and carry arms. The unit should have senior police personnel to assist when necessary. This senior staff should be assisted by two police inspectors, each working directly under an ASP, and they should be specially selected. As for staff training, they would require special training for staff. Funds would be needed for this as well as for sending senior staff for training aboard.

Wages and Career

The senior civilian investigator would be on the same pay scale as an ASP: [His pay would be] $600 plus allowances, as this would attract people of calibre. As for civilian investigators, they should be on the same rate as sub-inspectors of police. This is the same scheme for Special Branch personnel on special duties. Staff should be given a career path; that is, there should be opportunities for promotion. Hence, there was a need to create a small number of posts of levels between the civilian investigators and senior civilian investigator.

Unit Budget and Workspace

The unit would need an allocation (budget) for office furniture and stationery. There was also a need to acquire equipment for their work [as] the police force did not transfer the equipment used by the former CID ACB. The unit also needed funds to acquire a pick-up. As for workspace, the current staff were occupying the office of the original Special Investigation Team on the second level of the Supreme Court. Its offices were facing the High Street side of the building. The unit occupied two rooms (18x10 feet) and (9x10 feet). The PWD could add three more rooms (9x10 feet each). The new unit was to remain at this office space and the three new rooms were to be added quickly. The unit was expected to expand in the following year, and more spaces within the Supreme Court building would be carved out for this purpose. The unit's estimates (budget) would not be published, it would be included in a block vote under "Miscellaneous Services". Additional funds, when needed, could be placed under the Defence Services Supplement.

Naming the Unit

It was proposed to drop "anti-corruption" as well as "prevention of corruption" in the name of the new unit. Both had defensive slants. It was preferred that the new unit should bear the phrase "corrupt practices investigation". It was also better to use "Bureau" than "Secretariat" as a "Director" implied authority while "Secretary" did not.

▶ Laborious Birth

Richard Middleton-Smith, The Man and His Directorship[206]

When war came to Malaya in December 1941, Middleton-Smith was assigned to work within the Colonial Secretariat Office, where he remained for almost three weeks before being "released" to join the Straits Settlements Volunteer Force (SSVF) on 20 December 1941. He joined the SSVF as a private. Similarly, Mr William Allmond Codrington Goode — who later became Singapore's Colonial Secretary (1955–1957), last Governor (1957–1959) and first Yang di-Pertuan Negara in 1959 (before Yusof bin Ishak) — was also an MCS official who joined the SSVF as a private during the defence of Singapore. Like Middleton-Smith, Goode was also sent to the Death Railway during the Occupation years.[207]

During the battle for Singapore, Middleton-Smith was posted to a machine-gun post (pillbox) on the beach facing Keppel Harbour (Sentosa), training by day and guarding at night. After Singapore surrendered on 15 February, Middleton-Smith was taken away to the SSVF Headquarters the following days.[208]

From there, he was sent to the Changi Barracks. On 26 June 1942, he was taken away to build the Burma–Siam Death Railway line (about 3,000 prisoners of war (POWs) were sent from Changi in June 1942). Thousands of POWs perished building the Death Railway.

After the war ended, Middleton-Smith returned to England in February 1946. He came back to Malaya in October 1946 and was sent to Klang to reopen the government's Labour Office.[209]

Middleton-Smith finally arrived at Singapore in March 1950, when he was appointed Assistant Commissioner of Labour. In March–April 1952, the Colonial Secretary asked him to pull together a special team to investigate an opium heist at Ponggol. Following the submission of the report, his team was kept together to form the core of the new anti-corruption body — the CPIB to replace the CID's ACB. Middleton-Smith was appointed by the Colonial Secretary to organise and direct the CPIB.

Middleton-Smith declared that "the government decided that the police should no longer control anti-corrupt [efforts]". It was Middleton-Smith who conceived the Bureau's name — Corrupt Practices Investigation Bureau. He personally coordinated with the staff of the Supreme Court building to set up office there, and started interviewing people whom he could hire for the Bureau.

One of his first hires was his secretary, the wife of a police officer whom he considered to have been very good at her work. His core team included the original members the Special Team which came together in March–April 1952. After Middleton-Smith left the Bureau at the end of 1952, he went on leave back to England with his wife in May 1953.[210] When he returned in 1954, he was appointed Secretary for Defence and Internal Security, and then Deputy President of the City Council. He left Singapore in 1958.

Middleton-Smith's place in the CPIB's history is not diminished by the short length of time when the Bureau started active service during his tenure. He was to leave the Bureau before he could even complete a year within the unit and return to the Labour Department in early January to become its Deputy Commissioner.[211] The main reason for his swift departure was that his deployment to the Special Investigation Team, and his position in the CPIB, had been on a part-time basis. This was also the case for his deputy, Corridon.[212]

The CPIB's founding principles were the brainchild of Middleton-Smith. He was not a Special Branch officer like his colleagues but he understood the requirements and responsibilities of his service. As a member of the MCS, which is equivalent to today's officer of the Administrative Service, he was considered highly capable and of higher calibre.[213] Under Middleton-Smith, the Bureau's first task was to get its house in order. Till August 1952, the team had to plan its work and working space, including the unit's future expansion. It was during this time that Middleton-Smith put pen to paper for estimates for the unit (budget), its manpower policies as well its areas of responsibility and organisational hierarchy.[214]

▶ Laborious Birth

It was only during the last week of October 1952 that the CPIB started its core duties in earnest. The first task was publicity and "propaganda". Middleton understood that public education was important in the battle against corruption. People must know they could send complaints or information to the Bureau. So, he gave the Bureau's PO Box number to the press — 2222.[215] Within a week of the publicity blitz, the Bureau started receiving a good number of responses by people responding to the CPIB's appeal for information. On 28 October 1952, during a Press Conference, the Colonial Secretary laid out the Bureau's work thus far: the investigation into the 1951 Opium Heist had been completed. The Bureau had started Banishment proceedings for four Chinese, one of whom was involved in the heist. A corrupt policeman in the Attorney-General's Office had also been disciplined, and the Bureau had gained significant knowledge of the local opium smuggling racket since the time of the Special Investigation Team. He also revealed that the Bureau had 14 staff, five of whom were

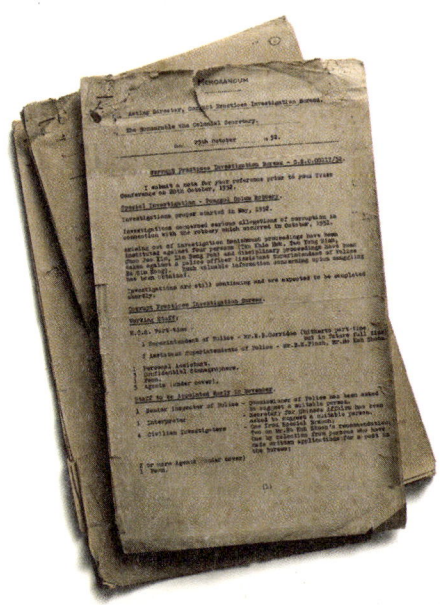

Official memorandum on the Ponggol Opium Robbery by Richard Middleton-Smith (then-Acting Director, CPIB), 25 October 1952.
Source: CPIB Archives.

■ 134

engaged in undercover work, and there were plans to increase the staff in a matter of months. Non-police personnel in the Bureau also carried warrant cards issued by the Colonial Secretariat. The Bureau reported to him directly as it was a department under the Colonial Secretariat.[216]

It was only in December 1952 that the Director of the CPIB met with the Governor to hear his views on the work of the Bureau and his expectations of the unit.

In this meeting, the Governor made it known that he was not expecting spectacular prosecutions or for cases to go to Court. He was perfectly satisfied if the CPIB could ensure that government procedures did not "invite corruption" — to spot "loopholes" and "eliminate them". The

Former Director of the CPIB Richard Middleton Smith hosting Commonwealth Parliamentary Association delegates in his capacity as Acting President of Singapore City Council in 1956.
Source: Ministry of Information and the Arts Collection, courtesy of National Archives of Singapore.

Governor emphasised that strict discipline among government staff was of utmost importance. He was quite content with dismissal of corrupt staff from the public service rather than prosecution — citing the practice in Hong Kong when the Colonial Secretary could at any time demand an explanation from a government staff when his "living standard" was higher than his salary scale. If the officer could not explain, he would have to resign. Fundamentally, the Governor had no problem with public servants buying expensive properties as a form of investment, but he could not condone unexplained expenses on luxury purchases. In response, Middleton-Smith said that he could delegate a senior staff to investigate government procedure and work with organisation consultants who might "over focus on efficiency and overlook possible corruption issues".[217] While Middleton-Smith was squarely focused on investigating "corrupt practices", the Governor's slant was "prevention of corruption".[218] By the time he left the unit at the end of the year, although Middleton-Smith's unit had not brought any cases to Court, he had undoubtedly led his Bureau across the starting line. It would be his former boss at the Labour Department who would run that race in earnest.[219]

Endnotes

[1] Clement Liew and Peter Wilson, *A History of Money in Singapore* (Singapore: Talisman, 2021), pp.164–65.

[2] *Straits Times* 15 Sep 1945.

[3] The Malayan Union plan was announced to the public in October 1945, a month after liberation. See *Straits Times* 12 Oct 1945; *Malaya Tribune* 15 Oct 1945.

[4] Clement Liew and Peter Wilson, *A History of Money in Singapore*, p.162.

[5] Japan's Emperor declared surrender on 15 August 1945, but the formal surrender only took place on 2 September.

[6] British Forces landed in Singapore on 4 September 1945. The formal surrender took place on 12 September 1945.

[7] Civilian police took control of all normal police duties towards the end of August 1945. They handled all cases except for looting and rioting. They could still call upon the Japanese military for help when needed, and they did. See *Straits Times* 8 Sep 1945.

[8] At the beginning of October 1945, a looting party of 20 Chinese armed with revolvers and knives raided a store on Cecil Street. Only three were arrested. See *Straits Times* 2 Oct 1945. In another raid on a shop on Upper Serangoon Road in October, the Police shot dead three looters, two men and a woman. See *Malaya Tribune* 15 Oct 1945. At this time, much of the island still had no electricity. Kerosene lamps had to be used. It was not surprising that more than 50 looters raided a kerosene store at Kallang BMA store in October 1945. Only a handful were discovered with kerosene in their possession. They were arrested. See *Straits Times* 17 Oct 1945. It was also in this month that about 50 Chinese looted Messrs Borneo Motor Co. Ltd. Only seven were arrested and they were sentenced to five months' rigorous imprisonment. Interestingly, it was in this case that two of the looters, Lim Ah Giam and Lim Tiang Song, attempted to bribe three Special Constables (Singapore Police Volunteer Reserve – Special Constabulary) with $200 to let them off. They were arrested and allowed bail of $500 each. See *Malaya Tribune* 20 Oct 1945.

[9] Retailing army supplies was illegal. The first hawker to be charged for this offence appeared in Court in early October 1945. He faced up to three years' imprisonment, or fined up to $2,000, or both. See *Straits Times* 3 Oct 1945. It was noted that members of the services had been responsible for supplying the black market in the months following liberation. They sold their possessions (allocations and personal kits) often at high prices and used the money gotten to purchase other stuff on the island. It was the locals who were the victims in this regime. See *Straits Times* 7 Nov 1945. There was a concentration of Allied troops in Singapore after the war because the Headquarters of the Supreme Allied Commander of the South East Asia Command (SEAC) relocated from Ceylon to Singapore in November 1945. The move cost the British £2,500,000, of which £1,000,000 was spent directly in Singapore. Hence, a great amount of cash was pumped into the island's economy. In addition to the wages spent by hundreds of servicemen assigned to the Command here, there was also their own allocated supply of cigarettes, food, clothing, mosquito nets and more. All these items flowed into the black market. Even the crew of the supply ships arriving with army goods were bringing in their own stash of goods for personal trades. These items also entered the Singapore black market. As a case in point, with regards to bartering at this time, it was discovered that a ship captain had offered 500 duty-free cigarettes as payment for a silk coat. As for the large private trades, when a cargo ship newly arrived at Singapore, "all night long" when the cargo was being unloaded on one side of the ship, "goods come down and money goes up" on the other side. A ship's officer would bring from India a certain amount of goods which he would offload at Singapore for a 500% profit. *Straits Times* 26 Nov 1945.

[10] *Straits Times* 10 Nov 1945.

[11] *Straits Times* 3 Oct 1945.

[12] *Straits Times* 29 Nov 1945.

[13] *Malaya Tribune* 17 Oct 1945. This was actually an improvement from the September–October 1945 labourers' wages of $0.60–$0.80 per day. In December 1945, following the interim findings of the Cost of Living, Wages Inquiry Committee appointed in early 1945, skilled and unskilled workers received an increase of their daily wages of about 10%, which then raised their income to

between $0.80 and $1 a day. By the end of 1946, even when some labourers' earnings rose up to $2 a day, the cost of most things was still prohibitive. See *Malaya Tribune* 3 Nov, 12, 23 Dec 1946.

[14] Penicillin was first discovered as an antibiotic in 1928 by Alexander Fleming. However, it was not widely used till the 1940s. In the 1930s, the German-produced Prontosil was the first commercially used antibacterial drug. It was only in 1845 that penicillin was used widely for bacterial infections.

[15] *Straits Times* 27, 29 Sep 1945.

[16] *Straits Times* 27 Sep 1945. Despite price control regulations, people were still selling rice and sugar above price control proclamation. In November 1945, customs officers arrested a number of these black marketeers. See *Sunday Tribune* 25 Nov 1945.

[17] *Straits Times* 27 Sep 1945. Prices indicated were derived from actual prices at Beach Road Market.

[18] By end October 1945, eggs and a loaf of bread, which before Occupation cost three and five cents, respectively, now cost 30 cents and $5, respectively. See *Straits Times* 23 Oct 1945. By early November 1945, prices of meat had reached their highest levels since the end of the Occupation. Pork which cost $2.60 a kati at the Beach Road Market in late October 1945 was $3.60 by the first week of November 1945. However, at Tiong Bahru Market, pork was sold at $4.50 to $5 at the same time. See *Straits Times* 6 Nov 1945. By mid-December 1945, the price of medicines had also reached levels unseen before. Tan Chin Tuan, member of the Singapore Advisory Council, appealed to doctors not to raise prices of medicines further, some of which cost 10 times pre-war levels. See *Malaya Tribune* 14 Dec 1945. It was noted that one cause of rising prices at this time was the great flow of money into the Singapore economy and market. Besides the shift of the SEAC Headquarters (HQ) from Ceylon to Singapore in November 1945, which saw infrastructural spending on the part of the military, the arriving HQ troops were augmented by thousands of returning displaced civilians (many had been in India during the Occupation) and the returning Dutchmen to the East Indies, expenditure on essential and other goods in Singapore rose to unprecedented levels. This stretched the already limited supplies on the island. There was more money than there were available goods. Prices shot through the roof. See *Malaya Tribune* 26 Nov 1945.

[19] *Straits Times* 23 Oct 1945. The British Military Administration (BMA) was perhaps one of the biggest "employers" in Singapore in late 1945. At this time, of the BMA staff under permanent employment, 340 earned more than $100, 257 received between $55 and $95, and eight who took home below $50. Under temporary employment, 352 earned between $50 and $100 and 117 received above $100. See *Sunday Tribune* 11 Nov 1945. Before the war, a government officer, at the executive level earning $240 monthly could support a large family of seven children, in addition to his old parents, all under one roof, as things were cheap then. See *Straits Times* 5 Jul 1946. Lim Chuan Geok, a member of the Singapore Advisory Council, raised the issue of hundreds of unemployed clerks and clerks suffering low pay. He pleaded with the BMA to introduce a cost of living (COL) allowance for these government clerks. See *Malaya Tribune* 13 Dec 1945.

[20] *Malaya Tribune* 3 Nov 1945.

[21] *Straits Times* 29 Sep 1945.

[22] *Malaya Tribune* 22 Dec 1945. Singapore's ration card system was modelled after the system implemented in England. An additional measure the BMA implemented to enforce food control was the deployment of more officers in enforcement work. See *Straits Times* 22 Dec 1945. At the same time, the BMA banned, from 1 January 1946, the public sale of bread, milk (condensed, evaporated or powder), rice, sugar, edible oil, vegetables (fresh, tinned or dehydrated) and wheat flour, cooked and uncooked, in "inns, public houses, restaurants, buffets, coffee-stalls, or any places of refreshments open to public". See *Malaya Tribune* 3, 5, 8 Jan 1946; *Straits Times* 3 Jan 1946.

[23] *Sunday Tribune* 23 Dec 1945. By the beginning of 1946, over 1,000 government employees received coupons to purchase affordable meals within government buildings. While the lower-paid staff bought 35-cents meal coupons, the better paid ones bought 75-cents coupons. See *Straits Times* 30 Dec 1945.

[24] Pyke's Committee also recommended "price control for essentials, and retailers had to display

prices. It also suggested the appointment of Price Control Inspectors who would enforce the measures. The Committee also supported the setting up of Government Shops that sold necessities to curtail profiteering merchants." See Clement Liew and Peter Wilson, *A History of Money in Singapore*, p.174. *Morning Tribune* 1 May, 28 Jun 1946; *Straits Times* 28 Jun 1946.

[25] The Singapore government created the first People's Restaurant in June 1946 to sell meals to any labourer for 35 cents. See *Straits Times* 28 Jun 1946. By the end of 1946, there were People's Restaurants in Tiong Bahru Telok Ayer and Outram Road. There were six People's Kitchens which prepared the 8,900 daily meals served at the People's Restaurants to feed wage-earning labourers. See *Malaya Tribune* 23 Dec 1946. In December 1946, the government also opened its first "Family Restaurant" to feed non-wage earners, including their dependents. Each meal cost only 8 cents in the Family Restaurants. The first was opened at the Maxwell Road Market. It served 2,500 meals a day. See *Singapore Free Press* 14 Dec 1946; *Malaya Tribune* 14 Dec 1946; *Straits Times* 14, 19 Dec 1946. From the start of 1947, Family Restaurants were also serving 10-cent breakfasts and the People's Kitchens sold bulk meals directly to the public. By this time, the government also established the island's first Children Feeding Centres. In 1947, the government reduced its 35-cent meals to 30 cents, while the People's Kitchen bulk meals were lowered from 30 cents to 28 cents. See *Singapore Free Press* 8, 20 Jan 1947; *Straits Times* 25 Sep 1948. Also see Clement Liew and Peter Wilson, *A History of Money in Singapore*, pp.175–76; *Singapore Free Press* 20 Jan 1947.

[26] *Morning Tribune* 22 Jul 1946. In the pre-war years, clerks of the lowest grade started at $55 in the first month and had a $5 monthly increment till their wage reached $95 and that became his annual wage. The next higher-grade clerk started at $100, had a $10 annual increment till he reached a ceiling of $160. The highest-grade clerk started at $160, his ceiling was $210. With the 1946 "reforms", a clerk's wage was between $65 and $75 monthly, and he was given a monthly cost of living (COL) allowance which was an additional $10 plus 10% of basic wage. In total, if his basic pay was $65, he took home $65+$10+$6.50, that is a total of $81.50 monthly.

[27] In August 1946, lower-rank government (British Government) and municipal servants (local government) had their COL allowance ceiling nearly doubled from $35 a month to $60. For monthly-paid employees, this meant that their COL allowance was raised to 20% of basic wage (1941 levels) plus $10. The minimum monthly basic wage in 1941 was $25. For daily-rated employees, it was an increase of 20% of their daily basic plus 40 cents daily — this was a total of 79 cents more daily. In 1941, the average take-home daily was 55 cents. The rates for female employees followed the basic rule of two-thirds the rate of their male counterparts.

[28] At this time, most teachers were still surviving on less than $100 monthly. So, they demanded higher pay. See *Sunday Tribune* 2 Jun 1946. As a case in point, the teachers of Nan Hua Girls School had an average wage of $95 per month, inclusive of COL allowances and a free meal a day. *Straits Times* 6 Aug 1946.

[29] *Straits Times* 10 Oct 1945. Before the fall of Singapore, Singapore's annual opium farm revenue was around $6,000,000 (Malayan).

[30] During the course of the war, in 1944, the Allies came together in Bretton Woods, New Hampshire, United States, to plan the future of the post-war era. The result of this Bretton Woods conference was the creation of the World Bank and the International Monetary Fund. It was also decided at Bretton Woods that the US Dollar (USD) would be the "trade currency" (and reserve currency) of the post-war world. This ended the "silver standard" regime of the pre-war years. As a result, most strategic resources at this time had to be paid for in USD (part of the Bretton Woods Agreement).

[31] Currency (Exchange) control was implemented almost immediately after the war. For more details see Clement Liew and Peter Wilson, *A History of Money in Singapore*, pp.178, 181–82.

[32] The real problem was that this was a chicken and egg question. Singapore and the Malayan Union (MU) could not wait till social order and progress had been achieved before introducing the measure that would earn them the funds that were needed to achieve those very goals in the first place. However, by 1947, the situation was

so critical that this additional income stream was needed to keep the administration afloat; it was not just a matter of replacing the loss of revenue from the opium excise farm. As such, the MU and Singapore government pushed through their Income Tax Ordinances in December 1947. The first assessment year would start on 1 January 1948 (to be paid in 1949). See *Straits Times* 11 May, 19, 31 Dec 1947; *Malaya Tribune* 4, 17 Dec 1947; *Singapore Free Press* 4 Dec 1947. The Singapore Income Tax Department was created in 1947 to administer the Income Tax Ordinance enacted during that year. https://www.iras.gov.sg/who-we-are/our-organisation/history-and-milestones.

[33] Barbara Leitch Lepoer (ed.), *Singapore: A Country Study* (Washington: GPO for the Library of Congress, 1989), p.42. Also in http://countrystudies.us/singapore/9.htm.

[34] Besides the tens of thousands of soldiers and labourers, as well as prisoners, sent abroad during the Occupation, there were perhaps even more who fled to India, Australia, England and other places. Many of them eventually returned to Singapore over the years. There were also thousands who were sent to the Endau and Bahau food-growing settlements during the Occupation. In late September 1945, there were still 10,000 Singapore Chinese in Endau still waiting to return. See *Straits Times* 20 Sep 1945.

[35] *Malaya Tribune* 5 Sep 1946.

[36] *Straits Times Annual* 1 Jan 1952.

[37] *Straits Times* 7 Aug 1951.

[38] *Straits Times* 2 Dec 1945, 7 Aug 1951.

[39] Security Branch members of the British Intelligence Service worked with the BMA's Civilian Affairs Police Department to send special officers across Malaya to collect evidence of atrocities and other criminal acts of Japanese and local officials in order to secure arrests. In the Malay States, within the Kuala Lumpur area alone, more than 500 police officers were dismissed, and many of them were placed under arrest. In Selangor, collaborators arrested included jailers, detectives, judges and other police officers. In Ipoh, the military police also arrested collaborators who were involved with the massacre of Chinese at Kampar. The Malayan Police Establishment was by and large depleted following liberation. As a case in point, Negeri Sembilan had only seven Asiatic policemen left after purging. Retraining of the remaining policemen was also a top priority. By October 1945, 1,000 men were undergoing short training sessions in police duties at the Kuala Lumpur Police Depot. This was part of the BMA's reorganisation of the Malayan Police Force. See *Malaya Tribune* 16 Oct 1945; *Straits Times* 6 Oct 1945; *Sunday Tribune* 21 Oct 1945.

[40] *Straits Times* 14, 24 Oct 1945.

[41] *Straits Times* 14, 23 Oct 1945.

[42] It was only in September 1946 that the Police would receive $178,000 to upgrade its facilities, and this was principally spent on the restoration of CID's operational capacity, which included the ACB. The amount seemed to be paltry in light of the Singapore government's rehabilitation fund (loan) of $25,000,000. See *Malaya Tribune* 5 Sep 1946.

[43] The main currency for international trade was the USD in the post-war period. Britain was also encumbered by a war loan it had to repay the Americans in USD. Hence, to secure the much-needed foreign exchange (USD) to sustain its foreign trade and to repay war debts, Britain imposed exchange controls throughout its colonies. In consequence, British colonies which needed USD to purchase economic and recovery resources, for example machinery, building materials and more, had to pace their efforts in accordance with the foreign currencies made available to them.

[44] The Police Volunteer Reserves (PVR) (Europeans) was first established in 1937. The Force was strengthened with the addition of an Asiatic contingent, the Asiatic Police Volunteer Reserves (APVR), in 1940. The officers of the Volunteer Reserves had remained in their post till the fall of Singapore. See *Straits Times* 5 May, 8 Nov 1940. In 1941, when war and instability threatened, the PVR force was given regular police authority and were "suitably armed" (Police Force Ordinance No. 39 of 1941). See *Morning Tribune* 1 Oct 1946; *Indian Daily Mail* 2 Oct 1946.

[45] *Straits Times* 15, 21 Sep 1945.

[46] The volunteers, now called Special Constables, served full-time eight hours daily. Asiatic inspectors were paid $165 monthly, while Sergeants received $75 and constables $45. See *Straits Times* 23

Sep, 30 Oct 1945. From 1 December 1946, the Sergeants' and constables' remuneration were raised to $90 and $60, respectively, with an additional COL allowance of $10 and 20% of their basic pay (this also applied to the Inspectors). The officers of the Special Constabulary were also offered transfer to the regular police force if they were found suitable. See Indian Daily Mail 23 Nov 1946.

[47] *Straits Times* 30 Oct 1945.

[48] *Straits Times* 17 Oct 1945.

[49] Amongst those arrested, in March 1947, two were charged in Court for theft and attempting to bribe the Special Constables; Siow Ang Koo and Siow Ah Moi had stolen $1,500 worth of cloth from the dock godown. They also offered a $2,000 bribe to two Special Constables guarding the area. The Magistrate set their bail at $2,000 each. See *Malaya Tribune* 20 Mar 1947.

[50] *Straits Times* 16 Jun 1946; *Singapore Free Press* 11 Apr 1947. By mid-1946, after the BMA had handed over control of Singapore to its civilian government, the SC was 250 strong, led by three officers who reported to Major Wee Kah Kiat, and he in turn answered to the Police Commissioner of Singapore. At this time, the SC wore jungle green and a number of them were attached to the CID as radio operators (radio patrols). SC constables received $1.50 a day, better than the lowest paid regular police officers who were receiving $26 a month.

[51] *Malaya Tribune* 20 Nov 1946, 3 May 1947; *Morning Tribune* 3 May 1947.

[52] *Straits Times* 3 May 1947.

[53] Yong had claimed that he found the rice on the beach during a raid on smugglers.

[54] *Malaya Tribune* 29 Aug 1946; *Straits Times* 24, 29 Aug 1946; *Singapore Free Press* 24 Aug 1946; *Morning Tribune* 4 Sep 1946. The exploits of Inspector Lee Cheng Teen and his fellow Special Constables started months before the Siglap case. On 25 May 1946, in the wee hours of the morning, Inspector Lee and two Special Constables boarded a boat at Clifford Pier and headed to Telok Ayer Basin where the SS Fort Abitivi was moored. The Inspector had received information that the government's sugar from the ship had been loaded onto lighters anchored next to the ship and were about to be robbed (this would also have defeated food control measures). So, Inspector Lee and his compatriots boarded the Fort Abitivi and waited. The robbers came and worked fast. Within minutes of jumping onto the lighters, they had already carried onto their boat 80 bags of sugar. The three SC men arrested 13 men on the spot. Three were convicted, receiving imprisonment of three to six months each. See *Morning Tribune* 4 Sep 1946.

[55] *Singapore Free Press* 8 Jul 1948; *Malaya Tribune* 30 Aug 1948; *Morning Tribune* 30 Aug 1948. The SC's recruitment was carried out at the Police Headquarters. Major Wee Kah Kiat interviewed each and every one. Of the 200 recruited by August 1948, 100 were immediately sent to the Police Training School for a two-month course before they were deployed for guarding and escort duties. Armed Special Constables were in great demand during the Emergency as Leftist sabotage became increasingly common. At its height, the SC had 400 men trained to guard godowns. However, by 1954, with the threat from Communist saboteurs greatly reduced, many of the local firms returned to using their own *jagas* and security guards. By this time, only 10% of the Force was deployed to guard duties. See *Singapore Free Press* 26 May 1954

[56] *Singapore Free Press* 1 Oct 1946; *Straits Times* 1, 2, 21 Oct 1946. *Malaya Tribune* 1 Oct 1946; *Indian Daily Mail* 2 Oct 1946; *Morning Tribune* 2 Oct 1946; *Sunday Tribune* 3 Nov 1946. VSC officers were sworn in under the provisions of the Police Force Ordinance No. 39 of 1941. When it started, ex-members of the pre-war SC were also invited to join. The Singapore Chamber of Commerce also submitted 100 names for consideration. At the same time, the Singapore Harbour Board also contemplated having their own night patrol volunteers.

[57] By 1950, the VSC had 900 officers and in the following year, the Police targeted to have 1,500 volunteers. See *Malaya Tribune* 27 Aug 1950; *Singapore Free Press* 26 May 1951.

[58] Barbara Leitch Lepoer (ed.), *Singapore: A Country Study*, p.42.

[59] *Malaya Tribune* 27 Oct, 13, 14 Nov 1945; *Straits Times* 27 Oct, 5, 13 Nov 1945. On 14 Nov 1945,

they met with Major General HR Home, Chief Civilian Affairs Officer, BMA, to kick-start their endeavour.

[60] *Straits Times* 10 Nov, 2 Dec 1945; *Malaya Tribune* 3 Dec 1945. It was suggested that the Anti-Corruption Department to eradicate corruption should be re-established.

[61] *Straits Times* 10, 15 Dec 1945; *Malaya Tribune* 12, 14 Dec 1945. Chen Su Lan pointed out that a verbal warning to public servants against corruption was not enough — "if they did not fear the Japanese, then they won't fear the British".

[62] *Malaya Tribune* 23, 25 Jan 1946.

[63] *Malaya Tribune* 4 Apr 1946. Almost immediately, on the day of the BMA's handover, plans were made to prepare for the island's first elections. A Committee was appointed to plan and organise the elections. See *Malaya Tribune* 1 Apr 1946; *Straits Times* 7 Apr 1946. The 1948 Legislature had 22 members; only six councillors were elected, the rest were civil servants and nominated members. Nomination and Polling days were on 16 February and 20 March 1948, respectively.

[64] *Straits Times* 1 Sep 1946.

[65] *Malaya Tribune* 5 Sep 1946.

[66] *Straits Times* 1 Sep 1946.

[67] Anti-Corruption Laws Tightened, *Malaya Tribune* 5 Sep 1946.

[68] *Straits Times* 12 Sep 1946.

[69] *Straits Times* 2, 25 Dec 1945; *Malaya Tribune* 3, 14 Dec 1945, 23, 25 Jan 1946.

[70] Tan Chin Tuan, who became a legislative councillor in 1948, noted that the quality of essentials, like rice, distributed by government had been of such low quality that they were "almost unfit for human consumption". He identified corruption as having played a great part in fostering this dismal socio-economic state. Accordingly, in early 1949, he asked if the government could reinforce the ACB. See *Singapore Free Press* 3 Feb 1949.

[71] Barbara Leitch Lepoer (ed.), *Singapore: A Country Study*. p.42. The poor socio-economic conditions had also fuelled the Communist-led strikes and work stoppages in public transport prior to the Malayan Emergency.

[72] The military police had been responsible for general law and order during the BMA period. As such, it was the military police who led all measures to suppress corrupt activities in the immediate post-war years. By the start of October 1945, the Australian Military Police (Provost) in Singapore had already arrested over 100 civilians involved in corrupt activities. They were all charged in Court. A military court had already opened in the former police court on 9 September 1945. See *Straits Times* 10 Sep 1945. The military police targeted street peddlers and hawkers who peddled army rations, medical supplies and drugs, and much more. They also had lots of tinned goods of every description, many with the inscription "for HMS ships only". Essentially, this mass retail sale of government goods, mostly pilfered from government supplies, had constituted the immediate post-war "black market", which the military police first prosecuted. This "black market" was a hawkers' enterprise. It was distinct from the syndicated black markets which were also in operation at this time. See *Straits Times* 3 Oct 1945. Most of the goods found in this massive black market had come from Allied troops who bartered for what they truly wanted with British military supplies. The British Army's Special Investigation Branch (SIB), the detective branch of the military police, was also fully engaged in suppressing this activity. By early November 1945, the SIB's raids on the black market resulted in the arrest of 100 persons. They recovered $100,000 worth of War Department property. Many of the black marketeers could be found in the vicinity of New World Park; at this site, 18 people were arrested with 254 tins of foodstuff, 184 packages of chocolates and 37 tins of cigarettes. At China Street, the SIB arrested two Chinese. One was fined $350 and the other was given six months of rigorous imprisonment. See *Straits Times* 10 Nov 1945. Besides servicemen stealing from their own stores, there were also cases where soldiers guarding the army's depot simply allowed thieves to enter and steal, after accepting a bribe. In March 1946, three servicemen did just that. They were subsequently convicted along with two civilians who stole 135,000 bedsheets from their depot on Mohamed Sultan Lane. See *Malaya Tribune* 24 May 1946; *Morning Tribune* 17 May 1946.

[73] In 1945–1946, one of the more popular military units to steal from was the Navy, Army and Air Force Institutes (NAAFI). The NAAFI was responsible for providing all the logistical needs of the servicemen and their families. They handled millions of dollars of military goods. In December 1945, the CID detained three Chinese who brought tens of thousands of cigarettes that belonged to NAAFI, in three lorries, to Merchant Lane for sale. They were fined between $1,000 and $3,000. See *Malaya Tribune* 14 Dec 1945. Just before the NAAFI cigarettes theft case, in November 1945, the ship's captain and seven of his officers of the ship Sam Freedom were caught selling the NAAFI's store they were hauling to Singapore: "80,000 cigarettes, 161 bottles of liquor, 10,750 razor blades, lots of toilet stuff, tobacco and much more". These "British pirates" did not even wait for their cargo to be offloaded on shore to sell them. They simply skipped the middlemen and sold their cargo to bumboat merchants who came up to the ship as it entered Singapore. The black market value of these goods was £2,000–£3,000. The lot received sentences that ranged from 1–12 months. See *Straits Times* 23 Dec 1945.

[74] Local Chinese leader, Tan Kah Kee, who was, after the war, also the Chairman of the Singapore Chinese Federation for Peace and Democracy in China (Leftist), supported the student strikes in China against the Kuomintang government. One of their demands (manifesto) was to remove corrupt officials. See *Indian Daily Mail* 2 Jun 1947. The British authorities had suspected that Tan had been involved in Communist activities, so they denied his entry back into Singapore in 1950. He then settled permanently in China and held various positions in the Chinese Communist Party (CCP). The British watched him closely. Tan was also a Director of the Bank of China during this period. See FCO 141/14432: Singapore. The Bank of China. Vol. I. Secret — Migrated Archives, in National Archives (Great Britain).

[75] *Sunday Tribune* 26 Jan, 9 Feb 1947.

[76] *Morning Tribune* 27 Mar 1947. The Singapore Traction Company busmen planned an earlier strike in September 1946. It was called off after its union came to an agreement to increase pay, allowances and bonuses. See *Indian Daily Mail* 11 Sep 1946. On the busmen's part, the union had agreed to put a stop to all corrupt practices. However, half a year on, another strike threatened when the union accused the company of not keeping to the agreement on the payments. The company responded by pointing out that the corruption had continued. In Court, the Union's Secretary provided a definition of what is considered a "squeeze" and "corruption", as per their September 1946 agreement; "Squeeze, was when some conductors collected money from passengers and issued less value tickets, while corruption was tea money paid by the conductor-applicants to whoever was in-charge of engaging them". See *Sunday Tribune* 29 Sep 1946.

[77] *Malaya Tribune* 4 Jul 1947; *Indian Daily Mail* 7 Jun 1947. This was the same fear in the MU — the point made by the Union Finance Review Committee. See *Malaya Tribune* 5 Feb, 27 Nov 1947.

[78] Legacy of Corruption, *Malaya Tribune* 3 Dec 1945; *Singapore Free Press* 14 Feb 1952. It was already noted weeks after liberation that "the germ of corruption, sown during the Japanese regime, has taken deep root among men holding responsible and 'paying' positions in the government or in civilian firms.... In abnormal times, 'we can make allowances for persons who had to accept bribes in order to make ends meet', but now things are returning to normalcy, should they still continue corrupt ways? Should they still ask for tea money? Or for the least favour?" See *Straits Times* 27 Oct 1945. Another problem was the laxity in government employment standards in the pre-war and post-war years. In October 1945, a filing clerk of the Colonial Secretary Office, RS Maniam, was caught and convicted for theft of books and stationery from his office. He sold them to a second-hand bookstore on Bras Basah Road. It was discovered during the trial that he had been convicted previously for cheating and theft in 1924, 1926, 1929 and 1939. How did a man of this "calibre" secure a job in the Colonial Secretariat Office? See *Malaya Tribune* 24 Oct 1945.

[79] *Straits Times* 16 Nov 1945; *Malaya Tribune* 20 Oct, 6 Nov 1945.

[80] *Morning Tribune* 26 Apr 1946; *Straits Times* 21 Sep 1946, 15 Jan 1947.

[81] *Morning Tribune* 14 Sep 1946; *Straits Times* 9 May 1948. Second-hand goods dealers were popular targets for corrupt officials in the early post-war years. It was the nature of their business that the provenance of everything they sold could be known. Thieves or looters would also find these dealerships a convenient way to offload their illicit items. Hence, these dealers were easily threatened with withholding of licences or confiscation of their goods. In early 1948, Detectives Koh Teng Han and Too Ah Seng were prosecuted for doing just that. On 2 and 8 March 1948, both detectives threatened to seize Phoon Kui's second-hand goods on Kelantan Road if they were not given something. They also took $18 from Phoon. Both were charged for committing extortion and for illegal gratification. They pleaded not guilty. See *Straits Times* 9 May 1948.

[82] On 1 Apr 1948, Frank William Norris, a building inspector of the Municipality's Architect Department, received $200 money from Ng Eng Kee (complainant), a contractor, to overlook the commencement of work on a building at South Bridge Road before plans were approved. He was found guilty and sentenced to four months' rigorous imprisonment. However, he was acquitted in March 1949 when he appealed his conviction at the High Court. See *Morning Tribune* 13, 22 May, 30 Jul 1948; *Singapore Free Press* 30 Jul 1948; *Malaya Tribune* 13 May 1948; *Straits Times* 22 May 1948, 5 Mar 1949.

[83] *Straits Times* 25 Jan 1948; *Morning Tribune* 19 Mar 1948. A Malay, Dhaik Mydin, gave $10 to a detective who said he was "hungry". Dhaik was charged. Two watchmen at the Rationing Office took $15 from P Pavadai to have his ration card altered speedily in March 1948. Pavadai was also charged.

[84] "Makan kopee". See *Malaya Tribune* 28 Aug 1946.

[85] *Straits Times* 16 Nov 1945; *Malaya Tribune* 20 Oct, 6 Nov 1945. It was believed that most policemen were corrupt during the Occupation. See *Straits Times* 30 Oct 1945. One of the more contentious issues in the latter part of 1940s, involving corrupt officials, was the allocation of Singapore Improvement Trust (SIT) flats. The SIT did not even maintain a register of applicants. See *Malaya Tribune* 4 Nov 1949. The lack of cooperation from the public was identified as a stumbling block in the fight against corruption, namely in the matter of bribery. *Malaya Tribune* 6 Nov 1945; *Straits Times* 5, 15 Nov 1945.

[86] An STC conductor caught organising an illegal gambling party offered a CID detective $2 coffee money, two cigarettes and a cup of tea. See *Malaya Tribune* 20 Aug 1948. In another case, LT Fernandez of Messrs George Wimpey & Co., Bukit Timah Road, took a bribe of a gold ring, six bottles of beer and a dozen oranges to favour the briber with employment. He was originally given three months' imprisonment and fined $1,000. This sentence was later set aside. The ACB's ASP PS Gordon had oversight of the case. See *Morning Tribune* 17 Mar 1948.

[87] *Singapore Free Press* 11 Jul 1946. EV Fowler, DCP, CID in 1946 pointed out that in the context of limited supplies, businesses (retail) often had to pay tea money to wholesaler clerks in order to be on their preferred list or these clerks would sell to others who were willing to pay the bribe. In a way, this was extortion.

[88] *Malaya Tribune* 30 Jul 1946. For instance, on 27 July 1946, a Chinese offered a clerk at the Victoria School Rationing Office a $2 bribe for the speedy renewal of his rice card.

[89] For example, on 24 February 1947, Baboo Sahib offered a bribe of $50 to a food control inspector at Raffles Place for a "favour". See *Malaya Tribune* 26 Feb 1947.

[90] For example, when the two marine police officers stopped Tan Choon Hee for carrying rice without permit, he offered them $8 to look the other way. See *Singapore Free Press* 5 Oct 1949. In August 1946, Inspector Ponniah Rajaratnam, a future Director of CPIB, was offered $10 *"makan kopee"* by Ho Ah Fook who was found illegally in possession of army supplies. Ho was arrested. See *Malaya Tribune* 28 Aug 1946.

[91] For instance, in May 1949, Leck Kwee Ser was fined $50 and sentenced to one month of imprisonment for giving a $4.20 bribe to a clerk in the Identity Registration Office. See *Malaya Tribune* 1 Jun 1949; *Straits Times* 26 May, 1 Jun 1949.

[92] The disparity in the penalty amounts could be due to the limits set for each respective offence in the Penal Code.

⁹³ For example, the STC conductor who offered $2 for his gambling infringement was fined $25 for gambling and $150 for bribery. See *Malaya Tribune* 20 Aug 1948.

⁹⁴ *Straits Times* 5 Apr 1946 — a Chinese offered a bribe to get out of a disorderly conduct charge.

⁹⁵ Two men offered a $2,000 bribe to two Special Constables who detained them for theft of $1,500 worth of cloth from a dock godown. See *Malaya Tribune* 20 Mar 1947.

⁹⁶ Tan Pai was found to have been in possession of 26 sacks of empty shells and a brass sheet (for export). He bribed a detective with $70. See *Malaya Tribune* 1 Feb 1947; Yeo Ban Soon was fined $5,000 for illegal possession of rice and given a six-month prison sentence for bribery. He brought in 90 bags of rice from Rangoon, and 130 piculs of Java rice in motor boat. The marine police caught him on 6 Nov 1947, and he offered them $500 to let him pass. See *Singapore Free Press* 14 Feb 1948; *Straits Times* 14 Feb 1948; *Sunday Tribune* 22 Aug 1948; in 1949, two carpet merchants, Mohinder Singh and Mohan Singh, offered bribes to the Assistant Executive Controller of Imports and Exports Department LJ Wood. He reported the matter to his superiors and to the ACB. Following the instructions of ACB's Inspector Roland Arthur Lawrence, a trap was set. Mohinder, who offered Wood $7,000, was fined $3,000, and Mohan, having given Wood $2,000, was fined $1,000. Following an appeal for a harsher sentence, the High Court added 18 months' imprisonment for Mohinder while Mohan got one year. See *Straits Times* 8, 12 Apr, 31 Aug 1949; *Malaya Tribune* 9, 12 Apr 1949; *Singapore Free Press* 8 Apr 1949.

⁹⁷ Chan Ann Kim arrived in Singapore without any documentation in May 1949. He offered Police Corporal Ibrahim bin Tahir $65 to look away. Chan was fined $300. See *Straits Times* 13 May 1949.

⁹⁸ Three men involved in a fatal motor-car accident in the Naval Base tried to get off scot-free by bribing a sub-inspector of the Naval Base Police with $200. They were sentenced to four months of rigorous imprisonment. See *Straits Times* 16 Jul 1949.

⁹⁹ In 1949, the Singapore soccer league was found to have been tainted by bribery. See *Sunday Tribune* 8 Sep 1949. The association was known as the Singapore Amateur Football Association (SAFA) on 14 May 1929 before adopting its current name, the Football Association of Singapore, on 13 January 1966.

¹⁰⁰ *Singapore Free Press* 1 Jul 1947, 6, 25 Feb 1948; *Malaya Tribune* 1 Jul, 7 Aug, 25 Sep 1947, 25 Feb 1948; *Straits Times* 1 Jul, 7 Aug 1947, 25 Feb 1948; *Morning Tribune* 6 Feb 1948.

¹⁰¹ *Straits Times*, 25 Sep 1947.

¹⁰² *Sunday Tribune* 24 Nov 1946; *Morning Tribune* 25 Sep 1947.

¹⁰³ *Singapore Free Press* 26 Sep 1947.

¹⁰⁴ *Malaya Tribune* 16 Jul 1947; *Singapore Free Press* 16, 23 Jul, 2 Aug, 25 Oct 1947, 2 Mar, 30 Apr 1948; *Morning Tribune* 24 Jul 1947; *Straits Times* 24 Dec 1947, 30 Apr 1948.

¹⁰⁵ In 1947, several Chinese were charged for bribing food inspectors. On 18 April 1947, Ho Loke Hui gave McPherson $600. At the same time, together with Ong Chin Ho, Ho also gave an additional $600 to two other food control inspectors. Ong gave $750. Both men wanted these inspectors to avoid taking enforcement action at Kreta Ayer Market. See *Straits Times* 15 Aug 1947.

¹⁰⁶ In June 1948, Detective Goh Nam Seng was caught taking $100 to take no action against *Chap Ji Kee* (illegal gambling) agents. See *Malaya Tribune* 22 Jun 1948. In May 1949, when Teo Cheng Lian was caught for having *Chap Ji Kee* slips, he offered the arresting detective $40 to be let off. He was fined $300 and given two months' rigorous imprisonment. See *Malaya Tribune* 1 Jun 1949; *Straits Times* 26 May, 1 Jun 1949.

¹⁰⁷ *Straits Times* 10 Nov 1945.

¹⁰⁸ *Malaya Tribune* 12, 14 Dec 1945; *Straits Times* 15 Dec 1945.

¹⁰⁹ *Straits Times* 25 Jan 1946.

¹¹⁰ *Straits Times* 25 Jan, 1 Aug 1946; *Malaya Tribune* 4 Jul, 1 Aug 1946; *Morning Tribune* 5 Jul 1946.

¹¹¹ *Straits Times* 28 Jul 1946.

[112] *Malaya Tribune* 5 Sep 1946 "Anti-Corruption Laws Tightened".

[113] *Straits Times* 12 Sep 1946.

[114] *Straits Times* 12 Sep 1946.

[115] *Straits Times* 25 Sep 1946, 25 Jan 1947; *Malaya Tribune* 14, 26 Sep 1946; *Morning Tribune* 14 Sep 1946; *Sunday Tribune* 24 Nov 1946. In August 1946, Shannon closed two separate cases of corruption by clerks of the Ration Office at Victoria School. These clerks put the "squeeze" on people who went to the Ration Office to renew their rice ration cards. In one of the cases, an elderly woman had placed $2 (*kopi* money) on the renewal form she handed to the clerk. He rejected it and pushed it back, so she re-tendered with $10. See *Straits Times* 1, 6 Oct 1946; *Sunday Tribune* 13 Oct 1946; on 2 August 1946, a government ship surveyor, while on inspection at the Telok Ayer Basin, was given a $500 bribe by a boat owner after completing his work. He reported the matter to Shannon. See *Straits Times* 1 Nov 1946; in the same month, a Chinese man asked a constable to assist in a case involving two men in an armed charge. The constable asked for money. After Shannon was informed, he set a trap using marked notes. The constable was arrested. See *Malaya Tribune* 26 Sep 1946.

[116] *Malaya Tribune* 6 Mar 1947.

[117] *Indian Daily Mail* 26 Aug 1949. In August 1949, Shannon was appointed as Superintendent in the CID Headquarters.

[118] *Singapore Free Press* 3 Jul 1947; *Morning Tribune* 3 Dec 1947.

[119] *Malaya Tribune* 12 May 1947. The CID's public communication about the ACB's work at this time was that the public must cooperate with the ACB if widespread corruption of the day was to be effectively checked. They could contact the ACB at 82322.

[120] *Singapore Free Press* 3 Jul 1947.

[121] *Singapore Free Press* 26 May 1947.

[122] *Straits Times* 25 Sep 1946; *Malaya Tribune* 25 Sep 1946.

[123] *Malaya Tribune* 15 Nov 1949.

[124] *Singapore Free Press* 26 May, 12 Jul 1947.

[125] For instance, in May 1949, a Police Corporal at the Court, Johan bin Salim, demanded $1 from a hawker who needed an endorsement on his bail receipt. An ACB detective witnessed the original incident, so a trap was set for the corporal. He went to jail for $1. See *Straits Times* 22 Jul, 20 Dec 1949.

[126] *Malaya Tribune* 6 Mar 1947.

[127] *Straits Times* 9 Sep 1947.

[128] *Straits Times* 27, 28 Oct, 25 Dec 1948, 23 Feb, 2 Mar, 14 Apr 1949; *Malaya Tribune* 28 Oct 1948, 23 Feb, 29 Mar, 14 Apr 1949; *Singapore Free Press* 27, 28 Oct 1948; *Morning Tribune* 23 Dec 1948.

[129] *Singapore Free Press* 26 May 1947.

[130] *Singapore Free Press* 15 Jul 1949; *Straits Times* 15 Jul 1949.

[131] Bretton Woods was the post-war agreement among the Western allies for the creation of a new currency standard (that is, the main currency of trade, reserves, exchange standards etc) would be the US Dollar.

[132] *Singapore Free Press* 21 Jun, 15 Jul 1949; *Straits Times* 15 Jul 1949.

[133] *Straits Times* 22 Sep 1949.

[134] *Morning Tribune* 22 Oct 1948; *Straits Times* 20 May 1949. EV Fowler also asked members of the Singapore Chamber of Commerce to report corruption cases in the commercial sector. See *Straits Times* 22 Sep 1949.

[135] *Malaya Tribune* 20 Oct 1949; *Straits Times* 14 Feb, 9 Mar, 23 May 1950.

[136] Fowler, as chief of the ACB, spearheaded the unit's anti-corruption drive in 1949. He informed the public that any complaints and allegations of corruption could be sent to the ACB and their complaints would be kept confidential. They could contact the ACB at 82322. See *Straits Times* 11 May 1949.

[137] *Singapore Standard* 17 Aug 1950.

[138] From March to September 1949, the ACB prosecuted about 80 anti-corruption cases. Yet, corruption remained widespread. See *Straits Times* 23 Sep 1949; *Malaya Tribune* 14 Oct 1949.

[139] *Malaya Tribune* 14 Oct 1959.

¹⁴⁰ *Straits Times* 23 Feb 1950. One impetus that pushed the government to reform the ACB was the pressure piled on by Inche Sardon bin Jubir, Legislator, unofficial member. He pointed out that the government should appoint a special anti-corruption committee to enquire into foreign exchange control regulations. *Straits Times* 10 Jun 1949; *Singapore Free Press* 20, 21 Jun 1949.

¹⁴¹ *Straits Times* 19 Aug 1950; *Malaya Tribune* 18 Aug 1950.

¹⁴² In 1949, the ACB investigated 290 cases of police corruption, which led to 105 persons being charged, of which 71 were convicted successfully. At the same time, 17 police detectives (Gambling Branch) were sacked and one Sergeant was deported. In 1950, three policemen and a Chinese detective were arrested for their involvement in opium smuggling. The case was ultimately dismissed owing to conflicting accounts.

¹⁴³ *Straits Times* 18 Sep 1951.

¹⁴⁴ *Straits Times* 2 Oct 1951.

¹⁴⁵ *Straits Times* 23 Aug, 21 Oct 1951.

¹⁴⁶ *Sunday Tribune* 16 Apr 1950. Following the promulgation of a similar Act in the Federation of Malaya, an attempt to amend the anti-corruption ordinance to allow the Police to check bank accounts had been in the pipeline since 1950, but nothing came of it.

¹⁴⁷ *Singapore Free Press* 15, 21 Jun 1951; *Straits Times* 10 Jan 1952; *Singapore Standard* 28 Aug 1951.

¹⁴⁸ *Singapore Free Press* 30 Apr 1952.

¹⁴⁹ *Straits Times* 30 Apr 1952.

¹⁵⁰ *Straits Times* 31 Oct 1952.

¹⁵¹ *Singapore Free Press* 15, 21 Jun 1951; *Straits Times* 10 Jan 1952.

¹⁵² *Straits Times* 14 Oct 1952.

¹⁵³ In September 1952, Toh Teck Him, a merchant, gave SIT clerk, Ee Sim Chwee, $500 to get a flat. See *Straits Times* 20 Sep 1952.

¹⁵⁴ *Straits Times* 30 Sep 14 Nov 1952; *Singapore Standard* 15 Nov 1952.

¹⁵⁵ *Straits Times* 16 Dec 1950, 16, 23, 27, 28 Feb, 10 Mar 1951; *Singapore Standard* 23 Feb, 7 Mar, 7 Aug 1951; at the inquiry of the Singapore Riot Commission at the end of February 1951, Detective Major Singh, CID, testified that several policemen, from two patrol cars, did not take action to aid some Europeans being attacked at the junction of Bras Basah and North Bridge Road. They said that they were waiting for reinforcement. So, he went to their aid instead. See *Singapore Free Press* 1 Mar 1951. In total, Singh was credited to have singlehandedly saved six Europeans during the riot. *Singapore Standard* 1 Mar 1951.

¹⁵⁶ *Singapore Standard* 21, 27 Dec 1950.

¹⁵⁷ *Singapore Standard* 21 Jan, 11 Apr 1951, 23 Jan 1952; *Singapore Free Press* 7 Feb 1951.

¹⁵⁸ *Singapore Free Press* 9 Aug 1951; *Singapore Standard* 9 Aug 1951. The whole reform was brought on by the failure of the police force during the Maria Hertogh riots. Pennefather's reform was aimed at making the Force more professional and efficient. Hence, he revealed that his plan was to create a people's police force rather than one run along military lines.

¹⁵⁹ *Singapore Standard* 22 Aug, 21 Nov 1951.

¹⁶⁰ *Straits Times* 15 Jan 1952; *Sunday Standard* 20 Jan 1952.

¹⁶¹ In reality, with all the roguing, sackings, retirements and resignations since liberation, by the later part of 1951, two-thirds of the Force was no longer composed of the pre-war police force. See *Singapore Standard* 8 Aug 1951.

¹⁶² *Straits Times* 7 Jan, 10 Mar, 2, 3 Jun 1951; *Singapore Free Press* 29 May 1951, 1 Aug 1952, 20 Jan 1953.

¹⁶³ *Singapore Standard* 20 Nov 1951.

¹⁶⁴ *Straits Times* 20 Nov 1951.

¹⁶⁵ *Singapore Free Press* 14 Feb 1952.

¹⁶⁶ *Straits Times* 23 Feb 1952.

¹⁶⁷ *Straits Times* 1 Dec 1951, 25 Nov 1952. Byrde had been the Police Radio Chief. See *Singapore Standard* 17 Aug, 16 Sep 1950.

¹⁶⁸ *Straits Times* 1 Aug 1952.

¹⁶⁹ The failure to see through the passage of a new

▶ Laborious Birth

anti-corruption ordinance in 1950–1951 was never more painfully felt than in 1952. The new law would have allowed the Attorney-General to authorise the Police to check the bank accounts of government officers, an advantage which was already in force in the Federation of Malaya. It would also increase the powers of police to search and enter premises, cutting out the delays involved in applying for warrants, as well as to allow the holding and questioning of a suspect. See *Sunday Tribune* 16 Apr 1950.

[170] Details in this section are derived from *Straits Times* 28 Nov 1951, 5, 6, 8, 11, 12, 13, 15 Mar 1952; *Singapore Standard* 27, 28 Nov 1951, 5, 8, 11, 18, 20 Mar 1952.

[171] Before the men left, Lee Peng Chong instructed Lim Hian Chye, to collect the opium the next morning but not to send the consignment to their boss, Tan Yong Siah.

[172] The preliminary court trial was in late November 1951.

[173] Lawyer RCS Bush, defended Lim Peng Koi, one of the six, while David Marshall defended four of the rest.

[174] *London Gazette* 15 Apr 1952, p.2240. Nicoll was appointed Governor and Commander-in-Chief of Singapore on 17 April 1952.

[175] This was the scheme to replace expatriates with locals in Civil Service positions.

[176] *Indian Daily Mail* 3 Jan 1950; *Straits Times* 3 Jan 1950; *Singapore Free Press* 7 Jul 1950; *Singapore Standard* 7, 8 Jul 1950; *Straits Times* 4 Oct 1954, 14 Aug, 11 Dec 1955, 29 Apr 1959, 9 Oct 1961.

[177] *Singapore Standard* 24 May 1951, 16 Jun 1953; *Straits Times* 11 Aug, 21 Sep, 21, 27 Nov, 15, 23 Dec 1951, 3, 27 Jan, 5, 26 Feb, 4, 5 Mar 1952, 14 May 1953, 26 May, 24 Aug 1954, 29 Nov 1955, 18, 19, 20, 21 Dec 1956, 13 Feb 1957.

[178] The story of Middleton-Smith and RB Corridon will be covered in the following pages.

[179] It should be noted that the Colonial Secretary assembled this special task force to inquire into the truth behind this heist when the police force was undergoing a wholesale reorganisation in 1952 as a result of the 1950 Maria Hertogh riot. The CID itself had been reorganised in 1951.

[180] *Straits Times* 24 Sep 1952, 5 Feb 1953, 12 Feb, 8 Mar, 15 Sep 1954; *Singapore Free Press* 31 Jul 1953.

[181] *Straits Times* 5 Jul 1952. A survey of contemporary sources up to two months prior to this news release shows no other cases of police misdeeds that had resulted in the suspension of police detectives.

[182] *The Singapore Standard* 8 Jul 1952.

[183] *Straits Times* 15 Oct 1952.

[184] *Straits Times* 29 Oct 1952.

[185] The following details were extracted from CPIB File 001 CPIB Early Organisation: The Special Investigation Team Report (Interim) — Opium Robbery, set up by the Office of the Attorney General, (undated). This Interim Report mentioned that the final report on the Opium Heist was being prepared. However, there is no trace of this document in CPIB archival files. The reported submission of "the Report" in May 1952 is likely this "Interim Report", as no other document on the matter had been submitted to the Colonial Secretary.

[186] However, Corridon remembered that they were brought together in April 1952. See CPIB File 001 CPIB Early Organisation: RB Corridon, Acting Director, CPIB, Correspondence with FK McNamara, Snr Asst Commissioner, CID HQ, Fed of Malaya, 28 Mar 1955, CPIB, 132/54, 13.

[187] CPIB File 001 CPIB Early Organisation: New Anti-Corruption Organisation: Establishment and Estimates, Organisation and Leadership (Sep–Dec 1952, and 1953), Minutes by Mr Middleton-Smith, CPIB's first Director, Sep 1952.

[188] *Singapore Free Press* 18 Mar 1952.

[189] *Singapore Free Press* 12 Apr 1952.

[190] *Singapore Free Press* 12 Apr 1952.

[191] *Straits Times* 7 May 1952.

[192] *Straits Times* 29 Apr, 6 May 1952.

[193] *Singapore Free Press*, 3 July 1951.

[194] *Singapore Standard* 28 Aug 1951.

[195] *Straits Times* 26 Sep 1951.

[196] *Straits Times* 6 May 1952. In late May 1952,

Governor Nicoll announced that the anti-corruption proposals were in the hands of the Attorney-General, and that a special team had been recently appointed to investigate allegations of corruption among public servants. The ACB would likely have mistakenly thought it was their proposal that was under review. See *Straits Times* 22 May 1952.

[197] *Straits Times* 15 Mar 1954.

[198] *Straits Times* 19 Dec 1952.

[199] CPIB File 001, CPIB Early Organisation: New Anti-Corruption Organisation: Establishment and Estimates, Organisation and Leadership (Sep–Dec 1952, and 1953), Minutes by Mr Middleton-Smith, CPIB's first Director, Sep 1952.

[200] There are several official files (microfilm) deposited at the National Archives of Singapore: Colonial Secretary's Office (CSO), Anti-Corruption Organisation, 1952, (C) 0117-52; Colonial Office Records, CO 1022/109: Measures taken against corruption in the Malayan Civil Service, (01/01/1952–31/12/1953), National Archives (Great Britain).

[201] *Straits Times* 14 Oct 1952.

[202] *Straits Times* 21 Oct 1952.

[203] CPIB File 001 CPIB Early Organisation: Corridon's reply to McNamara's dated (SR) 35/10/1/1 of 16 Mar 1955.

[204] This was perhaps to be expected, or should not be unexpected — after all, the unit had just completed a review of their colleagues involved in the Ponggol Opium Heist. Going forward, there was also a clear possibility that the CPIB would cast a watchful eye on the entire CID.

[205] CPIB File 001 CPIB Early Organisation: New Anti-Corruption Organisation: Establishment and Estimates, Organisation and Leadership (Sep–Dec 1952, and 1953), Minutes by Mr Middleton-Smith, CPIB's first Director, Sep 1952.

[206] Middleton-Smith shared his experiences in Singapore before and after the war, including his time in CPIB, with the National Archives not so many years ago. It reveals the character of the man. Details in this section were extracted from his oral interviews with the Archives: Richard Middleton-Smith, Oral Archives, National Archives of Singapore (NAS), The Public Service, Accession Number 002151.

[207] Richard Middleton-Smith, Oral archives, NAS, The Public Service, Accession Number 002151, Reel 1.

[208] Richard Middleton-Smith, Oral archives, NAS, The Public Service, Accession Number 002151, Reel 1.

[209] Richard Middleton-Smith, Oral archives, NAS, The Public Service, Accession Number 002151, Reel 3.

[210] Richard Middleton-Smith, Oral archives, NAS, The Public Service, Accession Number 002151, Reel 4.

[211] *Straits Times* 11 Feb 1952. Prior to joining the Special Team, he was the Assistant Commissioner of that department.

[212] CPIB File 001 CPIB Early Organisation: Memorandum, Acting Director, CPIB, to Col Sec 25 Oct 1952, CPIB CSO 00117/52.

[213] Richard Middleton-Smith's first posting in Malaya was in Klang, where he was the Assistant Controller of Labour in 1937. He was then sent to Kuala Lumpur to be the Acting First Magistrate in 1938 before returning to Klang in April 1939 to resume his former duties there. When the war ended, as a Lieutenant of the British Army, he travelled across Burma, Thailand and Malaya–Singapore from August to October 1945 to survey all POW and labour camps, taking note of their conditions and needs. After which, he was posted to Kedah to be the Deputy Commissioner of Labour till 1948. In that year, he was Appointed Senior District Judge of Kedah and the Chairman of the Kedah Defence Committee (Malayan Emergency) which was responsible for the implementation of emergency measures in the state. In March 1950, he was appointed Assistant Commissioner of Labour in Singapore, and he was appointed to the Riots Claims Tribunal (Maria Hertogh riot) in 1951. In April 1952, he was appointed to head the Special Investigation Team which then became the CPIB from September–October 1952, and he became Director. When CW Lyle was Commissioner

of Labour, Middleton-Smith was his Deputy. In 1954, he was seconded to the Singapore City Council as Deputy President. He finally left Malaya in 1957, after serving here for 21 years. See *Straits Times* 21 Sep 1937, 31 Mar, 9 Apr 1939, 3 Oct 1947, 30 Mar 1950, 27 Jun 1951, 25 Nov 1954; *Singapore Free Press* 6 Jul 1948; *Sunday Standard* 3 Mar 1957; Richard Middleton-Smith (Riots Claims Tribunal) to the Colonial Secretary, 6th April, 1951, CO 953/10/2; Private Papers of Lt Middleton-Smith, Imperial War Museum — https://www.iwm.org.uk/collections/item/object/1030012706.

[214] *Straits Times* 14 Aug, 15 Oct 1952.

[215] *Straits Times* 31 Oct 1952.

[216] CPIB File 001 CPIB Early Organisation: Memorandum, Acting Director, CPIB, to Col sec 25 Oct 1952, CPIB CSO 00117/52. Statement of Progress.

[217] CPIB File 001 CPIB Early Organisation: Notes by Middleton-Smith: Interview with HE the Governor on 9/12/52.

[218] CPIB File 001 CPIB Early Organisation: Note on Interview with HE the Governor on 9/12/52, by Middleton-Smith.

[219] Middleton-Smith passed on 25 December 2011. See https://www.legacy.com/obituaries/thetimes-uk/obituary.aspx?n=richard-middleton-smith&pid=155344083. Middleton-Smith kept a diary of his war experiences. This is deposited at the Imperial War Museum Department of Documents.

Part Three

Long & Winding Road
1953–1959

Established in 1952, the CPIB started on a long developmental journey that saw its status as an independent agency compromised and its integrity questioned by the major political parties of the day. The Bureau was after all created by the colonial regime and led by members of the ruling class. Although it was conceived as an institution independent of the police force, it was still an arm of the British Establishment. The Bureau would unexpectedly come under police oversight by the mid-1950s, which to some extent did not endear it to mainstream politicians of the decade; accordingly, the main parties created their own "report corruption" agencies. At a time when the sojourning and domiciled people of the island were on the cusp of self-determination, embarking on their first steps towards nationhood, the issue of corruption amongst government officers became the most important socio-political issue for the people. Never before could locals have chosen their own leaders by having a fully elected government. In this light, politicians were quick to champion a government free of corruption as an electoral platform to win the "hearts and minds" of the people.

It took an instance in 1952 to plant the seeds that founded the Bureau, but the task of creating a permanent, independent and incorrupt anti-graft body would take more than a decade to achieve. Following its establishment and into the 1950s, the CPIB had to navigate the turmoil of political and social changes that accompanied the birth of the Singapore nation.

Beginning as a colonial law enforcement establishment, the CPIB had to traverse the path from conception, birth and then to maturity as a national institution. Naturally, the CPIB experienced shifts, oscillations and twists in this most critical decade that could have at any time rendered it inert or caused it to disappear altogether if it was subsumed into the Police Establishment, just as the defunct Anti-Corruption Branch had been. The journey towards permanency and relevance was a long and winding road for the CPIB. The fight against corrupt practices had been an old and never-ending one; the decisive victory in this battle was not by chance, maybe with some luck, but certainly had been the choice of those good men of Singapore during those tumultuous years.

Chapter Twelve

On a Proper Footing

The Special Investigation Team's May 1952 report on the Ponggol Opium Heist, which exposed the involvement of police personnel, had helped the Colonial Secretary and Governor to conclude that the colony's anti-corruption agency had to be independent of the Police Establishment. Hence, even before the formal establishment of the CPIB in late September 1952, this Team, still without a proper name or portfolio, continued to investigate and pursue the perpetrators involved in the original opium smuggling part of the affair. The Court had discharged the lot, but did not acquit them. Meanwhile, Richard Middleton-Smith devoted his time, putting pen to paper, to draft a document detailing the possible scope and work of a new anti-corruption body which the Colonial Secretary endorsed. When the Anti-Corruption Branch (ACB) was dissolved in July 1952, the Team took over its responsibilities almost "incognito", as hardly anyone knew about the Team or what they were doing.[1] Little did anyone know that even the Special Investigation Team was uncertain of their own scope of work, the extent of their tenure or their responsibilities, till the last quarter of 1952. The entire Team had been in the unit as seconded staff, including the Director. When Middleton-Smith completed his main task of laying the foundation for the establishment of the CPIB as an independent anti-graft agency for Singapore,[2] he relinquished his Bureau post at the beginning of January 1953, returning to the Department of Labour as Deputy Commissioner.[3] As for the rest of the Team, by early 1953, only Richard Byrne Corridon remained with the Bureau while the rest returned to their parent services.

Determining Core Parameters and Responsibilities

The task of putting the new Bureau on a proper footing then fell on the shoulders of the next Director, Claude Wormald Lyle. He was also a member of the Malayan Civil Service (MCS), but unlike Middleton-Smith, he was appointed on a full-time and permanent basis.[4] It did not take long for the new Director to realise that his first task was to resolve certain legacy issues that the first CPIB team had no time to resolve. Middleton-Smith's September 1952 proposals for the constitution of the Bureau, which Corridon called the "Charter", specified only what the Bureau could do and not what its role was within the larger government machinery.[5] The Police Establishment, or specifically the Police Commissioner, still believed that they had oversight of corruption cases, especially with regard to those involving police officers. And since the Bureau was independent of the Police, there was a need to establish the lines and spheres within which the Bureau operated and cooperated with the Police; ergo, the CPIB still had to define its core work and responsibilities vis-à-vis the police force.

On 19 February 1953, Lyle met with the Colonial Secretary, WL Blythe, and the Commissioner of Police, NG Morris,[6] to clarify the role of the Bureau. It was agreed that the CPIB would handle serious cases of corrupt practices, mainly to investigate and conduct research, while it was more appropriate for the Police to deal with minor cases involving petty bribery, like those involving hawkers. At the meeting, on his part, Lyle reported that even though the Bureau's establishment up till this point in time had been small, it actually handled a wide array of corrupt practices involving opium smuggling; *Chap Ji Kee* gaming; graft in the Singapore Improvement Trust (SIT), the Customs, the Imports and Exports Department as well as in the Public Works Department (PWD) and within the City Council, especially in cases involving hawkers' licensing and the general solicitation of tea money by public servants. Lyle made it clear that, as things stood, there was a danger that the CPIB would become bogged down by the "mass of petty corruption", to the detriment of more important major cases. He was of the conviction that there was a need for the Bureau to concentrate on the "big rackets" like opium smuggling and *Chap Ji Kee* gaming as these were the sources of big-money corruption and had involved a great number of people. Lyle also believed that the CPIB should continue giving attention to corruption in government departments as the public's impression of these institutions had a direct impact on their perception of the government.[7]

In response, Morris declared that he would "form a section in the police force to deal with minor corruption". However, he did not indicate what form this "section" would take nor when he would do it. At the same time, the Commissioner opined that the existence of the CPIB as an independent unit was "enough deterrent" against public service corruption. As for staffing, since the Bureau was still composed of policemen, the Commissioner expressed his concern about the career prospects of police officers seconded to the Bureau; they were after all still part of the Police Establishment, but would not be deployed in police work.[8] Clearly, the Commissioner had diplomatically expressed his "discomfort" with this new agency. Nevertheless, Lyle was still able to work out the CPIB's sphere of responsibility during this meeting.

Essentially, the outcome of this meeting was the confirmation that the police force was still taking action against corrupt activities, parallel to the CPIB. The Commissioner had, in fact, raised the issue of coordination; he pointed out that there was a need for close liaison to ensure that the Police and the CPIB did not work on parallel lines. He suggested that the Police should deal with cases involving individuals, and the CPIB would only take over when they found that organisations or rackets were involved.[9] While Lyle noted the Commissioner's overall "guidance", he could not adopt these suggested "protocols" in its entirety. This was a critical moment for the CPIB. Had Lyle simply pulled back and just concentrated on the big cases, it would have been a very different CPIB that evolved. Fundamentally, it was not a turf war between the CPIB and the Police

Establishment. The main problem was the Colonial Establishment itself. By early 1953, with the police reforms completed and when things were less volatile, the Establishment was content to revert to managing corrupt cases instead of eliminating general corruption. The fact of the matter was that the Colonial Establishment had little political will to clean up the city. After completing their tour of service, almost all British expatriate officers would certainly return home to Great Britain. They had no personal stake in the island state.

Directorship of Claude Wormald Lyle

While the first Director had treaded carefully and employed bureaucratic niceties to get the unit started, it fell to his successor to develop the unit on a proper footing to deal with both large-scale and small-scale cases of corrupt practices, in spite of the terms of his "détente" with Morris. This agreement, however, was never going to "box-in" the CPIB as its new Director was not afraid to demonstrate a significant level of gumption in doing his job. Before the war, he had been the Assistant Protector of Chinese (Chinese Protectorate) in Pahang, where his duties included dealing with the Chinese secret societies. In fact, when he passed away in 1956, the press made it a point to mention that he was "feared by secret society members".[10] He saw action in the war while on duty in the navy. His ship was sunk by Japanese fighters, and he spent the rest of the war interned in Sumatra. Of course, as a Malayan Civil Service officer, he was counted amongst the upper echelons of British colonial administrators. He was therefore considered unquestionably intelligent and much was expected from his leadership.[11]

Lyle was the Director who laid the foundation of the CPIB's graft fighting legacy by defining and elucidating the Bureau's philosophy, policies and practices which would guide the organisation for decades to come. His approach, first and foremost, was to clearly identify and call out the real issues of the day as he perceived them. While the *Free*

Press described 1950s Singapore as a place and society where "almost everybody in this city appear to consider bribing as a part of the ordinary life", he confronted this narrative head-on by declaring that "it is not necessary to bribe to get things done. The public must drop the idea that bribing was an easy way to accomplish things."[12] Lyle had believed that the Bureau need not wait for complaints of corrupt acts in order to take action. He understood that in order to make real changes, the environment, attitudes and level of enforcement must also change. Hence, within a fortnight on the job, he issued an open plea to the "public not to give (bribes)",[13] and assured them that any information they may provide regarding corrupt practices in the city would be treated with "strictest confidence". Initially, Lyle even offered amnesty for information; "confess if you paid tea money" and you "will not be penalised".[14] However, by May 1953, he would realise that he could not guarantee a free pass for guilty persons who provided information. He could only assure them of their safety. Still, Lyle articulated the need for public cooperation for information, and that "any little scrap of information helps" as a chain of information could build knowledge which could help break up rackets. By the beginning of May 1953, Lyle's publicity efforts had reaped promising results. In just four months, the CPIB had amassed 87 cases; one case concluded with (government) departmental action, six were reported to the Colonial Secretary, one government officer was demoted, another transferred to a new department and 37 cases were still under investigation.[15]

By July 1953, the CPIB's work was not only noted by the public, but also by the press, which had earlier labelled the ACB as the "silent service" for its lack of presence and success.[16] The press described the new Bureau as an anti-graft agency which had great powers,[17] supposedly more than what the ACB possessed. This was, of course, a myth. While the Bureau's men worked clandestinely to catch corruptors red-handed, their work was not unknown to the public by mid-1953. By the end of that year, the CPIB's work was publicly noted. The local press started articulating their admiration for the "secret and painstaking efforts of a handful of 'cloak and dagger' boys working in the Corrupt Practices Investigation Bureau, in the Supreme Court Building".[18]

While the Bureau's core concerns had been identified in Middleton-Smith's "Charter", the first Director had had very little time or opportunity to see most of his initiatives bear fruit. Most of these concerns only made notable progress during Lyle's directorship.[19] In March 1953, Lyle listed the main areas and government entities that the CPIB had been investigating up till that month. These included: opium smuggling, police, Customs, Vehicles Registration Department, Immigration Department, SIT, Keppel Bus Company, City Council, military personnel, gambling syndicates, commercial entities and more.[20] The following summed up some of the major works and significant strides of the Bureau during Lyle's directorship:

Publicity

Within weeks of taking the helm, Lyle had more than 5,000 posters printed and displayed all over Town.[21] This was the CPIB's first major campaign against corruption. The posters were printed in English, Chinese, Malay and Tamil to achieve maximum outreach across all communities on the island. The multilingual aspect of this "propaganda" effort was perhaps not used at that time outside of election campaigning. The other important aspect of the poster was the publicity given to "PO Box 2222", the mail address of the Bureau to which information could be sent. Most people were fearful of exposing themselves while giving information. Hence, the letter box was the most pragmatic and safest means to connect with the CPIB and to retain anonymity. In this respect, the Bureau's public contact avenue had differed markedly from the ACB's; from 1947 to 1952, the way to contact the Branch was to personally call the Criminal Investigation Department (CID) at 82322.[22] This did not provide complainants or informants any anonymity. Indeed, few even had access to a telephone, or had ever used a telephone in those early days of the post-war years. The Bureau would only provide a phone contact together with its PO Box number from 1955 when the Bureau took on elections monitoring responsibilities. This contact information was highlighted in all of the Bureau's publicity posters which were the most popular "mass media" of the day. They were placed on walls and advertising spaces on public transport;[23] in addition to the original 5,000 posters, 150 smaller ones were printed for placement within omnibuses. These had different slogans. There were also 10,000 handbills distributed in four languages.[24]

Public Housing

The SIT at that time was the main government body developing and allocating public housing for the city's masses.[25] It had been fraught with corruption for years. When Middleton-Smith met the Governor in September 1952 to secure endorsement for the Bureau's first budget estimates, he indicated that the Bureau would be looking into the SIT's affairs.[26] The ACB had paid "serious" attention to the Trust every year, weeding out SIT officers who accepted tea money or monetary gifts in return for priority housing allocation to the bribers. Yet, the problem persisted. The CPIB took one step further to check the "larger-scale" corrupt practices of the Trust. An opportunity to hook a larger SIT fish (in terms of quantum of money) came in August 1953 when the Bureau took the lead to entrap an SIT officer who solicited thousands of dollars from an individual applying for "change of use" in a Trust's property. The affair, as things panned out, might have involved the "rank and file" of the Trust.

It must be remembered that the SIT, as a housing authority, was not only allocating new houses and apartments to applicants. It was also responsible for an array of licensing matters involving SIT properties. Similar to today's Housing and Development Board (HDB) shophouses and coffeeshops, different licences were required for different business types in these properties. In August 1953, Phua Hoon Sim, a barber, approached SIT officer, Tan Yook Suan, to apply for a change in the nature of business at a shophouse at Albert Street belonging to an old woman. The original registered business at this shophouse was a textile business. Phua also wanted to include the name of his business partner. Together, they had planned to start a hairdressing business at the premises, and this required a permit from the SIT. After Tan instructed Phua to submit his request in a letter, he informed Phua that $3,000 was required; $1,000 for the chief of the SIT, $500 each for two others and $1,000 for himself. He also rushed Phua for the money for the chief who was (supposedly) going on leave. Phua, having little means to pay this "extortion", and not knowing how high up the racket went, panicked and turned to his lawyer for advice. His lawyer told him to report the matter to the CPIB.[27]

At the Bureau, (Acting) Assistant Superintendent of Police (ASP) Ng Leng Hock set up a sting operation to catch Tan red-handed. He asked Phua to prepare $1,000 in $10 notes and he duly recorded their serial numbers. Ng then instructed Phua and his business partner to visit Tan at his Tiong Bahru flat to hand him the money. Standing by outside the flat were CPIB officers Ng,[28] Inspector Peter Tay and two civilian investigators.[29] When the team did not receive the prearranged signal that the money had been taken, they entered the flat on the pretext that they were checking identity cards. The marked bills were found on Tan's bedroom table. Tan was arrested on the spot.[30] Clearly, in this instance, the bribe was not offered but solicited, and this affair was not simply another case of run-of-the-mill petty corruption.[31]

Customs Department

It was during Lyle's tenure that a real clampdown on corrupt customs officers occurred. By September 1953, the CPIB had successfully identified and reported corruption amongst five customs officers. They were sacked for graft. The approach in this instance was to allow the Customs Department to manage their own affairs; the CPIB had simply passed the cases to the Department after investigation had concluded and proof had been secured. The Customs Department, of course, was only too pleased to announce that they had uncovered these corrupt officers while working closely with the CPIB.[32] Lyle had a special interest in the dismissals and suspensions at the Customs Department. It was believed that large-scale smuggling and trafficking activities were invariably linked to "someone in the know" or those connected in strategic areas like the Customs. It was in this area that Lyle had hoped that the offer of a reward for information would tip the scales.[33] Hence, he believed that anti-corruption measures in the Customs Department were an important step in their endeavour "to stamp out corruption" in the public domain as "there were more opportunities for corruption in the Customs Service than in any other government department, even the police". The CPIB was contented to simply provide the Customs Department with information in order for them to self-manage corruption in their ranks. Accordingly, the Customs seized the opportunity in 1953 to publicly announce that they were using three ways to combat corruption in their ranks: job rotation, closer supervision and staff education that included topics on ethics of the service, their duty and the consequences of corrupt practices. Following this, the Customs Department also put up notices at all Customs' examination stations encouraging the public to report any illegal demands for money. They declared that "it takes two to corrupt", and that they needed cooperation from the public.[34]

Large-Scale Smuggling and Rackets

Even before Lyle assumed his post, the CPIB had already been deeply involved in pursuing big-money opium cases.[35] In fact, since the days of the Special Investigation Team, the Unit had pursued the perpetrators of the smuggling racket in the Ponggol Opium Heist. By March 1953, the Bureau was investigating several large-scale smuggling rings (mainly opium). Lyle considered these rackets as important cases which had significant webs of connections.[36] They were highly organised and had large resources to offer the biggest bribes to collaborating officials. Under

Lyle's directorship, the CPIB paid more attention to the "source and method" of these opium syndicates and not how smuggled commodities were disposed of. In this regard, by working closely with the Customs and the Anti-Narcotics Departments, the Bureau enjoyed some early successes in apprehending offenders.[37]

In the 1950s, all large-scale opium cases inevitably involved some form of bribery of law enforcement officers, especially amongst customs officers; large values or volumes of opium often involved large bribes. Sometimes high-level officials were also involved or implicated. In such cases, investigations or surveillance normally stretched over lengthy periods. One particular case handled by Lyle, which started in August 1953, was only concluded and brought to trial in July 1954.

Besides the opium syndicates, the CPIB identified the *Chap Ji Kee* gaming racket as a major source of corruption in Singapore in the 1950s.[38] *Chap Ji Kee* was not just a simple gaming pastime. Like all forms of private gambling in Singapore, it was illegal. However, the organisers of the *Chap Ji Kee* were able to amass significant wealth and had ample means to bribe their way out of any tight spot or to evade detection. As a case in point, during a raid at Florence Road by the Gambling Suppression Branch on 15 April 1952, more than $257,500 worth of *Chap Ji Kee* stakes were seized.[39] Triad members were also known to have provided the muscle for these outfits. In 1953, the CPIB detected two Chinese *kongsi* operating the *Chap Ji Kee*: Tai Poh Kongsi and Siu Poh Kongsi. While the former, which operated for the Hokkiens, had almost been broken up at this time, the latter that involved the Hokchias, was flourishing. One reason for this, as the Bureau discovered, was that certain officers of the CID's Hokkien Sub-Branch had only been arresting the dens of the Tai Poh Kongsi because the officers were on the take, and in cahoots with the Siu Poh Kongsi. The Bureau, however, did not go after the corrupt officers within the Hokkien Sub-Branch directly. Instead, it chose to tackle the Siu Poh Kongsi first by collecting intelligence on this group, as collecting information on the corrupt officers would have been more daunting. So the Bureau first gathered information on known individuals of the Siu Poh Kongsi: the six shareholders of the Siu Poh Kongsi, the identity of the *kongsi*'s "two treasurers, a gang of fighters employed by the leaders, and the names of eight of the schedule collectors". The CPIB then uncovered the names of police personnel involved, which included detectives and those of higher ranks. They allegedly protected the Siu Poh Kongsi.[40] Even with constant surveillance and suppression, *Chap Ji Kee* remained prevalent for decades. Winners could win up to 100 times their bets. In Singapore, this game was popularly known as the "housewives' opium".[41]

City Council Elections (Municipality)

Dealing with graft involving the City Council was not one of the major undertakings that Lyle had expected to handle when he arrived at the CPIB. Between 1949 and 1953, 18 of the 27 Council seats were elected. Investigating allegations of electoral fraud and related corrupt activities could potentially drag the Bureau into a political quagmire. Accusations could have been politically motivated or the result of poison pen letters. Nevertheless, as all corruption accusations were made public, the CPIB had to step in to perform its duty. In July 1953, CC Tan, a Legislative Councillor and President of the Singapore Progressive Party, accused members of the City Council of receiving bribes of $2,000 each to support applications for licences and concessions. The CPIB had to investigate this accusation.[42] The only way was to check the Councillors' bank accounts or to have them declare their assets. Naturally, the Councillors objected and resisted. The whole affair dragged on for months and wasted much of the CPIB's time.[43]

Then, in the December 1953 polls for the 1954 Council, the CPIB was dragged into another round of tension with the city councillors, but in this instance, the Bureau could not tread gently. It was reported in November 1953 that people had approached candidates to guarantee blocks of voters, from 100 to 1,000 votes. The Bureau warned each electoral candidate that they must report such offers.[44] Although the City Council at this time was composed partly of officials and elected members, "democracy" was still at stake. There was a chance that criminal organisations or syndicates could influence the outcome of the polls, and therefore, manipulate elected officials (government). It was also reported that gangs were guaranteeing votes and attempting to alter the outcomes by sending out children at night to tear down political posters of candidates opposing their "clients". Candidates who did not want their efforts sabotaged might also relent and pay these gangsters the money they demanded. The candidates themselves reported that during their house-to-house campaigning, some people could be heard shouting, "Why come and bother us here. No money, no votes. There are people who can pay us."[45] Around this time, the CPIB also received letters (in Chinese) reporting outright vote buying for the City Council elections. Votes could be bought between $5 and $10. The CPIB promptly warned the public that the Bureau would go after buyers and sellers of votes.[46] Following this, the CPIB received more information about racketeers in bars and coffeeshops offering $15 per vote.[47] This worried the CPIB. There were 45,000 people who could participate in the City Council elections which offered five elected seats in this round of polls. It was difficult to police this crowd and the event. The Elections Ordinance at this time had specified that no candidates could "entertain" voters. This meant that the candidates could not even buy drinks for potential supporters.[48] As Lyle saw it, the fundamental problem at this time was not just social or moral ethics; Singapore was still a "nation in making". Most of the population at the time were residents not citizens. They had no stake in Singapore and did not need to concern themselves with the politics of the day. So, if someone offered to pay for their vote, it was unlikely that they would feel any disgust. More likely, many would see an opportunity. The problem for the CPIB, and the government, was that criminal elements, and even the Communist insurgents,[49] could manipulate elections for their own benefit.

Other Government Departments

In the first months of Lyle's directorship, the CPIB received over 60 complaints about corrupt public servants, mostly in letters sent to the Bureau's PO Box 2222.[50] Amongst these, some were about criminal offences rather than corruption. These were forwarded to the Police. The Bureau handled the rest, which mostly involved petty bribery in the form of *kopi* money. Essentially, from the outset, the Bureau tackled all corrupt practices in the government, and did not only deal with large-scale cases as suggested in the February 1953 *entente cordiale* with the Police Commissioner. One reason might have been because the Bureau's public information programme, namely through the thousands of posters across the city and on public buses, had provided the public with necessary information to contact the Bureau directly. Of course, public education worked both ways; public servants were also well aware that the CPIB was on the job and watching. One interesting case the Bureau prosecuted in 1953 involved a complaint from a public servant that a member of the public had offered a bribe. A Chinese stallholder attempted to "lubricate" his application at the Immigration Department for an entry permit for his wife, who was arriving from Hong Kong. He passed a $50 bribe to an Immigration Department staff who duly reported the matter to her European boss. Her boss informed the CPIB. The offender was arrested and charged on the same day.[51]

One reason the Immigration staff and her boss were so quick to turn in their briber might have been because of the controversy surrounding another case that played out around the same time. The Bureau sent one of its own as an "agent provocateur" to create an opportunity for a public servant to demonstrate his honesty, or corrupt disposition. It was said that Lyle had been the first graft fighter to employ this method of law enforcement in Singapore.[52] On 25 June 1953, the Bureau's civilian investigator went to the government's Chemistry Department to arrange for a tin of milk to be tested. The investigator told Government Chief Clerk Lim Joo Soo that he needed the test results quickly. Lim had told him the process needed a week to complete. The investigator replied, saying that he did not mind paying for "overtime". When he returned on 2 July, Lim told him that the report would be ready in the afternoon, and the official fee was $40. The investigator paid the fee and slipped an envelope containing another $25 to the chemist. Lim accepted the envelope. The CPIB then swooped in and arrested the chemist. The Lim case was the first time law enforcers in Singapore employed an "agent provocateur" to set a "trap".[53]

Ng, the CPIB officer sent to arrest Lim, demonstrated that the money in Lim's possession was indeed the bribe money. The Bureau had marked the notes with a special powder that would glow in the dark. Although Lim was sentenced to 10 months' jail, and the judge ticked him off for the offence as he held "a very senior position", the judge also bemoaned the way the CPIB set the trap as "utterly contemptible".[54] This was echoed in the press, which added: "at present, it looks dangerously as though the Bureau is looking for work to do if its only objective is to create corruption in order that it can be stamped out". There was "no need for the Police to create crime".[55]

Singapore Traction Company (STC)

Although dealing with corrupt practices within the private sector was not specifically mentioned in Middleton-Smith's conception of the Bureau, its predecessor, the ACB, had occasionally taken on this task, especially when public interest had been at stake. In 1947, a general STC strike was sparked, paralysing the city, when the government pressed hard to end corrupt practices. It was serendipitous that in December 1953, Lyle himself caught STC conductors red-handed pocketing fares. Instances of bus conductors receiving fares without issuing tickets, or issuing lower value tickets to keep the proceeds, had been a common occurrence for years.[56] Lyle recorded the conductor's number and personally made a report of the matter. Following this, two detectives took the same ride on 24 and 25 November, and saw the conductor keep the money that he had received as fares. The Police was sent to arrest the conductor, Loi Wee Tong. He was charged with criminal breach of trust of 10-cent fares and sentenced to five months' jail.[57]

Lyle's Reflections on the Work of the CPIB[58]

After nine months on the job, Lyle put pen to paper to record his thoughts on the work of the Bureau and state of corruption in Singapore in 1953. In his view:

Causes of the Problem

Corruption is not new in Singapore. It had increased greatly since the pre-war days partly because many people were forced to supplement income by wit and dishonest means during the Japanese Occupation. The most common form of corruption is the bribing of officials to turn a blind eye. The most insidious example of this is the offering of gifts (money and in-kind) for services rendered by the officials who were supposed to provide the same services as part of their duty. Most people do not see the evil or abnormality in doing so. Initially, these gifts may have been a matter of gratitude, but later, offending officers may come to expect it and would react negatively when gifts were not presented. With increased government control over day-to-day necessities, like in the case of Food and Exchange Controls, there would be processes, for example, documentation, which the average person may not understand. So, they would offer some incentives to "lubricate" the wheels of the government. This was seen as a legitimate expense to get ahead or to move on. So, the fault lies not only on the side offering the bribe. Singapore is a commercial city, full of people engaged in business making money. There will be officials who will be tempted to take advantage of this to enrich themselves.

Types of Corruption

Roughly, there are two types of Corruption; the large-scale well organised rackets, for example opium and gambling, and the small-scale ones that involved the corruption of police, civil servants and city council employees. As for the rackets, these do not seem to have any single directing authority. These normally involved just a number of smaller organisations operating in certain areas. They are largely dependent on secret societies or gangsters for power, and will use knives or guns to eliminate rivals or informants. These groups will engage in wholesale bribery of government officers, especially police and customs officers to turn a blind eye to their activities or to inform them of impending government action. As for the small-scale corruption, this was more visible and widespread. Even though only small sums were involved in this instance, these types of corruption affect the public more; payments to foot police or traffic patrol or to inspectors of food control departments, or to city council employees for ease of business with the government.

Difficulties in Combating Corruption

The most important hurdle to fighting corruption is public attitude. While some people frown on giving evidence against others who had rendered them services, others admire those who are able to get away with it as they feel that everyone is entitled to make money. So far, the best information received by the Bureau come from one of the two parties — those who fell out, mainly over demand for payments, and bribers who found the demand of the bribed having been overly excessive. Yes, this is a sad commentary on public morals, but unless social attitude changes, the Bureau can make no permanent progress. The current legislation, based on Ordinance 41 of 1937, is insufficient as wide powers are needed. There is a need for a new Ordinance. One is being prepared now, based on the Federation's Ordinance 5 of 1950.[59]

Methods of Combating Corruption

For the large-scale cases, we will do research and gather intelligence on the source of the corruption rather than on those on the receiving end. If a racket is suppressed, the corruption in this area will go away. In such cases, we may have to work with external parties like the British Embassy in Bangkok which could provide information on the movement of individuals to and from Siam. In the case of small-scale corruption, this can be difficult to track down. The public can report these through PO Box 2222. For most of these types of corruption, as their modus operandi are well-known, the Bureau can set traps. The Bureau has created some posters which have been distributed in public spaces like on STC buses. We have attempted using cinema slides and going on Radio Malaya. But so far, these approaches have yielded little results. Successful court cases are a more effective deterrent. Nevertheless, we will continue to use public promotion methods, but we will get professional advertising firms to handle this aspect.

Staff Selection

The Bureau is helmed by one Director, and he is assisted by four specially selected police officers and six civilian investigators. As most of the civilians are new to this work, they require training. It is hoped that the new legislation will grant them the status of police inspectors.[60]

Action Taken

It is difficult to catch persons or organisers of gambling and opium rackets. They work in the dark. Nevertheless, when sufficient information has been gathered, we will issue arrest warrants to bring them to Court. Such convictions, as far as the public is concerned, have more deterrence value. However, not all cases brought to Court have been successful. In pursuing government staff, we always prepare a second charge which can be used in departmental discipline and result in dismissal.[61] Or, in some cases, when corruption is still suspected but cannot be proven, the government departments will receive a CPIB report that recommends transfer to other posts, thus removing the opportunity for corruption. Although the briber and receiver are both guilty, the Bureau has so far not prosecuted the persons who provided the information, which were mainly the briber. As for the civil servants, they always suspect that the offeror of the bribe is an agent of the Bureau. So, when a bribe is offered, or demanded, those who want to report the offence must do so as soon as possible. The use of "traps", by agent provocateurs, is not a method that the Court likes. But we have little options. If the Bureau depends just on public information, we would *get nowhere. Although the use of traps is often criticised in the press and by the Court, there are also supporters of the Bureau who praise such methods. Basically, it's in the hands of the public to prevent corruption.*

Lyle left the Bureau in mid-1954. He was the last Malayan Civil Service officer to ever head the CPIB. From this point till Lee Kuan Yew became Prime Minister, the Bureau would be headed by career police officers.[62]

Chapter Thirteen

Constable at the Helm, on the Eve of Change

The 1950s was a milieu of change for Singapore. The Cold War had started, Britain was in the midst of decolonialisation and all war-ravaged nations and territories had to rebuild; in many places, this transformation included the socio-economic and political landscape. In Singapore, this slow journey towards nationhood created difficulties at many levels. For one, from the early 1950s, locals were already being trained to replace the withdrawing British governing elites, who were now known as expatriates.[63] This process was executed in phases over the length of the decade. The British withdrawal directly impacted the Bureau's progress from the mid-1950s. The concept of an independent CPIB was pivoted on civilian leadership, and this was dependent on the administrative Malayan Civil Service (MCS) providing senior officers for the job. When Claude Wormald Lyle ended his tenure in mid-1954,[64] the British MCS had no more senior staff available to assign to the Bureau. By this time, the man behind the creation of the CPIB, Colonial Secretary WL Blythe, had already stepped down, and the other champion for the Bureau, Governor JF Nicoll, was on the verge of retirement.[65] Under these circumstances, Richard Byrne Corridon was appointed Acting Director of the Bureau until 1955. This change marked the beginning of the transition of the CPIB as an independent agency to becoming part of the Police Establishment. Unfortunately, senior British police officers were also leaving Singapore. This created a situation where the leadership of the Bureau changed hands constantly until the early 1960s.

In his parting words, Lyle declared, "Although a police officer is taking over, there is to be no change in the Bureau's policy. It still remains the independent body it has always been. It just happened that Mr Corridon was available for the job." Corridon was not appointed permanent Director because his public service status was far below the MCS rank assigned to the directorship of the Bureau. He was also a career police officer seconded to the Bureau, and not considered a civilian even if he had occupied a post intended for civilian leadership. Nevertheless, as the last member of the original Special Investigation Team still in the Bureau, he continued to run the Bureau in the spirit of the agency conceived by Richard Middleton-Smith and developed under Lyle. However, Corridon could not forestall the forces of change. By the time his tenure ended in 1955, the Bureau was not just helmed by a police officer; it had become a unit deferred to the Police Commissioner. As such, Corridon's directorship was perhaps a bridge in this transition. Administratively, the Bureau under Corridon continued to report to the Colonial Secretary directly.

Bureau Operations[66]

When the Bureau was made a full agency in September–October 1952, Corridon was "number two" to Middleton-Smith. He was then appointed Deputy Director of the CPIB during Lyle's directorship.[67] He became Acting Director when Lyle moved on in mid-1954.[68] In March 1955, Corridon provided an insight into the workings of the Bureau when he was asked to provide a briefing on the operations of the CPIB to his counterpart in the Federation of Malaya where their prevention of corruption body was still an anti-corruption bureau within their Police Establishment.[69] The Federal Police was in the process of instituting reforms across the Causeway. It was in this briefing that Corridon first described Middleton-Smith's September 1952 minutes of his meeting with the Colonial Secretary, which contained his proposal for the establishment of the Bureau as the document that "embodied" the CPIB's "Charter".[70] He also revealed that up till his directorship, the objectives of the CPIB had not digressed from Middleton-Smith's conception of the Bureau. The only point in Middleton-Smith's "Charter" which Corridon did not agree with was the arming of civilian investigators. He believed that these investigators should not behave or act like detectives. In any case, Corridon contended, they should not be "in imminent danger as they go about their tasks".[71]

Corridon also reiterated that the CPIB was not a police unit even though a number of its staff had been drawn from the Police Establishment. The Bureau took direct instructions from the Chief Secretary and the head of the Bureau, who was a senior MCS officer.[72] Hence, although Corridon was at this time the (Acting) Director of the Bureau, he considered himself just a caretaker as he was waiting for the appointment of the next MCS Director. There was some uncertainty surrounding the Bureau as Singapore was on the cusp of "impending changes"; political-constitutional developments in Singapore and Malaya resulted in the introduction of the Malayanisation programme which was the initiative to replace expatriate British officers with locals. The process had reduced the number of MCS senior officers across Singapore and the Federation.[73]

In his briefing, Corridon also revealed his dilemma as the Director of CPIB and a career police officer. He was of the opinion that police officers should not staff the Bureau. He felt that "police officers should not be seconded to this work regardless of how brilliant they are at their work. No policeman should be seconded, in my opinion, to work of this nature if there is the least suspicion that he has been corrupt at any time or lived above his income, or has more than one family. Our Asian officers have been subjected to enormous pressure through relations and friends at times, for private information, and only a carefully nurtured belief in the importance of the work they are doing has led them to resist such approaches and report what has happened." This was how Corridon felt about the personal cost police officers had to suffer to become a CPIB officer.[74]

Corridon also confessed that he had a bias for the Special Branch personnel doing the job: "CPIB work suits Special Branch types of proven integrity." The Bureau also needed officers who were fluent in several Chinese dialects as most of the large-scale corruption in Singapore had involved organised crime syndicates like Chinese triads. Bureau officers, therefore, needed to have a flair for languages, as well as some standard of education in Chinese. In 1955, of the CPIB's three inspectors, only one had Special Branch experience. Corridon also hoped that the Bureau would always have one Chinese officer with Special Branch experience.

By early 1955, a considerable part of the CPIB's work had been devoted to research. This aspect of the work, which was described in Middleton-Smith's September 1952 minutes, was led and directed by Corridon himself, while the actual research work was undertaken by a senior civilian investigator and two registry assistants. The Bureau's first and only senior civilian investigator was Mah Kah Kee, a Supreme Court interpreter whom the Bureau considered to have been a person of great integrity. Corridon had himself convinced Mah to join the Bureau as he had been a bank manager before joining the Court. Corridon considered Mah a great asset as his knowledge of banking and business was an advantage in the work relating to circumvention of Exchange Control measures and preparation of investigation papers on banking and financial matters.

As for the Bureau's two registry assistants, they were Chinese-educated and former teachers. They helped the senior civilian investigator to handle top secret records, many of which were materials gathered about Chinese triads. The Unit had to employ six civilian investigators. They were from "all walks of life"; one was Indian and five were Chinese. In Corridon's opinion, the Bureau's Chinese civilian investigators had to "have knowledge of" and "be fluent in two Chinese dialects or know Chinese characters", or they would be useless to the Bureau, unless they were also good at surveillance work or had technical skills. Hence, Corridon was unwilling to mandate that his civilian investigators should have an English education qualification. He was happy enough that "they pass part one of the law exam". None of the six civilian investigators had "Senior Cambridge" (A-Level) passes. Corridon also had not filled six vacant posts for civilian investigators on account of the financial stringency he was forced to adhere to during his tenure. The Bureau's additional six establishment posts for investigators had been frozen due to budgetary constraints. His hope, and plan, was to hire three more civilian investigators who had better educational qualifications when these posts were freed up. His only reservation was that he believed that the higher educated ones might be more "inclined to be smart alecks", and might not mix well with the rest of the team. He considered that a solution to this problem would be to recruit the better educated ones straight out of school as they would still be considered junior to the older staff.

The Bureau also employed a number of non-establishment staff as "watchers". They formed the core of the Bureau's surveillance troopers, whose identities were protected. The Bureau recruited them young, around 18 years of age. Corridon was hopeful that among these "watchers", there would be some good enough and keen to remain in this work, to eventually become civilian investigators.

As for the Bureau's physical assets and equipment, Corridon felt that the Bureau was still in its "early days" and evolving. So, he advised against "acquiring too many technical equipment". In this respect, the CPIB had received tremendous help from the Special Branch with their work in the rural districts and within the Town area. Accordingly, the Bureau had only one piece of equipment asset — a tape recorder, which at this point was being used at Police Headquarters and serviced by radio experts. Nevertheless, the Bureau continued to budget for such items in its annual estimates even though the allocation was seldom utilised during Corridon's tenure. The Bureau also did not possess any vehicles as the police officers of the Bureau had their own. Civilian investigators who used their own vehicles were offered mileage allowances.

Corridon had to run the Bureau on a tight budget because of the policy for financial stringency in the 1950s. In this decade, as Singapore emerged from World War II financially stretched and lacking reserves, annual deficits had been a norm for the government. As such, Corridon held back on hiring additional clerical staff and interpreters. Also, the Bureau's office accommodation at the Supreme Court had been modest, and there was insufficient space for more staff. Hence, the Bureau's civilian investigators had to do their own interpretation and paperwork; Corridon jested that it gave them "good training doing interpreter duties". The team created their own index of Chinese characters with translations in English to aid their work. As for staff training, for example in surveillance skills, the Special Branch helped by conducting such training in-house to save costs. A Police Superintendent also gave weekly lectures on Singapore's laws in the Bureau's office.

Another critical aspect of the Bureau's operations was the reliance on informants. While public information on corrupt practices of government officers had been an important resource in combating corruption, either by disgruntled bribers or aggrieved victims, leads provided by civil servants on graft by their colleagues were even more valuable as they could contain details which might aid the Bureau's successful action against the infringer. However, whistle-blowers often, and rightly so, feared reprisal at the workplace, which might end in harassment, isolation or even dismissal. Hence, often, the Bureau had to use forms of affirmation, encouragement, appeals to moral courage or even rewards as inducement.[75] Still, the fear remained and informants preferred to remain anonymous.

In early 1955, Corridon received just one of such anonymous whistle-blowing correspondences that came in the mail (PO Box). Normally, the Director would "pay no attention" to information from unknown sources. However, in this instance, the letter signed by *Zorro* contained details of an open case that corroborated with what the Bureau already knew about corruption in a government department, but did not have enough evidence to pursue further. Corridon was hopeful that the informant knew something more useful. So he placed an advertisement in the newspapers for *Zorro* to call him personally — *Zorro, Please Ring 5110*. The Bureau paid $10 for this advertisement.[76] Interestingly, Corridon received five calls claiming to be *Zorro*. Corridon was certain that the first caller had been the real *Zorro*, but the caller put down the phone soon after several cryptic exchanges with the Director. So, Corridon turned to the newspapers once more, this time passing his message through an interview with a reporter. The Director spoke clearly and unreservedly to the pressman, knowing it would be reproduced in verbatim; Corridon openly called out to *Zorro*, "if he can contact me once again..."[77]

Though the whole affair seemed to have panned out in slow motion, and had been cumbersome and non-linear in approach, it was part of the whole regime to protect the informant — maintaining distance and anonymity to ensure security. From another perspective, the methodology of communicating through the press, messaging in plain sight, seemed to have been straight out of the cloak and dagger playbook. The use of agent provocateurs by the Bureau was another hint of this influence. Perhaps the fact that two of the four founding members of the Bureau had been members of

Five 'Zorros' called — but real one hung up, *The Straits Times*, 9 February 1955, p. 8.
Source: The Straits Times © SPH Media Limited.
Permission required for reproduction.

5 'Zorros' called — but real one hung up

"ZORRO, please ring 5110......" said a personal advertisement in the Straits Times.

The advertisement was inserted by Mr. R. B. Corridon, director of the Corrupt Practices Investigation Bureau, Singapore. The number is his office number.

Five people who claimed to be "Zorro" phoned 5110 on Saturday and a sixth, a woman, phoned to ask for "Zorro".

Mr. Corridon believes that only the first caller was the real "Zorro."

"I asked him for what he was famous and he replied: 'I flew a kite', which means to put forth

PERSONAL
Zo Waithe (sp Yunketeers).
ZORRO Please Ring 5110...

The advertisement

a tentative idea. I then told him my identity and he immediately rang off." Mr. Corridon said.

"But," he added, "I am hoping 'Zorro' will phone or write to me again. I would very much like to know who he is and have a talk with him."

"Zorro", whoever he may be, wrote a letter, containing allegations of bribery, to the head of a Government department. The letter was referred to Mr. Corridon.

"Normally I pay no attention to anonymous letters." Mr. Corridon said. "but parts of his letter corroborate things I already know and there is a strong chance that he has some special information that will assist our investigations.

"If he will contact me again he can be assured we will meet under secure arrangements," Mr. Corridon added.

177

the Malayan Security Service, which became the Special Branch, had influenced the way the Bureau operated in those early days. The Bureau continued its approach of having Special Branch (now known as Internal Security Department) officers in its ranks.

Big-Money Syndicates, Beyond Borders

It was spelled out in Middleton-Smith's "Charter" that the Bureau would "seek out, identify and bring to justice the large-scale corrupters. These corruptors included the organisers of opium and gold smuggling, those who organise gambling activities, and others engaging in illegal activities involving large sums of monies... Their money seeps through all grades of the government and their power inspires fear."[78] What Middleton-Smith did not fully realise was that these goals were far beyond what a single organisation could achieve alone. Corridon had gradually realised that the Bureau had to work closely with all government departments to stamp out corruption, even though some of those departments suffered chronic corruption themselves. Soon after becoming Director, he declared that since the establishment of the Bureau, the CPIB had learnt many lessons and collected lots of valuable information which would be helpful for the future.[79] And many of these lessons were learnt by working with others.

Lyle had already taken this first step by working with the Customs Department in dealing with the big-money corruptors involved in opium smuggling. In the process, the Bureau also aided the Department to clean up its own backyard by purging corrupt customs officers. It was Corridon who started the next significant step — to hit at the source of the smugglers' supply by pursuing the culprits beyond Singapore's borders.

In the early 1950s, much of the opium coming into Singapore originated from Burma.[80] The first break in tackling the problem came in late 1952 when a "mystery man" in Siam wrote anonymously to the CPIB. He provided information on a man in Bangkok who was supplying "black currency" to opium and gold smugglers in Singapore to pay for their opium suppliers in foreign countries. In the 1950s, even smuggling syndicates needed foreign exchange to pay for goods they wanted outside of Singapore. It was near impossible to obtain these currencies legally as declarations had to be made to get them.[81] The CPIB gathered intelligence on these syndicates for more than a year before a house in Singapore was identified and raided in January 1954. It was during this raid that the CPIB discovered pieces of paper in a wastepaper basket that contained more names of individuals involved in a ring that spanned Singapore and Burma.[82] Accordingly, Corridon informed the Bureau of Special Investigations (BSI) in Burma, and they arrested two men and brought them to trial. At the same time, Singapore's Customs, in coordination with the Burmese, raided 20 houses in Singapore. However, the "big boy" they were after eluded arrest. It was believed that he was in hiding in the Federation. Corridon then made a trip to Burma to liaise with the BSI for further action. This led to the arrest of eight Chinese in Singapore. They were banished (deported) and five customs officers were dismissed for corruption. In addition, in August 1954, $254,000 worth of opium from Burma was seized from three ships moored at Singapore.[83]

By September 1954, Corridon had smashed an opium smuggling ring that had spanned the territories of Malaya and Burma. Two wealthy businessmen in Singapore had been taken to Court for their part in this international opium smuggling ring. The BSI also described their successful crackdown as their first international case.[84] A month later, in October 1954, Singapore's Customs seized another ship with a consignment of Burma opium that was worth $155,200.[85] It was also in this month that the Bureau was able to arrest a young Chinese businessman. He was presumably the elusive "big boy" who had been a major player in the trafficking of opium in the East. Corridon detained the man under the provisions of the Banishment Ordinance, which instantly placed him on the banishment list. From this point, the Customs Department assumed the lead in the continuing battle against the opium syndicates, of course in coordination with the CPIB.

Following this, opium smuggled into the island came in smaller packages,[86] which also carried less value and therefore less profit as well. Hence, the smugglers had fewer opportunities to resort to bribery of customs officials to get their products through. As a case in point, in an earlier incident that occurred in 1954, when a lorry carrying 3,000 lbs of opium was stopped at the Customs, a man in the vehicle offered an officer $35,000 to turn a blind eye.[87] When shipments started entering in small consignments, the opium smugglers could not offer such enticing inducements. By July 1955, the Customs was able to announce that they had the opium gangs on the run after their big haul.

The sudden "awakening" of the Customs Department in 1954–1955 was in no small part due to the efforts of the CPIB to set things in motion. There was perhaps a sense of inertia and defeatism before this time as few believed that corruption could be eliminated. When the Bureau provided the investigative and enforcement breakthroughs, the Customs Department gained the confidence and rode on the impetus for change. In October 1954, soon after the Comptroller of Customs revealed that there had been few complaints about customs officers in the past months, following the dismissal of six officers for corruption involving opium, tobacco and liquor smuggling, and discipline of two others,[88] he also announced that the Department was undertaking a staff reorganisation. This would see the Department shedding over 100 junior staff over the next three years. Only 32 new officers were to be employed to cover the work of the retrenched officers. These new officers were to be better educated: university graduates or holders of Senior Cambridge certificates (A-Levels).[89]

While cooperation with the Customs Department and the Police had been critical to the Bureau's successful handling of corruption surrounding the opium rackets, Corridon's decision to leverage the provisions provided by the Banishment Ordinance to deal with "corruptors" had also been a critical factor.[90] In retrospect, the Bureau during Lyle's and Corridon's directorship had employed both an iron hand as well as a reward system in managing cases. They employed the proverbial carrot and stick approach to produce results. For instance, when the case involving the Burma opium smuggling network had had some success, the Bureau openly declared in August 1954 that they were still waiting for their "mysterious" informant from Siam to contact them as they had a $1,000 reward for the man who had helped bust this international opium ring.[91] By making this known publicly, Corridon had given the Bureau the best advertisement it could ever hope to have: one should provide information, not only because it could effect real changes as far as the fight against corrupt practices was concerned, but one could be rewarded handsomely for it as well.

Elections, Politics and Corruption in 1955

The 1950s was a time when everyone was caught up with the politics and elections of the day; while some saw the opportunity to participate in building nation and home here, others were nonchalant about the political jostling and outcome of the polls. In the case of the latter, many of them did not frown at being rewarded to vote one way or another. Nevertheless, the elections in the early 1950s involved smaller electorates, thus the scope of corrupt practices in the polls had not been great in those years. The problem became more serious in the mid-1950s when more people were allowed to be registered voters. This dynamic socio-political climate of the times had a significant impact on the work of the Bureau. Corridon lamented years later, recalling how "there were many corrupt politicians around, waiting to gain power for themselves".[92]

There were two political platforms in the 1950s that involved electing representatives: the City Council and the Legislative Assembly elections. There were already allegations of corruption in these polls. In fact, during the 1950 Municipal (later City Council) elections, calls were made to resist corrupt practices at the polls; one even declared, "Don't sell your souls for 300 silver $."[93] As for the Legislative Assembly elections, it was already noted in the 1948 polls that corruption had been a "menace".[94] It was during the 1951 legislative elections that things became heated and allegations of bribery and dirty practices were flung in every direction by electoral candidates.[95]

These incidents, however, were considered mild in comparison to those from 1955. In the early 1950s, there were more appointed official members in the City Council and Legislative Assembly than there were elected representatives. The electoral body was also very small. In the 1949, 1950 and 1952 Municipal/City Council elections, only 8,688, 22,325 and 44,896 residents, respectively, were eligible to cast a vote. This naturally limited the reach and impact of any "corruptor". In the 1953 City Council elections, only 6 out of 18 seats were elected. It was not until the 1957 City Council elections, when all seats were contested and there were no more government appointees, that the electoral body grew to half a million. And the allegations of corrupt practices exploded during this poll.

Nevertheless, the Bureau had its first test dealing with electoral improprieties during the 1953 City Council polls. In July 1953, the Progressive Party warned that there were people offering city councillors $2,000 each to support their applications for work licences issued by the government. The city councillors denied accepting bribes and demanded to know details of the allegations made.[96] Lyle was obliged to investigate and enquire into the veracity of the allegations.[97] The Assemblymen and Councillors protested, questioning the necessity of making them declare their assets. They did not "understand" how that would prevent corruption.[98] Nevertheless, a year later, the Labour Front had all their representatives in the Council declare their assets so as to "purify politics".[99] Meanwhile, the new CPIB Director in 1954, Corridon, vowed to continue watching for signs of corruption amongst "government and City Council officials in Singapore".[100]

Things escalated during the 1955 Legislative Assembly General Election which saw the majority of the seats elected. This was the occasion when the Rendel Constitution was adopted and the people of Singapore voted for their very first local government (Limited Self-Rule). This was the first election that stretched the resources of the Bureau. The earlier legislative polls, in 1948 and 1951, only saw 22,334 and 48,155 persons, respectively, who were eligible to vote. In the 1955 polls, the electoral body was expanded to 300,299. And by 1959, when Lee Kuan Yew came to power, the electoral body had grown to 586,098.

The real mud-slinging and recriminations had already started in the months leading up to the 1955 Election. The government's Public Relations Secretary, George G Thomson, had to go on radio and newspapers to tell people to safeguard their own democratic rights and to warn them about the danger of accepting bribes —"Let us act to ensure that the right to vote, the greatest political right in a democratic constitution, shall not be bought and sold." The promulgation of the 1954 Singapore Legislative Assembly Elections Ordinance (Ordinance 26 of 1954) had already made corrupt practices illegal during the legislative elections.[101] In his radio broadcast, Thomson specified the types of electoral corruptions: "offering voters meat, drink, refreshment or provision, or the money, or ticket, for them, to influence a voter; undue influence — using force or threat of harm to influence voters; and bribery — give, lend, promise or offer money or valuables to influence electors."[102] This Ordinance provided the government an effective tool to fight or deter electoral graft. In addition, the Ordinance also mandated that only persons whose names were on the electoral register could vote and persons convicted of corruption could not be on the register.[103] This was a small step towards a clean election. The electoral affairs in 1955, nevertheless, kept the CPIB very busy.[104]

In the end, the Bureau could not verify any of the allegations of corruption made by politicians and electors against poll candidates.[105] Interestingly, court cases involving politicians in the 1955 election "season" had centred more on libel than they were about corrupt practices. In February 1954, the first case under the 1954 Singapore Legislative Elections Ordinance was brought to the courts. Lim Koon Teck, the Singapore Progressive Party candidate for Paya Lebar, reported Tan Eng Joo and

Chuang Hui Tsuan of the Democratic Party for making false statements that affected the outcome of the polls. This was considered a "corrupt practice" under Section 57 (d) of the Elections Ordinance.[106] A month later, Lim sued Tan and Chuang for slander.[107] It was also in March 1955 that City Councillor Chan Kum Kee took his accusers to Court (High Court) for false allegations of corruption against him.[108] Even David Marshall, who had already been installed as Chief Minister by this time, had to endure a deluge of accusations and charges of corruption from opposing politicians. Police reports were made against him.[109] It was not surprising that Corridon attempted to stay above the fray amidst all these accusations and counter-accusations of corruption.

Nevertheless, Corridon still had to establish if there were real instances of corrupt practices amidst all the "noise". Among the improper activities linked to the April 1955 Legislative Assembly elections to which Corridon paid extra attention included the case of the "2,000 taxis". The CPIB had credible information that politicians had "booked" hundreds of "pirate" taxis to ferry electors to polling stations to cast their votes for "preferred" candidates. They were offered $150 to $200 per day when their normal earnings had been between $20 and $25 a day.[110] Although such practices had allegedly occurred in previous elections, the magnitude of the 1955 "free taxis to the polls" electoral maleficence was three times greater than previous instances. It was also believed that many of these "taxi" drivers were members of political parties.[111] Corridon had also received information that people had been paid $10 to $25 to vote for certain candidates; some would just take the money but still vote how they wanted. Although Corridon had received many reports of this occurring, he could not prove any of them. Still, Corridon assured the public that his small team of nine assistants could handle election-related corruption cases.[112]

One unexpected outcome of the 1955 Election was that it brought to the surface existing fault lines between the CPIB and the Police Establishment with regard to the oversight of corruption matters. During the polls, while the CPIB reminded the public to cooperate with the Bureau because it was aided by the staff of the Attorney-General's Office,[113] Commissioner of Police NG Morris also provided alternative police contact information even though he would include a line that said the public could also "contact the CPIB" for cases of electoral graft. In late February 1955, Morris also announced that the Police would be making special arrangements for the people to report election corruption.[114] Soon after, he announced that he had assigned Superintendent EJ Linsell to assist Legislative candidates and members of the public who may need "advice" during the election period, stating that he could be reached at 25550 (Police Headquarters) or by writing to PO Box 5000 (Police). Of course, Morris added that one could also contact the CPIB directly.[115]

Nurture or Nature, Society or Culture

It was during Corridon's first tenure (1954–1955) as CPIB Director that fundamental issues affecting the state of corruption in Singapore were brought to the forefront of public debate. Through the 1955 election period, the government had to remind and educate the public of the importance of their rights to vote their own government and to have a fair election. They had the responsibility to protect these rights by guarding against treats, threats and bribes.[116] However, this was not an easy message to convey in the 1950s when there was not yet a nation or a citizenry, nor did the people of Singapore share a common ethos. Many still considered themselves part of a diaspora. Nevertheless, the process of change had started. Corridon understood that it was not only about morality and values, but also attitudes, habits and norms that had to change.

It was common for people to offer *kopi* money to public servants even when not asked. As a case in point, at the beginning of 1955, Corridon handled a case of a man who gave a mortuary staff of General Hospital $10 to claim the body of a relative. Other relatives of deceased patients complained to the CPIB when they found out. But the man offered the money without being asked! As a result, the hospital put up two notices in five languages telling the public that no extra payment was needed.[117] Giving something to "lubricate" a transaction was somewhat part of the social culture of the day. On one side of the continuum, it was a show of appreciation, and on the other side, it was corruption.

However, during the 1955 Singapore Traction Company (STC) Strike, also known as the "Great STC Strike" which lasted 142 days (September 1955 to February 1956) and was considered "the longest" strike in post-war Singapore, the socio-economic condition in colonial Singapore was identified as an important factor for corruption that afflicted the public transport sector of the day. While the busmen complained of low wages and wanted better pay, the management of the STC (who were Europeans) took the position that corruption amongst bus drivers could never be eradicated because of the corrupt nature of the locals.[118] The STC Union revealed another facet of the story. About 2,800 STC employees had been on strike for months. The company paid the lowest wages amongst all transport employees. While an STC driver was paid $5.63 per day, the drivers of the Changi Bus Company were paid $11.10 for an 8-hour day. The strikers vowed to continue their industrial action till they were given decent wages. They pointed out that till the strike started, 187 STC conductors had been sent to jail for corruption.[119] Devan Nair, Singapore's future President (1981–1985), who was then the legal advisor of the STC Employees' Union, pointed out to the Passenger Transport Commission that low wages had forced conductors to commit crime.[120] The union argued that "poverty, low wages and poor living conditions are the primary reasons which engender corruption", and "the blame for whatever corruption that existed in Malaya could not be laid on the people, but on those who created the social and economic conditions which gave birth to corruption".[121] The Commission, on the other hand, suggested that the triads had been behind the busmen's corrupt actions.[122] The bosses of the other bus companies felt that "pocketing money without issuing tickets" was likely linked to union activities. The conductors, in their opinion, were siphoning money into a strike fund. They pointed out that of the

57 transport strikes in the year, half were unannounced sudden strikes, which were illegal.[123]

There was no consensus as to the cause or source of general corruption; was it a matter of nurture or nature, a social condition or cultural norm? In any case, one cannot ignore the fundamental truths of the day; socio-economic and political changes had to occur for improvements to be made. The Police Establishment instituted reforms in the early 1950s, reorganised, changed systems and increased wages, believing it would eradicate police corruption and inefficiency. Yet, there were still corrupt police officers, just as there were corrupt staff in many government departments. Would wage increase change anything in the STC? These were issues which the CPIB could never resolve on its own. The war against corrupt practices was never going to be easily won. Corridon left at the end of 1955. He would helm the Bureau once more from 1963–1968, after his retirement from the police force.

Chapter Fourteen

Stormy Seas & Rugged Road

Change and Challenges

The CPIB was founded in the early days of Singapore's journey towards nationhood. It was a difficult period of change for everyone. It was a time to forge a national identity and to create shared socio-cultural norms that would bind the tapestry of a multicultural immigrant society while the concept of citizenry took root. Among the fundamental changes occurring across the Singapore–Malayan landscape was the transition of the island's political and administrative leadership. The ruling British elites which formed the echelon of the old colonial society, now expatriates, were leaving, and locals filled the vacuum and responsibilities created by their departure. The sojourning and immigrant society of the days of old was also paving the way for the emergence of a rooted society. In this context, the domiciled communities of Singapore could no longer ignore or dismiss imperfections in a place where they were building their home and they were no more simply guests. It was through multiple elections in the decade that the citizens of this new polity could choose a government and society they needed and wanted. However, this democratic process came under threat from various quarters that employed corrupt means in order to steer the outcome of the polls. The Bureau was therefore engaged in a struggle, not only to rid the emerging nation of corrupt practices, but also, in the process, to safeguard the democratic rights of the people.

However, the process of decolonisation had a more profound impact on the CPIB than its founders could ever expect. Both the Colonial Secretary and Governor could have never envisaged that their tenure would not last beyond the mid-1950s. As such, they took no steps to place the Bureau on a more permanent footing. It was, after all, created simply based on an executive order. Consequently, its trajectory would also be as tenuous; the Bureau could also be closed simply based on an executive order. This state of insecurity critically afflicted the men of the Bureau in the late 1950s.[124] But more importantly, the socio-political changes of the decade would greatly impact CPIB's leadership. In particular, the Malayanisation scheme left the colony short of European leadership at all levels of the colonial administration, including the CPIB's. There was no Malayan Civil Service staff to take over from Director Claude Wormald Lyle. So Richard Byrne Corridon occupied the seat as an Acting Director. From the end of 1955, since Corridon left, to mid-1957, in less than two years the Bureau would be helmed by no less than five new directors, who were mostly posted on a temporary basis. Most of them were also expatriates who were on the Malayanisation scheme.

Former Director CPIB, Richard Byrne Corridon, *The Straits Times*, 11 September 1963, p.11. *Source:* The Straits Times © SPH Media Limited. Permission required for reproduction.

Former Director CPIB, Sardar Singh. *Source:* The Straits Times © SPH Media Limited. Permission required for reproduction.

Former Director CPIB, John Le Cain, *The Straits Times*, 22 March 1963, p.1. *Source:* The Straits Times © SPH Media Limited. Permission required for reproduction.

The First Decade
Directors, CPIB: 1952–1963

Mar–Sep 1952	Richard Middleton-Smith, Leader, Special Investigation Team
Oct–Dec 1952	Richard Middleton-Smith (Acting)
Jan 1953	Claude Wormald Lyle
Jun 1954	Richard Byrne Corridon (Acting)
Dec 1955	Sardar Singh (Acting)
Aug 1956	Andrew Howat Frew
Mar 1957	WJ Parks (Acting)
Apr 1957	OO Griffiths
Jul 1957–Mar 1959	John Le Cain
Mar–Oct 1958	Basil St John Hickman (Acting)[125]
Mar 1959	Sardar Singh
Oct 1959–May 1960	Ponniah Rajaratnam[126]
Jun 1960	Khong Heng Ngee
Dec 1960	Ponniah Rajaratnam[127]
Apr 1962	Michael Chong[128]
Dec 1962	Khong Heng Ngee (Acting)[129]
Sep 1963	Richard Byrne Corridon[130]

In its first decade, up till 1959, the Bureau changed directors a total of 12 times. It is not difficult to imagine just how this could have affected the stability of the unit. The transient leaders would not have been expected to formulate long-term plans for the Bureau. When the Bureau had its first Asian director, ASP Sardar Singh, in late 1955, he was also assigned temporarily, holding an Acting post.[131]

Police Assumed Oversight

Following Corridon's departure, the Bureau effectively became a unit of the Police Establishment, although this status would not be formalised until 1957. Fundamentally, the issue was the Bureau's independence. As early as in 1953, when the Singapore Association asked the Secretary of State for Colonies to appoint an independent Commission of Inquiry to look into the state of corruption in Singapore,[132] the issue of the independence of the local anti-corruption department was already raised. The Association noted that because the department had been part of the local government, even when it acted independently, "it does not appear to the public to be independent". The Association was of the opinion that "little could be done to combat bribery and corruption until an anti-corruption department independent of local government and having the widest powers was set up".[133] The question of independence was therefore not only a matter of status, but also the reason for the establishment of the CPIB. The crux of the problem was the general perception the public had with regard to corruption in the police force. Having been placed within the Police Establishment from 1956, the Bureau underwent a bit of a crisis. For one, civilian leaders in the Legislative Assembly were quick to point out that "for evils of corruption in colony to be rooted out, the CPIB should not be manned by policemen". This was because "the public was reluctant to come forward to report cases to government officers [who were themselves corrupt]". As such, William Tan, Assemblyman from the Liberal Socialist Party, suggested in 1957 that the Bureau should be "reconstituted".[134]

This was a dark time for the Bureau. It faced a general trust deficit from the public as well as politicians who might one day assume political power. Coupled with the constant change of directors within the Bureau, the staff of the CPIB suffered low morale through the rest of the 1950s. For one, all the civilian investigators in the Bureau were hired on a temporary basis. By 1958, most of them faced retrenchment. Most of them had been with the Bureau for several years, but in that time, the status of the Bureau itself was impermanent. This was due to the way the unit was created — from an executive order. By this year, the Bureau's ever-changing directors could only tell the staff that the government was still "assessing the efficiency of the Bureau" before deciding on the unit's permanency. Compounding the staff's difficulties was their pay scale. Almost all the civilian investigators had reached the wage ceiling of $500. As they had no avenue for promotion, they could have no further progression in their jobs, and therefore, there were to be no more increments. It was a "dead end" job. Yet, they worked as hard as the police officers compiling the Bureau's investigation reports.[135] In March 1957, when OO Griffiths was Director, following his discussions with the Customs, it was decided that the CPIB would no longer deal with narcotic smuggling matters. As a result of this policy change, Senior Civilian Investigator Mah Kah Kee was made redundant. Furthermore, of the Bureau's 12 civilian investigators posts, six were permanently abolished in 1959. The impending elections which would see the creation of a fully elected local government was also another event that might see the Bureau's termination. Hence, there was no certain future for the staff of the Bureau.[136]

The formal transfer of the Bureau from civilian to police oversight took place in mid-1957 when the Deputy Chief Secretary of Singapore endorsed the move. The Bureau was to be treated as part of the police force as far as administration and discipline were concerned. The Director of the CPIB, whether he was a police officer or not, would be a subordinate of the Commissioner of Police, although he retained the right to have direct access to the Chief Minister. He was also still entitled to withhold information from the Commissioner of Police. These recommendations were sent to the Deputy Chief Secretary on 20 March 1957 and he replied with his approval on 4 April 1957.[137] When Sardar returned to the Bureau in 1959 to become Director for a second time, he found the arrangements made for the Bureau most unsatisfactory. Up till January 1958, the Bureau was placed directly under the Chief Secretary. In this arrangement, the Bureau came under the Attorney-General for investigations and the Commissioner of Police for Administration and Discipline. Sardar found that having to answer to "two heads" was not "a happy situation" for the Bureau.[138] In any case, Sardar then proceeded to "clean out" the Bureau of its core staff in 1959 — those he considered as being inefficient and ineffective and had to be transferred. They included two ASPs, three Inspectors and all five civilian investigators. The civilian investigators were told they had six months to improve or they would be replaced.[139]

Operation Dagger

Weeding out corruption from the mid-1950s had become more challenging for the CPIB. Coming under police oversight placed the men of the Bureau in an impossible conundrum. At this time, many in the public, including contemporary politicians, had little faith in the Police. Hence, when the Bureau lost its independence, both the public and politicians also distrusted the CPIB.[140] Historically, crime, corruption and conspiracy have been long-time bedfellows. This was no exception in Singapore. Since the nineteenth century, gaming syndicates and Chinese *huey* members had colluded with corrupt police officers to break the law. And there were also instances where police officers had been behind criminal enterprises.

By the mid-1950s, Chinese secret societies, and the thugs associated with them, had become so brazen that they started interfering in local politics by tying up with political parties.[141] These triads also started to have a hand in seemingly "legitimate" businesses, often in cahoots with public officers. In mid-1955, the Bureau, in cooperation with the Anti-Vice

CPIB: Establishment and Development 1952–1965

National Development	Period	Directorship	Leadership	Government Oversight	Legal Authority	Milestones	Other Anti-Corruption Institutions/Measures	Locality
Colony	1952–1954	Malayan Civil Service (MCS)	Civilian + Police	Colonial Secretary & Governor & Attorney General Office	1937 Ordinance 1946 Amendment Provisions within Banishment Ordinance	Mar–Apr 1952 Started as Special Investigation Team	Anti-Corruption Branch, CID, up till Jul 1952	Room at Labour Building to Level 2 Supreme Court
Colony & Limited Self-Rule	1954–1955	Supt of Police	Civilian + Police		Provisions within, Legislative Assembly Elections Ordinance, 26 of 1954		Transport Commission 1955–56 addressed STC corruption	Level 2 Supreme Court
	1956–1959	Senior Police	Police	Chief Secretary (from mid-1955)		Malayanisation — Exodus of Expatriates in Government Service	Commission I May 1957 - Government, Local, Led by Justice Chua[1] Commission II Aug 1957 - Colonial govt — probe 1957 by-election — aka Elias Commission[2] Complaints Bureau 1957 - City Council	
Self-Rule	1959–1963	Senior Police	Police	Home Affairs	1960 Ordinance	June 1963 Reforms — Team System — Police Headed	Central Complaints Bureau 1962	From Supreme Court to Stamford Road
Merger	1963–1965	Civil Servant	Civilian	Prime Minister's Office	1966 Ordinance no. 27	Singapore Police Federalised Oct 1963 Police pulls out Team System retained	Audit Department Instruction Manual	Stamford Road
Independence	1965			Attorney General Office				

[1] Justice Frederick Arthur Chua, MJ Namazie and Teh Say Koo See were appointed to the Commission in May 1957. They sent their report to Governor Sir Robert Black in November, see *Straits Times* 8 Nov 1957.
[2] Commission led by SHD Elias (Chairman) had members GH Kiat and CR Dasaratha Raj. It was appointed to investigate allegations of corruption during the 1957 Assembly by-election.

Branch, uncovered a prostitution racket operating out of a hotel. It was discovered that the "operation" had been ongoing for five years, and the hotel had generated at least $5,000,000 in profit. Upon interrogation, the hotel owner revealed that the racket involved both secret society members and "government men" whom he called *cheng-hu-lang* (in Hokkien). On average, the enterprise raked in $30,000 monthly for the "consortium".[142] This was perhaps one of Corridon's last big-money cases before he left. By the beginning of 1956, when the Police started assuming oversight of the CPIB, although there were still large smuggling cases with lots of bribe monies involved, these were dwindling with increased enforcement. The Bureau fell back to its usual run-of-the-mill corruption cases.[143] However, it was also in 1956 that things turned more severe with the criminal underworld when a number of millionaire *towkays* were subjected to kidnappings, house robberies, death threats, extortion and much more. Most of these crimes involved secret societies. In June 1956, a bar fight between rival secret society gangs in Chinatown created the spectre of open gang warfare in the streets of Singapore.[144] Things were getting out of hand. It was time to suppress the *hueys* and to take to task their affiliates — corrupt police officers. Operation Dagger was launched on 15 July 1956. While the Criminal Investigation Department (CID) went after the secret society thugs, the Bureau went after the police officers who had been aiding the thugs.

Three days after Operation Dagger was started, 234 gangsters had been detained.[145] Police targeted the main money earning syndicates of the secret societies: gambling, vice, narcotics and smuggling of opium.[146] By August 1956, Operation Dagger was widened with a general manhunt that rounded up thugs. It was believed that removing the main players in the *hueys* would have been fruitless if "vacancies were filled by desperate recruits", and as "most society men turned to crime only because of big money to be made", the Police would continue to target these hoodlum "industries", which included extortion and prostitution rackets. In just over a month, Operation Dagger had already "hit the Colony's big-money smugglers".

Opium smuggling had almost stopped, and the illegal importation of liquor and tobacco was also greatly reduced.[147]

By mid-October, over 1,000 suspects had been questioned and 70 had been convicted and imprisoned. Gurkhas were deployed in heavy police patrols; protection rackets which provided the *hueys* great leverage over businesses had been greatly reduced.[148]

However, the initial shock and impact of Operation Dagger seemed to have tapered off by the first quarter of 1957 and armed robberies started increasing once again. The gangsters started returning to the streets as Operation Dagger seemed to have "lost its thrust".[149] Singapore faced a new crime wave. So, the Police intensified Operation Dagger once again from mid-1957.[150] The last thrust of Operation Dagger took place on September 1957. From then, the anti-triad drive was renamed "Operation Preksah" to reflect its shift in emphasis to target crime in general. On 6 October 1957, in a span of 24 hours, the Police rounded up 300 gangsters in one broad sweep. By November 1957, a total of 24,108 people had been stopped and searched, of whom 520 were detained for screening and four charged in Court.[151] It is no wonder that the authorities found that the secret societies intensified their involvement in the local political parties around this time. The police clampdown had seriously impacted their ability to operate with impunity, and having an influence in future political leaders might provide some breathing space. However, their presence in the electioneering processes, seen as political corruption, only pushed the government to intensify Operation Dagger to make a final thrust into the *hueys* from June to September 1957.[152]

While the police crackdown on the *hueys* seriously impacted their ability to generate huge incomes with which they could bribe officials, the other aspect of the corruption nexus that had to be dealt with was the corrupt police officers who worked hand in glove with the triads. In late August 1956, during Operation Dagger, Police Commissioner NG Morris finally ordered "stern action [to be taken] to break a 'link' between certain members of the police force and secret society gangsters".[153] Just before this, Morris had dismissed an anti-vice police sergeant for taking bribes from a secret society. This was certainly the result of the CPIB's investigative work. Morris realised that the CID's Secret Society Sub-Branch had been taking protection money from gangsters. It was also alleged that many officers had been connected to the secret societies before they joined the Police. Therefore, there was a need for Operation Dagger to include cleaning up the Police from within, and in this instance, Morris gave the CPIB top priority to investigate police corruption.[154] However, Morris placed a caveat on the Bureau: the CPIB had to inform the Commissioner before taking action on any officer it was investigating.[155]

In any case, Morris' new position struck fear in most police officers, especially among detectives. Now they feared the CPIB as it had the backing of a top brass. Interestingly, in reaction to their new predicament, police detectives started avoiding their regular drinking spots and "favourite waitresses" for fear of being questioned by the Bureau and put on corruption charges. Waitresses around the Jalan Besar area were informed by their detective "boyfriends" that they had to stay away, at least, for the moment. When Operation Dagger started, the Bureau had questioned a number of detectives from various divisions in the Police, including the CID's Anti-Vice and Anti-Gambling Sub-Branches. Of course, the Bureau also realised that *huey* members who informed on corrupt officers could also be taking advantage of the situation to smear detectives in order to escape the tightening noose of Operation Dagger.[156] So, the CPIB treaded carefully. It is difficult to establish the extent that the Bureau's hands had been tied during its sojourn within the Police Establishment. But one thing for sure was that to successfully combat corruption in Singapore, it was imperative that the police force itself had to be cleaned up, with repeated follow-up. This vigilance had to be "constant".[157]

In any case, the cleaning up of the police force started in earnest. Corridon would return in 1963 to helm the Bureau once more till 1968. He was in a unique position to provide a perspective on corruption affecting Singapore and its police force, in the 1950s and 1960s, and of the changing nature of the Bureau's work[158]:

"*The police force was so manifestly corrupt.... The public had no more trust in it. And then there was a Court case (Ponggol Opium Heist) ... in which the evidence... in the Court was cooked up and so clever lawyers were able to destroy it.* [It was] *an important case against notorious criminals* [which] *broke down. And then I think the final thing that led to my being taken out of the Special Branch* [to form the Special Investigation Team] *was when a shipload of opium was landed, I think on Changi Beach (actually Ponggol), late one night. It was landed for the Teochew Section of this CID. And once it had been loaded, detectives from the Hokkien Section moved up to the lorry driver and said, 'Now, go or you'll be killed. Not killed tomorrow or the day after, you'll be killed now.' They probably showed him a revolver.... He got out and went. He was going only to be paid to drive this van. And they took this whole van of opium over to other interested... so they all shared the money of this great importation of opium. That kind of thing was possible. One section of the CID working against its brother officers... it was very very corrupt, and Mr Middleton-Smith was taken out of the Secretariat to be the Director of the Special Branch (Special Investigation Team), and I was chosen, and I was told to choose officers I wanted, that I could trust. So gradually, we built up the CPIB.*"[159]

"*By this time (1963) ... it (Police) was very much better. Anything that we investigated in respect to the Police no longer had to do with senior police officers, say, Assistant Superintendent of Police officers, ...* [it was] *much more the rank-and-file type of corruption which you will always have.... There was a constable who got a commendation for the way he was bringing in motorists who failed to stop at the double-white line, in one of the roads of Bukit Timah Road. And he brought in, case after case there, it was a very busy junction, and we heard just a rumour that this constable was corrupt. So, we had him watched and we found that he stopped, car after car, some he passed on after a talk through a window with the driver, and some he wrote up a booking. And after about three days surveillance of this kind of thing, it was clear that he* was both sort of protecting himself by booking a number of people in the course of his duty at that point, as well as taking bits of money off them, about 10 dollars a time. And so, 10 dollars and you're not worried with a court case, or having to face some senior official who would impose a fine. We brought him to book for having been corrupt in this way, and he was making a lot more money than the cases he was reporting in. He had allowed two cases to pass with taking 10 dollars each, and then, with every third case, he booked and reported. It was a very good source of income. Just standing on a road, making money.... The CPIB, at this time, was answerable to the Prime Minister. Yes, we used to... keep him informed of very much what we did, but our senior officer was the Attorney-General, or the Solicitor-General. One or the other would always take our work and deal with it."[160]

The New Racket, 4D Characters Lottery

Gambling is such a part of human nature that almost everyone would have gambled at some point in their lives, be it by placing a bet, rolling the dice in a game, buying lottery numbers or simply daring someone to a bet. Gambling syndicates had always been a bane to the authorities in Singapore. Although not every gaming house had been syndicated or part of a *huey*, they all had the potential to amass significant wealth, and with it, the propensity to corrupt any vulnerable official, or even a whole government department. Seldom would there be a new game invented in modern times that would entice the masses. But this was exactly what happened in 1959. In early February that year, the Bureau uncovered a four-digit (4D) number racket at Empress Place; several government employees in the building were runners for the racket. There was also a big bookie amongst them, a civil servant, who took bets from the employees of the building. The crackdown by the CPIB started on Saturday, 24 January 1959, after a runner, a peon in the Treasury located in the building, was found to have had betting slips on him for the Bukit Timah Saturday races. Names of government officers and clerical staff were on the slips. The CPIB then searched the Accountant-General's Office in the building and carted away incriminating documents. After interrogating the peon, CPIB Director John Le Cain decided it was a departmental matter. As for the other government employees who were interrogated, Le Cain submitted a report on them to the Permanent Secretary. This was the first time the CPIB had dealt directly with a 4D racket. The problem Le Cain faced then was that the game was so new that it was not yet a criminal offence to make bets in the game, although the Federation had already made it an illegal gaming activity. Nevertheless, it was at this point a disciplinary issue as the government had issued a departmental circular in June 1958, stating that any government employee found gambling at work could be dismissed. In this instance, the Bureau found that 4D lottery had been rife at Empress Place for months.[161]

Politics and Corruption

In every milieu, there would always be contemporary causes and sources of corruption. While the construction boom and the associated public spending in the pre-war years, spurred by the war reparation, created the conditions for corruption linked to this industry, the extreme shortages in the post-war period created the right setting for black marketeers. This gave rise to all the associated corrupt activities to circumvent official control, or simply for the man on the street to acquire essentials whichever way he could get them. By the 1950s, when decolonisation started and constitutional development was afoot, politics, or political power, became the concern of the day. When the electoral processes started, from small municipal polls to the colossal General Election, the stake for politicians and people on the ground also increased exponentially. In this context, not all instances of corrupt activities or practices involved money. The CPIB was already compelled to check such activities during the directorship of Lyle and Corridon. Going beyond the mid-1950s, corruption in the political arena would take on new dimensions. Local politicians started politicising the issue of public corruption. Jonathan Rauch, an American author, wrote, "In politics, hypocrisy and doublespeak are tools. They can be used nefariously, illegally or for personal gain… but they can also be used for legitimate public purposes…"[162] In post-war Singapore, when a great majority of the masses lived in poverty, and corruption in society and in government departments had been rife, causing further hardship to the general public, it was popular for politicians and political parties to adopt an anti-corruption platform in the polls. The Labour Front Alliance, the party that won the 1955 General Election that paved the way for Singapore's Limited Self-Rule, was quick to champion anti-corruption initiatives within their party as well as in government departments serving the masses.[163] What is significant here was not that the incumbent proceeded to make good on its campaign promises, but that, in doing so, other political parties also took on functions directing the anti-corruption franchise and agenda instead of leaving it to the state's apparatus like the CPIB. In the latter half of the 1950s, the Bureau would appear less prominently in the prevention of corruption while the political institutions seized the day to champion cleaning up corruption in the government.

In mid-1956, the Labour Front Alliance (Parliamentary Committee) lobbied the government to appoint a three-men commission to immediately probe corruption in public services, including the Police and City Council.[164] This "Commission of Inquiry into Bribery and Corruption" which was to be a "full scale war" against corruption, remained just a public narrative.[165] In 1957, the Labour Front adopted an anti-corruption platform for the Legislative Assembly and the 1957 City Council elections. The party argued that the government, which they led, should have a clear policy to wipe out corruption in government departments and in the City Council. Not only did the Front applaud the government's initiative in 1957 to set up the commission of inquiry into the alleged corruption in the Council,[166] it even took the position that the battle against corrupt practices should not end there, and that it was only just the beginning. Lim Siew Chuan, the Front's City Council candidate for Tanglin, even pledged to wipe out corruption in the Council as his party stood for honesty, integrity and efficiency.[167] The elimination of corruption was also given top placing in the United Malays National Organisation's (UMNO) (Singapore) 10-point City Council election manifesto.[168] Similarly, the People's Action Party (PAP) nine-point manifesto included the pledge that the party's candidates "have been chosen for their integrity and loyalty and they will clean up the corruption and maladministration" and that they would "stop the oppression of hawkers, trishaw riders and taxi drivers by corrupt officials".[169] On the surface, most political parties had made similar promises to better the lives of the electorate. Be it simply bravado or honest politics, the real difference between them, in terms of combating corruption, was political will.

Another phenomenon of party politics in the 1950s was the courage local Asiatic leaders had in questioning the Establishment. Backed by a party, and an electorate, local politicians started calling out public officers for their shortcomings in the public service. In December 1957, William Tan, a Liberal Socialist Party Assemblyman, accused CID officers of being thugs who had links to secret societies. He also asserted that the CPIB was useless, now that it was under the supervision of the Police, because junior officers would not have the courage to investigate senior officers; they would certainly risk their "rice bowl" if they filed a report against their superiors. While EP Shanks, the Attorney-General, denied that this would happen, ST Stewart, the Acting Chief Secretary of Singapore, asserted that junior officers in the CPIB would not be transferred if they offended senior officers. In reply, Tan asked, "How can we stamp out corruption when we have the CPIB entirely staffed by police officers?" Tan added that he had forwarded many complaints to the Bureau for investigation but nothing had come out of them. Shanks had no answer to this point but assured Tan that the CPIB was housed separately from the main police force and was staffed by specially chosen men from the Force.[170]

In April 1958, Lee Kuan Yew decried the Singapore government for not taking action against the Personnel and Welfare Manager of the

Singapore Harbour Board. Lee pointed out that the CPIB had submitted a report on the man's alleged graft. Shanks claimed that he had read the CPIB's report and no action would be taken. Lee then asked Shanks if it was because the manager had recently received the Order of British Empire (OBE). Shanks said no. So, Lee asked if the man would be disciplined by his department. Shanks said no. Lee then asked if the Attorney-General could share what advice was given to him on the matter. Shanks said no. To this, Lee shouted "Shame!"[171]

Clearly, the patronising treatment local politicians received in the 1950s, especially when allegations of inefficiency and corruption in the public service had been made, truly underscored the real issues preventing fundamental changes which would put an end to the corruption in the government — the Colonial Establishment itself! Despite years of complaints and prosecution of SIT officers, Tan Theng Chiang, the Assistant Minister for Lands and Housing, remarked in April 1958 that the accusations and attacks on the SIT for being corrupt were unwarranted, unfair and unethical. He asserted that the local government had so far received no specific complaints, and neither had the Corruption Commission nor the CPIB.[172] In September 1958, when Assemblymen William Tan and Lim Cher Kheng pointed out that the SIT was still filled with corrupt officials, the SIT Local Officers Association challenged Tan and Lim to report them to the CPIB, accusing Tan and Lim of politicising housing issues and engaging in "soap-box talk" with their allegations for the "eyes of their electorate".[173] It is clear that while corruption had become a political matter in the decade, broaching the issue publicly had also surfaced the real issues behind the pervasive corruption in society and government.

Anti-Corruption Measures Politicised

Just as corruption had become a political issue in the 1950s, the politicians also did the same with anti-corruption measures. The presence of these "other" institutions that handled corruption issues had the effect of lessening the function of the CPIB in the latter half of the 1950s.

The Bureaus

In 1955, when David Marshall was Chief Minister, he became the first political leader to collect public feedback and complaints outside of the Government Establishment. Marshall started his Public Advisory Bureau in mid-July 1955. It functioned like a "meet-the-people session", dealing with dozens of cases daily,[174] although his Labour Front had its own "meet-the-people session".[175] Basically, the Advisory Bureau was Marshall's platform to render real assistance to the grassroots, although many of the issues tackled were not all related to inefficiency and corruption in the public service. The fact that the people sought the help of the Advisory Bureau instead of government departments said a lot about the level of public service people on the ground were receiving. Amongst the many complaints were poor service from public servants.[176] In June 1956, the Advisory Bureau received a complaint about prison officers denying prisoners good food if they did not donate blood to the blood transfusion centre.[177] Marshall's Advisory Bureau folded in November 1956, several months after he stepped down as Chief Minister and left the Front.[178] Had it lasted, it might have effected some real changes. In 1958, when the PAP took control of the City Council, it also introduced its own in-house bureau — the Public Complaints Bureau. This institution would become a full City Council department and function to receive feedback on corruption and inefficiency of public services.[179]

League for the Prevention of Vice and Corruption

This was essentially a citizens' league against vice and corruption. The social condition in Town areas in the late 1950s had been rather dismal. Amongst the middle-class residents in the City, a number of "civic-minded citizens" were concerned about the state of affairs. They also did not have much faith in the anti-corruption establishment on the island. They were led by AG

Benedict, a building inspector with the City Council. They proposed the establishment of a "League for the Prevention of Vice and Corruption" for Singapore and they wanted the Police and the CPIB to support it. They realised that many residents were unwilling to report corruption cases to the authorities as they could be required in Court. This was in itself a dangerous thing in colonial Singapore. So they conceived the idea of the League, as the group could pass information to the authorities without fear that individuals would be targeted.[180] In the end, nothing came out of this proposal. It is likely that many of such civic-minded citizens could have ultimately left Singapore under the Malayanisation scheme. But more importantly, their concerns shone a light on why the CPIB was not more successful in the latter half of the 1950s — most people still distrusted the state's apparatus and the government had done little to ensure the safety of informants other than a verbal assurance.

The Justice Chua Commission[181]

This was the first of two Commissions of Inquiry appointed in 1957 to deal with corrupt activities in the government. Officially known as the Commission of Inquiry into Allegations of Corruption in the City Council, it was made up of three members: Justice FA Chua (Chair), MJ Namazie and Teh Say Koo. It was originally thought that this Commission would be the start of the "full-scale" war on graft that the government spoke of in 1956. After all, the Commission would look into the corruption amongst public servants in all government departments. However, when this long-awaited Commission started work in earnest, it became clear that it was more exploratory than prosecutorial. Although its Terms of Reference covered instances of corruption in both the legislative and administrative branches of government,[182] including assemblymen, city councillors and other government officers,[183] the Commissioners decided that it should also pay special attention to three specific cases of suspected graft in the City Council: the Council's delimiting of taxis in Town, the permits granted to build Katong Cinema, and the issuance of licences to bus companies to operate certain bus routes.[184] Chua then issued a public notice and went on radio to appeal to people to come forward to submit evidence, in person or in writing; Chua declared, "Singapore must have honest officials.... The success of a self-governing Singapore depends on honest officials, but it is up to the public to ensure that they are honest."[185]

The proceedings of the Commission, held in the High Court, started in August 1957 and lasted a couple of months. By the first week of November, the Commission had completed its work and submitted its report to the Governor.[186] The Commission of Inquiry, which everyone had hoped to be the tip of the spear in the "full-scale" onslaught against graft in the government, reported that it found no evidence of corruption![187] Basically, Chua found that many did not come forward to testify because they feared reprisals.[188] Therefore, the Commission also made no recommendations for further action. Perhaps the most useful outcome of the exercise had been the information that the Commissioners had gathered with regard to the indebtedness of public servants in Singapore,[189] a condition which provided an opening for corruption and exploitation.[190] Although the Justice Chua Commission did not surface guilty corruptors or result in the cleaning up of any part of the public service, it had been a most revealing exercise that surfaced the fundamental truth about the state of affairs in colonial Singapore: the people were fearful because the threats were real. If the public did not cooperate with this Commission, they would not have assisted the CPIB either. The problem of corruption in society, and within the government, was not only about the lack of morals and honesty, it was also about courage and the will to change.

The Elias Commission

The second Commission of Inquiry of 1957 was assembled by Governor Sir Robert Black to inquire into allegations of corruption and illegal practices in the June 1957 by-election. The 29 June 1957 Cairnhill and Tanjong Pagar polls followed the resignations of David Marshall as Chief

Justice FA Chua at ceremonial opening to mark beginning of the legal year outside the Supreme Court, 17 January 1967. He was a member of the Commission of Inquiry into Allegations of Corruption in the City Council in 1957.
Source: Ministry of Information and the Arts Collection, courtesy of National Archives of Singapore.

Minister on 7 June 1956, and Lee Kuan Yew, who took up Marshall's challenge for him to resign and seek re-election.[191] It was during the days of electoral campaigning that supporters of all the candidates got involved in "questionable" activities. When the dust settled, allegations of vote buying, illegal gratifications, sabotage, collusion, intimidation and much more surfaced.[192] While it would be logical that the CPIB should have led the investigation and prosecution of those who committed offences during electioneering, most of the major political parties during the polls of the late 1950s shared the same sentiments that the CPIB could not be trusted to do its job.[193] Lee had been the first political leader who requested the appointment of a Commission of Inquiry to investigate political corruption in Singapore. He made this call in June 1957 even before the polling day of the Cairnhill and Tanjong Pagar by-election. In fact, when Lee raised the issue at the Legislative Assembly, he asked whether the Justice Chua Commission could extend its scope of investigations to include corruption cases in the by-election. The government replied that it would appoint a separate Commission to look into electioneering issues.[194]

The three-men Commission of Inquiry investigating corruption in the 1957 legislative by-election was appointed in September 1957;[195] its members were GH Kiat, CR Dasaratha Raj and SHD Elias who chaired the Commission. Public hearings, which started on 15 October 1957, saw 40 witnesses examined in four months.[196] On 15 April 1958, the Elias Commission submitted its findings in a 40-page report.[197] Witnesses from various political parties told of secret societies' involvement and interference, influencing and intimidating voters, selling "block" votes of residents in blocks of flats they controlled, canvassing for politicians, offering payments for votes, taking voters to polling stations, sending them home by cars and more.[198] It is perhaps interesting that all these by-election infringements would only be reported at the Commission, and not to the Police or the CPIB during the polls. William Tan, Liberal Socialist Party's Assemblyman, while testifying at the Commission, explained why the party did not report to the authorities an incident involving a boy they caught tearing down their posters. He said that the boy was hungry and out of work. The boy was paid $5 to tear down their posters.[199] Tan then said that he had not made a report simply because "he had no faith in the Corrupt Practices Investigation Bureau in dealing with corruption" as the Bureau "did not investigate corrupt cases he sent to them". Tan asserted that he had in the past reported such cases to the CPIB and that these reports "were 'killed' at the investigation stage". Therefore, he did not trust the Bureau, and he did not expect any outcome if he had reported the incident.[200]

The Elias Commission had found that the parties of both winning candidates of the Cairnhill and Tanjong Pagar by-election had flouted election laws. When questioned about the basis of these assertions, the Commission simply stated that they had been from "reliable" sources.[201] This peeved Lee. He criticised the way in which the Commission conducted its investigations, using "secret allegations in their report" without allowing accused persons to know or to cross-examine witnesses.[202] The Elias Commission also refused to respond to these criticisms that came hard and fast after the release of its report, saying instead that it could not comment as the report was in the government's hands. The government, now under Lim Yew Hock, also found it expedient not to comment.[203] So Lee took it to the Assembly, where he repeated his criticisms of the Commission and made it known that, originally, he had been one of the first to voice out that there were anomalies in the by-election, and that guilty parties should be prosecuted, if the Police had evidence.[204] The Attorney-General replied that he had no evidence. So Lee withdrew his motion. Lim then reminded the Assembly that the Commission's integrity and efficiency should not be questioned because the Commission was not the one on trial.[205] Herein lay the blatant contradiction between the findings of the government's Commission on the by-election and the state's position: one claimed to have "proven" that there had been corruption and collusion, while the other stated unequivocally that there was no such evidence. It is no wonder that the PAP and the other political parties took the position that they had no faith in state institutions like the CPIB, which at that time was still answerable to the Attorney-General despite having come under police oversight.

The government accepted the Elias Commission's report and adopted almost all of its recommendations as the basis for a new Bill for fair and honest elections. Changing election laws on campaigning was intended to wipe out corruption and illegal practices at the polls.[206] The new Bill was debated in the Assembly, offering politicians another occasion to address the deficiencies of the Elias Commission's findings. However, Lee was once again stopped from speaking out about the corrupt practices that the Commission had found which now shaped the formulation of the new law; this time by the Speaker of Assembly.[207] Nevertheless, the Bill was passed and became law — the Local Government Election (Amendment) Ordinance, 1958.

Chapter Fifteen

PAP's Philosophy & Measures Against Corruption

The People's Action Party's (PAP) ethos for an honest and efficient government was conceived years before Singapore's Independence in 1965. These values were forged during the tumultuous struggle for self-determination in the later years of 1950s, even before attaining internal self-government in 1959. Although the CPIB would temporarily fade into the backdrop during this period of constitutional and political development, this phase of the nation's history was nevertheless critical for the Bureau's transition from a colonial institution into a critical national agency that became the bulwark against corrupt practices which continued to threaten the birth of this new nation.

Managing the City Council, 1958

The first time the PAP had been elected into a leadership position was during the December 1957 City Council elections. This was also the first time the City Council was constituted entirely of elected representatives from 32 constituencies.[208] Although the PAP did not secure the majority of the Council seats, as a party it won the greatest number of seats. By forming an alliance with the United Malays National Organisation (UMNO) which held two seats, the PAP was able to take control of the City Council and appoint Ong Eng Guan as Mayor.[209] It was through the Council that the PAP would first implement their vision of a corruption-free "local government". Although the City Council had been the instrument of municipal administration, it was not the colony's government. Singapore's government was at this time under the Labour Front coalition following their success in the 1955 Legislative Assembly elections, the island's first General Election where the majority of seats had been filled by elected representatives.[210] Nevertheless, in 1957, all city councillors were also elected to their seats, and each councillor contested the polls under the banner of their own political party, notwithstanding the independents. This anomaly of having two centres of authority elected through popular polls — despite the fact that the government was undisputedly the final authority and the Council was subservient — would eventually be

Foreground from right, Chief Minister Lim Yew Hock introducing British Prime Minister Harold Macmillan to Deputy Mayor Ong Pang Boon, Mayor Ong Eng Guan and his wife at Singapore's City Council Steps, 12 February 1958.
Source: Ministry of Information and the Arts Collection, courtesy of National Archives of Singapore.

Crowd outside City Hall during the Singapore City Council's first meeting, 24 December 1957.
Source: Ministry of Information and the Arts Collection, courtesy of National Archives of Singapore.

permanently resolved after Singapore attained self-government in 1959. In the meantime, Ong, as Mayor, would put the extent of his mandate and authority to the test right at the start of his term when he announced that his administration would clean up the City Council of corrupt officials and improve efficiency in serving the people. Notably, the new Mayor did not declare that he would utilise or work with the CPIB for this purpose. He could not since the Bureau reported only to the government and not the municipality (city). But more importantly, could the Mayor take these steps unilaterally?

It was not surprising that Ong's stance alarmed the Singapore government. Almost immediately, the Minister for Local Government, Lands and Housing, Abdul Hamid bin Jumat, made it known through the press that the Mayor was just the "chairman" of the Council and it was not his "duty to run the administration" and "direct city council officers".[211] Interestingly, it was the response to Ong's manoeuvres by the rank and file of the government and municipality that shone a light on the real source of corruption and inefficiency afflicting public services in Singapore in this milieu. Instead of cheering the Mayor's resolve to improve efficiency and "to stamp out corruption in the council services",[212] they bemoaned the impending dismissals. As early as January 1958, Ong had already announced the creation of a "new bureau" to weed out corruption within the City Council, making it "unnecessary" for the government to appoint any "special committee to investigate alleged corruption in the Singapore City Council".[213] Nevertheless, the Mayor faced a barrage of obstacles from the staff of the Council itself; members and staff of the previous City Council, many of whom were still employed in the Council, denied Ong's accusation that they had been inefficient and corrupt, and had left the city a legacy of neglect and maladministration.[214] In April 1958, the Singapore City Council Services Union challenged the Mayor to "take all corrupt Council officials to Court and charge them", or withdraw his allegations if he could not prove wrongdoing.[215] And when the Mayor proposed making the Public Complaints Bureau a permanent department within the Council,[216] the "opposition" non-PAP members of the Council accused him of trying to set up a "permanent gestapo department in the Singapore City Council… merely to create ill-feeling".[217]

While many of the obstacles Ong faced from the non-PAP Councillors would have been politically motivated in obstructing reforms to improve efficiency and remove corruption, these Councillors essentially reneged on the campaign promises they made during the 1957 City Council polls that had helped them to secure their seats. All of them, including the PAP, had pledged to eliminate corruption in the Council if they were elected. In short, they had all, before the City Council elections, acknowledged that corruption and inefficiency were real and present problems in the

Council. Yet, when the Mayor took action on actual cases of dereliction amongst City Council staff, the "opposition" Councillors voted to reverse the disciplinary measures already meted out. In August 1958, three of the Council's health inspectors were reported by a Councillor who found them in a coffeeshop discussing "gambling and corruption" matters during office hours. Ong issued a stern warning to all staff about their gambling and betting activities during work hours. Instantly, the Singapore City Council Services Union defended the three inspectors and issued an open reminder to members that they should seek the union's assistance if they were "booked for disciplinary action" by the authorities.[218] Not surprisingly, the gambling problem persisted. In October 1958, when an officer at City Hall was found to be a bookmaker during work hours, Ong had him dismissed. Opposition Councillors, however, reversed his dismissal, allowing the man to resign instead. This allowed him to continue to receive his Provident Fund benefits. Of course, these Councillors outvoted their PAP colleagues who argued hopelessly that if such cases went unpunished, there would be "chaos and all sorts of maladministration in the City Council". The non-PAP Councillors also reduced the punishment of two other officers, who lost five wage increments each for dereliction to just one increment.[219]

From one perspective, the non-PAP Councillors, and their parties, had really been soft on tackling corruption and inefficiency. From another perspective, all their election promises were simply bravado or rhetoric. Whichever the case, it was clear that on the eve of the 1959 General Election that gave Singapore self-government, none of the political parties, including the PAP, had considered the CPIB a partner in their endeavour to end corrupt practices in the public service. In fact, the "CPIB" was conspicuously absent in all their social and political narratives at this time, except for a few instances when they dared each other to report their alleged wrongdoings to the CPIB.[220] The creation of the Public Complaints Bureau within the Council was perhaps a declaration that the PAP-led City Council had preferred to depend on their own graft buster instead of the government's anti-corruption body. The main reason for this was perhaps due to the PAP Mayor's nationalistic anti-colonial stance. In February 1958, a clash arose between the City Council and the Public Service Commission (PSC) on staffing matters. On the surface, it appears that the City Council had wanted to exercise autonomy when it declared that it considered the role of the PSC as only advisory,[221] but the reality was that the Council would only promote officers on the basis of merit, honesty and efficiency, while the norm in the government then had been based on seniority. In this instance, it divided the Council. The non-PAP members, once again, outvoted the PAP Councillors by 19 to 13. Ong saw this as the weakness of the colonial condition; even *Straits Times* had been critical of the Council as it could not shake off the fundamental flaws of the old practices, which unquestionably had been the source of inefficiency and corruption in the public service. Ong put it simply: it was because it was a "European-owned *Straits Times*".[222] Ong also described the Council staff who were from the previous Council as being "colonial agents".[223] Ong's perspective that the men and institutions which were "European" and "colonial" were obstacles to progress was illuminating. Calling Ong's anti-corruption Public Complaints Bureau a "gestapo agency" also reinforced the notion that the real problem was the old establishment itself. It wanted to retain the status quo and it resisted fundamental changes. This could explain the limited success of the CPIB in the latter part of the 1950s. Also, none of the political parties had fully endorsed the Bureau, probably because the Police had oversight of this institution, and many did not consider the Police Establishment as being honest at this time. The CPIB was essentially still a colonial institution. Also, if the Complaints Bureau, as an agency of change, was considered "gestapo"-like, then the CPIB would also have been seen in the same light. It was time for change.

Running the City Council had been more than a time of service for Ong and his PAP Councillors. The party had used the opportunity to introduce and test the social and political philosophies which it would put in place from 1959 when it came to power. Ong did not hide the fact that even as Mayor, he continued to take instructions and followed his party's ethos in managing the Council.[224] In particular, the Mayor's, and the PAP's, emphasis on honesty and efficiency would become national values for the new nation.[225]

Public Complaints Bureau

Originally, the Complaints Bureau was framed as the City Council's "anti-corruption bureau" as it was intended as a channel, or "administrative measure", by which the public could complain or give feedback on poor Council services or corrupt officials. In this way, the Mayor could receive the necessary information to clean up the Council.[226] Although it was not planned for the Complaints Bureau to be an alternate body to the CPIB, the creation of this Bureau reduced the need for the CPIB to look into wrongful practices among the employees of the City Council as the new agency could handle issues in-house,[227] notwithstanding those cases requiring prosecution which it referred to the CPIB. Nevertheless, the PAP Mayor had used the Complaints Bureau, instead of the CPIB, to weed out corruption amongst public servants within the Council. The Complaints Bureau had also functioned as the Council's general feedback unit, handling issues relating to hawkers, squatters and workers. Such issues became more regular after June 1958 when the Mayor's meet-the-people sessions ended,[228] and he personally urged the public to utilise the Complaints Bureau instead.[229]

The City Council's Public Complaints Bureau officially started services on 13 January 1958. It began as a "one-man show" at the first-floor entrance of City Hall. The Mayor appointed Loh Pui Kay, who was also the Assistant Accountant in the City Treasury, to be the Bureau Chief. His instructions were "to open eyes and ears" to corruption and rudeness in the Council. The complaints he received went immediately to the Mayor.[230] The Public Complaints Bureau remained a temporary set-up till June 1958 when the Mayor raised the matter with the Council to make the Public Complaints Bureau a permanent department within the Council as it had already been an effective check on corruption within the Council. In Ong's plan, the permanent Bureau would have a Director, an Assistant Director, two clerks and a runner.[231] Besides the main office at City Hall, Ong also envisaged establishing a branch of the Complaints Bureau at the Registry of Vehicles Office at Middle Road.[232] The Registry of Vehicles had been a Council department where corruption had been rife.[233] By mid-June 1958, despite the objections of the non-PAP Councillors, the Public Complaints Bureau was made a permanent feature in the City Council when the Council's Finance and General-Purpose Committee voted four to three to support the move. However, the new Bureau had to broaden its scope to deal with all public inquiries and complaints. It was renamed the Public Complaints and Inquiry Bureau,[234] and it even had a hotline number — 39333.[235] By the end of 1958, the Mayor was delighted to report that through the work of the new Bureau, much had been done to stop the "squeeze" and rudeness associated with the Council's services.[236] The next significant step taken by the Complaints Bureau occurred in early 1959 with the creation of a mobile unit which visited all of the 32 City Council wards to register public complaints. Ong was particularly excited about the small successes of this unit in the context of the fight against corruption and inefficiency. He found the mobile unit most effective in keeping in touch with the public at large. Through the 1950s, many had been reluctant to come forward to report instances of corruption they witnessed. The mobile unit brought the "listening ear" to them. Ong opined that "unless they give their active support, there is very little the Council can do".[237] Nevertheless, it would seem that the PAP's City Council had done more on the front of cleaning up City Hall and all its affiliated staff and public services than the CPIB during the last years of the 1950s. The real poser at this time was whether the PAP, after attaining political power, would retain the CPIB or simply build on their own institutional successes.

End of the Experiment

The PAP's time in the City Council had been a fruitful period, albeit a short one in terms of tenure. Ong became Mayor in January 1958, and the entire PAP contingent in the Council would resign *en masse* by April 1959. It was not just the opposition Councillors who had continuously blocked or obstructed the efforts and reforms the PAP Councillors tried to put in place in the City Council. Strong resistance also came from the rank and file of the Council staff, the public servants. By November 1958, the level of success enjoyed by Ong's team in cleaning up the City Council of corrupt practices and inefficiency had an inverse response from the Council's employees. There was disquiet and discontent. Opposition Councillors seized this opportunity to accuse their PAP colleagues of causing disquiet within the Council and creating an environment where "people worked in fear". A mini crisis ensued. The Mayor defended his team by reiterating his party's working ethos: "It is our aim to eliminate corruption and raise efficiency, to build this council into a fine public institution to serve the public and to make the basic necessities of life, like water and electricity and health, available to every man and woman, young and old, Malay or Chinese, Indian or Eurasian."[238] It was at this juncture that Ong attempted to strengthen his mandate and authority by pushing for the dissolution of the Council and calling for fresh polls.[239] However, the PAP Councillors were defeated, by 18 to 14, when the Council put the motion to a vote.[240]

And so, the polemical relations within the City Council persisted and continued into 1959, until March that year when things came to a head. When Ong uncovered questionable acts by PC Marcus, the City Council's Chief Administrative Officer, he brought the matter up to the Council's Finance and General-Purpose Committee for action. It was suggested that the case should be handed over to the CPIB. Marcus responded by insisting that the Committee had no power to charge him and he would not answer to their charges. Instead, Marcus accused the Mayor of "fault-finding with ulterior intent".[241] Meanwhile, the non-PAP Councillors, particularly those from the Singapore People's Alliance (SPA) objected to the Mayor's suggestion that the case should be turned over to the CPIB, and when the Mayor wanted to put it to a vote, the non-PAP Councillors opted not to participate.[242] There was really nothing the PAP Councillors could do to break the deadlock except to continue the verbal exchanges.[243] It was around this time that the PAP's "experiment" and effort to reform the government service from within was nearing its end. It was towards the end of March 1959 that the Ministry for Local Government started stripping the authority and responsibilities held by the City Council when it transferred some functions and powers of the Council to the Ministry. While the City Council was still responsible for the maintenance of essential municipal services, it had little legal means to discharge those duties.[244] Then the final blow came at the beginning of April 1959, when the Governor appointed yet another Commission of Inquiry. In this instance, it was to inquire into the workings of the City Council and its leadership. Once again, SHD Elias was appointed to the Chair of the Commission (Elias Commission, 1959) in search of corrupt practices. This time, it was a one-man Commission that was tasked to inquire into any possible misconduct of the Mayor's administration of the City Council. It was to report whether any irregularities or improprieties were involved in the appointment, dismissal and discipline of staff; whether the Mayor had interfered in duties of Council employees; whether he had also used Council properties and monies; and whether he was involved in the acceptance and rejection of tenders.[245]

The new Elias Commission first received evidence from the non-PAP Councillors.[246] Many twists and turns followed,[247] but even before the dust could settle, all PAP Councillors, including the Mayor, resigned *en masse* on 18 April 1959. Officially, they stepped down because the government had already stripped the Council of much of its authority and all the PAP Councillors had to vacate their seats in order to contest in the upcoming General Election.[248] The new Elias Commission would continue into May

1959, even after Elias himself withdrew from the Commission and another chairperson was appointed.[249]

Lee Kuan Yew's Reflections

The founding father of modern Singapore had said many things about the substance and soul of this nation. Before he became Prime Minister, Lee Kuan Yew had been sidestepped or shut down on many occasions when he attempted to register his thoughts in the Legislature on the real state of corruption in colonial Singapore. His conviction and beliefs regarding a clean Singapore could be summed up succinctly without going into a diatribe on the local government's shortcomings in dealing with corrupt practices or providing a lengthy discourse on his speeches. For Lee, the big picture of the times was the threat corruption posed to an emerging new nation. There were two distinct dangers on the eve of self-government: forces corrupting the political process of the nation and corrupt politicians becoming leaders of future Singapore.

In 1958, Lee shared his views at a University of Malaya forum: "As a negative force, [secret society] gangsters made a mockery of the democratic system." The threat to the whole body politic was real because the "bulk of the population was not prepared to stick their necks out to combat the menace… because of their self-preservation complex, the gangsters are prepared to intimidate and plunder the people." So, we have to fight on three fronts: sociological, economic and psychological. In order to tackle this problem, we need "honest political leadership as well as the determination and ability to see that the menace is not only stifled but completely eradicated".[250]

A year earlier, when Lee had still been trying to establish his case in the Legislative Assembly, he said, "However good the democratic system, if the dramatis personae consist of clowns, buffoons and nincompoops, it must fail." Lee expressed his greatest fear that "… in the next election, if we allow these types to win, then I say within five years you either knock them out completely and start a revolution before they do damage, or within five years the damage that they would have done would be of such a permanent nature that you would never get the people to believe in a democratic system."[251]

There was still a Long Road ahead and each step was just a beginning for the nation. Perhaps it was an even more difficult one for the CPIB at this time. Just as Singapore had started its journey to evolve from its colonial roots to become a sovereign nation, the Bureau, also, had to transcend its own colonial origins to become a national institution.

Endnotes

[1] *Straits Times* 6 May, 21 Jun, 14 Oct 1952. When the Colonial Secretary and Governor first revealed the existence of the new unit that was to replace the ACB, the public was not given any details. All the press could see was that the unit was operating from the High Court building and a sentry stood guard at the agency's main door, which had no name attached. They speculated that these "Special Investigators" had extensive powers to tackle senior civil servants who were corrupt. So they operated within a "hush, hush" environment — "cloak and dagger" stuff. Also see *Sunday Standard* 22 Nov 1953.

[2] This independence was stressed by Colonial Secretary Blythe soon after he announced the existence of the Bureau in October 1952. He emphasised that it was under Governor JF Nicoll and himself and had no connection with the Police or any other government department. See *Singapore Standard* 19 Oct 1952.

[3] *Straits Times* 27 Jan, 11 Feb 1953. Within a month of returning to the Labour Department, Middleton-Smith initiated legislative reforms to better the working conditions and wages of labourers in Singapore.

[4] It was never intended for Middleton-Smith to hold the post permanently. The Special Investigation Team was neither a police unit nor a government department. It was at best a "project team" or a composite "task force" where members still belonged to their departments of origin. Hence, when Middleton-Smith was appointed, or transited, to directorship of the new CPIB, he was essentially still in the Labour Department. Hence, he described himself as an "Acting Director". His role was simply to lay the foundation of the new agency. See File 001 CPIB Early Organisation: Memorandum, Acting Director, CPIB, to Colonial Secretary, 25 Oct 1952, CPIB CSO 00117/52. Statement of Progress.

[5] CPIB File 001 CPIB Early Organisation: New Anti-Corruption Organisation: Establishment and Estimates, Organisation and Leadership (Sep–Dec 1952 and 1953), Minutes by Mr Middleton-Smith, September 1952.

[6] CPIB File 001 CPIB Early Organisation: Meeting notes for 19 Feb 1953, Colonial Secretary with the Commissioner of Police, NG Morris, and the Director CPIB, Lyle, signed by WL Blythe, Colonial Secretary, 24 Feb 1953: CSO. Conf.0117/52/63.

[7] CPIB File 001 CPIB Early Organisation: Meeting notes, 19 Feb 1953, Report by CW Lyle, 19 Feb 1953.

[8] It should be noted that Commissioner Morris had also been a member of the Special Branch earlier in his career. See CPIB File 001 CPIB Early Organisation: Meeting notes for 19 Feb 1953, Report by CW Lyle, 19 Feb 1953.

[9] CPIB File 001 CPIB Early Organisation: Meeting notes for 19 Feb 1953, Report by CW Lyle, 19 Feb 1953.

[10] *Straits Times* 19 May 1956.

[11] After graduating from Oxford University, CW Lyle joined the Malayan Civil Service in 1935 and was appointed the Assistant Protector of Chinese (Chinese Protectorate) in Pahang. When the war started, he remained in Malaya and joined the Malayan Royal Naval Volunteer Reserve. When the Japanese invaded, Lyle was serving on board an anti-submarine vessel, the *Siang Wo*. On 13 February 1942, the ship was hit by Japanese warplanes and it was beached at Bangka Island. He became a prisoner of war and was interned in Sumatra. See Donald A Bertke, Gordon Smith & Don Kindell, *World War II Sea War, Vol 5: Air Raid Pearl Harbor. This is Not a Drill* (Bertke Publications, Illustrated edition, 2013), p.336. After the war, Lyle was appointed Secretariat for Chinese Affairs in Selangor and Johore. In 1950, he was appointed Deputy Commissioner for Labour in Singapore. In 1951, when he became Acting Commissioner for Labour, Middleton-Smith was appointed his Deputy. When Middleton-Smith left to head the Special Investigation Team assembled by the Colonial Secretary, Lyle was made the Secretary for Chinese Affairs. In January 1953, Lyle succeeded Middleton-Smith as the Director. He remained in this post till June 1954 before returning to the Labour Department to become its Commissioner once again. In 1955, he sat on several posts — the first being the Secretary of Internal Affairs, before his appointment as Registrar of Societies. In November 1955, he became the Acting Deputy Chief Secretary. Then in February 1956, he was made the Governor's Secretary and Clerk to the Council of Ministers. He fell ill within months and returned to England where he passed away on 16 May 1956 in London.

[12] *Singapore Free Press* 12 Jan 1953. Lyle said it with a slight difference the following day — "The public must get rid of the idea that giving and taking bribes is a part of everyday life." See *Straits Times* 13 Jan 1953.

[13] *Straits Times* 13 Jan 1953; *Singapore Free Press* 12 Jan 1953, 8 May 1953.

[14] *Straits Times* 24 Jan 1953.

[15] *Singapore Free Press* 8 May 1953. By May 1954, just before Lyle's tenure ended, he had taken 28 cases to Court and in that month, the Bureau had 67 cases still under investigation. See *Sunday Standard* 9 May 1954.

[16] *Malaya Tribune* 14 Oct 1949.

[17] *Singapore Standard* 11 Jul 1953.

[18] *Sunday Standard* 22 Nov 1953. Initially, when they learnt of the existence of the CPIB, they lamented that the Bureau had been too "low profile" as they seemed to be working secretly as an anti-corruption unit headed by government officers to catch government officers. They opined that such a unit should not be in the hands of officials. Non-officials, civilians, should be better suited for the job required. See *Singapore Standard* 22 Oct 1952.

[19] CPIB File 001 CPIB Early Organisation: Memorandum on the Work of CPIB 19 Sep 1953, by CW Lyle.

[20] CPIB Monthly Report, Mar 1953. The Bureau's inclusion of corrupt acts amongst commercial entities was already revealed in October 1952 by Colonial Secretary Blythe. See *Singapore Standard* 29 Oct 1952.

[21] This was one of the major initiatives mentioned in Middleton-Smith's September 1952 proposal for the Bureau. However, the proposal was also the very document he was using to apply for a budget for the unit.

[22] *Malaya Tribune* 12 May 1947; *Straits Times* 11 May 1949.

[23] *Singapore Free Press* 22 Jan 1953. Anti-corruption posters were displayed on STC buses and on walls across Town. See CPIB Monthly Reports, Jan to Mar 1953.

[24] *Sunday Standard* 18 Jan 1953.

[25] Governor Nicoll revealed that the government was not only interested in cases involving corruption in government housing but also in private housing as well. In January 1953, he appointed a committee to enquire into the high rental demanded by landlords in the city. He noted that no one had yet reported the matter to the CPIB. See *Singapore Standard* 27 Jan 1953.

[26] CPIB File 001 CPIB Early Organisation: Notes by Middleton-Smith: Interview with HE the Governor on 9/12/52.

[27] *Straits Times* 5 Jan 1954; *Singapore Standard* 5 Jan 1954.

[28] ASP Ng Leng Hock joined the police force in 1941. He joined the Criminal Investigation Department (CID) after the war and was promoted to Acting ASP around 1950 and then posted to the CPIB in 1953. In November 1953 he was sent to Scotland Yard for training. He was promoted ASP on 13 June 1956, then promoted to Superintendent a few years later. In 1960, he was made Commandant of Police Training School, and a year later, he was concurrently appointed Commandant of the Volunteer Special Constabulary (VSC) as well as the Commandant of the first Police Cadet Corp (later National Police Cadet Corp (NPCC)) with the first units formed at Siglap Secondary School and Serangoon Garden Government High School. In 1964, he became the Superintendent of Police A Division, before retiring in 1971. See *Straits Times* 13 Nov 1953, 13 Jun 1956, 9 Jul 1961, 25 Aug 1964, 1 Mar 1971; *Singapore Free Press* 3 Aug, 21 Dec 1961.

[29] Inspector Peter Tay Kim Leng became an inspector after the war and was posted to the Kandang Kerbau Police Station. He joined the CPIB in 1953. Tay remained with the CPIB till 1956. In 1957, he was sent to the United Kingdom for a police course at the Metropolitan Police Training School in London, which he passed in March 1958. In the early 1960s, he was promoted to the rank of ASP and posted to the Special Branch. See *Sunday Standard* 16 Sep 1951, 19 Oct 1957; *Singapore Free Press* 14 Mar 1958; *Straits Times* 14 Mar 1956, 21 Dec 1963.

[30] *Straits Times* 27 Nov 1953.

[31] Following a trial in late 1953, Tan Yook Suan was fined $2,000 and sentenced to six months'

rigorous imprisonment. See *Singapore Standard* 7 Jan 1954. However, when Tan appealed, on account of mistakes made during the trial, his conviction was reversed in mid-1954. See *Singapore Standard* 6 May 1954.

[32] *Straits Times* 4 Sep 1953.

[33] *Sunday Standard* 28 Jun 1953. RS Tufnell, Acting Controller of Customs, admitted that corruption in his department had been a real problem, but they had been working with the CPIB to handle the situation. He attributed the recent successes against corruption in the Customs to public information.

[34] *Straits Times* 13 Mar 1953.

[35] In 1953, the Bureau had given much attention to gambling and opium rackets. See *Sunday Standard* 22 Nov 1953.

[36] The pursuit of "bigger elements" following the CPIB's investigation was noted in Blythe's briefing to the press in October 1952. See *Singapore Standard* 29 Oct 1952. When asked about his handling of small cases and why the Bureau had yet to prosecute any cases by January 1953, he pointed out that following the small players may "lead to the principals of rackets". See *Singapore Standard* 14 Jan 1953.

[37] *Straits Times* 11 Mar 1953.

[38] CPIB Monthly Reports, Jan 1953.

[39] *Straits Times* 29 May 1952. The game "involved betting on six red and six black playing pieces in a game of Chinese chess. The red pieces were engraved with the Chinese characters — field marshal, prime minister, minister, chariot, horse and cannon, while the black pieces consisted of the characters general, scholar, elephant, chariot, horse and cannon." See Janice Loo, "Desperate Housewives: The Lure of *Chap Ji Kee*", in *BiblioAsia* Oct–Dec 2015, Vol 11, No. 3: 8–13. It is believed that the game was popular in the late nineteenth century amongst Chinese women of Singapore. The rich ones held private card parties and gambled high stakes. An attempt was made in 1896 to suppress this form of "entertainment". See GT Hare, "The Game of Chap-Ji-Ki", *Journal of the Straits Branch of the Royal Asiatic Society*, No. 31 (Jul 1898): 63-71, 48.

[40] CPIB Monthly Reports 1953.

[41] https://kajomag.com/the-history-of-illegal-gambling-and-chap-ji-kee-in-sarawak/.

[42] *Straits Times* 28 Jul 1953.

[43] *Singapore Standard* 30 Jul, 1 Sep 1953.

[44] *Singapore Free Press* 10 Nov 1953.

[45] *Straits Times* 10 Nov 1953.

[46] *Straits Times* 15 Nov 1953.

[47] *Singapore Standard* 22 Nov 1953.

[48] *Straits Times* 22 Nov 1953.

[49] As a case in point, a CID detective, Liu Soo Hoe, was caught taking $150 from Ng Khai Chun to halt an investigation into his activities. He was allegedly a Communist. Although it was uncertain what Ng had been doing specifically, the incident demonstrated just how easily corrupt officials could inadvertently aid insurgents to circumvent detection. See *Singapore Standard* 5 Jan 1954.

[50] CPIB Monthly Reports, Jan to Mar 1953. As early as October 1952, the Bureau had already received a significant volume of information regarding corrupt individuals and corruption in government departments. See *Indian Daily Mail* 29 Oct 1952.

[51] *Straits Times* 29 Jul 1953. And what of his $50? It was given to the Police Reward Fund.

[52] This method was spelt out by Director Lyle in 1953. See CPIB File 001 CPIB Early Organisation: Memorandum on the Work of CPIB 19 Sep 1953, by CW Lyle, Director CPIB.

[53] It is interesting to note that Corridon declared during a luncheon meeting with the Rotary Club in July 1968 that the CPIB had never used agent provocateur in corruption cases, and would never do so. See *Straits Times* 12 Jul 1968. In fact, towards the latter part of 1955, when Corridon was still Acting Director, the Bureau sent its Civilian Investigator, Chew Soon, as an agent provocateur to lay a trap that caught a counterfeiter of rupiah notes in Singapore. See *Singapore Standard* 22 Oct 1955.

[54] *Straits Times* 30 Aug 1953; *Singapore Standard* 28 Aug 1953.

[55] *Straits Times* 3 Sep 1953.

[56] *Singapore Standard* 29 Jan 1953.

[57] *Straits Times* 10 Dec 1953. In the original incident witnessed by Lyle, the conductor pocketed a 20 cents fare without issuing a ticket. See *Singapore Standard* 10 Dec 1953. The public had complained in January 1953 that the CPIB had not been doing its duty as STC conductors had returned to their old tricks of not issuing tickets after a short spell of being honest. See *Singapore Standard* 29 Jan 1953.

[58] Extracted from CPIB File 001 CPIB Early Organisation: Memorandum on the Work of CPIB 19 Sep 1953, by CW Lyle, Director CPIB.

[59] Lyle had revealed that the Bureau had already been working on a new legislation since early 1953 as the Bureau's powers had not been as extensive as the ACB's and the Federation's Police. *Singapore Standard* 30 May 1953.

[60] By November 1953, the Bureau had four police officers (two Chinese and two Europeans) and seven civilian investigators (six Chinese and one European). See *Sunday Standard* 22 Nov 1953.

[61] Colonial Secretary Blythe had made it public knowledge in October 1952 that disciplinary action within government departments would be one possible outcome of the Bureau's investigation, although it would not be the only course pursued. See *Singapore Standard* 29 Oct 1952.

[62] Lyle also revealed that the Bureau was working on a draft of a new Anti-Corruption Ordinance which was based on the Federation's Anti-Corruption Ordinance. See CPIB Monthly Reports, Jan to Mar 1953.

[63] *Singapore Standard* 31 Jan 1952.

[64] After leaving the CPIB, Lyle became Deputy Chief Secretary and then Singapore's Secretary for International Affairs. He passed away in London in May 1956. See *Straits Times* 20 May 1956.

[65] Blythe was succeeded by William Allmond Codrington Goode (Colonial Secretary, 1953–1955; Chief Secretary, 1955–1957), who also became the last Governor of Singapore from 1957–1959. Nicoll retired in 1955.

[66] Details in this section are mostly contained in the following file: CPIB File 001 CPIB Early Organisation: RB Corridon, Acting Director, CPIB, Correspondence with FK McNamara, Snr Asst Commissioner, CID HQ, Fed of Malaya, 28 Mar 1955, CPIB. 132/54, 13, paras 6–13.

[67] *Straits Times* 11 Aug 1948; *Singapore Free Press* 4 Jun 1954. In 1939, Corridon served in Army Intelligence where he remained (Intelligence Corp) till the end of war. In 1945, he was appointed Adjutant of the Motor Transport Staff, CAS Police Depot, Negapatam, India before being sent to Kuala Lumpur to serve in the Malayan Security Service (MSS) which was tasked to restore law and order in Singapore–Malaya. When the MSS morphed into two separate entities at the start of the Malayan Emergency, the Malayan and Singapore Special Branches were created on 1 August 1948. The MSS was absorbed into the respective police CID establishments as special branches. Corridon was therefore placed in Singapore's Special Branch, from where he was seconded to the Special Investigation Team from March 1952. ASP Corridon was awarded the Colonial Police Medal for Meritorious Service in January 1952. Corridon was conferred MBE (Member of the British Empire) in December 1952 months after CPIB was officially set up. See *Straits Times* 12 Jan, 5 Jun, 21 Dec 1952. In March 1964, after returning to helm the CPIB once more, he was invested the Pingat Jasa Gemilang (Meritorious Service Medal) by Yang di-Pertuan Negara, Tun Yusof Ishak.

[68] https://www.unithistories.com/officers/Army_officers_C02.html; Corridon would remain in charge until the end of 1955. He then returned to the Special Branch as Assistant Superintendent, where he was promoted Superintendent of Police within the Special Branch. In 1963, Corridon returned to the CPIB once more, this time as full director (after retiring from the Special Branch) and he remained at the Bureau's helm till 1968. In 1970, he returned home to the United Kingdom, moving to Addlestone, Surrey.

[69] CPIB File 001 CPIB Early Organisation: RB Corridon, Acting Director, CPIB, Correspondence with FK McNamara, Snr Asst Commissioner, CID HQ, Fed of Malaya, 28 Mar 1955, CPIB. 142/54, 13, paras 1–5. Corridon's reply to McNamara's (Federation) request for information (SR)35/10/1/1 — 16 Mar 1955.

[70] Corridon's reply to McNamara's letter dated (SR) 35/10/1/1 of 16 Mar 1955.

[71] Corridon joked that one of their civilian investigators wanted to do his rounds with a

Sten gun on one shoulder and a portable tape recorder on the other. He was undoubtedly overly enthusiastic.

[72] Following the April 1955 General Election which saw more elected representatives in the Legislative Assembly (following the recommendations of the Rendel Commission, 1953–1954), the position of the Colonial Secretary was renamed Chief Secretary. William Allmond Codrington Goode, who was Colonial Secretary at this time, became the new Chief Secretary.

[73] It should be remembered that the CPIB was started by the British Establishment. It was, after all, a colonial apparatus reporting to the colonial hierarchy in Singapore. There was no guarantee that the elected local government would retain the Bureau.

[74] At the point Lyle handed over directorship to Corridon in June 1954, Lyle declared "it still remains the independent body it has always been". Clearly, by Corridon's description of the Bureau in March 1955, the Bureau was already being identified more closely with the Police Establishment — a reality which he felt with discomfort. He was convinced that no policeman should be seconded to do the CPIB's work. It is important to note that Corridon did not object to police officers doing the job, but not as police officers. That is, they become CPIB officers and not seconded police officers.

[75] In October 1952, when Colonial Secretary WL Blythe announced the existence of the Bureau, he had already announced that a reward would be given for information received. See *Singapore Standard* 29 Oct 1952.

[76] *Straits Times* 4 Feb 1955.

[77] *Singapore Standard* 9 Feb 1955; *Straits Times* 9 Feb 1955.

[78] CPIB File 001, CPIB Early Organisation: New Anti-Corruption Organisation: Establishment and Estimates, Organisation and Leadership (Sep–Dec 1952 and 1953), Minutes by Mr Middleton-Smith.

[79] *Straits Times* 28 Aug 1954.

[80] As a case in point, in April 1954, just before Corridon became director, the Singapore Marine Police chanced upon a motor-sampan smuggling opium through the Kallang River. The value of the opium seized was $30,000. See *Straits Times* 9 Apr 1954.

[81] *Straits Times* 28 Aug 1954.

[82] *Straits Times* 28 Aug, 23 Sep 1954.

[83] *Straits Times* 10 Sep 1954. On one ship alone, the *Phillip Q*, $225,000 worth of opium had been seized by the "Preventive Branch" of the Customs (CPIB). See *Straits Times* 18 Aug 1954. Corridon had forged a close working relationship with the Burmese, exchanging information freely. This was the CPIB's first cross-border cooperation. See *Sunday Standard* 9 May 1954.

[84] *Straits Times* 23 Sep 1954.

[85] *Singapore Free Press* 5 Nov 1954.

[86] By mid-1954, the fear of government action and arrest forced big-time smugglers to abandon their old modus operandi of using chartered ships, and turned to seamen to land their contraband along the longer Singapore coastline in smaller consignments. Corridon attributed this change of pattern to the recent success of the Customs Department — more than $12,000,000 worth of opium had been seized by then; eight millionaires involved in opium smuggling were arrested in 1953, the result of the cooperation between the Customs and the CPIB. See *Sunday Standard* 29 Aug 1954; *Singapore Standard* 24 May 1954.

[87] *Straits Times* 25 Nov 1954. The Customs noted that the success of the "Preventive Bureau" (CPIB) in tackling opium trafficking led to the rise of opium prices. *Straits Times* 19 Oct 1954; *Sunday Standard* 29 Aug 1954; *Singapore Standard* 24 May 1955.

[88] *Singapore Free Press* 6 Oct 1954.

[89] *Straits Times* 19, 30 Oct 1954.

[90] The Bureau had already started using the threat of banishment in 1953 against the perpetrators of the opium smugglers of the Ponggol Opium Heist. See CPIB Monthly Reports, whole of 1953. The Bureau saw this as a useful tool to eradicate bribery. See *Singapore Standard* 24 May 1954.

[91] *Straits Times* 28 Aug 1954.

[92] RB Corridon, Oral Archives, National Archives of Singapore (NAS), The Public Service, Accession

Number 000044, Reel 11. This interview was conducted in 1980.

[93] *Malaya Tribune* 1 Aug 1950. In the 1949 municipal elections, a candidate, Cheah Kim Bee, was charged for corruption. She was subsequently acquitted and discharged. See *Straits Times* 26 Mar 1949. After Singapore was granted city status 1951, the municipality was renamed City Council. In the first City Council elections, allegations of corruption were again heard. See *Straits Times* 1 Dec 1950.

[94] *Sunday Tribune* 14 Mar 1948.

[95] *Malaya Tribune* 22 Aug 1950; *Straits Times* 8, 14, 21 Apr 1951; *Singapore Free Press* 31 Mar 1951; *Singapore Standard* 28 Mar 1951.

[96] *Straits Times* 27 Jul 1953.

[97] *Straits Times* 28 Jul 1953; *Singapore Standard* 28 Jul 1953. Lyle contended that the CPIB could do nothing about the matter without specific information.

[98] *Singapore Free Press* 21 May 1954

[99] *Straits Times* 10 Nov 1954.

[100] *Singapore Standard* 22 Jun 1954.

[101] Ordinance 26 of 1954, Singapore Legislative Assembly Elections Ordinance 12 November 1954. The Bill was published on 28 October 1954. See *Hansard, Singapore (Legislative Assembly Elections) Volume 531*: debated on Wednesday 27 October 1954, col. 279 — On the electoral register for Singapore; House of Commons Debates 27 October 1954, vol. 531, cc278-9W 278W. The first legislative assembly election was slated for early April 1955. Singapore's present Parliamentary Elections Act (Chapter 218) evolved from Ordinance 26 of 1954.

Interestingly, Director Lyle had said in May 1954 that a new legislation was being prepared to give the CPIB more powers to look into the bank accounts of individuals (he must have meant politicians). No new anti-corruption legislation was created in that year. It is likely that the prevention of corruption measures he alluded to finally materialised in the provisions encapsulated within the Singapore 1954 Legislative Assembly Elections Ordinance. See *Singapore Free Press* 3 May 1954.

[102] *Straits Times* 24, 25 Feb 1954; *Singapore Standard* 26 Feb 1955.

[103] *Straits Times* 11 Mar 1955. Under Section 51 of 1954 Elections Ordinance, people convicted of corruption or illegal practices cannot participate in the April 1955 Election.

[104] CPIB File 001 CPIB Early Organisation: RB Corridon, Acting Director, CPIB, Correspondence with FK McNamara, Snr Asst Commissioner, CID HQ, Fed of Malaya, 28 Mar 1955, letter dated (SR) 35/10/1/1 of 16 Mar 1955, CPIB. 132/54, 13, paras 1–5. *Straits Times* 25 Feb 1955; *Singapore Free Press* 24, 25 Mar 1955.

[105] *Straits Times* 25 Feb 1955.

[106] *Straits Times* 24 Feb 1955.

[107] *Straits Times* 31 Mar 1955.

[108] *Straits Times* 24, 25 Mar 1955.

[109] *Straits Times* 29 Mar, 26 Jun, 3 Jul 1955.

[110] *Sunday Standard* 6 Mar 1955; *Straits Times* 18 Mar 1955. Pirate taxis, or non-licensed taxis, were common in the day. They usually operated by pooling multiple passengers who were heading in the same direction. This allowed each person to pay less in fares. They were essentially private hire public transport which were illegal in those days.

[111] *Singapore Standard* 6 Mar 1955.

[112] *Singapore Free Press* 11 Mar 1955. Corridon was more interested in the case of the hire cars or taxis booked to take voters to the polls. He reminded the public to call the CPIB on 5110 or 25550 or write to PO Box 2222.

[113] *Straits Times* 27 Feb 1955.

[114] *Straits Times* 25 Feb 1955; *Singapore Free Press* 24, 25 Mar 1955.

[115] *Straits Times* 26 Feb 1955. In George Thomson's communication with the public on 24 February 1954, he actually said call 5110 (CPIB) or write to PO Box 5000 (Police). See *Straits Times* 24, 25 Feb 1954; *Singapore Standard* 26 Feb 1955. It was soon after the elections that several policemen received commendations from Morris for their work on corruption cases, including Senior Inspector J Payne and Detective Inspector George Prior. *Straits Times* 17 Jul 1955. While there is

no public information on what cases Payne had worked on, Prior (Singapore Harbour Board Police) was involved in the case of the corruption case involving Deputy Superintendent of the Singapore Harbour Police Ray William Walters and a Chinese who offered to bribe him with a total of $2,200 in 1953. Prior was also involved in taking down opium smugglers who were bringing the drugs into Singapore on board arriving ships.

[116] *Straits Times* 24 Feb 1954.

[117] *Straits Times* 27 Jan 1955.

[118] *Straits Times* 13 Nov 1955.

[119] *Straits Times* 21 Oct, 13 Nov 1955.

[120] *Straits Times* 13 Nov 1955.

[121] *Straits Times* 13, 14 Nov 1955. In June 1955, just months before the Great STC Strike, an STC employee was charged in Court for CBT of ten cents. Two hundred STC drivers and conductors turned up to support their comrade. See *Sunday Standard* 12 Jun 1955.

[122] *Straits Times* 13 Nov 1955.

[123] *Straits Times* 6 Dec 1955.

[124] Discussed in the next section.

[125] John Le Cain was also the manager of the Police Cricket Team. The entire team had been competing in Hong Kong in the first half of 1958. Hickman was Acting Director in his absence.

[126] Rajaratnam was appointed Registrar of Citizenship in April 1960. See *Singapore Free Press* 29 Dec 1961.

[127] *Singapore Free Press* 15 Dec 1960.

[128] *Straits Times* 16 Apr 1962.

[129] *Straits Times* 6 Jan 1963. Khong was reappointed Director of CPIB on 1 December 1962. On 1 Jan 1961, ASP Khong was promoted to DSP. See *Straits Times* 1 Jan 1961. In April 1963, DSP Khong was promoted to Superintendent of Police. See *Straits Times* 7 Apr, 11 Sep 1963.

[130] *Straits Times* 11 Sep 1963.

[131] *Singapore Standard* 10 Dec 1955.

[132] After World War II, the Straits Settlements (Singapore) Association was succeeded by the Singapore Association. See https://eresources.nlb.gov.sg/infopedia/articles/SIP_1174_2006-08-31.html.

[133] *Singapore Free Press* 29 May 1953.

[134] *Singapore Standard* 20 Dec 1957.

[135] *Singapore Standard* 26 May 1958.

[136] CPIB File 001 Director CPIB, Sardar Singh to Senior Attorney-General, 30 Jul 1959, p.5.

[137] CPIB File 001 Director CPIB, Deputy Chief Secretary to Commissioner of Police, 1 Mar 1957, p.6.

[138] CPIB File 001 Director CPIB, Deputy Chief Secretary to Commissioner of Police, 1 Mar 1957, p.6.

[139] CPIB File 001 Director CPIB, Deputy Chief Secretary to Commissioner of Police, 1 Mar 1957, copy to CPIB Director, 30 Jul 1959, p.6.

[140] *Straits Times* 18 Dec 1957.

[141] The government had warned of the political infiltration by secret society gangsters as early as January 1956. A year later, former Colonial Secretary, BL Blythe, highlighted the problem directly with local political parties. See *Straits Times* 16 Jan 1956, 25 Jan 1957.

[142] *Sunday Standard* 14 Aug 1955.

[143] Among some of the cases the Bureau handled in the first half of 1956 were persons using counterfeit Indonesian Rupiah notes to trade in Singapore. See *Singapore Standard* 27 April 1956; *Singapore Standard* 26 Apr 1956; There were also cases of police officers and inspectors taking *kopi* money to settle traffic and other offences. See *Singapore Standard* 14 Mar, 6 May, 13 Jul, 21 Nov 1956; *Straits Times* 14 Mar 1956; *Sunday Standard* 6 May 1956. As for the big-money smuggling activities which Corridon tackled during his tenure, mainly involving gold and opium, these would be overtaken by liquor and tobacco as the most trafficked contrabands. By this time, as a result of the Customs and the CPIB's enforcement measures, there were fewer instances of large-scale illegal opium smuggling-importing into Singapore. See *Singapore Standard* 3 Dec 1956. In fact, by late 1957, it was said that most of the "opium kings" had left Singapore for Siam, in part

due to Operation Dagger in 1956–1957 which dealt a severe blow to the secret society–corrupt police nexus that protected and perpetuated this crime. See *Straits Times* 11 Sep 1957; *Straits Budget* 18 Sep 1957.

[144] Following a triple stabbing incident at a bar at Upper Pickering Street in early June 1956, the Police detained a man at Cross Street, which was then famed for being a *huey*-controlled area. He was walking publicly with a knife in his hand and had three henchmen by his side. The brawl had involved 20 men who fought with knives, bottles and chairs. The Police feared that the incident would develop into a full-scale war between two rival *hueys*. See *Straits Times* 10 Jun 1956.

[145] *Straits Times* 18 Jul 1956. By 19 July, 339 had been arrested. *Straits Times* 20 Jul 1956.

[146] *Straits Times* 2 Aug 1956.

[147] *Straits Times* 5, 19 Aug 1956. The Customs Department revealed that the new Merdeka Bridge and Nicoll Drive had helped in the anti-smuggling war: the bridge and coastal road had cut off coastal areas used by smugglers to land contraband. Smugglers using the waterfront in the area had been greatly affected. Continuous checks by the Customs had also discouraged financiers of illegal opium imports because they had to seriously consider the risk they were undertaking. Police roadblocks and street screening during Operation Dagger had also resulted in contraband consignments being seized and had hindered opium from being moved from street to street. By August 1956, the Police had already investigated 900 tattooed men under Operation Dagger. See *Straits Times* 31 Aug 1956.

[148] *Straits Times* 17 Oct 1956. Gangs flourished when they intimidated and collected protection money from small shopkeepers. Operation Dagger affected this enterprise. The results were clear: in June 1956, 731 serious crimes were reported. In July, this had fallen to 660. By August, it was 610, and September, it fell further to 582. See *Straits Times* 15 Feb 1957. Out of the 12,439 cases the Police handled in 1956, 2,413 (20%) cases involved secret societies. In that year, 5,382 gangsters were arrested, most of them during Operation Dagger. See *Straits Times* 21 Mar, 2 Aug 1957.

[149] *Singapore Free Press* 20 Mar 1957; *Straits Times* 20 Mar 1957.

[150] *Singapore Free Press* 15 Jul 1957.

[151] *Singapore Standard* 7 Oct 1957; *Singapore Free Press* 12 Nov 1957; *Straits Times* 13 Nov 1957.

[152] *Straits Times* 10, 11, 13 Jun 1957. In mid-June 1957, the Police had detained 170 Secret Society members in the Cairnhill and Tanjong Pagar districts, the two wards involved in the 29 June 1957 by-election.

[153] *Singapore Standard* 28 Aug 1956.

[154] *Singapore Standard* 25, 28 Aug 1956.

[155] *Singapore Standard* 20 Oct 1957.

[156] *Straits Times* 31 Aug 1956.

[157] *Sunday Standard* 27 Oct 1957.

[158] RB Corridon, Oral Archives, NAS, The Public Service, Accession Number 000044. NAS interview, 1980.

[159] RB Corridon, Oral Archives, NAS, The Public Service, Accession Number 000044, Reel 13. In Colonial Secretary Blythe's description of the Bureau's work in October 1952, he had revealed that the CPIB had already uncovered a "great brotherhood of corruption". Presumably, this would be the network of corrupt policemen that Corridon noted in this interview. See *Indian Daily Mail* 29 Oct 1952.

[160] RB Corridon, Oral Archives, NAS, The Public Service, Accession Number 000044, Reel 11.

[161] *Singapore Standard* 3 Feb 1959.

[162] A line by Jonathan Rauch, quoted in an article by Ilya Somin, "Opinion: Why politicians lie", *Washington Post* 25 Oct 2016.

[163] *Singapore Standard* 2 Nov 1955.

[164] *Singapore Standard* 13 Jul 1956; *Straits Times* 29 Sep 1956.

[165] *Straits Times* 29 Sep 1956; *Straits Budget* 4 Oct 1956.

[166] The "Commission of Inquiry into Bribery and Corruption" proposed by the Labour Front did not materialise, but there was still need for one in early 1957. In March 1957, Lim Cher Keng, Democratic Party Assemblyman for Changi,

sponsored a motion at the 24 April Assembly session for the appointment of a commission to eradicate corruption in public services. See *Singapore Free Press* 30 Mar 1957; *Straits Times* 29 Mar 1957. David Marshall, who was now in the Workers' Party and no more in the Labour Front, also made a similar call in the Assembly. However, on 24 April, the Chief Minister Lim Yew Hock announced the creation of a three-men corruption commission in the Assembly before Marshall's and Lim Cher Keng's motions could be debated. See *Straits Times* 25 Apr 1957; *Straits Budget* 2 May 1957.

[167] *Straits Times* 19 Sep, 21 Nov 1957; *Singapore Standard* 19 Sep 1957.

[168] *Straits Times* 19 Nov 1957.

[169] *Straits Times* 11 Nov 1957; *Singapore Standard* 11 Nov 1957. The condition of hawkers, in particular, had been very bad. Singapore had yet to industrialise in the 1950s and therefore there were more people than there was work available. The post-war baby boom also exacerbated the employment situation. In this context, hawking became the best option for most families who found it hard to secure jobs. In 1953 alone, there were 25,000 hawkers in the streets. Every month, 3,000 of them would be brought to Court for street obstruction or hawking without a licence. And they were the very class of people whom corrupt officials often targeted for *kopi* money or offered bribes so that officers might close an eye to their infringements. See *Singapore Standard* 25 Aug 1953.

[170] *Straits Times* 18 Dec 1957.

[171] *Singapore Standard* 23 Apr 1958.

[172] *Singapore Standard* 25 Apr 1958.

[173] *Singapore Standard* 14 Sep 1958; *Straits Times* 15 Sep 1958.

[174] *Straits Times* 17, 19 Jul, 23 Oct, 6 Nov, 11 Dec 1955.

[175] *Straits Times* 1, 31 Dec 1955.

[176] *Straits Times* 16 Oct 1955.

[177] *Straits Times* 24 Jun 1956

[178] *Straits Times* 25 Jun, 4 Nov 1956; *Singapore Standard* 28 Feb 1956.

[179] The Complaints Bureau is discussed in greater detail later in this chapter in the section on the 1958 City Council.

[180] *Singapore Standard* 29 Mar 1957.

[181] Commission appointed in May 1957, under the provisions of the Inquiry Commissions Ordinance (Cap. 52).

[182] Commission's terms of reference, GN No. S 1324/1957 — Commission 1957, dated 28 May 1957 — https://www.global-regulation.com/law/singapore/146333/commission.html.

[183] *Straits Times* 11 Aug 1957.

[184] *Straits Times* 12, 13 Jun, 5 Jul, 2, 3 Aug 1957. The case of the delimitation of taxis in the city first surfaced in 1956. A city councillor allegedly discovered how taxi owners paid $2,000 each as a gift to pressure city officials to abolish the ceiling on number of licensed taxis permissible in Town. See *Straits Times* 1 Nov 1956. Detailed in Public Notice, Commission of Inquiry, *Straits Times* 13 Jun 1957.

[185] *Singapore Standard* 6, 11 Jul 1957; Public Notice, Commission of Inquiry, *Straits Times* 13 Jun 1957.

[186] *Straits Times* 8, 13 Nov 1957.

[187] The Commission found no proof of corruption in the City Council's dealings (in the three cases), despite multiple allegations by city councillors and assemblymen. The Commissioner also did not offer recommendations to combat corruption. From the beginning, Justice Chua found the public's response to his call for information disappointing, even after public broadcast. See *Straits Times* 13 Nov 1957.

[188] *Straits Times* 6 Jul 1957.

[189] From the start of the inquiry, bankrupt government employees would declare their bankruptcy before Justice Chua. The total debts of 10 government officers who declared themselves bankrupt in mid-August 1957 was $34,298, the smallest individual debt being $696, while the highest was $6,748. See *Straits Times* 17 Aug 1957. Up till this point, the Commission found that bankrupt public servants had liabilities that amounted to $71,255.50 See *Singapore Standard* 24 Aug 1957; *Straits Times* 17 Aug 1957. In late

September 1957, there were 20 bankrupt public servants whose total liabilities stood at $58,000. See *Straits Times* 21 Sep 1957.

[190] In the 1950s, the government had already issued two general orders against indebtedness amongst government officers. The cause of this problem, according to a committee of government and staff representatives, was "not poverty but extravagance — gambling and living above means". Hence the two orders: public servants cannot gamble at their workplace, and they could not place bets using office phones. All public servants also had to sign a declaration every three months to state that they were free of debt. It was recognised that indebtedness was an opening to corruption. See *Straits Times* 9 Jul 1957. Yet, numerous public servants made their way to Justice Chua's Commission to declare bankruptcy during the length of his proceedings — certainly hoping their admission before the Justice would save them from any accusation of making false declarations in the office. In this instance, not only was policy and practice essentially not synonymous, it was literally incongruous.

[191] Lee Kuan Yew resigned his seat on 26 April 1957.

[192] *Singapore Free Press* 16 Apr 1958; *Straits Times* 16 Apr 1958.

[193] *Singapore Standard* 19 Oct 1957; *Straits Times* 19 Oct 1957.

[194] *Straits Times* 4 Sep 1957.

[195] *Straits Times* 13 Sep 1957.

[196] *Singapore Standard* 16 Oct 1957, 10 Apr 1958.

[197] *Singapore Standard* 4 Oct 1957; *Straits Times* 16 Apr 1958. Lee Kuan Yew testified at the Commission on 29 October 1957. See *Straits Times* 29 Oct 1957.

[198] MB Brash, a member of the Liberal Socialist Party, testified that secret societies waited at polling centres. He declared the secret societies as being the biggest menace to the elections. Although the secret societies took payments before the elections, but they continued taking after elections. Payments did not stop, as from time to time, they would demand for more. There were also some voters who took money from "promoters of all candidates" and then placed a cross on all of them; Goh Chew Chua, PAP Assemblyman, said that many told him of people buying votes at $5 per vote. However, he did not report the matter to the Police, or to the CPIB, because he had no proof and had not witnessed this personally. Also, Chinese voters who took the money would not admit to it to the authorities. Goh also claimed that Koh Choon Hong, a candidate of the Tanjong Pagar by-election, had used a "bad woman" (of ill repute) to canvass votes for him. Commissioners also heard from Lim Choon Mong, leader of the Liberal Socialist Party, that "gangsters" wearing "Labour Front symbols" had intimidated voters at Keok Street to prevent them from coming out to vote in the Cairnhill by-election. He also claimed that students led by girls, all wearing PAP insignia, had gone house to house along Banda Street to solicit votes by using veiled threats. Lim also claimed that a member of his party caught a boy pulling down posters put up by the party. The boy confessed that he had been paid to do so. However, Lim did not report the matter to the Police or the CPIB. Lee Kuan Yew told the Commission that the Liberal Socialist Party candidate for Tanjong Pagar, Chong Wee Ling, offered voters $5 to $7 for a vote. However, he told the Commission that he did not make a police report. See *Singapore Standard* 18, 30 Oct, 13 Nov 1957, 4 Jan 1958; *Straits Times* 18 Oct, 13 Nov 1957.

[199] *Singapore Standard* 19 Oct 1957; *Straits Times* 19 Oct 1957.

[200] *Straits Times* 19 Oct 1957. Tan claimed that the boy's parents pleaded with him, so he did not make a police report.

[201] *Singapore Free Press* 16 Apr 1958.

[202] *Straits Times* 17, 18 Apr 1958; *Singapore Standard* 17 Jul 1958. Lee reminded people that it had been the PAP who first called for the probe. William Tan had also learnt for the first time in the report that some of his friends were secret society members.

[203] *Singapore Standard* 18 Apr 1958.

[204] Up till early 1957, most politicians, including Lee, had taken a different position on the secret societies' presence in local politics. In January 1957, former Colonial Secretary BL Blythe informed Singapore's politicians that secret society bosses were courting them, the future

leaders of Singapore, in the hope they would make it legal for them to function again in the future. In return, the secret societies offered their support for politicians. David Marshall, at this time, declared that there was no evidence. Lee opined that if Blythe had evidence, he could reveal it and then have an official commission to probe the matter. See *Straits Times* 25 Jan 1957. By mid-1957, soon after the Justice Chua Commission had been appointed, Lee questioned the Commission's ability to get people to come forward with information on corrupt practices of officials. He jested that the Commission could get the secret society bosses to cooperate. Clearly, Lee was aware the secret societies had been involved in local politics. See *Straits Times* 19 Jul 1957. By October 1957, in his testimony during the Elias Commission, Lee himself raised the issue of secret societies being involved in the by-election. Lee believed that the political parties which had been less organised for the by-election might have turned to secret societies for help; they put up posters for candidates that hired them and tore down posters of others, and intimidated campaign workers of other parties. See *Straits Times* 30 Oct 1957.

[205] *Straits Times* 17 Jul 1958. Interestingly, even though Lee had withdrawn his motion, the *Singapore Standard*, which could not be more different from the "European-owned *Straits Times*", declared that the Assembly had rejected his motion. Perhaps the way in which the government had sidestepped Lee's attempt to seek redress through the legislature, forcing him to withdraw his motion was, in reality, rejection of Lee's motion by those in power — the Colonial Establishment. See *Singapore Standard* 17 Jul 1958.

[206] Elections canvassing was prohibited on polling day, starting at midnight before polling day; it was an offence to "borrow or hire motor vehicles to convey people to polling stations"; offering food, drinks or any other treats during campaigning was forbidden; it was illegal to bribe to influence voting, or "to bribe a person to stay away from voting". The fine for breaking any of these laws was $1,000. The only recommendations not adopted were making voting compulsory and making polling day a holiday. See *Singapore Standard* 16, 23 Jul 1958; *Straits Times* 24 Jul 1958.

[207] The Elias Commission's report noted that during the Tanjong Pagar by-election, Ho Beh Swee, a PAP committee member, had supplied food to the Eng Hiong secret society of the 108 group to get them to put up posters for the PAP. He was also accused of having 14 secret society members acting as his stewards at his elections rally on 16 June 1957. However, Ho had already withdrawn from the elections. Also, the witnesses were police officers, so, Lee Kuan Yew opined, their testimony should not be taken in secret as they should not have to fear being identified as witnesses. The report also claimed that Soh Ghee Soon, who was returned to Cairnhill, had secret society gangsters at his rally at Tank Road on 13 and 24 June 1957. But he had not had a rally at Tank Road on that day. See *Singapore Standard* 17 Jul 1958.

[208] The last City Council elections held before the 1957 polls took place in 1953. From 1949 to 1957, the Municipal Commission, which then became the City Council following Singapore attaining city status from September 1951, was composed of 27 elected and appointed members; 18 elected representatives from six wards (three seats each) and nine members appointed by the British colonial government. As the PAP was only founded in 1954, the first opportunity to participate in the City Council's poll was in 1957.

[209] The PAP and UMNO held 13 and two seats, respectively. Although the alliance was still two seats short of a simple majority in the 32-seat Council, the opposition was hopelessly divided at this point. This presented the PAP the opportunity to appoint Ong Eng Guan as the first Mayor in Singapore. The other members of the Council included elected representatives from the Labour Front, Workers' Party, Liberal Socialist Party, UMNO and two independent candidates.

[210] The PAP won only four seats (after an independent candidate joined the PAP) of the 25 seats available for contest in the 1955 Legislative Assembly. There were also seven appointed officials in the 32-member Assembly. Essentially, the PAP was an opposition party in this Assembly.

[211] *The Straits Budget* 22 Jan 1958.

[212] *The Straits Budget* 15, 22 Jan 1958. The English press demonised Ong, portraying his efficiency

drive as the Mayor who was sharpening his "axe for City staff", and the "PAP-controlled Singapore City Council" retrenching "redundant" employees "to cut down expenditure and raise efficiency."

[213] *The Straits Budget* 26 Feb 1958. In May 1957, the government appointed a Commission of Inquiry (Justice Chua Commission) to look into allegations of corruption within the City Council.

[214] *Straits Times* 10 Jan 1958.

[215] *Singapore Standard* 8 Apr 1958.

[216] *Singapore Standard* 12 Jun 1958.

[217] *Singapore Standard* 19 Jun 1958.

[218] *Singapore Standard* 30 Aug, 16 Oct 1958; *Straits Budget* 10 Sep 1958.

[219] *Straits Times* 17 Oct 1958.

[220] *Singapore Standard* 22 May 1959.

[221] *Straits Times* 22 Feb 1958. The Council was not fully autonomous. It was under the Minister for Local Government.

[222] *Straits Times* 1 Mar 1958. The non-PAP Councillors agreed that seniority had been the basis of promotion in the past, and during the election, all parties had supported ending "the maladministration of the past 10 years". However, they pointed out that the PAP alone could not decide on the measure of honesty.

[223] *Singapore Free Press* 25 Mar 1958.

[224] Ong revealed this during a session with the Southeast Asia Foreign Correspondents' Association. He said that he did not see how this would bring him into conflict with his duties as Mayor. See *Straits Times* 23 Jan 1958.

[225] Opposition Councillors opposed Ong's sessions with the people. They reminded him that meeting the people was not Council's work. So, if he wanted more staff to help run the sessions, they insisted that he should do it on his own money. See *The Straits Budget* 23 Apr 1958; *Straits Times* 14 Apr 1958. As Mayor, Ong even held "meet-the-people sessions", and he spoke of the need to create a governing system which was more suited to "Asian conditions". See *Straits Times* 10 Nov 1958.

[226] *Straits Times* 12 Jan 1958.

[227] One interesting fraud incident the Public Inquiries and Complaints Bureau handled itself was the case of a man who posed as a City Council employee to trick people into paying him their electricity, water and gas bills. The victims complained to the Bureau. See *Singapore Free Press* 3 Oct 1958.

[228] *The Straits Budget* 23 Apr 1958; *Straits Times* 14 Apr 1958.

[229] *Singapore Standard* 3 Jun 1958.

[230] *Straits Times* 15 Jan 1958.

[231] *Singapore Standard* 12 Jun 1958.

[232] *Singapore Standard* 3 Jun 1958.

[233] Corruption in the Department of the Registry of Vehicles had been so prevalent that almost all Councillors, regardless of political affiliation, had agreed that it must be resolutely tackled. In fact, the city councillors felt that the department itself had to be reorganised to achieve this end. And they believed that a "right man from outside" should be appointed as the new Registrar, and if possible, this person should be a university graduate. See *Singapore Standard* 20 May 1958. It is interesting that all the Councillors did not think that this logic should apply to all City Council departments.

[234] *Singapore Free Press* 17 Jun 1958. The opposition councillors would continue to object to the creation of the Bureau all through the term of the Council. See *Straits Times* 18 Nov 1958.

[235] *Singapore Standard* 23 Aug 1958. From this point, it was the PSC that appointed the new department's staff. Loh Pui Kay, who had been manning the Complaints Bureau since the beginning of 1958, was made the Director and Koh Ah Bah, who had been the clerk in the City's Architect and Building Surveyor's Office, was appointed Assistant Director of the new Bureau. See *Singapore Standard* 9 Sep 1958. The Bureau opened daily from 9.00am to 4.30pm without a lunch break. See *Straits Times* 20 Oct 1958.

[236] *Straits Times* 29 Nov 1958.

[237] *Straits Times* 1 Nov 1958, 1 Jan 1959.

[238] *Straits Times* 18 Nov 1958.

[239] *The Straits Budget* 26 Nov 1958. While fresh polls would have helped the opposition majority in the Council to resolve the continuous impasse they faced with the PAP Councillors, they might have been fearful that fresh polls may actually strengthen the PAP's hands instead. It was only in July 1958 that the PAP won the Kallang ward of City Council by-election. The seat was vacated by the Workers' Party Councillor. All political parties had considered the Kallang by-election, the last poll before the landmark 1959 General Election, as the watershed poll which would indicate in which direction the future electorate would be leaning. All political parties considered the Kallang by-election as the first skirmish before the impending General Election. See *Straits Times* 23 Jul 1958. The PAP won this by-election. Therefore, agreeing to a fresh poll for the whole Council would have been an unmitigated risk for the opposition Councillors. See *Straits Times* 27 Jul 1958.

[240] *The Straits Budget* 26 Nov 1958; *Straits Times* 20 Nov 1958.

[241] *Singapore Standard* 26 Mar 1959.

[242] *Singapore Standard* 26 Mar 1959.

[243] The Marcus affair was brought up during the proceedings of the Commission appointed by the Governor in April 1959 to inquire into the affairs of the City Council. Lee Kuan Yew acted as counsel for Ong Eng Guan during this inquiry, while Marcus' counsel was LAJ Smith. See *Singapore Standard* 22 May 1959.

[244] *Singapore Standard* 1 Apr 1959.

[245] *Singapore Standard* 3 Apr 1959; *Straits Times* 29 Apr 1959.

[246] *Singapore Standard* 4 Apr 1959.

[247] *Singapore Standard* 14 Apr 1959; *The Straits Budget* 15 Apr 1959; *Straits Times* 8, 11, 18, 22, 23, 28 Apr 1959; *Singapore Free Press* 10 Apr 1959.

[248] *The Straits Budget* 15 Apr 1959; *Singapore Standard* 11 Apr 1959.

[249] *Straits Times* 29, 30 Apr 1959; *Singapore Standard* 29, 30 Apr 1959. *Singapore Standard* 30 Apr 1959.

[250] *Singapore Standard* 28 Aug 1958. The Director of Information Services, GG Thomson, concurred, as he opined: "the real antidote to gangsterism is the development of a healthy civic consciousness among the citizens," there was a need to build up "some civic enthusiasm and courage…. Gangsters threat to politics presented a major challenge on the broad front of self-government".

[251] *Straits Times* 19 Jul 1957; *Hansard, Singapore (Legislative Assembly Debates)* 18 Jul 1957.

Part Four

Nation-Building Journey
1959–1989

Attainment of full internal self-government on 3 June 1959 marked the birth of the Singapore nation, although the British continued to control all external affairs of the island, namely foreign affairs and defence. It was from this point that the Singapore colony became a self-governing democratic state which had a fully elected legislature, with its own Prime Minister (PM), Cabinet, Constitution, state flag, National Anthem[1] and most importantly, a Head of State.[2] This political and constitutional milestone fundamentally transformed the status of all state institutions and agencies of Singapore. Be it the police, healthcare, postal, education, social, housing or any other public and state apparatus, all government bodies had become "national" instead of colonial institutions, including the CPIB. The maintenance of law and order and basic services was no longer solely for the purpose of their stated functions. From the time of self-rule, all government institutions had become an extension of the state's, or ruling party's goal, endeavour and aspiration to build a nation. One reason the people of the island gave the mandate to the People's Action Party (PAP) in the 1959 General Election was precisely because the Party espoused their hope for self-determination.[3] So the nation-building enterprise commenced. The success of this endeavour was dependent on the ability of the island's pioneering leaders to create and accentuate a sense of common purpose and identity; a national identity, to shape the mindset of the citizenry that Singapore was not only their home, but also their homeland. This noble goal, however, required the people to want to change, and for the leaders to have the political will to implement and follow through policies, in particular those that were promulgated to change the culture of corrupt practices among the local populace. The socio-political conditions for this transformation, however, were not present during British times.[4] This was the reason that no fundamental changes to better the lives of the people of the island, especially in the area of corruption, could be successfully enacted during the colonial period.

The new Government of Singapore was under no illusion that their nation-building enterprise was going to be easy and quick; the journey towards nationhood could only be achieved in the long haul, and there was no certainty of success in this endeavour. In this light, corruption in society constituted an insurmountable obstacle to any effort to forge a community spirit and shared ethos, the very building blocks that were needed to build a nation out of a multicultural society. As such, the PAP commenced governance by starting the process of "cleaning up" Singapore. Interestingly, the PAP's stance on a corruption-free government and society was first tested during the Party's tenure in the City Council. In retrospect, Mayor Ong Eng Guan's "Keep Your City Clean Campaign" in 1958,[5] when he led a couple of thousands of City Hall employees to sweep clean the streets of Singapore, was more than a political exercise and demonstration of leadership and will; it was also the PAP's metaphoric statement on its intent to forge a nation rid of corruption, if it came into power. And when the Party did come into power, the new Minister for Culture, Sinnathamby Rajaratnam, enunciated just how the soul of this new nation was pivoted on a clean society. This was symbolised in our national flag: "The white colour on the state flag was to serve as a constant reminder to the people to guard against such corruption and other anti-social elements."[6]

The work of cleaning up corruption in Singapore started almost immediately after the PAP came into power. While Lee Kuan Yew slashed excessive allowances of senior government officers,[7] he also dismissed and suspended dozens of corrupt officials within the City Council.[8] Then the police force was reorganised, corrupt officers removed and the CPIB itself underwent significant manpower and structural changes going into the 1960s. The cleaning up of the country's civil and statutory bodies was a necessary first step if the nation-building aspiration was to succeed.

Chapter Sixteen

Beginning with the Cleaning Up

The Prelude

Several major corruption scandals exposed just before the 30 May 1959 General Election that brought the People's Action Party (PAP) to power had given the contesting parties an ominous preview of what might await the people of Singapore if the wrong party formed the next government. The most serious of these was the corruption scandal surrounding Chew Swee Kee, the Singapore People's Alliance's (SPA)[9] Education Minister. The PAP had come to know in September 1958 that the Minister had $500,000 deposited in the First National City Bank of New York under his personal name. Initially, neither the Minister nor the Government provided an explanation for the source or purpose of the money. This fuelled speculation of corruption, foreign aid or intervention in local politics and more. The government also did not investigate it even as a matter of tax evasion cast a cloud over the whole affair. In March 1959, under pressure, Chew resigned as Minister as well as from his seat in the Legislative Assembly and his Party. The PAP made the point that his resignation only gave credence to the allegation of foreign interference and did not clear the air surrounding the matter.[10] In fact, soon after Chew stepped down, the truth of the matter, and much more, came to light. Based on evidence from bank account transactions,[11] Chew had received $300,000 in 1957. It was believed that the Labour Front (that joined the SPA Coalition in 1958) had used this money to fund its activities during the 1957 City Council elections. The $500,000 that Chew deposited in his account in 1958 was another sum that the SPA used in that year's City Council polls. The money was a "gift" from a foreign country. It was also brought to light that some part of the money was used to purchase private properties for third parties and to invest in tin mines in Malaysia. Lee Kuan Yew insisted that Chew's resignation was really an admission of guilt.[12]

The whole affair had become politically toxic and by this time, even the SPA assemblymen themselves were demanding a public enquiry into the matter to clear up allegations of "dishonesty and corruption". Lee was also calling for the SPA-led government to resign![13] Unquestionably, this scandal ultimately cost the incumbent government led by Lim Yew Hock their success in the 1959 General Election.[14] The affair would certainly also strengthen Lee's conviction that his Party, and his government, if he was to form one, had to be corruption-free. Interestingly, even though the affair had played out in full view of the public, none of the political parties in the Legislature, and obviously as well as the government, having been itself embroiled in the scandal, had instructed or suggested that the CPIB should look into the matter. The government had been discredited just before the 1959 General Election. As the CPIB was created by the Colonial Secretary, and not by an elected local government, it also did not enjoy much credibility with the public, and certainly not with the PAP.[15]

Although the Chew affair had been a critical blow to the SPA government as far as public confidence was concerned, the SPA government would suffer greater trust deficit with the general public right up till the May 1959 General Election. It was also in March 1959 that the public learnt of the CPIB's investigation into the disbursement of money by the Ministry of Education to teachers and headmasters. The Bureau unearthed large-scale irregularities, mostly involving overpayments made to the staff of Chinese schools.[16] Of course, the Minister for Education at this time was the "man of the hour", Chew. Then, a month later, soon after the Governor appointed SHD Elias to convene a "one-man" Commission of Inquiry to look into the conduct of the PAP City Councillors and the Mayor, the whole affair turned into a farce. Elias was forced to remove himself from the Commission when Lee revealed that the Commissioner was biased and had a conflict of interest in the proceedings since he had personal dealings and pecuniary interest in the City Council over a tender matter.[17] By April 1959, the importance of a clean government could not be clearer to the politicians contesting in the upcoming General Election which would put in place a fully elected government.

Cleaning Up the Public Service

Corrupt practices, both large-scale and petty acts, had been so deep-rooted in society and within the public services that no one, including the indomitable Lee, could possibly eradicate it immediately. But the clean-up had to start, and it took great will and courage to see through this very endeavour. The PAP's City Council "Keep Your City Clean Campaign" in 1958, serendipitously, was a preparation on the part of the future ruling leadership to show Singaporeans the pathway to make this island their home. It was not only a health and cleanliness campaign, but also a message that this journey had to be walked together. Time and again since the post-war years, police leadership, as well as the first directors of the CPIB, had emphasised that the community had to cooperate in order for corrupt practices to be successfully checked. What Mayor Ong Eng Guan did in his cleaning-up campaign was to show public servants in municipal services that the change in societal values had to start from above. So, he led more than 2,000 public servants across the streets and lanes of Town and in the kampongs to show the public, and the government officers, that a responsible government could make real changes that seemed impossible in colonial times.

After coming to power in June 1959, the new PAP Government made plans for their first steps — to clean up the Public Service. From the beginning of August 1959, about two dozen inept and corrupt City Council staff were dismissed or suspended. Most of them were long-serving and held high positions. The Bureau was activated in this clearing-out process.

Following this, the new Government then channelled its energy to clean up the government ministries and various other statutory boards and departments. In this endeavour, great attention was placed on staff and service efficiency.[18] It was common among the public in post-war Singapore to face lengthy delays and unexplained obstacles which were often resolved with a little *kopi* money. This had to change; public servants could go slow so as to put the squeeze on or incompetent public servants would naturally push desperate members of the public to offer some "grease" to hasten processes, even when unsolicited. Either way, such practices were anti-social and created dissonance amongst local residents. Initially, the new Government took big and small steps to improve public service efficiency which it hoped would go some way to removing opportunities for corrupt practices. One of these first small steps was taken in September 1959, when the Government declared that mail sent to seven government departments did not require postage stamps. And this included letters to the CPIB.[19] The purpose was to make feedback and communication with government bodies easier and to do so without fear.

Reforming and Restoring the Bureau

The continuous change of the directorship of the CPIB in the 1950s did not help the progress of the Bureau, and neither did it cease when the PAP formed the new Government in 1959. While the departure of senior European officers during that decade had been responsible for the situation then, beyond achieving self-government, the Government still had problems identifying capable and suitable local candidates who could helm government departments. The issue with the Bureau was that its leadership had become tied to the larger problem of police leadership because, since the mid-1950s, senior police officers had to be seconded to the Bureau to serve as directors. Hence, any "movement" within the police force hierarchy could also see the Bureau's Director returning to the Force. This was exactly what occurred just before the 1959 General Election; following the retirement of Special Branch Director Khaw Khai Boh, the Bureau's Director, John Le Cain, was promoted to Assistant Commissioner of Police (Detachments).[20] Sardar Singh was redeployed back to the Bureau from the Traffic Police to cover the departing director. Essentially, the Bureau was once again helmed by yet another acting director, which did little to improve the sense of uncertainty and low morale encumbering the staff at this time.[21] Sardar's subsequent "clear out", "shape up or ship out" policy at this time further exacerbated the situation within the Bureau just when the PAP came into power.[22]

Prior to self-rule, it was no surprise that political parties occasionally questioned the efficacy and impartiality of the CPIB during days of electioneering. However, from June 1959, with a fully elected government of local leadership and representatives, all public institutions, including the CPIB, had become state agencies as they were no longer colonial institutions.[23] In this context, the CPIB had an important role as an extension of the Government; it was the new regime's goal to create a nation free of corruption, or at least a nation that frowned upon corrupt practices. But the new regime had to first "clean up" and then restore the Bureau so that it could be part of the Government's nation-building endeavour. So, not long after gaining power, the PAP Government "closely scrutinised" the police force and the CPIB in its anti-corruption drive. This was the first salvo, and it resulted in the dismissal of several CPIB civilian investigators.[24]

The plans for reforms were announced by the Minister for Home Affairs, Ong Pang Boon, in July 1959. The actual reorganisation took place on 6 September 1959 in conjunction with the reorganisation of the police force; the entire uniformed section of the Bureau was posted back to the Police and a whole new set of seconded veteran policemen was sent to replace them. At this point, although a senior police officer remained at the helm, the Bureau was placed under the supervision of the State Advocate (Attorney-General) Inche Ahmad bin Ibrahim.[25] Among the new uniformed officers of the Bureau were Superintendent Ponniah Rajaratnam, who was a secret society expert; two homicide squad men; Inspectors Tan Chin Wooi and Phang Cheow Hock; the former Chief of Anti-Vice Squad ASP CJR Mason and two inspectors who had been part of the original CPIB team in 1953, Richard Tay and Fong Ying Loong.[26] Not long after this reorganisation, following Lee's tour of all government departments, the Bureau was reorganised once more when it was placed directly under the Ministry of Home Affairs.[27] At the same time, Rajaratnam was promoted to Assistant Commissioner of Police and appointed (Acting) Director of the CPIB in place of Sardar Singh who had gone on long leave.[28] Although it was not ideal for the Bureau to continuously change leadership with the unending appointment of acting directors, the new nation needed time to identify and train suitable persons to fill the posts of expatriate senior public servants who had left or would eventually leave. Hence, government departments, including the Police, would continue to be deprived of a permanent leadership for several more years. Rajaratnam himself was posted out even before a year's stay at the Bureau when he was appointed Registrar of Citizenship in mid-1960. He was replaced by Khong Heng Ngee.[29] Within half a year, Khong was posted out and Rajaratnam returned once more to lead the CPIB. This time, Rajaratnam remained as Director for a year and a half before being replaced by Michael Chong in April 1962.[30] Once again, within half a year, the acting directorship changed hands. Chong was posted out and Khong returned at the beginning of December 1962.[31] Khong was the last of the "impermanent" directors. In September 1963, Richard Byrne Corridon returned to the Bureau for the second time to take up directorship of the CPIB.[32] This time, he was appointed permanent director, the first since Claude Wormald Lyle left in 1954.

The process of putting things right at the Bureau, especially with regard to its leadership, was a long-drawn journey. It partly explained why the Bureau was not more successful after Corridon's return to the Special Branch in the mid-1950s. While constant changes to the Bureau's leadership during the latter part of the 1950s could be seen as a lack of seriousness in dealing with deep-seated corruption in society and in the public service, and that it was a symptom of the colonial period,[33] the continued uncertainties beyond 1959 had other root causes. The new Government needed time to consolidate and develop necessary resources, including human capital, for the whole Government. Every government department needed capable and suitable new leaders, and the new regime needed time to identify its people and to place them where they were needed most at differing points of time. But there were not enough locals who were experienced in senior positions in those early years. This was the fundamental issue hindering the proper "resetting" of the CPIB from 1959. Also, the Bureau was no longer just an anti-corruption agency that fought graft mainly within the Public Service and areas of public interest. The CPIB would be a critical component in Singapore's nation-building journey, if the incumbent Government chose to continue its existence.[34] Aside from the unceasing leadership changes and the handful of uniformed personnel who were rotated en masse before and after the General Election, the Bureau also lost a number of its civilian investigators. There were just not enough men to do much more. And this was no state secret. The Government's strategy, in this instance, was not to simply augment the CPIB but to fix the Bureau's issues together with, and in context of, the broader war against corrupt practices within the nation.

    This opportunity presented itself in early 1960 when the Government pushed for the passage of a new Prevention of Corruption Bill in the Legislature; the new legislation was to strengthen the law suppressing corruption as well as the enforcers of this law. The Government pointed out that the shortage of officers and inadequate laws in the past had hampered the fight against corruption.[35] It was during the process of tabling the 1960 Prevention of Corruption Ordinance (PCO) in the Legislative Assembly that Ong Pang Boon was given the opportunity to inform the law makers, and the nation, that the Government intended to do all it could to "eradicate bribery and corruption in the country, especially in the public services". Part of this policy and "movement" to root out malpractices within the Government was to make Singapore's Public Service the best in the world for "ability, efficiency, honesty and incorruptibility". It was in this context that the Government would enlarge the staff strength of the Bureau in order to enable it to succeed in its responsibility to enforce the law as espoused in the new PCO. The Minister then made it known that future civilian Special Investigators of the Bureau would be better prepared for their tasks as new officers would undergo six months of training at the Police Training School.[36] These new Special Investigators would allow the Bureau to play a larger role in helping the Government "to intensify the cleaning up of public services of malpractices and to ensure they remain incorrupt".[37] The recruitment of five more civilian Special Investigators started as soon as the PCO was brought into operation in June 1960.[38] This was a fundamental shift as far as the Bureau was concerned. For the first time, the Government made provisions for the recruitment of university graduates for the post of civilian officers.[39] Also, prior to the 1960 PCO, civilian investigators of the Bureau were only given three-year contracts, to be renewed at the end of each contract term. They were not permanent staff in the Public Service Establishment. However, from 1960, civilian officers were part of the regular Establishment. Each new civilian officer started with a three-year probation period,[40] and he or she had to undergo six months of training at the Police Training School. The net effect of the new law and personnel arrangements was that the Bureau was given more "bite" and its manpower situation stabilised.

In September 1960, the Bureau moved to its new home at Stamford Road, where it would remain till the 1980s.[41] In many ways, 1960 marked the beginnings of a new chapter for the CPIB, in no small part due to the promulgation of the new PCO in that year. All these changes were initiated by the new Government which was bent on tackling corruption in Singapore head-on.

The CPIB office at Stamford Road from 1960 to 1984. Often cited as the "White House", it was home to CPIB officers for 24 years, the longest tenure thus far.
Source: CPIB Archives.

Staff at the CPIB's Stamford Road Office.
Source: CPIB Archives.

A social gathering at the 1971 Annual Staff Dinner.
Source: CPIB Archives.

New Prevention of Corruption Ordinance[42]

Singapore's main anti-corruption legislation prior to self-rule had always been the Straits Settlements' Prevention of Corruption Ordinance No. 41 of 1937. This law was updated in its 1946 Amendment, and since then the Bureau had functioned under the provisions of this law. After attaining self-rule, the PAP had realised that the old anti-corruption legislation could not meet the needs of this new nation. Fundamentally, the "old PCO" had contained the laws required to combat corrupt practices, but it was in great need updating in order to make the Ordinance relevant to the times. The "old PCO" had a glaring gap — it did not provide for the establishment of an anti-corruption body. The 1937 PCO was created simply as a law which the colonial Police Establishment could use to combat corruption crimes in the pre-war years. It was only in 1941 that the Anti-Corruption Branch (ACB), a branch within the Criminal Investigation Department (CID), was created to give greater attention to corruption crimes. The ACB was the first official body to use this law. When the CPIB came into being in 1952, it was created from an Executive Order and was not based on any legislative act. Hence, the oversight of the Bureau could be easily transferred from one governmental body to another without consideration of the laws in which it operated. This was the reason the Bureau suffered great uncertainty during the decolonisation processes of the 1950s, when the very executives who gave life to the Bureau were themselves exiting the island permanently.

After coming into power, the new PAP Government realised that if it chose to retain the CPIB as an anti-corruption agency of the state, it had to have legislative underpinnings which other government bodies enjoyed. Therefore, the "old PCO" was repealed and a new Prevention of Corruption Ordinance (No. 39 of 1960) was created, not only to add more bite in its war against corruption, but also to give the Bureau the legal existence it required to become a truly effective and independent entity. And from this point, the position of the Director of the Bureau, as well as those of its core staff, were gazetted by law.[43]

The 1960 PCO was the new Government's demonstration of political will to effect real changes. While the departing British did indeed create the CPIB in 1952 to tackle corruption crimes as they occurred, or were discovered, there was no effort to root out the causes of corruption in the public services or to eradicate the sources of corruption afflicting society then. In fact, time and again, when corruption cases reached the Court, successful prosecutions were not the norm, particularly in instances where expatriates were involved.[44] These became "scandals" of the day and they added public scepticism that any action against corrupt persons was not genuinely intended to punish everyone involved in wrongdoing.[45] The elections of the 1950s which saw accusations of corrupt activities being thrown around and against all political parties also did little to lend confidence in the law enforcement and justice system. The fact that Commissions of Inquiries were set up to look into electoral corruption, and a complaints bureau started to collect complaints about corrupt officials, instead of relying on the Bureau to investigate all allegations, spoke volumes about how little the people trusted the Government of the day. Even though much had been said publicly about vote-buying throughout the 1950s, the CPIB had always returned a "no evidence" verdict. In the end, the Chew affair was perhaps that last straw that broke the camel's back for the credibility of the Lim Yew Hock's government.

The new PAP Government was determined not to allow its anti-corruption stance become just another electioneering rhetoric, or half-measure that would change nothing. Minister Ong Pang Boon, while championing the 1960 Prevention of Corruption Bill in the Legislative Assembly declared, "The Government is deeply conscious that a Government cannot survive, no matter how good its aims and intentions are, if corruption exists in its ranks and its public services on which it depends to provide the efficient and effective administrative machinery to translate its policies into action. We have only to look at post-war Asia to realise how evil and damaging the scourge can be... It is of interest to note that in post-war Asia, where the public service in a country has been undermined and demoralised by corruption, the rule of dictatorship follows inevitably. If we do not wish to see the same pattern being repeated in this country, then adequate power must be given to deal effectively with the problem."[46] Ong also made the point that even though Singapore's Public Service was generally better than most other nations then, it would be foolhardy to believe that corruption did not exist in this land. It was the Government's conviction that they had to maintain "unceasing vigilance".[47]

The CPIB could have been abandoned, and so this colonial edifice had to be made a useful and effective weapon that the new state could deploy against corrupt practices. The new PCO would have provided the Bureau the ordnance it required to do the job well. In the new law, the Bureau's civilian Special Investigators are given "the power of arrest, and search of the arrested". It also allowed magistrates or the Director of the CPIB to issue warrants. However, if the usual route to securing a warrant resulted in a delay that would "frustrate the object of a search", police officers and

Special Investigators would be empowered to enter, search, seize and detain incriminating documents. At the same time, the public prosecutor might authorise the Director of the Bureau and Special Investigators to inspect the bankbooks of public servants, their wives, children or agents to ascertain if evidence of corruption could be found in their books. Government employees and their families would also be required to account for all assets owned, including those sent out of Singapore. The public prosecutor was also empowered to contact the Comptroller of Income Tax to acquire the income information of civil servants and their families, and to require bank managers to supply copies of bank accounts. The new PCO also "relieved" the Court of the "restriction of using evidence provided by accomplices". Prior to the new PCO, evidence provided by such persons, "people of bad character", was to be considered "unworthy of credit unless corroborated". It was felt that "such evidences were tainted". However, since "bribery and corruption" were usually "committed in secret", and only the briber and receiver were present, it became a stumbling block to many prosecutions if the accomplices' account could not be considered. Notably, all offences under the PCO were deemed seizable offences.

The far-reaching powers provided in the 1960 PCO were unprecedented. It was certainly the Government's declaration that it was giving no quarter in its war against corruption. Under this new Ordinance, the Court had the power to order the persons convicted of accepting illegal gratification to pay a penalty equal to the gratification, on top of other punishments imposed. In other words, nobody could gain from any gratification they had received during the commission of corrupt acts; it was now an offence for any person to offer, to take, to agree or to promise to receive, to give or to solicit any gratification. Anyone found obstructing the effort to prevent and suppress corruption was also liable to a fine "not exceeding $2,000 or jail up to a year or both". The new PCO also clearly stated that public officers to whom "a bribe is corruptly given, must arrest the giver or are liable to a maximum of six months' jail or must pay $500 fine, or both".

It was clear that the 1960 PCO had true bite, and that the Government meant business. Not surprisingly, the Opposition in the Assembly also supported the Bill.[48] But more importantly, the Bureau was now empowered with far greater authority than ever. It was also after the passage of the PCO that there were no longer any contract-based civilian investigators in the CPIB. From this point, all civilian investigators were called Special Investigators,[49] raising their public profile.

The 1960 PCO was just the beginning of a very long and protracted fight against corruption in Singapore. It was not a magic wand nor a be-all and end-all instrument to clear the path for building a nation. The real work was just beginning. The law and the agency needed to carry the fight forward had been given a more solid foundation, but much more still had to be done. In 1962, the Government made it known that it was considering another new law to compel all civil servants and assemblymen to submit details of their annual incomes and assets to the CPIB. Ong Pang Boon started the ball rolling by announcing that all ministers had already done so on the day of their installation. They submitted their declaration to the Yang di-Pertuan Negara, while all Parliamentary Secretaries submitted theirs to the Prime Minister (PM).[50] The Government was resolute that the battle against corrupt practices would be led from the front. And it was this conviction that shaped the nation's policies and direction for the next few decades, including the high standards of honesty and integrity to which senior civil servants and ministers were held. For the CPIB, this meant that it could depend on the incumbent Government to back the Bureau in the conduct of its duty, **without fear of reprisal**.

Total Approach

The approach against corrupt practices before self-rule was to see corruption as simply a wrongful act, criminally or simply disciplinarily. Hence, the main emphasis of government bodies in tackling corruption before 1959 had been enforcement; detection, arrest, disciplinary action and prosecution. In this system, the war against corruption was fought in silos by individual government departments, and where cooperation was required, the CPIB would participate in enforcement action. When the CPIB had been the lead, relevant departments joined the investigation. In this administrative culture, there was no "strategic" thinking by the government hierarchy. This would change from self-rule, largely due to Lee's tough walk-the-talk and no-nonsense approach. He had promised to establish a clean government and forge a nation free of corruption. Hence, Lee adopted a holistic approach in governance; it was every government department's responsibility to prevent corruption, and there were multiple agencies and processes to ensure that there were no opportunities for corrupt practices. From the time the PAP formed the Government, and for several decades thereafter, overlapping responsibilities and fields of checks and counterchecks were put in place so that corruption in the Government would be discouraged or prevented; this included checks by the Audit Department, guidelines specified in departmental Instruction Manuals (IM), the Public Service Commission's filtering and hiring of honest government officers, having the Central Complaints Bureau received feedback and information from the public, the Commercial Affairs Department to ensure financial crimes did not slip through the cracks, and more. The CPIB would assist with its investigative skills and when prosecution was the next step. By the 1980s, it would be said that Singapore had "one of the most effective anti-corruption mechanisms in Asia".[51]

Putting in place the right mechanisms within the Government was just the first step in checking corrupt practices amongst public servants. It was also clear to Lee that the right men were to be employed in the Public Service, especially among the upper echelons of the political and administrative leaders. When these men failed, or caved in to temptation and faltered, the Government had to have the gumption and political will to take them to task, even if they were serving ministers in the Government. In this respect, Lee was unyielding, and the CPIB was given all the backing it needed to carry out its duty.[52]

Beyond checks and enforcement, the Government's total approach encompassed facing off with the very corrupt social culture that afflicted the Public Service since the days of Stamford Raffles. The first step to remedy this was to provide the public services with the correct spirit of service and a positive ethos. Such an approach could supplant the corrupt tendencies ever so rooted in the Public Service of the day. One of the hallmarks of this anti-social culture was the practice of offering or receiving *kopi* money. On one end of the continuum, it was a show of appreciation. On the other end, when gratification became an expectation, and one that was solicited, it was a "squeeze", or an extortion bid, that was disdained and discredited by the Government. While the 1960 PCO covered all angles of corruption — to give, to take, to offer, to ask or to pressure — it could not tackle social attitudes that tolerated, accepted and were ambivalent to such practices. Change from the ground was necessary, but again, this had to start from the top. The Government had identified embryonic symptoms that provided the right conditions for breeding corrupt practices — the lack of public efficiency and courtesy in the Public Service. These traits were by and large considered unimportant, or even innocuous, during the colonial period. But they fed the culture of corruption. A rude officer could withhold or disrupt service to the public who might then feel they had to offer some inducements to move along. There were also many instances where officials delayed services in order to solicit gratification. Were they rude and inefficient because they were corrupt, or were they just rude and inefficient? The truth behind such behaviour was not easy to uncover. In any case, it started with a condescending government officer behaving badly. So the PAP Government met the problem head-on by launching a public service courtesy campaign in December 1960, with the slogan "Courtesy by citizens for citizens".[53]

Spearheaded by Goh Keng Swee, the Finance Minister, the campaign saw a gathering of over 40 top government officers from nine ministries, which included 28 heads of department, to plan how the Public Service could be more courteous towards the public. One could not be courteous and act like a bully at the same time. Goh reminded civil servants that courtesy was "implicit in the contracts of every civil servant" and that "courtesy made the act of helping not an expression of superior condescending to inferior". He emphasised that the Public Service was the "instrument of the people and not against the people".[54] In May 1961, the Government took a gigantic leap with the campaign by making an order. It warned that civil servants could be dismissed if they received complaints from the public that they had been rude and difficult. The Government also assembled a nine-men committee to compile a courtesy code for civil servants.[55] Although it was not explicitly stated, the Government understood that if public servants espoused a "better than thou" attitude in dealing with the public, because they had the authority and power to affect their lives, then they would also have the propensity to bully or to demand gratification.

The new reality for the Bureau in the 1960s was that it was not the main gatekeeper against corrupt practices in Singapore. The Government was itself gatekeeping. One important government body that the administration depended on for information on corrupt or inefficient officials was the Central Complaints Bureau (CCB), a legacy "concept" from the days of Ong Eng Guan's City Council. It was created to provide an avenue for the public to complain or to get information and guidance on government processes without having to deal with "lawmen" or "government men" whom the general public tended to fear and avoid. Following a review by a PAP committee appointed on 18 May 1961 to look into the workings of government departments, the PAP gathered "significant feedback" that there was still public resentment simmering. There were still delays, discourtesy and "outright bullying" by public servants. The committee reported that "people have been made to pay several visits to government offices for services that ought not to have taken more than several minutes... in some cases, there were allegations of incipient corruption among certain classes of civil servants. Civil servants, denied of opportunities to be corrupt, have enforced laws and regulations with a strictness calculated to rouse popular animosity against the Government."⁵⁶ So the committee recommended that the CCB be established to "improve the relationship between public and bureaucracy" and to fight "petty bureaucratic tyranny" in the Civil Service.⁵⁷

When the CCB eventually opened at City Hall on 3 July 1962, it was first called the Public Enquiry & Complaints Bureau. Part of its original mission was to provide information to members of the public who needed help with municipal processes and paperwork. A great number of them were illiterate or non English-speaking. As such, they could easily fall victim to unscrupulous public servants who took advantage of their situation — often making these victims believe that they had to pay for services which actually cost nothing. While the public servants involved could face departmental action or prosecution, it changed nothing as far as the victims were concerned. They still needed help with their transactions with government bodies. Hence, with the CCB helping to provide correct information and guidance, corrupt practices by public servants could be prevented. And as the keeper of this gate, the CCB office was where members of the public could get government tender documents and employment forms, "free of charge", without having to pay additional costs or *kopi* money.⁵⁸ And as the complaints bureau, the CCB functioned as a filter and check; complaints arising from a lack of understanding or miscommunication with government bodies were tactfully resolved by CCB staff. Legitimate complaints about inefficiency or unjustified foot-dragging by civil servants were investigated by the CCB which submitted their findings to the ministries concerned for follow-up action. And where corrupt practices were apparent, the CCB submitted their report on such cases to the CPIB.⁵⁹

Chapter Seventeen

Tackling the Culture of Corruption

Corruption in a Nation-State

The CPIB's major cases in the 1950s involved keeping criminals at bay to ensure that the rule of law was not subverted by syndicates and individuals who had the resources to corrupt public servants. In this decade, the Bureau enjoyed some successes against big-money rackets like the opium and gambling syndicates which had no problem bribing corrupt officials. However, the most prevalent corruption cases of the day that inundated the Bureau were not the large-scale highly organised crimes which had unlimited resources. The most widespread corrupt practices in the 1940s and 1950s were mostly linked to the socio-economic conditions of the period — the shortage of everything. People bribed in order to circumvent control regulations, for guards to turn a blind eye, for enforcement officers to turn their heads, for government clerks to facilitate or speed up the renewal of ration cards or licences, and much more. The flipside was also true — officers and clerks had also solicited gratification to do, or not to do, their jobs. While the adverse socio-economic conditions of the post-war years had by and large disappeared going into the 1960s, and the large-scale big-money syndicates had now given way to smaller players, the infractions, greasing and *kopi* monies nevertheless continued almost unabated beyond the colonial period. These anti-social "practices" had become acceptable values for some and a social norm for most, creating a culture of corruption within the new nation-state. It became clear that attaining self-rule was not an automatic solution to ending corruption;

now that locals, or citizens, occupied the upper echelons of government, things were not immediately better than when the British were in charge. For some in the Government, it was thought that things were *same old same old*, especially during the time of the David Marshall and Lim Yew Hock administration (limited self-rule). So graft among government officers continued. But things were not the same as before. Prior to 1959, locals were not entirely in charge, but after the People's Action Party (PAP) came into power, a government with a clear vision of forging a nation was now at the steering wheel. This new government was determined to "clean up the City" by resolutely pursuing corrupt officers (regardless of cost and resources) and changing social values. The Government, over time, put in place a system and network of agencies and processes preventing corruption. At the same time, the CPIB was empowered by law to be an extension of the Government's policy on eliminating corruption. Government agencies like the CPIB had become an aide to the Government's nation-building effort.

In the 1960s and 1970s, while citywide petty corruption cases remained a staple for the Bureau, they were no longer just run-of-the-mill instances of corrupt practices. This was a period of socio-economic, urban-demographic and communal-political changes.[60] It was a most exciting time for citizens as opportunities abounded and hard work, education and skills could produce rags-to-riches stories, or at least help many escape the poverty cycle. This was the beginning of Singapore's industrialisation, which saw the rise of a middle class, an improvement of education levels and educated masses, improved standard of living, and much more. In sum, a greater number of people had money in their pockets and there was generally more money in circulation. However, this also meant that people had more cash to gamble or be involved in other vices. Although there were more opportunities to earn stable wages, the pay for normal folks was not high, especially among public servants. Among the lowest paid public servants at that time were teachers, policemen and clerical staff. So, on the one hand, the improving general conditions fostered greater "wants" in society, while on the other hand, the inability to earn enough also created a propensity for many to seek other means — gambling had been a way for many to "buy hope". Essentially, corruption before the 1960s had been greatly spurred by vices and needs, and after by values and wants. And so corruption continued and the Government knew that it would be a never-ending battle; the only way to lessen the instance and impact of corrupt practices on the state's nation-building endeavour was to ensure state anti-corruption agencies like the CPIB remained steadfast and continually vigilant, while the Government pressed on with its efforts to change social norms. In other words, the Bureau's overarching role at the birth of the Singapore nation was to hold the line until social values improved and the culture of corruption was checked.

Old and New Legacy Issues

The changing socio-economic scene in Singapore saw the Bureau handling new staple cases on top of the "old types" of corruption cases. For one, the CPIB encountered a greater number of corruption cases in the private sector. Some of these cases had the potential of sullying the reputation of the island state as well as eroding the confidence that this was a safe place for businesses. The more serious of such concerns involved Singapore's strategic resources and services. In 1970, the CPIB received its first hint that something was amiss at Shell Oil Refinery at Pulau Bukom when an employee at the island made a report to the CPIB about corruption at the refinery. A gang who had warned him against it had attacked and stabbed him three times at Jalan Besar the day after he went to the Bureau.[61] Then in 1977, the CPIB was called in to investigate Shell Oil Company's loss of millions of dollars of petroleum.[62] The Bureau discovered that Shell staff had abetted the theft of petrol oil from the company's installation in Woodlands for several years. The siphoned petrol was resold to contractors and transport firms in the Lim Chu Kang and Choa Chu Kang areas at 10% below market price. Another big-time commercial scandal the Bureau

Tackling the Culture of Corruption ◀

handled in the 1970s was the Singapore Airlines $1,000,000 graft case involving four senior officers of the company. The CPIB launched an investigation following a tip-off in early 1977. The Bureau discovered that the staff took $1,000,000 in kickbacks to favour several local companies to only purchase goods, machinery and equipment from them over a period of three years, from 1974 to 1976.[63]

There was also an interesting case of a conspiracy between a private clinic and a travel agency. The clinic supplied blank vaccination certificates to the agency which then issued them to its clients who had booked tour tickets but lacked the health papers to complete all arrangements on the spot. Travellers could then present their endorsed certificates, with the doctor's signature and clinic stamps, to the Port Health Authority for endorsement without having to be vaccinated for smallpox or cholera or both. When the CPIB received a tip-off, the travel company was raided and the clinic's doctor questioned. In this instance, the CPIB submitted its report to the Singapore Medical Council.[64] In light of today's Covid-19 pandemic, it is not too difficult to imagine what harm could have resulted from this conspiracy to circumvent health regulations back then.

These acts of securing gratifications, big or small, were not symptomatic behaviour of a society composed of many people who were in need, and who were desperate to get on with making a living or getting by — these corrupt individuals had money, but wanted even more.

Going into the 1960s, one vice that continued to be a lucrative source of bribery was *Chap Ji Kee* gaming. Generally, all forms of gambling had been prevalent since the nineteenth century, but right up to the 1950s, it was *Chap Ji Kee* which offered the most handsome rewards for its players. This helped the vice to become ultra-resilient to suppression, and it was certainly one of the vices that corrupted government officers. In this instance, it could be said that Singapore's "gambling culture" was near synonymous with the island's "culture of corruption". The Bureau was therefore kept vigilant and busy in tackling the *Chap Ji Kee* rackets. There were occasions when a good police officer informed the CPIB when the big-money *Chap Ji Kee* corruptors came knocking,[65] but increasingly from the 1960s, the big-money syndicates became magnets for crooked cops. The irony here was that the game's racketeers and runners were so numerous that they also became easy targets of extortion by corrupt enforcers. And often, when the policemen's squeeze on the illegal gamers had been excessive, they would turn the table on the cops instead, and report the corrupt cops to the CPIB despite knowing that they could also be "taken down" for gaming.[66] A judge presiding over one such corrupt police case in 1961 opined, "It has been said that the responsibility of maintaining an incorruptible police force rests upon members of the Force as well as the public. All the accused have not recognised this responsibility. It has been said by an eminent Chief Justice in Singapore that an offence of this nature strikes at the root of the impartial administration of the criminal law. This, if widespread, will destroy the foundation of the Government."[67]

The CPIB's relentless prosecution of corrupt police officers from the 1960s also created an unexpected phenomenon that impacted the Bureau's work; criminals knew that the CPIB would go all out to investigate any information of collusion between corrupt officers and criminal enterprises. So false accusations against enforcement officers became a common occurrence. For instance, *Chap Ji Kee* promoters caught red-handed by the Police in the late 1960s would occasionally "turn informers" by volunteering information of police officers who had taken bribes from them.[68] In fact, the use of false accusations as a form of distraction became a common practice for many criminals, not just illegal gamblers. These cases were treated seriously by the CPIB. Accused officers were often suspended and their wages docked till they were cleared of all wrongdoings. It became part of the Bureau's responsibility to speedily exonerate wrongfully accused officers,[69] and this added to the Bureau's daily workload.

Among the old corrupt practices to which the Bureau paid scant attention until the 1960s were the old behavioural shortcomings; many did not consider such behaviour as wrongdoings, yet it was at the core of the corrupted social culture of the day. The Government was adamant that no supernumerary remuneration should be given to or taken by public servants who were already paid for their job. Of course, there were many angles to this; should staff of the service industry accept the occasional tips, or taxi drivers keep the change, regardless of quantum? Would it be wrong for a cleaner or runner in a firm or a government department to accept a reward of little food or a cup of coffee, or a Christmas gift or an *ang pow* (red packet containing cash) during Chinese New Year from the office? To many, these are not considered improper, and perhaps even expected. These had been the socio-cultural values of the people on the ground. In the 1960s and 1970s, the Government's position was crystal clear for government employees. They should not accept any form of gratification even if these were unsolicited, as tokens of appreciation by members of the public. At the heart of the matter was the knowledge that what was considered goodwill today could become an expected practice — the very nature of the *kopi* money culture so prevalent in the 1940s and 1950s amongst food control and municipal staff. It was this culture of expectation of token gifts that was at the heart of the endemic corruption afflicting the Public Service in the post-war years and was still present in the 1970s. It was in the mid-1970s that the CPIB started looking into such cases of small-value gratification involving government street-cleaners and postal workers in order to prevent these practices from developing into larger issues in years to come. The Bureau first received information in 1975 that postmen had been going house to house demanding *ang pows* during Chinese New Year. The CPIB sent its investigators to spot-check and actually saw postmen receiving the red packets from residents.[70] However, it was not clear if they had solicited these gifts in 1975. So, the Bureau prepared itself to catch these men red-handed during the next Chinese New Year. And that they did, successfully. A number of postmen delivering mail in Chinatown and North Bridge Road were caught and fined by the Court, and so were the shops and individuals who offered them *ang pows*. In this instance, the Bureau found only one case of a postman who solicited an *ang pow* from a shop. The rest had simply received and kept the red packets,[71] which was also considered improper. Nevertheless, the Bureau believed it had to tackle this problem before a situation arose when a postal worker might decide not to deliver mail to persons who did not offer him the customary *ang pow*. Yet, despite the clampdown in 1976, the practice continued among postmen.[72] In 1978 alone, six postmen were arrested by the CPIB for accepting *ang pows* from the public. Four of them were convicted in Court and dismissed. More had to be done. In December that year, the Postal Department issued a circular reminding its staff that it was an offence to receive gifts and money from the public. Then in 1979, the Amalgamated Union of Public Employees (AUPE), to which 800 postal workers were affiliated, warned its members against accepting red packets.[73] The case of the postmen and Chinese New Year red packets clearly demonstrated just how difficult it was to try to change old habits, particularly over small amounts of monies which could never make anybody rich. Still, there was a potential for greater harm if such practices went unchecked.

Conspiratorial Servants

It was from the 1960s that another phenomenon of the local corruption culture emerged amongst government employees.[74] The traditional large-scale corruption enterprises had been pivoted on cooperation between government officers and syndicated outfits. The 1960s, however, saw the emergence of syndicates involving civil servants, organising illegal enterprises on their own, forming their own "brotherhood" in crime. Generally, any form of esprit de corps amongst public servants would be considered a positive development, especially in the context of Singapore's nation-building journey, but the spirit of collusion in corruption found its way into Singapore's public services despite all of the state's efforts to change this anti-social culture. In early 1965, the CPIB uncovered a racket involving hundreds of public servants from different government departments who had been forging medical certificates (MC) for their collective since late 1963. The ringleaders, junior government employees, had scores of other junior officers involved in selling MCs to other junior public servants at a rate of a dollar for a day's MC. Their network of middlemen sold the MCs to malingerers. In just a few months after the CPIB started its investigation, more than 300 forged MCs were found, submitted by public servants from the Government Printing Office, Public Works, Postal Services, Education Ministry, Airport Police, the General Hospital and more. The largest number of forged MCs were found to have been submitted by employees of the Singapore Traction Company. The conspiracy began unravelling when an employee of the Printing Office submitted one of the forged MCs from the General Hospital to his boss. It was serendipitous that his boss spotted the name of the doctor on the MC, who happened to be his friend. But the signature was not correct. So he reported the matter to the hospital, and the hospital traced the MC to a hospital attendant. The CPIB was informed. When the Bureau realised just how extensive the conspiracy had been, it put almost all its investigators on the case. The Bureau then sent out a directive to all government departments to check the MCs they had received going back 18 months, especially from Division 4 employees. The Bureau's big break came following a raid of the homes of General Hospital attendants and staff of the Government Printing Office; pads of General Hospital MCs and rubber stamps were found. The CPIB discovered that MCs were sold openly. Even though they were badly forged, no one had noticed for over a year. While most of the malingerers faced departmental action, the ringleaders were prosecuted.[75]

The other big scandal of the period involving the connivance of public servants was the 1970–1971 Traffic Police's "protection toll" conspiracy. This single event forced the Bureau to introduce new measures to fight corrupt practices within the police force. Prior to the scandal, most corruption cases involving the mobile Police were simply just the taking of *kopi* money to let off traffic offenders. The Bureau occasionally prosecuted these officers.[76] There were times when corrupt traffic officers were caught committing more serious offences, like helping to cover up accidents, even in cases where there had been deaths.[77] However, regardless of the scope of the corruption, the Government's position was that all forms of corruption by public servants had serious implications. In December 1963, during the sentencing of a police officer for accepting a bribe from a motorist, the First Criminal District Judge remarked that "policemen are the guardians of the law, and if the public cannot trust policemen not to be corrupt in discharging their duties, then ... 'the public may ask who shall guard the guardians?'... corruption in the Public Service 'eats away' the foundations of a stable society and must, like cancer or any other disease, be stamped out..."[78] Certainly, in the scheme of things, the CPIB "guarded the guardians". And this responsibility was never more felt than in 1971 when almost the entire Traffic Police squad had to be investigated by the Bureau.

It was towards the last months of 1970 when some "enterprising" traffic cops chanced upon an idea to levy their very own "toll" for transport vehicles. There had been concerns regarding air pollution by vehicles spewing excessive exhaust smoke since the early 1960s. In 1968, fines were imposed for infringements. In August 1970, the fine was raised from $20 to $50.[79] The Government, hoping to remedy the "excessive smoke" situation quickly, empowered the Mobile Squad in November 1970 to book vehicles for the infringement without having to send them to the Registry of Vehicles for inspections first.[80] This literally handed the corrupt officers the perfect opportunity to abuse their authority.[81] Initially, the measures seemed to have achieved some level of success as the numbers fined decreased over time. However, no corresponding improvement in air quality had been achieved at that time. The truth of the matter was that the decline in the total number of motorists fined was not due to greater compliance but a reduction in the numbers caught! The CPIB had taken notice of the irregularities in traffic fines as early as September 1970 and so, it started surveillance and investigations of the Mobile Squad.[82] In the days that followed, the CPIB discovered that about two dozen traffic cops were at the core of a syndicate that let off smoking lorries belonging to companies that joined their "traffic toll" system. In all, 36 transport companies which had a combined fleet of 15,000 lorries paid a monthly "toll" of only $30 for each vehicle in order to avoid "harassment" by the traffic cops. The CPIB suspected that most of the 155 Mobile Squad cops were involved in one way or another. Accordingly, the Bureau's 16 Special Investigators were put on the case, assisted by divisional police inspectors and the Police Reserve Unit. They helped the Special Investigators to fan out across Singapore raiding the offices of 25 transport companies.[83]

Essentially, these cops ran a policemen protection racket for the transport companies. They took advantage of the transport companies which were buckling under the heavy fines they were receiving for their smoking lorries. The CPIB received its first direct tip-off about the scam in September 1970 when 35 policemen from various police divisions were sent to the Police Training School for two months of additional training in order to boost the strength of the Mobile Squad during the Commonwealth Heads of State Conference held in January 1971. When these officers joined the Mobile Squad, "transport agents" were sent to make friends with them and to offer them the option of joining their "toll syndicate". One of these new mobile officers was offered $800 as a joining fee. He declined and informed the CPIB. Then the break came in February 1971 with the arrest of three traffic cops who were seen taking money from a lorry driver off Bukit Timah Road. It was in the course of investigating the accounts of the company of this lorry driver that the CPIB found that the company's account books contained numbers which corresponded to the badge numbers of traffic policemen. The Bureau learnt that the syndicate sent out off-duty policemen to collect the monthly payments from the participating companies. Each of them collected about $800 every month for the syndicate from each of the 36 companies involved. This was an average of $28,800 a month, or $345,600 annually. And each officer involved received from the syndicate a remuneration of at least $150 monthly. No wonder the Bureau suspected that the entire Mobile Squad was involved.[84] The Bureau also found that a number of policemen had been using this system to receive payments from the companies for several years, before the syndicate even started.[85] Presumably, they had already been taking monies from these companies for other offences. This was a perfect example of how minor cases of graft, if not checked, could snowball into something more serious. But more importantly, not only did the Police "toll syndicate" impact public confidence in the Police and Government, the state's anti-pollution efforts had been compromised and the Government had also been deprived of the income it would have earned from the compound fines collected.

When the dust settled, the Bureau blacklisted 100 men from the Mobile Squad, the Anti-Pirate Taxi Section of the Traffic Police and the section in charge of warrants and summons at Maxwell Traffic Police Headquarters.[86] At the same time, the Police Commissioner started his own inquiry into the affair. He collected statements from all 150 Mobile Squad officers.[87] In mid-February 1971, the CPIB handed 20 names and badge numbers to Police Headquarters. Three probationary inspectors and 21 men from Mobile Squad were transferred out of the Traffic Police Division.[88]

The story of conspiratorial public servants in the new nation-state is not complete without reference to clerks of works (CoW) employed by the Government. While working alone, a single CoW may do very little as they were more often than not part of a whole team that supported professionals like architects and electricians. They had to work in concert to defeat any system put in place to deter wrongful practices, or at least till they were found out by the more vigilant others. In this regard, the story of the Housing and Development Board's (HDB) CoW stands out in the chronicles of the corrupt conspiracies. While the PAP Government assumed correctly that discontinuing the Singapore Improvement Trust (SIT) and establishing the HDB as the new housing authority would eradicate all the corrupt practices associated with the SIT, the Government would come to appreciate how greed could make ordinary folks extraordinarily scheming and irresponsible, even in the new HDB. In an era of massive developmental works, just like in the pre-war defence works period, large funds were in circulation. Opportunities were aplenty for those willing to work hard, as well as for those in search of opportunities for wealth by other means. It was in this context that developers and contractors could always find a not so well-paid CoW and other government staff to facilitate their shortcuts or short-changing. In the mid-1960s, the CPIB was kept busy investigating the usage of substandard materials, and improper short-piling, in the construction of apartment blocks in HDB housing estates. In this area of investigative work, the Bureau had to seek the assistance of architects and electrical engineers.[89] It was no secret that builders could get away with shoddy works if the CoWs and other officers tasked to ensure compliance and inspect quality of material and works also collaborated. Given the scope of each building project, there was always going to be more than one HDB staff assigned to each site. Coordinating collaboration within the group, even in cases of graft, had to be an "inside" process. The first of such scandals occurred in 1963. HDB CoWs were found to have falsified pile-driving records at the MacPherson Road (South) piling site. A similar incident then occurred at Toa Payoh in 1965. The site was under Gammon Construction Limited. It was their own site agent who provided false pile-driving information to the company. At the same time, three HDB CoWs were found to have used pile-driving records with false information to mislead the HDB. When the CPIB launched their investigation of the piling works done at Toa Payoh in August 1966, all their wrongful acts and conspiracies were uncovered. After the Bureau completed its investigation in 1967, a total of 12 HDB CoWs were dismissed for their part in the Gammon affair. Nevertheless, the company took responsibility for the shoddy works and paid the HDB $2,700,000 in compensation.[90]

What is mind-boggling about corrupt practices in this area is that substandard works will always show up eventually. While shoddy work was easily done, it was never easy to get away with. Nevertheless, the perpetrators still tried. The Bureau continued to uncover many such conspiratorial practices in the 1970s, and some of them had come with new twists. In 1974, while the contractors became creative in providing CoWs with gratification in the form of entertainment in posh nightclubs and hotels, the Bureau also discovered how the lure of such glamour would lead CoWs to request that contractors provide them with such luxuries. In this instance, contractors were known to have provided such gratifications on a monthly basis.[91] Interestingly, corrupt CoWs were often ambivalent to the danger of substandard building works that they had facilitated in developing while they partied. In 1976, a whole Jurong Town Corporation (JTC) factory at Gul Avenue had to be torn down due to substandard piling works. The CPIB kept watch on the CoWs involved in the project. The Bureau found them living beyond their means; driving expensive cars and visiting expensive nightclubs regularly. Some of them were also found to have large sums in their bank accounts.[92] These sorts of corruption, although not linked to the dangerous underworld, were equally harmful to the island state.

Covetous, Meek and Helpless

As a state institution, the CPIB had to handle a vast array of domicile cases, from the most basic to the most benign forms of corruption. This was because, in a new nation-state, corrupt practices had permeated all levels of life. Not all corruption cases had serious national implications, nor were they always about conspiracies, or had been highly organised or syndicated. For one, corrupt habits tended to be resilient to change and would not simply go away when an arrest had been made or a law to prevent it had been introduced. Often, it was simply just about greed, greed and greed. Can there be different kinds of greed? Fundamentally, there has always been only one form of corruption, but many kinds of people who ply their corrupt acts in different ways.

Corrupt acts by the lowest kinds of characters need no justification or explanation. In 1959, the Bureau tackled a case where several police detectives had simply accepted $100 each to look away from a secret society gangster who had just robbed another citizen of $40,000.[93] There was no solicitation or affiliation, it was just corruption. Then, within weeks of the first police case, another detective was arrested by the Bureau for extorting $50 from a man he falsely accused of attempting rape.[94] The detective did not even know the man. Then in early 1962, the Criminal Investigation Department (CID) found amongst its own ranks that senior officers were running an illegal bookie operation within the CID itself. At least 10 officers were involved, and most of them held the rank of Assistant Superintendent of Police! In this instance, the Bureau was instructed by Ong Pang Boon, the Home Affairs Minister, to lead the investigation.[95] These officers conducted their gaming activities within their group without involving any members of the public or criminals. Nevertheless, they were still manifestly corrupt and covetous, and probably malingerers as well.

In the 1960s and 1970s, the Bureau also encountered corruption within social and communal institutions which were essentially the very organisations that functioned to build bonds and provide stability within the nation. The long tentacles of corruption did not spare them. In 1964, the leadership of the Singapore Manual and Mercantile Workers Union (SMMWU), which had 20,000 members and was a component part of the National Trades Union Congress (NTUC), was suspended for corruption involving the Union's funds.[96] In 1968, the scandal of corruption also afflicted the Singapore Family Planning Association (SFPA). The CPIB, with the assistance of the Audit Department, found $100,000 of the Association's funds missing. In consequence, the Singapore Family Planning and Population Board had to take over the running of the SFPA.[97]

Among the more appalling cases of corrupt practices that fell into the lap of the Bureau in this decade were those that cheated and bullied the poorest and helpless. It was with these people that the criminally corrupt officials saw opportunities for profit. Often these intelligent public servants would get away unscathed while their victims were left stranded with nothing left or had to face the law since they were still guilty of corrupt acts, even though they had been lured into their predicament. Such cases were the very antithesis of the Government's nation-building agenda. In this light, the Bureau also had the responsibility of protecting the meek and marginalised who had been taken advantage of by public servants.

One such case that angered even the Chief Justice occurred in 1961. Wong Cheong Kim, a street hawker, encountered extreme difficulties in his application for a hawking licence from the City Council. He was repeatedly told by the superintendent of the Council's Markets and Hawkers Department, Loh Pui Kay, to return another day after having waited from dusk to dawn for several days. In desperation, on 21 and 24 November 1961, Wong offered Loh two bribes. The Bureau prosecuted Wong and he ended up having to pay a fine of $1,200. Wong's appeal against his prosecution was turned down by the Court. But the whole affair left the Chief Justice, Alan Rose, indignant. While the law had to punish Wong for his corrupt act, the judge felt that the real culprit was Loh, even though the CPIB could find no wrongdoing on his part, with the exception of gross inefficiency.[98] Rose noted that on one occasion, when Wong met Loh, the latter had assured Wong that he would try to recommend Wong for a licence. And on another occasion, Loh told Wong that he would be informed when it was approved, which gave Wong the impression that his application had been approved and was awaiting the completion of some processes. So Wong waited and waited, till he concluded that his problems at the Council stemmed from the absence of a little *kopi* money.[99]

The Bureau could not conclusively prove that Loh had put the squeeze on Wong. Rose, having rejected Wong's appeal, observed that Loh's conduct in the circumstances had contributed to Wong's perception that a bribe was impliedly sought. The Chief Justice held that "there had been considerable delay in dealing with the application for the licence, and when the hawker had exhausted his patience, he probably thought a bribe was required. It was important that a government department must not only be incorruptible, but must also manifestly appear to be incorruptible. It is not enough to track down the culprit after the act of corruption or to preach to the public. The real remedy lies in prevention, and the main and necessary ingredient is efficiency."[100] Following this scathing criticism of the Council's Markets and Hawkers Department, Loh was suspended, even though Rose also noted that he believed the delay was "due to incompetence and not corruption".[101]

In another heart-wrenching case, in 1970, more than 50 squatter families fell prey to a scheming junior public servant and his compatriots who told them to pay for land and housing on a site that, in reality, did not belong to the Government. They lost everything. The CPIB was given the unenviable task of getting to the bottom of the matter. The affair, which was then called the Bukit Gombak Housing Fraud, was the brainchild of a single junior officer from the Inland Revenue Department (IRD). The CPIB was called in and found that 80 families had paid a junior officer of a government department for an "official permit" to reside on an empty plot of land at Bukit Gombak. They paid between $60 and $200 each, and many of them had also paid for or set up their zinc-wood structures in December 1970. They did not know that the land was still the property of the British Military. In any case, the "IRD officers" produced official letters sanctioning the land sales which also declared their structures legal. When the British Ministry of Defence found these illegal squatters and structures on their land, they lodged a complaint upon which the Ministry of National Development ordered that all their wooden huts be demolished. When the desperate squatters went to the Bukit Panjang district's Member of Parliament (MP) Pathmanaban Selvadurai for help, the whole scam came to light. They showed their MP the "official letters" they had received from the IRD. During the CPIB's initial investigation, which included interviewing all the families involved, it was revealed that middlemen "liaising" with the IRD had gone around their villages to induce them to join the housing scheme. He distributed official letters from the IRD, signed by the Comptroller of Property Tax. This middleman collected money on the spot.[102] The squatters were also given registration forms for erecting structures after they had paid for their lots. The tricksters even produced property tax forms to claim concession rates for their temporary structures. They all paid cash to the bogus government officers. The victims of the scam, mostly hawkers and farmers, lost their life's savings after paying the scammers. The scammers had even erected 46 unauthorised buildings which they then sold to the squatters. In total, these structures cost the squatters thousands more — only to be eventually demolished by the Government. Interestingly, the junior public servant who worked with the bogus officers only faced disciplinary action, even though he had used legitimate government forms in his scam.[103]

Then there was the case of the $1 pass racket at the Woodlands Checkpoint. Many lorries with perishable goods came through the Causeway where long queues and delays were frequent. It was not uncommon to hear of lorry drivers losing a part of their goods on account of the delays and the long waits under the hot sun. There were days when many of them were desperate for faster checks and clearances. In 1978, two customs officers,[104] separately, decided to render help to these lorry drivers by speeding up their clearances at the checkpoint for a small "toll" of $1 each way. The CPIB discovered their racket during a spot-check at the Woodlands Checkpoint. The Bureau's Special Investigators found wads of $1 notes in the customs officers' lockers for which they had no explanation.[105]

Negotiating Challenges

While a new PCO and the resetting of the CPIB in the early 1960s had been critical in preparing the Bureau for its fight against corruption in the decade, the Bureau was not without obstacles in moving forward.[106] For one, it remained a very small outfit throughout the 1960s. The Bureau's investigative team, including its seconded policemen, was never more than 15 officers.[107] When the police component pulled out towards the end of 1963, the Bureau was temporarily shorthanded. When Singapore merged with Malaysia in September 1963, the police force was federalised. The Federal Police wanted all officers returned to the Force. Generally, it was believed that the Bureau's small establishment had limited its work.[108] Then, Richard Byrne Corridon returned to head the Bureau — slowly but surely, he recruited more Special Investigators and restored the Bureau's staff strength to 15. He managed to retain that number till the mid-1970s when staff strength reached 25, and by 1978, the Bureau had 28 officers.[109] Meanwhile, Corridon, with his small band of good men, all "worked a seven-day week". The Bureau's men were driven by the belief that their work was important to the nation, and in particular to their Prime Minister (PM). In fact, Corridon shared, "The Prime Minister has many a time told me that he doesn't care who the corrupted person is. He wants to know — and he wants action."[110]

In the year that Singapore left Malaysia, the CPIB had already achieved a reputation for being efficient, effective and incorrupt. In fact, in May 1965, pressmen labelled the Bureau's men "The Incorruptibles".[111] In no small part, Corridon had played a big role in stabilising the Bureau after the policemen ended their secondment. But importantly, the Bureau's credibility reached new heights during his directorship, so much so that in January 1969, the Hong Kong Police sent its anti-corruption team to Singapore to study the CPIB's methods. They took back to Hong Kong copies of Singapore's PCO, the Criminal Procedure Code and the Disciplinary Procedure Code for their civil servants to consult. In 1974, the Hong Kong Government established their now famous Independent Commission Against Corruption (ICAC).[112] Corridon's reappointment to the Bureau's directorship in 1963 was not without problems. At that juncture, Singapore was on the verge of joining Malaysia as a state within an independent nation. It was no longer just a self-ruling territory within the British Empire. Most of its expatriate leaders had already left. In fact,

Lee Kuan Yew had to remind the Legislature, when Corridon's appointment was questioned, that Singapore was no longer in the "phase of chasing white men out". Corridon was given a two-year contract which would have kept him on the job till 1965, and if there were still no locals who had the experience and skills by then, Corridon's contract would certainly have been extended.[113] Lee also made the point that the Government still had other expatriates in the service then, citing the Public Utilities Board and the Port of Singapore Authority.

Several measures the Bureau employed to navigate its manpower challenges going into the 1970s included the recruitment of female Special Investigators and the raising of staff pay.[114] Like most other government departments, the Bureau's staffing was overseen by the Public Service Commission (PSC) and therefore could not independently raise its officers' grade and pay scale. However, in 1976, the Government helped by raising the baseline status of the Bureau's officers. The rank of all CPIB Special Investigators was raised from Division 2 in the Civil Service to Division 1.[115] More supervisory positions were also created to facilitate rank promotions.[116] Unfortunately, from the late 1970's to the early 1980s, the Bureau would be rocked by massive resignations. The situation was so bad that at one point, more than half of the Bureau's staff had been in service for less than a year.[117] One reason for this rough patch was the reality of the Bureau's work — it was tedious and the hours were long.[118] Nevertheless, the Bureau remained calm and pressed on. Clearly, all the occasions when the CPIB staff had to remain especially vigilant, working long and irregular hours, and all the times when the Bureau called for all-hands-on-deck, had taken a toll on the staff. This happened during a time where there were rackets involving fake medical certificates (1965), Bukit Gombak housing fraud (1970), traffic toll cases (1971) and more.

Another challenge that the Bureau faced in the 1960s, at a time of national development, was corruption by political and community leaders. There was no certainty, from the perspective of the public, that public servants would do their jobs without fear of reprisal from superiors or government leaders. While corruption in the political sphere could impact the credibility of the Government, taking to task community leaders could also potentially surface communal fault lines and affect social stability. At the core of these concerns was the credibility of the law enforcement agency itself — the Bureau had to demonstrate that it was impartial, had courage and would show no favour. Could the incumbent government walk the talk? The PAP had seen how the Chew affair had led to the discrediting of Lim Yew Hock's government, and had probably cost them the 1959 General Election. Hence, the Government backed the Bureau to do what it had to do, without fear or favour. Besides, the PM had already made it known that he did not "care who the corrupted person" was.

The Bureau was given a chance to demonstrate its resolve when one of its own was involved in a bribery case in 1964. The story started with two men, Chua Boon Swee and Lim Meng Wee, who joined the CPIB together in 1962. They became good friends. Chua resigned on 7 May 1964, on account of the low wages of $300 per month at the Bureau. Lim stayed on. Several months later, Chua contacted Lim and introduced him to Yip Thim Choy, a building inspector who was under CPIB investigation at that time. Chua wanted Lim's help to have a look at the investigation papers on Yip. Chua said that Yip could pay $5,000 for the favour. Lim informed his superiors about Chua's approach and they set a trap for Chua and Yip. Both men were caught red-handed when they brought the bribe money to meet Lim on 1 December 1964. Chua was sentenced to 18 months' imprisonment.[119]

Then came the first big test for the PAP Government. Tan Kia Gan, a former PAP minister, was removed from all functions in government in 1966 when his activities put him under a cloud of suspicion for being corrupt. He had become the Minister for National Development in August 1960. The PAP had suspended the previous Minister for National Development Ong Eng Guan in July 1960, and later expelled him for misconduct. In 1963, following Tan's defeat at the General Election, Tan vacated his ministerial post and was appointed Chairman of the HDB. Then, at the beginning of 1966, Tan moved over to the Tourist Promotion Board as its new Chairman. At the same time, he was the Deputy Chairman of the Economic Development Board and Singapore's representative on the Board of Malaysian Airways. On 12 August 1966, at a board meeting of Malaysian Airways, Tan raised his objection to the airline's purchase of new Boeing planes. He suggested chartering instead. But days later, an acquaintance of Tan approached the Singapore branch of the First National City Bank, Boeing's bankers, to inform the company that he knew someone who could help Boeing resolve its impasse with the Malaysian Airways with regard to the sale of their aircraft. This man also revealed that he had intended to set up an agency to sell Boeing airplanes. The bank reported the matter to the Government on suspicion that there was corruption involved in the whole affair. On 27 August, when the PM was informed, he spoke to Tan to seek an explanation and told him that he would be investigated by the CPIB. After questioning this "acquaintance", there was no conclusive evidence that Tan was in collusion. But Tan did not reveal his connection with this acquaintance when Lee Kuan Yew spoke to him. So, not convinced that everything had been above board, Lee took action to remove Tan from the Board of Malaysian Airways and all of his other government appointments as well, because he had "not discharged his duties beyond reproach".[120] By November 1966, Tan had been removed from all his statutory appointments after coming under suspicion of corruption.

A couple of years later, another sensitive case surfaced. The Assistant Director of the Social Welfare Department Abdul Aziz HM Nor was found to have taken money to approve the application of a Hong Kong woman to remain in Singapore permanently. This was discovered when he instructed his subordinate, Lee Poh Heng, to "backdate and write out" the interview they had had with the woman, and then to send this "favourable report" to the Immigration Department which was looking into the woman's marriage of convenience to a local resident. Lee Poh Heng complained to the CPIB and Aziz was found out. The matter was serious because he was a senior civil servant who had been in the service for 29 years, but it was sensitive because Aziz was well-known in his community. He had been running night classes from 1946 for the community. Three of his students had become ambassadors of Malaysia. In Singapore, one was a serving MP, and another a leading trade unionist. He was, nevertheless, convicted and jailed three years in 1969 for accepting a $2,000 bribe.[121]

The Bureau's biggest "political" case up till that time occurred in 1975. Wee Toon Boon, the Minister of State (Environment) was charged with five counts of corruption, with a combined bribe amount totalling $839,023. The CPIB, after extensive investigations, found that on 5 May 1972, when Wee was the Minister of State (Defence), he accepted the installation of a new galvanised roofing for his house. Then, on 16 January 1973, while Wee was Minister of State (Environment), he accepted from Atang Latief, the owner of a property development firm, a personal guarantee for an overdraft of up to $200,000 for his father. This was granted to his father for the purchase of shares through the Chase Manhattan Bank in Singapore. Following this, on 14 April 1973, Wee accepted another offer of guarantee from Latief for an overdraft from the same bank that was worth $100,000. Then in August 1973, Wee accepted the gift of a two-storey bungalow house from Latief. It was then valued at $532,000.[122]

What did Wee do to receive all these "gifts"? For one, each time Latief needed help with immigration matters, Wee acceded by contacting relevant government departments. These included Latief's application for permanent residency in Singapore and for his family servant who was an illegal in Singapore. And in instances when Latief's company faced problems with their $20 million housing project at Jalan Binchang, Wee arranged meetings between Latief's company and government planners, architects and others. On occasions, Wee would show up at the meetings unannounced. Eventually, someone in all these government bodies would highlight Wee's intervention in their affairs.[123] The maximum penalty for Wee's offences was five years' jail or a $10,000 fine or both.[124] He was sentenced to four years and six months, but this was reduced to 18 months when he appealed.

The last "political test" of the decade for the CPIB occurred on the last day of 1979,[125] when Phey Yew Kok, PAP MP for Boon Teck, took flight after being charged. He eluded arrest for years. This tested the tenacity and persistence of the Bureau's men for more than three decades. When the CPIB's investigations started in mid-1979, besides being an MP, Phey was the President of the National Trades Union Congress (NTUC); the General Secretary of the Singapore Industrial Labour Organisation (SILO), Pioneer Industries Employees' Union (PIEU) and Singapore Air Transport-Workers Union (SATU); the President of the Singapore Amateur Boxing Association and Singapore Mercantile Co-operative Thrift and Loan Society.[126] Devan Nair, then Secretary-General of NTUC, was also Phey's mentor.[127] Clearly, there was every reason for the Bureau's Special Investigators to tread carefully with this case.

The whole affair started when the CPIB investigated Phey after a SILO car was sold and $8,000 of the proceeds were credited into Phey's personal bank account. Although the sale occurred in 1974, it only surfaced in 1979. When the CPIB confronted Phey about the matter in September 1979, he claimed that a mistake had been made then and the money had been returned to the union. In fact, he got the SILO treasurer to forge documents to cover up the matter. After that, the Bureau dug deeper and discovered that in 1975, Phey had misappropriated two cheques meant for SILO. The Bureau also found that in September 1978, Phey used SILO's money to purchase shares in a supermarket without the approval of the Government, breaching the rules of the Trade Unions Act. The CPIB arrested Phey on 1 December 1979. On 10 December he was charged with four counts of criminal breach of trust involving $82,520 and two counts under the Trade Unions Act for using $17,745 of union funds to buy shares in the Forward Supermarket. In total, he misappropriated $100,265 of the union funds. He was scheduled to return to Court in January 1980, but he absconded.[128]

On 22 June 2015, old, sickly and alone, Phey surrendered himself at the Singapore Embassy in Bangkok, 35 years after he fled. The very next day, CPIB officers escorted him back to Singapore, and he was eventually sentenced to 60 months' imprisonment.[129] He had absconded and he had hidden, but he could not evade justice forever. The CPIB's file on Phey was certainly old, maybe it was a little dusty, but was never mothballed; the original Special Investigators had scrupulously and meticulously documented their research, and carefully packed all the paperwork for their successors at the Bureau, knowing one day they would apprehend Phey.[130] When Phey finally turned up, the Bureau's men were instantly ready.

The Government understood that tackling the culture of corruption in Singapore had to start from the top. The prosecution of top government men for corruption in the 1960s and 1970s had demonstrated this resolve. Few people remembered that Lee Kuan Yew himself had shown what it meant to be incorruptible; in 1960, the American Central Intelligence Agency (CIA) attempted to "buy him" over with a bribe. The whole affair started when a CIA agent attempted to bribe a Special Branch officer with "a large and continual sum" to provide information to the CIA. The officer rejected the offer and reported the matter to his superior, who in turn reported it to Lee. Lee instructed his men to lay a trap for this agent and to record everything. The agent was arrested. During negotiations to close the affair quietly and amicably, Lee suggested that the Americans could provide Singapore US$100,000,000 in economic aid; the Americans instead offered the PAP US$10,000,000. Now the CIA was trying to bribe the Party! The situation was truly reminiscent of the Chew affair. Lee had to decline the political gift. Lee, nevertheless, did not expose the intrigue till after Singapore gained Independence in 1965.[131]

Chapter Eighteen

Vanguard!

A most vital and often underappreciated function of the CPIB during Singapore's nation-building journey was the role it played in assisting other government departments to keep their own houses clean; reviewing government processes, lending an investigative hand and recommending disciplinary measures. Beyond enforcement, arresting and prosecuting corrupt parties, the Bureau had the duty of ensuring the nation kept on its path towards becoming a society that did not accept corruption as a norm in life.

From late 1966, a number of government departments which encountered allegations of corruption in their ranks were reorganised after receiving investigation reports from the CPIB.[132] In one such instance, the CPIB had to look into the affairs of HDB staff dealing with contractors who were suspected of questionable practices that led to irregularities in short-piling works.[133] In another case, after allegations of corruption, the CPIB investigated the Public Cleansing Department under the Ministry of Health. It was announced that a reorganisation was forthcoming; the daily-rated workers of the department were malingering and only showed up on Sundays and public holidays when the daily rates were higher. They were absent on weekdays. These workers also pilfered items they had picked up while on the job and sold them to junk shops.[134]

In 1967, the Ministry of Finance (MOF) Trade Division's Import and Export Office was reorganised after investigations by the CPIB; the Bureau received complaints of irregular delays in the approval of applications in the department. Suspicion of impropriety arose after it was found that some applications took a long time to receive approval as compared to others. So, the MOF streamlined and reorganised the department "to eliminate opportunities for corruption and to provide an efficient and quick service to all applicants". The public was also warned against providing "inducements". During the course of the CPIB's investigation, 11 officers, including a few senior men, were suspended. A year earlier, the Timber Section and the Supplies Unit of the MOF's Trade Division were also reorganised following the CPIB's investigation and report on their activities.[135]

Since the 1960s, the Bureau had continued to aid any government department that needed its investigative skills and expertise to resolve in-house matters or to help implement preventive measures in order to clean up and make proper their affairs. Beyond the new millennium, the Bureau also conducted occasional departmental assessments that produced Review Papers which were submitted to the relevant government departments.[136] This was one way the Bureau demonstrated vigilance amongst government bodies.

Quis Custodiet Ipsos Custodes

"Who will guard the guards themselves?"[137] In Singapore's journey towards nationhood, besides ensuring that politicians remained clean, the state also had to make certain that the law enforcers of the country were also free of corrupt practices. Eventually, the Police Establishment would be able to check itself, but till the 1970s, the CPIB had to play its part to "guard the guards" when required. Although the Bureau remained a small outfit of no more than 15 staff till the mid-1970s, it was still able to thoroughly handle large-scale corruption amongst law enforcement officers, as in the case of the 1970–1971 police "traffic toll" scandal. It was around this time that the CPIB's Special Investigators became "feared" law enforcers, especially amongst corrupt cops.

It was not possible to always follow up on all cases of corrupt enforcement officers when they surfaced. These were simply too random, and certainly were occurring too often in the 1960s and early 1970s. In 1971, the Bureau, in coordination with the Public Service Commission (PSC), checked for corrupt practices amongst government officers by inquiring into their indebtedness. This followed the PSC's dismissal of a high-ranking customs officer who had been under the CPIB's surveillance for a year. The PSC, having found the officer living beyond his means, instituted an inquiry and had the CPIB investigate him.[138]

Indebtedness was considered a condition that fostered corruption among public servants. Under Government General Orders,[139] police officers had to declare indebtedness twice yearly while the rest of the Civil Service did it annually. Any civil servant could be dismissed if they were indebted. Yet, in the early 1970s, the Government still found that many of its employees were indebted. The CPIB discovered that a finance company had liberally given out loans to public servants, with high rates of between 15% and 25% monthly. This was despite the fact that authorised moneylenders could only loan up to 18% annually. Nevertheless, many civil servants still took high loan rates from this finance company despite their annual declarations. Amongst these indebted public servants were many police officers. Hence, the CPIB sent the Assistant Commissioner of Police (Administration) a memorandum containing the details of each officer and the amounts they took from this company. The Bureau had gathered these names by examining the books of the finance firm. The CPIB also sent memoranda to various government departments which had staff who were also listed in the ledgers of the company. Most of them were junior officers who had taken loans years ago, and were now just paying interest. They had no way out.[140] When the People's Action Party (PAP) Government started enforcing the General Orders relating to indebtedness and bankruptcy from 1960, hundreds of public servants had already been dismissed across the decade.[141] Yet, the issue remained pervasive among public servants through the 1970s, and the police force was no exception.

In 1971, following probes by the Bureau, and a police internal inquiry into members of the Force who were in the books of the finance company that offered liberal loans, scores of police officers were found to have been indebted.[142] The CPIB realised from this period just how important it was working with the other enforcement agencies to effectively root out deep-seated corruption. In this light, the CPIB and the police force formed a joint task force in late 1976 to start "monitoring the assets, incomes and expenditure of all officers and men". The goal of this task force was to weed out corruption in the Force. It was in December 1976 that instructions were given to a number of commanding officers to submit returns of their assets, incomes and expenditures of all officers under their charge. This included ownership of houses, vehicles, their spouses' occupation and salaries. The task force wanted to determine if any of them had been living beyond their means. At the same time, the Police also sent special teams to pay surprise visits to police stations and units to conduct checks on officers doing their jobs, and to inspect documentation and records. The joint task force also identified existing "corruption hazards" and recommended measures to prevent them.[143] In any case, while these measures went some way to check corrupt tendencies, they were never going to completely eradicate corrupt practices in the country.

In the 1970s, besides the police force, the other important "guardians" of Singapore were those who safeguarded our national borders — the immigration and customs officers who controlled access to, and exit from, Singapore. Before Independence, most corruption cases regarding border control involved collusion of officers with criminal enterprises in smuggling activities. In the 1950s, such activities mainly involved opium and other contraband. Of course, criminal syndicates also valued forged Singapore passports which opened doors for anyone travelling within the British Commonwealth. By the 1960s and 1970s, the main reasons to get past border controls in Singapore were more economic in nature. Offenders tried to circumvent and evade excise controls, and to facilitate entry or overstaying in Singapore where work and profit opportunities were more abundant than they were in other parts of the region. Hence, the nature of corrupt activities among border control officers in the post-Independence period was fundamentally a more direct threat to Singapore's development than the period before. In this context, the CPIB had to be ever more vigilant in ensuring Singapore's border control services remained corruption-free.

In an era where the Customs control protected Singapore's trade and industries by ensuring no one bypassed excise and fiscal measures, border control staff also played a crucial part in Singapore's economic progress. Excise taxes contributed hundreds of millions of dollars annually to Singapore's coffers. Excise income was an important revenue stream that supported the state's infrastructural and other works.[144] Hence, ensuring that the borders were adequately protected had been central to Singapore's nation-building efforts. Yet, there were still customs and immigration officers who continued to fail to do their duty decades after Independence.

Circumvention of excise duties saved individuals and companies thousands of dollars annually, and perhaps millions over several years. There was, therefore, always the motivation to bribe border officials to avoid paying excise duties. And there were government employees who would fall into temptation to earn a few dollars. In the 1960s and 1970s, the CPIB would uncover many instances of this collusion between businessmen and customs officers at the Woodlands Checkpoint. Such collusion was distinctly different from the "$1 toll" cases in which junior customs officers on the ground were collecting from lorry drivers to ease their clearance. Excise evasion often netted the corrupt officers more than a $1 toll and tended to involve more coordination. If big importers offered bribes, the officers at the checkpoints just had to quietly accept the *kopi money* to close one eye; this was especially in cases where the casual traveller did not declare goods that were dutiable. In late 1971, the CPIB investigators kept watch on three custom officers, including a senior staff at the Woodlands Checkpoint. They were found to have taken money to facilitate smoother clearance or non-payment of duties. In this instance, the CPIB officers uncovered the nefarious activities which proved most interesting. Posing as travellers from West Malaysia, the Bureau men mingled with commuters and motorists to pass through the checkpoint daily.[145] The customs officers were eventually caught red-handed in full view of the "travelling" investigators.

Bureau men assigned to "guard the guards" at the checkpoints would have seen everything. Amongst the common tax evaders at the border, notwithstanding the regular liquor and cigarette "importers", there were also people importing monosodium glutamate (MSG), and even women's undergarments. For most people today, MSG is simply a flavour enhancer (gourmet powder). However, in the 1970s, when people were less health-conscious, MSG was a highly sought-after commodity, especially by those in the food and beverage industry. The one impediment they faced was a duty of $2 per lb placed on this "salt". This was enough motivation for individuals, and even customs officers, to organise MSG smuggling "gangs". The Bureau uncovered such a gang in 1972 when it tailed cars loaded with MSG, driven by Customs men travelling from Malaysia into Singapore. In one car, the CPIB found 800 lbs of MSG and in another, 1,200 lbs. The total "street" value of these "salts" was $20,000, while the dutiable value was $4,000. Seven customs officers were detained in this instance. The tip-off that busted open the case came from a rival "MSG gang" (non-customs officers).[146]

Another dutiable item in 1970s Singapore was clothing. Singapore was a manufacturing hub at this time. There were excise taxes on imports of similar items made locally; the duty on imported shirts was $2 per piece or 15% of the value, whereas a 25% duty was imposed on stockings and pantyhose. Local importers of clothing items would make immense savings if they were importing large quantities of clothing and could avoid taxes on all of them. So, what is a small bribe to get their consignments through, tax-free? In retrospect, while these anecdotal examples of corrupt officers and their dealings with saucy and trifling items for monetary gain seem to be light-hearted accounts of what border control staff would do for extra money, it must not be forgotten that they were, and still are, the guardians of the gateways into Singapore. Although the corrupt officers that aided these excise "cheaters" might have only received small amounts of *kopi* money, in doing so, they left our doors wide open to the illegal siphoning of millions in potential state income that was to be used for the development of the country, if one considers the total amount of all the taxes evaded.

There was also a darker side to the complicity of corrupt officers who rendered our borders porous; it also allowed the illegal movement of men, women and children across borders. In early 1971, the CPIB detected and arrested two policemen involved in an illegal immigrant smuggling syndicate. They aided smugglers who brought in Indonesian labourers by facilitating their landing along Singapore's coastline: Ponggol, Tanah Merah, Siglap and West Coast Road. A shortage of labourers in Singapore made this "trade" highly lucrative for these modern-day "coolie agents". General workers were paid between $5 and $10 per day depending on their skills. Not only were the Indonesian labourers willing to take half of this rate, their "employers" also did not have to pay them the obligatory Central Provision Fund (CPF) contributions. Even though these illegals were willing participants in this "scheme", it did not change the fact that their agent-smugglers, employers and the corrupt officers that facilitated their arrival had all been exploitative in the affair.[147]

While investigating the illegal immigrant labour affair, the CPIB also uncovered and smashed a regional racket smuggling Indonesian children into Singapore via Riau. The CPIB and the Police discovered how the syndicate, after bringing the children into Singapore, would get their counterparts in Johore Bahru to forge Malaysian birth certificates for them. The smugglers would provide the Malaysian forgers details of the children such as their ages and ethnicity. The birth certificates would include the names of Singapore citizens who would become actual "adopting" parents. Such details helped the forgers to "custom" and date the certificates correctly in order to match the children and their prospective parents. The certificates would enable the children to apply for blue identity cards (issued to permanent residents) which would then facilitate their admission into Singapore schools. All this while, the children never left Singapore after they reached the island. The syndicate, which had been in operation for several years before being exposed, had charged $4,000 to provide this "turnkey" service for each child smuggled in. The CPIB and the Police arrested a number of the syndicate's men in early 1972.[148]

The Bureau had to be at the forefront of the battle against the human smuggling racket in the 1970s, not because it was the CPIB's core work, but because corrupt officers in the Customs and Immigration Departments had opened the gateway for criminal syndicates to enter and use Singapore for their unlawful activities. The moral depravity they brought constituted a threat to our nation-building enterprise and the social fabric of Singapore society. Besides smuggling, another serious threat uncovered by the CPIB was the Woodlands Checkpoint passport racket; corrupt customs and immigration officers colluded with operators of adult entertainment and prostitution rackets to allow women in the trade to continuously extend their stay in Singapore. These operators were by and large also triad members. The passport racket had been so extensive that it literally sustained the progress of the underground illegal immigrant and sex trade, and subverted the island's anti-vice operations. Yet, despite continuous suppression, and the prosecution of border officers, the corruption continued. It was like a cancer which could not be permanently stopped,[149] and it returned repeatedly. The Bureau had to remain vigilant, always on alert to keep corrupt practices at the border in abeyance.

The CPIB was actually already well aware of a passport racket among the immigration officials before the 1970s.[150] However, it was not until February 1972 that the racket was fully exposed. The Bureau detained five immigration officers at the Woodlands Checkpoint for taking bribes to facilitate travellers holding restricted Malaysian passports. They were mostly women who were granted visit passes, but overstayed to work as call girls, bar waitresses and cabaret girls. In 1972, the CPIB "turned" a taxi driver to testify against three immigration officers who illegally endorsed passports. The driver had been ferrying prostitutes from Johore Bahru into Singapore and had helped other prostitutes to get their passports extended by the three officers.[151]

The continual suppression of the brothels by the Police and the CPIB's smashing of the passport rackets for call girls in 1972–1973 saw hundreds of call girls expelled while others fled or returned to Malaysia. This inevitably created a crisis among the triad gangs who operated the brothels. They lost thousands of dollars in revenue and their vice activities had been seriously crippled. Consequently, in late 1973, major triads from both sides of the Causeway organised a "summit" in Singapore to discuss how they could remedy the situation. The boss of Kuala Lumpur's biggest secret society, the *Loong Foo Tong* (Dragon and Tiger Society) was to be in attendance. A gathering of this magnitude could not be kept a secret. Eventually, the Police and the CPIB received news of this mega event as it was happening. The "generals" met in a shop at Albert Street, guarded by a dozen fully armed men. They discussed how they could "bring about closer, smoother and more lucrative criminal operations and cooperation between Malaysian and Singapore gangs". It was suggested that they could "restructure" their racket so as not to attract the attention "from government men". However, when the Police were about to commence their operation to detain all the "generals" at the gathering, the gangs received a tip-off that a raid was forthcoming. The "generals" managed to scatter before the Police arrived.[152] Interestingly, just like cancer, despite all the "heat", attention and clampdowns, the immigration officers' passport racket continued unabated into the 1970s.[153]

Despite major clampdowns occurring almost every other year, the CPIB uncovered yet another passport racket involving immigration officers in 1976. A Malaysian man had organised another passport-forging syndicate involving several immigration officers; he collected $100 from each prostitute and shared the money with co-conspiring corrupt immigration officers at the Woodlands Checkpoint. The scheme was discovered when the CPIB was informed that some fake endorsement rubber stamps were found in a house in Johore Bahru. Several immigration officers were questioned and two were detained, while others went into hiding. The Malaysian man was arrested in Singapore. The CPIB also found more fake rubber stamps in his house at Tanjong Pagar. Following this, brothels in Chinatown and Geylang were raided. Of the 10 prostitutes arrested, eight had passports with forged endorsement of social visit passes. And they were also on the Immigration Department's blacklist.[154]

It is perhaps noteworthy that it was in the 1970s that the CPIB had become a force to reckon with. While it was not uncommon to hear about crooks impersonating police officers in the days of old, it was in the 1970s that it became more "in vogue" to impersonate CPIB Special Investigators. In a 1973 incident, imposters pretended to be Bureau men to waylay a businessman at Joo Chiat. They forced him into a car and, at gunpoint, robbed him of $5,000 and a $200 watch.[155] In July 1977, another crook, a carpenter who needed money for his impending marriage, posed as a CPIB Special Investigator to cheat a widow of $5,000. The woman had needed help to recover some property swindled from her late husband. The carpenter posing as a Special Investigator took advantage of her predicament. The carpenter was jailed 15 months.[156]

At Any Cost

The pursuit and prosecution of Gerald Fernandez from 1969 to 1971 was, at that time, Singapore's most costly corruption case ever. It was an important case for the state not because Fernandez was an important figure, politically or otherwise, nor did his crime involve millions. But he was one figure that the Government decided it had to pursue and bring to justice at any cost! Unlike the future Phey Yew Kok case (1979–1980), Fernandez could be found, and there was a case to be made about dishonest public servants who thought they could outsmart enforcement officers.

Fernandez, the Malaysia–Singapore Airline (MSA) Secretary and Legal Officer,[157] committed two acts of corruption in 1966 and 1968, which in total involved $11,000. When his crime was discovered, he had already resigned from MSA and had returned to Malaysia. He was arrested in Kuala Lumpur on 24 July 1969 after the Singapore Government applied to the Malaysian Court for a warrant of arrest under the Commonwealth Fugitive Criminals Act (1967).[158] Fernandez was allowed bail while the Malaysian Court deliberated whether he should return to Singapore to stand trial. His bail was set at $15,000. The hearing for the Court's decision was set for 15 September 1969, but he absconded.[159]

The whole affair had started in early 1969 when the CPIB received complaints alleging corruption among the staff of MSA (Singapore). After months of discreet investigation focusing on the airline's insurance, advertising and aircraft servicing, the Bureau decided in June 1969 that it had enough evidence to proceed further with investigation. On 16 June, with all hands on deck, about 20 CPIB officers raided the MSA (Singapore) Robinson Road office and carted away all relevant documents and account books. Every effort was taken to carefully handle the search and seizure at the airline's office as it was partly owned by the Malaysian Government.[160] However, the Malaysian Government was peeved as they felt prior notice was warranted as a matter of courtesy since the CPIB was seizing MSA documents and they were concerned that the affair might affect the image of the MSA.[161]

At the same time the CPIB raided MSA's office, it also searched the office of the airline's insurer, Edward Lumley and Sons (S) Pte Ltd.[162] The Bureau consequently found evidence that Gerald Fernandez had received gratification from the firm in 1966 and 1968 that totalled $11,000. The two payments, $6,000 and $5,000, respectively, were given to Fernandez for favouring the firm in its bid for the airline's aviation and legal liability insurance contract for the period from April 1965 to March 1968. The contract was for the extension of insurance coverage for 18 months. After the contract was awarded on 13 July 1966, Fernandez approached the firm, through Quek Cheng Choy, the firm's agent, for a $6,000 loan to buy furniture. By the end of 1966, when the loan was not repaid, the firm issued a payment voucher backdated to 13 July 1966, and posted the voucher into the MSA commission account for 1967. Then, on 5 August 1968, when the firm found out that Fernandez was leaving the MSA, the firm gave him $5,000 as a parting gift for services rendered.[163] The CPIB had conducted thorough investigations which were supported by documentary evidence of all these transactions.

After fleeing Kuala Lumpur, Fernandez made his way to London where he lived as a free man for more than a year. It was after his arrival in Britain that Fernandez wrote to the Malaysian Attorney-General asking to be tried in Malaysia instead of Singapore, and he even attempted to appeal to the Malaysian Yang di-Pertuan Agong.[164] Meanwhile, the Singapore Government also applied to the British Government for his extradition. In October 1970, just as the Malaysian authorities had decided to try Fernandez in Malaysia, the British authorities granted Singapore's request for extradition. So, in October 1970, Fernandez was once again arrested; this time, he was jailed in London where he contested his extradition order.[165] He had engaged a Queen's Counsel (QC) to argue his case, and so had the Singapore Government.[166] It was during the proceedings of his extradition order that Fernandez made his most extraordinary claims that his charges in Singapore had been trumped-up because of his religious and political views![167] Fernandez argued that the Singapore Government was out to "eliminate" him and that the monies he got from Quek were simply personal loans.[168] In short, Fernandez claimed that he had been watched by the state, and that he was being persecuted. This necessitated Singapore's QC to put the CPIB's former Director and Director of the day on the stand in December 1970. Both men testified that Fernandez had never been on their watchlist, nor had they known of him in the 1960s.[169] The British Court rejected Fernandez's argument.[170] On 6 June 1971, Fernandez's final appeal against the extradition was rejected and he was sent "home" in July 1971, escorted by CPIB Assistant Director Ronald Naidu.[171]

Fernandez was finally convicted in Singapore on 9 September 1971, after a 26-day trial.[172] He was sentenced to 26 months' jail and fined $5,000, the quantum of the gift he received from the insurance firm in 1968. He was never charged for the $6,000 "loan" he took from the firm to buy furniture, which he never repaid.[173] For the Singapore Government, apprehending and convicting Fernandez had been about making a point. It did not matter who you were, what resources you had, who you knew, how far you ran and for how long you were gone. Moreover, in his attempt to get off scot-free from his corruption charges, Fernandez had also attempted to stir sentiments in Malaysia. He had resorted to discrediting the Singapore Government with accusations of conspiracy and persecution in relation to religious and political issues. In the end, apprehending and successfully prosecuting Fernandez cost the Government more than a quarter million dollars as well as invaluable time and resources.[174] The price of failing to convict Fernandez would have cost immeasurably more for Singapore's reputation.

Chapter Nineteen

Headwinds

Moving from the 1970s to the 1980s, Singapore faced new challenges in the nature of corrupt practices amongst citizens. Naturally, these became challenges for the CPIB as well. Generally, while old forms of corruption became more complex, new kinds of corruption also added to the challenges of the day. Also, to compound matters, the CPIB investigated all forms of rackets involving public servants and monies. Above all, not only did these emerging trends open a window to the sign of the times, they also gave a hint of the headwinds the Bureau would face in the coming decades.

White-Collar Rackets

It was during the CPIB's investigation into allegations of corruption at the Malaysia–Singapore Airlines (MSA) that the CPIB uncovered a racket that was such a brilliant "con job" that it duped almost every government department and Civil Service organisation that encountered it. It was, unfortunately, overshadowed by the Gerald Fernandez affair. Simply put, the "con" involved convincing government and private bodies to pay for advertisement space in souvenir publications for events or causes that either did not exist or for events and causes invented or organised by the tricksters. It was during the CPIB's second raid of the MSA office[175] that the truth of a scam relating to advertisements the airline had paid for came to light. Basically, the scam started with a printing firm sending out canvassers who would give businesses the false impression that they were printing a government or a government-sponsored publication. The canvassers also gave the impression that if they refused to advertise in these magazines, the relevant government department, or individuals in that department, would not be pleased. Although this might lead to resentment against the government, businesses tended to accede, especially if they had dealings with that particular department. This helped the "bogus canvassers" to collect advertisements for a publication that might or might not be printed.

Another modus operandi of the printing firms in the scam was to pressure a government employee to organise an event such as a body-building contest, which more than 10 government departments were invited to participate in. The firm would then publish a "souvenir programme" for the event, in the name of all the participating government departments which were invited, even though only a handful might eventually join the event. The bogus canvassers would then approach the shops, factories and businesses which required licences from these departments to buy advertisements in the souvenir or to make donations for the event. This was a subtle form of intimidation. Sometimes, these canvassers also carried so-called official letters which gave the impression that they were officers of those participating departments and that the proceeds of the event would go to the National Defence Fund or to charity.[176] When the CPIB delved into the modus operandi of one such printing firm in 1969, the firm claimed that it had collected $54,000 for a government department's souvenir programme. However, it only gave $1,000 to the department, $500 to the National Defence Fund and none to charity. The firm pocketed the rest. The CPIB believed that they had collected much more than they claimed. Interestingly, the Bureau found that the firm continued canvassing for advertisements for "new editions" of the souvenir programme even after the event was over.[177]

In another case the Bureau found that a trade union and statutory organisation had set up a "mythical" building fund for its "souvenir magazine". The printer collected thousands of dollars but deposited the money into a private bank account. In yet another scam, canvassers used the name of a Civil Service recreation club to produce a film show. In total, $30,000 was collected but only $8,000 went to the club. Also, the club's bank had been authorised to transfer funds into the publishing firm's account. A printer even tricked a well-known professor to help solicit funds for a charity that he was not familiar with; he did not even know if it was legitimate. Some Civil Service union officials were found to have been sending out letters to collect contributions for "souvenir magazines". Each magazine project netted the canvassing firms between $50,000 and $100,000. The number of such magazines being produced for fictitious causes and events annually was so large that the CPIB could not tally just how many had been printed. The staff of a government department, as well as the MSA, had produced such magazines on a monthly basis. One Civil Service association even produced a magazine of advertisements that was three inches thick. It earned the publisher close to a quarter of a million dollars, yet the association itself received less than $5,000. As part of the scam, printing firms had government organisations sign contracts which allowed the printers to include an unlimited number of advertisements and to collect and retain all monies connected to the advertisements.[178]

As a result of the CPIB's unravelling of this multi-million-dollar advertisement racket, the Government issued new instructions in mid-1969 that forbade civil servants and employees of statutory boards to give "patronage" to publications; in their personal or official capacity, or as a semi-government employee or staff of Civil Service associations, recreational clubs and so on. No public servant was allowed to be associated with any publication with paid advertisements. This instruction was entered into the Government's departmental Instruction Manuals. As a result, the racket was checked, and the CPIB had a new front against public service corrupt practices to monitor vigilantly. During its investigation, the CPIB raided printing presses, publishing firms and civil service organisations. Advertising canvassers were picked up and questioned by the Bureau in its Stamford Road headquarters. There were numerous complaints from the public. The Government's image was tarnished. The Ministry of Finance sent out its own circular to all Permanent Secretaries to be alert to such scams.[179]

The problems associated with printers, publishers and advertisers did not end with the CPIB's crackdown on the industry in 1969. In mid-1975, the Bureau started to investigate the affairs of an officer of the Singapore Tourist Promotion Board (STPB) who was believed to have received gratification from a leading advertising agency. The CPIB probe lasted several months and 15 people from the STPB and the advertisement agency were questioned. The Bureau discovered that the officer had received gratification from hotels and departmental stores as well. In total, it was believed that he had collected more than $300,000. So the CPIB checked his bank accounts and looked into his lifestyle to ascertain if he had lived beyond his means. Upon completion of its thorough investigation, the CPIB handed its research report to the STPB for further action.[180] Clearly, in industries and sectors flushed with funds and monies, corrupt practices tended to follow, even in places of glamour and not sleaze. This was a fact of life that was not lost on the Bureau.

Jail House Rock

It was in the mid-1970s that the prison service encountered an unprecedented situation — almost all the major drug "kingpins" were behind bars at the same time. While this attested to the success of the police force against the drug syndicates at this time, the new reality was that the prison system was now home to syndicate bosses who were not short of resources to make their lives better behind bars. Gone were the days of petty bribes of a cigarette here and some chocolate there. The transition started around January and February 1974, when the Central Narcotics Bureau arrested 15 notorious opium smugglers islandwide. It was about three months after their detention that their relatives and henchmen started approaching prison officers whom they had become familiar with during their frequent visits to offer rewards for helping to make the lives of their loved ones and bosses better. Initially, the officers asked for at least $20,000. After negotiations, they settled for $10,000 for each kingpin; four families accepted the arrangement while others who felt that the sum was too high simply backed out. The money was paid secretly in cash, in denominations of $25, $50 or $100, at prearranged locations outside Queenstown Prison. The kingpins whose families paid received better food, medical treatment and prison facilities. CPIB Special Investigators and prison authorities busted the bribery racket in early 1975 after keeping watch on the officers, the relatives and henchmen of the detainees for a month. Ten family members and five prison officers were involved. One outcome of this case was that it led the CPIB to contemplate monitoring the family members of other prisoners at Queenstown and Changi prisons.[181]

The corrupting effects of drug money in the prison service also affected Changi Prison in 1974. The CPIB and prison authorities kept a close watch on the drug traffickers who were inmates at Changi. So, it was difficult for them to bribe the prison warders there. Nevertheless, it did not deter three traffickers who were brought into Changi in July 1974 from trying to beat the system. Instead, they bribed the prison's male nurse with $1,000 to smuggle in food, cigarettes and letters, and to help them keep these items in the clinic wards rather than in their cells where they would be found. The traffickers, instead of approaching the nurse directly, initially avoided discovery by getting their own "contact men" to work things out with the nurse within a fortnight of reaching Changi. When the nurse was given his $1,000 outside the prison, the CPIB moved in and busted the ring.[182]

Even drug addicts got into the prison bribery racket. In 1976, the CPIB uncovered a racket among five warders who sold cigarettes spiked with opium for $15 a stick to inmates of the Telok Paku and Jalan Awan drug rehabilitation centres.[183] While investigating this case, the CPIB also uncovered another "inflated" cigarette price scam at the Telok Paku

Rehabilitation Centre that was used to disguise an inmate's way of bribing a warder. The inmate received treats in the centre: roti prata, fried mee and cigarettes. And when this arrangement worked out, and trust was gained, the inmate agreed to give a direct loan to the warder. The inmate got his wife to deliver $50 directly to the warder's house. The loan was never repaid. The warder was arrested by the CPIB and the judge handed him a nine months' jail sentence.[184]

Sembawang Opium Heist

In the annals of the CPIB's history, the October 1951 Ponggol Opium Heist would be considered the pivotal moment that led to the creation of the Bureau itself. It would be a surprise that history, or the level of such conspiracies amongst enforcement officers, would be repeated. But it was, 20 years later, at Sembawang. The story began on 12 September 1971 when customs officers seized about 2,200 lbs of raw opium at a beach in Sembawang which was worth more than $250,000 in the black market. It was the biggest haul in 10 years. The drug, brought from the South China Sea, was popularly known as "Yunnan Opium". Smuggled by a well-organised international syndicate, the opium was packed in 50 large polythene bags and buried in two shallow holes off the Sembawang coastline, four feet from the sea. One hole had 37 bags while the other hid 13. Each bag had 10 smaller packets. In all, there were 500 packets. The customs officers who found the loot had made no arrest. According to the Customs Department, six officers from their Preventive Branch, led by Chief Customs Officer Inche Ibrahim bin Haji Agnam, set up an ambush at Sembawang seacoast at around 10pm on 11 September 1971. The team included Senior Superintendent Lim Kee Sion, head of the Land Division, and his assistant, Acting Superintendent Yap Swee Siang. They waited all night and into the wee hours of the morning, but no one came. So, soon after 6am on 12 September, they surrounded a hut at the beach, believing that smugglers could be inside. But it was empty. They then searched the area around the hut and found the pits where the opium was hidden. The holes were covered by a layer of gunny sacks. Almost a ton (2,200 lbs) of opium was found. The value of opium at this time was $120 per lb.[185]

Although nobody had actually been caught with the loot, the raid itself was successful in uncovering the hidden opium. The customs officers involved in the raid then circulated a story that the opium had belonged to a drug lord who had been betrayed by his men, who had been the ones who provided the tip-off of the stash in Sembawang. According to this narrative, the men had stolen a much larger consignment of opium from their boss. And to deflect attention from themselves, they left 2,200 lbs of the drug to be found by customs officers, while they got off with the actual loot. It was a double-cross to hide their part in the theft from their boss. The gang had supposedly double-crossed another gang who was supposed to steal the hidden opium in Sembawang, and they had hoped that their tip-off would lead to their arrest by the Customs. In this way, their boss would have specific persons to blame for the loss of his opium. But the gang they set up did not turn up. Apparently, the drug syndicate importing the opium had been robbed several times earlier when they transported their drugs on fast boats down the Straits of Malacca. Hence, their tale of a hijack by another gang would not be unbelievable. The twist occurred in 1974, when the drug lord first learnt of the supposed "double cross" by his own men and hunted them down for their betrayal. According to the customs officers, members of this gang were still at large in 1974.[186]

The whole conspiracy by the Customs men crumbled when the drug boss went on his rampage. The CPIB started its investigation of the Sembawang Opium Heist in 1975. The Bureau found that the customs officers involved in the recovery of the raw opium at Sembawang beach in 1971 had conspired in order to claim the $30,000 reward for the tip-off which they shared. They had faked a tip-off, crediting it to one of their own regular informers so that the man could claim the reward and split it with the officers. Several top customs officers who were on the original "raiding team" were implicated. One officer was immediately suspended and a departmental inquiry started.[187] These officers had actually found the opium by chance. However, instead of reporting their find, which meant that no one would be rewarded as there was no real tip-off by an informant, they decided to "cook up" the whole story about betrayal and a botched heist... and an actual heist. Following this scandal, the Customs Department tightened its reward system; informers had to be registered to prevent fraudulent claims by customs officers.[188]

Non-Monetary Gratification

The early 1970s saw a new trend in the form of corrupt practices among civil servants. The new breed of corruptors simply offered expensive entertainment and parties. No money was exchanged. This was a period when a middle class was emerging in Singapore. Many civil servants had some money, though not a lot, and were less inclined to be tempted by a little *kopi* money, especially amongst higher division public servants. But many were enticed by glamour and lifestyle.

The CPIB started its investigation involving several Public Utilities Board (PUB) staff in August 1970 when it was found that tax-free underground cables for the Jurong Power Station had been imported in excess of requirements. So the Bureau raided the offices of two electrical contractors and found that the excess cables had vanished. Because the cables had been imported by the PUB, no tax was attached. The excess 20,000 yards of cable was not subjected to the 40% tax that the private sector had to pay. When the CPIB probed further, it discovered that these electrical contractors were sponsoring "lavish parties" for senior PUB officers at posh nightclubs. The Bureau submitted a preliminary report to the PUB which then set up a disciplinary board led by a lawyer.[189] Consequently, the PUB reorganised itself and a number of senior officers were asked to leave.[190] The CPIB also found a similar trend at the Port of

Singapore Authority (PSA). In this instance, the Bureau found that PSA staff had been attending lavish parties and fraternising with businessmen after office hours for several years. These businessmen would send chauffeur-driven limousines to fetch PSA staff to clubs and nightspots. Six senior officers were found to have been involved. PSA Chairman Howe Yoon Chong issued a warning to these senior officers following the CPIB's report.[191] By 1971, the CPIB started paying greater attention to such posh parties, keeping both senior civil servants and businessmen under surveillance.[192] And what the Bureau discovered! Three high-ranking police officers were found associating with a foreign businessman. They were questioned by the CPIB. The Permanent Secretary of the Ministry of Home Affairs was informed that the police officers had accepted gifts from an Indonesian tycoon.[193]

The Bureau also found that two junior staff of the Telecommunications Department had been on the "payroll" of Indonesian businessmen who also paid for their parties at night clubs and hotels. They were suspended.[194] After this, the CPIB raided the department to secure and check its books. As a result, 12 more Telecommunications Department staff were suspended. It was found that they had received gifts from the tycoon for services rendered. There were three supervisors in this group of women.[195]

The 1970s saw more and more instances of corrupt practices by public servants which did not involve monetary gratification. Besides parties, there were cases involving sex in return for favours. In 1976, a Housing and Development Board (HDB) officer agreed to help a woman's husband to secure a hawker stall in return for sexual favours. Her husband did not know of the deal. After that, he also helped the woman and her husband to secure a flat from the HDB. It was during the CPIB's investigation, which started after a tip-off, that the officer's affair with the married woman surfaced. The CPIB handed its investigation report to the HDB which convened a commission of inquiry. The commission recommended that the officer be sacked.[196]

Lure of Horses: Bookies, Cops and Guns

Greed has always been the root of all evil. But it is the thrill of the draw in the game of chance, the lure and temptation that is the real cause of corruption cancer. Historically, gambling syndicates had consistently been a source of corruption of law enforcers; gaming tables, gambling dens and triad-controlled gambling. Most of these activities had at one time or another bought protection from corrupt police officers or paid a constable to close one eye. It was only towards the late 1950s that betting on horse races became a corruption problem,[197] together with the related four-digit betting racket.[198] It was around 1957 that illegal bookmaking started to become a serious issue for the Turf Club. It was time to amend the law to deal with the problem. However, the Government realised that any measures taken to deal with off-the-course betting required coordination between Singapore and the Federation authorities, without which any legislation in Singapore could be circumvented. By this time, there were hundreds of bookies in this multi-million-dollar racket; they operated mainly from coffeeshops, bars, restaurants and even offices.[199] It was around this time that bookmakers started bribing police officers, and police officers started offering protection for the betting racket. It was in late 1959 that the CPIB started monitoring the situation at the Bukit Timah Turf Club, which was also in line with the People's Action Party (PAP) Government's stance on indebtedness of government officers.[200] The Bureau found government officers attending race meetings during working hours. Some of them had submitted medical certificates on the day they went to the Turf Club. The CPIB submitted the names of all these officers to the respective government departments for further action. Amongst these public servants were a number of police officers. In the following investigation, the CPIB found two detectives operating as bookmakers at the racecourse.[201] Soon after, at the start of 1960, the Government placed a heavy police presence at the Turf Club on race days to "wipe out" onsite bookmaking. Thereafter, the bookmakers avoided the Club.[202]

The corruption cancer reappeared at the Turf Club with a vengeance in 1971. In that year, illegal bookmaking emerged as the new big-money racket behind many corrupting malpractices of the day. At this time, the Singapore races were linked to the races in the Federation of Malaysia. So, the Singapore punters could bet on the races in the Malaysian turf clubs and vice versa. It was towards mid-1971 that the CPIB successfully prosecuted eight kingpin bookies, five of whom were Malaysians. They were charged in Court for bribing the Turf Club's Chief Security Officer, Wilfred Douglas Anthony. They wanted him to allow them to continue their bookmaking activities at the club during race meetings. Five of them pleaded guilty to nine bribery charges which they committed on 10 and 16 January 1971, which totalled $230. The rest offered Anthony bribes totalling $450 between 21 November 1970 and 10 January 1971. They offered Anthony $50 per race day to avoid harassing them and to release them if they were picked up. Anthony, who had already informed the CPIB of the bookies' overtures months earlier, gave the men up on 16 January 1971 and handed all the money given to him to the Bureau's Assistant Director, AJ de Silva. On 17 January, all the bookies, except for one who escaped the dragnet in Singapore and fled to Penang, were arrested. De Silva, with the assistance of the Malaysian Police, flew to Penang and escorted the top kingpin of the bookmaking syndicate back to Singapore. A big betting racket operating between Malaysia and Singapore, which also bribed local officers, was broken after eight months of investigation by the CPIB, and with the help of one good and honest man, Anthony.[203] By June 1971, the CPIB had taken to Court and convicted 10 of the biggest bookies on both sides of the Causeway. In total, they paid a fine of $139,000.[204]

Following the CPIB's takedown of these kingpins, the Bureau and the Police launched a major crackdown within the grounds of the Turf Club in June 1971. The Bureau did not realise at this point that it would stir up a hornets' nest. Between 27 and 29 June 1971, the CPIB and Police task force picked up 180 bookies at the Turf Club. When the operation commenced, all exits of the club were sealed off. All detained bookies were then photographed and had their thumbprints taken.[205] During the following week, starting 5 July 1971, another 195 bookies were picked up, photographed and and also had their thumbprints taken. In all, the two weeks' illegal betting turnover that was seized amounted to $5,400,000.[206] The operations paused momentarily — but the task force returned to the Club in full force in mid-September. Over 100 more bookies were caught. In total, since the crackdown had started in July 1971, 480 bookies had been booked. They were all placed on the Turf Club's blacklist. The CPIB believed that the reason the bookies kept coming back despite the mass arrests seemed to be because "third and fourth grade" runners were trying to fill the gap of the big bookies who were absent in the latter raids.[207] In December 1971, the Turf Club itself undertook another crackdown on illegal bookies on its premises.[208]

In 1972 and 1973, the Turf Club continued to show hundreds of suspected bookies out the door at every meeting. Most of those caught red-handed were small-scale operators and they were placed on the club's blacklist. Yet, the lure of betting on horses was so great that new bookies filled the places of hundreds of barred bookies almost instantly. After the 1971 CPIB–Police crackdowns, the large-scale syndicated bookies from Malaysia had actually withdrawn from Singapore. But in the years following, these syndicates repeatedly tried to restart their operations at the Bukit Timah Turf Club. And one man continuously stood in their way — Anthony.[209] Separately, the bookies also bribed the club's security officers while on the grounds. In each case, Anthony reported all solicitations to the CPIB. All of the club's corrupt officers were dismissed and some of them were charged in Court, fined and jailed.[210]

The Bureau kept a close watch on the Turf Club in the early 1970s partly because of the presence of the bookmaking syndicates, but mostly out of concern that civil servants who lost big bets would turn to corruption to resolve financial difficulties. So during race days, the CPIB's Special

Investigators mingled with the punters in order to spot any civil servant who might be falling into a debt trap at the Turf Club.[211]

By the mid-1970s, while the CPIB kept one eye on the Turf Club, the Bureau had the other eye on corrupting activities involving off-site illegal bookies. It was around April 1976 when the CPIB received a tip-off that three police officers had been receiving bribes to turn a blind eye to the activities of a huge bookmaking syndicate in Tampines. Apparently, this ring of bookies had been operating in full view of the public "with total disregard for police patrol" because they were protected by a number of policemen who had accepted their bribes. Consequently, the CPIB's Special Investigators launched an operation to surveil the policemen from a distance to gather evidence; they positioned themselves at the top of an HDB block in Tampines, using binoculars and cameras with telephoto lenses. The four-men CPIB surveillance team took more than 200 photographs. They discovered that the bookies had been paying $15–$30 to each policeman on their payroll every weekend, and other policemen $50 monthly. Armed with the 200 photographs taken at Tampines, the Bureau's men went to various police stations to identify the officers and detectives involved.[212]

Within a month, the CPIB had questioned more than two dozen policemen, mainly detectives. As a result, the Bureau discovered that there was an extensive policemen–bookies protection racket existing in the eastern part of the island. Amongst the first detained cops were four sergeants and eight men from the Criminal Investigation Department (CID). It was suspected that at least 60 policemen and detectives were on the bookies' payroll. Operating from a house near the Tampines Close Market, 10 bookies and a syndicate "paymaster", Kee Ah Chee, were also arrested by July 1976. And this was just the tip of the iceberg.[213] Eventually, Kee testified against the officers. He revealed that he had bribed 18 policemen, including two detectives, while at the Tampines Market where eight to nine bookmaking groups were operating an illegal horseracing gambling racket on racing days. Kee was not just taking bets at the market;

it was also his job to pay the policemen. The money was given not only to protect the bookies there, but also to guarantee that the officers would not disturb the punters in the market or arrest anyone. By the end of 1976, 13 policemen and detectives had been charged in Court for their complicity in the Tampines bookies corruption scandal.[214]

While still dealing with the Tampines case, the CPIB had gathered enough leads to start investigating another similar racket in Joo Chiat in November 1976. Five detectives were called up for questioning and at least 20 policemen and detectives were alleged to have been implicated in the Joo Chiat bookies syndicate. This ring also operated brazenly in public in marketplaces. The CPIB kept watch and found policemen and detectives frequently fraternising with the ring's members and taking bribes. They were on the bookies' payroll; each officer received $20 to $50 per month from the Joo Chiat bookies.[215]

While the Tampines and Joo Chiat crackdown on the police protection racket for bookmakers had been well publicised, and the punishment for the policemen concerned was severe, the corruption cancer linked to gambling and bookmaking made this vice persistent and resistant to suppression. At the same time, the corrupting agents, the bribers, were becoming more and more intense. There were incidents when, if the briber could not bribe, he would resort to coercion. In 1976, while taking action against the Tampines bookies-police racket, the CPIB had handled a case where certain betting kingpins hired gunmen to threaten and beat up jockeys who had refused to cooperate with them to fix races. These assaults also occurred in Ipoh and Penang. However, as the jockeys at Bukit Timah could not identify their assailants, the CPIB could make little headway with the case.[216] It was therefore no surprise that such threats continued. In May 1977, a gun-wielding gang threatened the lives of two foreign jockeys, Chris Gwilliam and George Podmore. They were placed under police protection after they received two warning notes with "live" bullets.[217]

Low-Tech Corruption

The tentacles of the corrupting punters and bookies found a new ally in the 1970s — telecommunication lines. In those days, races were not broadcast live on public radio; the Turf Club had a "closed-circuit" system that broadcast races only within the club. Hence, whichever way the bookies could get race commentaries ahead of time would give them a tremendous advantage. In the early 1970s, corrupt bookies targeted employees of the Telecommunications Department to tap into closed-circuit race commentaries, feeding them, over the telephone, to the bookmakers. However, at this time, it was not easy for most people to understand the workings of this scheme. The staff of the Telecommunications Department continued to enjoy the lavish parties in night clubs and hotels provided by an Indonesian businessman, despite knowing that the CPIB was watching public servants (who were receiving entertainment gifts).[218]

In June 1977, the situation escalated with scores of Telecommunication Authority of Singapore (TAS) staff caught providing illegal assistance to bookies. The CPIB arrested about 50 TAS employees for tapping closed-circuit race commentaries and passing the information to bookmakers. This involved $5,000,000 worth of bets each race day. The Bureau raided four telephone exchanges simultaneously to pick up the errant staff and collect evidence. Some escaped the dragnet by scaling over walls and fences. It was believed that the CPIB's raid and arrests broke the syndicate and saved the Government and the Turf Club about $200 million in annual revenue. To crack the case, the CPIB worked with the Turf Club's Chief Security Officer, Anthony, for more than a year to discover how the bookies were getting direct race commentaries. The CPIB, Police and the TAS could not understand how the syndicates were getting around the Turf Club's system. Their big break came when Anthony discovered the wiring system of the club's closed-circuit broadcasts had been tampered with, turning it into a transmission system that could be accessed at telephone exchanges.

Anthony was certain that TAS technicians were involved. After investigating further, the CPIB found technicians, artisans, office boys and senior officers were all involved.[219]

The cleaning up of corrupt practices within government and society, which started when Singapore commenced its nation-building journey, reached a critical point in the 1970s. By this decade, the Bureau's Special Investigators had become famed corruption fighters; the CPIB did not work alone, but with government bodies and the good men and women within them. Still, corrupt practices among public servants and the public seemed to have been undaunted by the Government's efforts to keep them at bay. In this instance, it was not that the state's direction, or the Bureau's efforts, had been benign. It was because Singapore was now confronting the heart of the corruption culture that afflicted most nations of the milieu. A new ethos had to be fostered to replace the old values of the day. The 1970s was that make or break phase in Singapore's history where the creation of a meritocratic and democratic society based on integrity and clean government was at stake. Central to this national endeavour was the Government's ability to keep corrupt practices in check in order that the citizenry might have faith in its administration, and above all, that they might believe in the nation that they were building together. Therefore, the CPIB's task and responsibility at this time were tremendous and heavy. The new trends of corruption in the 1970s constituted a serious headwind hindering Singapore's nation-building efforts. Fundamentally, the Bureau had to confront the new reality that corruption in the new nation could stem from normal citizens working in concert and not just about syndicated big-money corruptors subverting people,[220] systems and laws of the land. As such, the Bureau's men and women had to remain steadfast and vigilant at all times.

Chapter Twenty

For Home & Country

There was a marked change in the social environment in 1980s Singapore. Generally, the crimes and cases of corruption involving public servants had seen a noticeable decline. A perusal of press reports and CPIB files in the 1980s shows a general improvement,[221] although there were more reported cases of graft in the private sector. The biggest case of the decade, which the CPIB handled, involved football match-fixing, mainly in relation to the very popular and important Malaysia Cup. The only other case that dominated all conversations and discussion in public was the corruption case involving Minister Teh Cheang Wan. These two cases had surfaced major issues that had to be resolved in order that the Singapore nation could continue to grow and prosper.

Developing Capacity and Bandwidth

Few Singaporeans know that the famed Hong Kong anti-corruption agency, the Independent Commission Against Corruption (ICAC), which was established in February 1974, had actually studied the Singapore prevention of corruption models prior to their founding.

In early January 1969, the Hong Kong Government sent its anti-corruption team to Singapore to study the CPIB's methods. They also took back with them Singapore's Prevention of Corruption Ordinance, Criminal Procedure Code and the Disciplinary Procedure Code for Civil Servants. At this time, in Asia, Singapore was already considered a leading example of how corruption could be fought. The Hong Kong press in the 1960s credited Lee Kuan Yew for Singapore's success in this field.[222] The Singapore Government would build on this success. By the mid-1980s, crediting Singapore as having one of the most effective anti-corruption mechanisms for its Public Service in Asia, the pressmen identified "four agencies" which were pivotal in "regulating the conduct of public officers": Public Service Commission (hiring), Audit Department (accountability), Central Complaints Bureau (efficiency) and the CPIB (enforcement).[223] This overarching view of Singapore's anti-corruption measures elucidated the CPIB's role in the larger scheme of things; the Bureau did not work in silos, but was part of a larger anti-corruption "ecosystem".[224] Yet this well-oiled system did not develop automatically. The Bureau had to work hard, remain steadfast and press on when everything seemed overwhelming in the 1970s.

The CPIB's first major step forward in the 1970s was to increase and improve its staffing. The significant increase in cases handled by the Bureau was well beyond the capacity of a department of 15 investigators.[225] This was essentially just a few more men than what the Anti-Corruption Branch (ACB) had in the early 1950s, when they had had far less work to handle. Before staff numbers were increased, the Bureau created more supervisory positions to allow for progression through promotion and opened the door to hiring female Special Investigators.[226] By 1976, the Bureau's establishment of investigators was increased to 25, and at the same time its Special Investigators' substantive grade was also upgraded from Division 2 to Division 1 in the Civil Service, bringing the officer's scale in line with Police Inspectors. This upgrade was aimed at better reflecting and appreciating the increased workload of the CPIB's staff as well as to boost their morale and efficiency. The new status also meant that the Bureau's Special Investigators were eligible for first class wards and treatment in government hospitals, holiday bungalows and priority allocation of Housing and Development Board (HDB) flats.[227]

These improvements for CPIB employees were timely as well as being too little and too late; from May 1978 to August 1979, at least 14 of CPIB's long-serving staff resigned on account of the workload and working conditions. While the new status and perks saw the number of CPIB investigators grow to 29 by early 1979, the difficult conditions of the decade saw the Bureau challenged as far as efficiency and workload were concerned. In 1979, less than half of the Bureau's staff had even a year's experience in the CPIB.[228] Things would have been far worse for the Bureau had the 1976 improvements not been implemented. One administrative measure the Bureau put in place to slow the turnover was a two-year bond requirement for new hires.[229] In 1978, CPIB Director Ponniah Rajaratnam addressed the truth and reality that the Bureau could do nothing about: "Officers of the Bureau are required to work long and irregular hours because corruption does not occur only during office hours." The truth of the matter was that the work of the Bureau was not for just anyone. A special kind of person who was willing to put in the sacrifice for a noble cause was needed. This was a sentiment Richard Byrne Corridon echoed in 1954 when he opined that the average police officers were not suited for the job. Corridon was not keen on secondment of police officers to the Bureau. He had much preferred direct hires. Rajaratnam's staff were direct hires. Clearly, the commitment required of CPIB's Special Investigators during the "cleaning up" phase of Singapore's nation-building years had been extraordinary. When Evan Yeo became Director in 1980, he also faced another possible exodus of staff. Once again, a number of the Bureau's staff complained about the difficult conditions and long hours. He assured them that he would look into all their grouses, including giving everyone full days of time-off in lieu of Sunday and public holiday duties that they so often performed.[230] Indeed, the Bureau's staffing issues stabilised during his directorship.

In the early 1980s, the CPIB received a much-needed boost on the anti-corruption front. While there had been a decline in public sector corruption cases, there was an increasing number of complex graft cases in the commercial sphere. In the past, graft in commercial cases was handled either by the Bureau or the Commercial Crime Branch of the Criminal Investigation Department (CID). In 1973, the Branch was refashioned and renamed the Commercial Crime Division (CCD). However, this was still not the gamechanger in the fight against white-collar crimes. Things changed in 1984 when the Ministry of Finance (MOF) set up their Commercial Affairs Investigation Department, which was later renamed Commercial Affairs Department (CAD). The CCD and CAD (Finance) were merged in 2000 to form today's CAD, which is within the Police Establishment.[231]

In 1984, the CPIB moved its office to the newly built Hill Street Centre on 2 July. As part of Singapore's urban renewal process in the 1980s, the Stamford Road office, also known to the Bureau as the White House, had to give way to the development of a carpark needed for the area. So the Bureau relocated to the sixth floor of Hill Street Centre. The immediate two floors below were carpark spaces, while the bottom two levels was where the hawker centre was located.[232] The Bureau would remain here for a decade.

The CPIB office was located at the sixth floor of Hill Street Centre from September 1984 to 1998. This site (co-located with a hawker centre) offered many sumptuous food choices for the CPIB officers.
Source: CPIB Archives.

Duty Officer Room in CPIB Hill Street Centre premises between 1984 and 1998, where complaints were taken.
Source: CPIB Archives.

The 1980s heralded a new phase in Singapore's corruption story. While there were still corrupt practices at various levels of society, graft amongst public servants seemed to have been greatly reduced. *Kopi* money had not been wiped out, but it was no longer openly given or accepted. After decades of suppression, campaigns and enforcement by agencies like the CPIB, and with the help of the CCB, public service corruption had clearly been reduced, although other forms of graft still existed. It nevertheless changed the tone in Singapore society. The repeated raids in the Turf Club had now altogether disappeared, or become unnecessary, although bookmaking outside the club was still rife. The fact that the CCB itself "closed shop" attested to this change in general tone with regard to the Public Service. And this was confirmed by the accolades Singapore received in the mid-1980s as having had the best "anti-corruption mechanisms for its Public Service in Asia". However, to borrow a catchphrase from the Singapore Police Force, "low crime does not mean no crime"; in 1980s

Singapore, less corruption did not mean no corruption. The CPIB had to remain vigilant.

There were new forms of syndicated corrupt practices emerging. For instance, the new corrupting bookies of the day betted on soccer rather than horses, although the latter still existed. The CPIB first saw this emerging trend in mid-1977 when a gambling syndicate attempted to fix the outcome of the Malaysia Cup[233] for Penang to win by two goals. This enterprise, which was connected to the "criminal underworld", had planned to offer $60,000 to certain Singapore team players to ensure that goal margin in the Finals. After getting a tip-off, the Bureau started investigating the bookmaking ring involved. Singapore won 3–2 in Kuala Lumpur on 23 May 1977.[234] A little more than a month after the Finals, the CPIB picked up three national players who were implicated in the June Malaysia Cup match-fixing racket. The CPIB also picked up three others, including two first division club officials, one of whom had allegedly travelled to Malaysia to try to "fix" a match for the gambling syndicate.[235] Of course, receiving gratification for throwing a match was not a new thing in Singapore. It was popular knowledge that such practices were common decades before. The difference in the 1970s was that it did not occur only at the club level, but accusations of *kelong* (match-fixing) now tainted the national team as well. At this level, the stakes were higher but the country's reputation was also at stake.

The issue of *kelong* involving national team players exploded in 1981. After the Singapore National Team was defeated by Selangor by 4–0 in the 1981 Malaysia Cup Finals held at Kuala Lumpur, almost immediately, shouts of *kelong* rang out loud as Singapore had been favourites to win, let alone lose by such a margin. Things turned for the worse when Jita Singh, the Singapore team coach, revealed that before the kick-off he had been told that "five Singapore players had sold the match". The CPIB investigated.

As a result of all these cases, CPIB Special Investigators made their presence felt in the following year's Lion City Cup and Merlion Cup. And indeed, they found attempts to fix matches at these events.²³⁶ The "*kelong* culture" would remain with Singapore for years to come,²³⁷ like a cancer. A national coach said years later, *kelong* was "not a way of life in Singapore… but it is a fact of life that it exists here".²³⁸ So, the CPIB had to remain steadfastly vigilant. But what is most pertinent in the 1981 and 1982 episodes was that the Singapore public clearly did not appreciate or tolerate corrupt practices in their "most favourite game", but at the same time, it was rife to the extent that it became a "negative culture" — blame everything on corruption. The 1981 Malaysia Cup Finals fiasco clearly illustrates this point. Upon learning of the CPIB's findings that there was no "foul play", national player, Samad Allapitchay, lamented, "Singaporeans must learn to take defeat and not find scapegoats."²³⁹ The episode showed the Singapore public that the Bureau was not just out to prosecute everyone it investigated. It also played an important role of exonerating the wrongly accused. Although it had played this role for years, this aspect of the Bureau work had remained understated.

Graft in soccer was only one of many private sector cases handled by the CPIB. The 1980s saw an increasing number of cases from the private sphere. One sector with recurring corruption was Shell petroleum. Its construction manager in the 1970s, William Stewart Wilkinson, was jailed 18 months and fined $267,142.50 for accepting a £20,000 bribe for favouring a contract to a Japanese firm. He also accepted gifts from other contractors.²⁴⁰ In November 1981, another Shell executive, Chan Wing Cheong, was fined $3,000 on 24 charges of corruption, 23 of which were in relation to the Pulau Bukom Shell hydrocracker project. His lawyer, in trying to explain Chan's actions, declared that it was "somewhat a way of life in Pulau Bukom for gifts to be given".²⁴¹ It was also in 1981 that the CPIB started clamping down on hotel staff for taking bribes from syndicates to supply "massaging girls" to hotel guests.²⁴² Before the MOF established its Commercial Affairs Investigation Department (later CAD) in 1984, the Bureau also handled complex commercial and financial cases. In 1982, the CPIB probed a number of banks in Singapore, in conjunction with the Monetary Authority of Singapore, for flouting bank reserves regulations. Guilty banks were fined between $500,000 and $1,200,000.[243] The 1980s was also a time of massive resettlement of rural areas, when farms gave way to housing estates. In the Government's compensation packages, fruit-bearing trees on the land were also taken into account. A number of residents started planting trees anywhere and everywhere to inflate their claims. In 1989, the CPIB charged a number of them and brought them to Court.[244] Although, by and large, most of these private sector cases had not been on the scale of those involving public servants, they nevertheless tainted the social tone of the times and had the potential of affecting the good reputation they worked so hard to earn.

Political Leadership

The biggest corruption case that the CPIB had tackled in the 1980s was the Teh Cheang Wan debacle. Although he was not the first sitting Minister and Member of Parliament to be investigated for corruption, his suicide before the resolution of the case necessitated the Government to explain the matter for public interest. Teh had maintained that he was innocent till his end. He was never formally charged. Teh was the Minister for National Development from 1979 to 1986. The CPIB investigated Teh for taking two bribes of $500,000 each in 1981 and 1982. In November 1986, Lee Kuan Yew himself cleared the path for CPIB investigators to look into Teh's activities. In the larger context of Singapore's nation-building journey, and its journey towards becoming "corruption-free", the Teh affair had to be properly addressed in the public domain. What was at stake was the question of the government's resoluteness in maintaining a clean government, and whether the leadership had the gumption and political will to see through changes, regardless of difficulties. This was the reason why the CPIB was put in the spotlight when Lee appointed a Commission of Inquiry to look into the Bureau's conduct in the Teh affair.[245]

Teh's graft was discovered when the CPIB started its investigation on Hock Tat Development Company in April 1986. The son of the company's director, Pek Chee Kee, filed a civil suit against the company for paying out $560,000 improperly in 1982. Apparently, the sum given was to prevent a piece of land they owned from being acquired by the Government. Someone who had access to the affidavit sent the CPIB a tip-off. So Pek and three company directors were questioned. It was only in November 1986 that Pek informed the CPIB that the money was given to Teh, through "Liew", who turned out to be Liaw Teck Kee. Liaw then confessed that he was also the middleman who passed Teh a second $500,000 on behalf of Keok Seng Company, the developer of Riverview Hotel. On both occasions, Liaw claimed that Teh kept $400,000 and gave him $100,000. Then, when Teh's taking of the bribe came to light on 26 November 1986, a friend of Teh's, Liu Cho Chit, offered Liaw $1,000,000 to avoid implicating Teh.[246]

The CPIB questioned Teh for the first time on 2 December 1986. Lee was informed of the Bureau's findings after the interview, and Teh was asked to "take leave" till the end of the year. But Teh took his life on 14 December 1986. Reflecting on the case in Parliament a month later, Lee said, "There is no way a Minister can avoid investigations, and a trial if there is evidence to support one. Teh Cheang Wan chose death rather than face a trial on the charges of corruption which the Attorney-General had yet to settle. The effectiveness of our system to check and to punish corruption rests, first, on the law against corruption contained in the Prevention of Corruption Act; second, on a vigilant public ready to give information on all suspected corruption; and third, on a CPIB which is **scrupulous, thorough, and fearless** in its investigations. For this to be so, the CPIB has to receive the full backing of the Prime Minister under whose portfolio it comes. But the strongest deterrent is in a public opinion which censures and condemns corrupt persons, in other words, in attitudes which make corruption so unacceptable that the stigma of corruption cannot be washed away by serving a prison sentence."[247]

Lee had placed such importance on a clean and effective government that till today, PAP Members of Parliament still wear white shirts and slacks to "symbolise purity and honesty" just as they had in June 1959 when they took their oath of office at City Hall.[248]

Prime Minister Lee Kuan Yew and his Cabinet outside City Hall after the swearing-in of the new Government of Singapore, 5 June 1959.
Source: Ministry of Information and the Arts Collection, courtesy of National Archives of Singapore.

Endnotes

[1] Singapore's National Anthem, *Majulah Singapura*, was originally composed by Zubir Said in 1958 to be used during official functions at City Hall. It became Singapore's anthem after the island became self-governing in 1959. It was the PAP's Mayor Ong Eng Guan who commissioned Zubir Said to compose the anthem.

[2] The last British Governor of Singapore, Sir William Goode, was temporarily appointed the Yang di-Pertuan Negara, the island's first "Head of State" who was also Singapore's representative of the British Crown. Goode vacated his seat on 3 December 1959 when Yusof bin Ishak was appointed as Singapore's first local Head of State.

[3] The PAP won 43 of the 51 contested seats.

[4] Even if the Labour Front had shared the same conviction in the 1950s, real changes were not possible because in the context of limited self-government, only a part of the Legislature was elected, and the local government had limited control of administrative functions. Also, the real provision of amenities and other public services had been under the City Council, which was another partially elected body. These were essentially still colonial institutions.

[5] *Singapore Free Press* 4 Oct 1958; *Straits Times* 8 Jun, 1, 21 Oct 1958. The October–November 1958 campaign to clean up Singapore's streets, from the City to the kampongs, was led by City Hall, the municipal government.

[6] *Singapore Free Press* 3 Dec 1959. Rajaratnam was the Minister for Culture from 1959 to 1963.

[7] *Singapore Standard* 17, 19 Jun 1959; *The Straits Budget* 24 Jun, 1 Jul 1959; *Singapore Free Press* 24 Jun, 18, 21 Aug, 19 Oct 1959. Civil servants' variable allowances, for both local and expatriate staff, were cut.

[8] *Sunday Standard* 5 Jul 1959; *Singapore Free Press* 6 Jul, 24 Aug 1959. Cutting the variable allowances of about 6,000 public servants saved the PAP Government $12,000,000 annually. As a result of these cuts, a number of civil servants (middle-class) had to let go of their "maidservants, *amahs* and car cleaners". In a sense, this was a reality check for the Public Service. Before self-government, the British regime functioned with a significant level of excesses. This was also part of the mess that the new government had to clean up.

[9] The Singapore People's Alliance (SPA) was created when the Labour Front (LF) and Liberal Socialist Party (LSP) came together to form a political coalition in 1958. The LSP was itself a coalition of the Progressive Party (PP) and the Democratic Party (DP). The LF, PP and DP had all won seats in the 1955 General Election. Their combined numbers (as SPA) gave them a comfortable majority in the Legislature. The LSP also won the 1957 Cairnhill by-elections, giving the coalition another seat. The LSP and LF also won nearly half of the seats in the 1957 City Council elections.

[10] *Straits Times* 19 Feb, 4, 6, 8 Mar 1959; *Straits Budget* 25 Feb 1959.

[11] RP Newell, the General Manager of the First National City Bank of New York (Singapore Branch), provided details of Chew's bank account activities: The account was started in October 1957 with a deposit of $2,000. On 30 October 1957, $519,083.96 was credited into the account via telegraphic transfer. There was no indication of source of the fund. In April 1958, another $182,509.51 was credited into Chew's account by order of Yu Kuo Hua for Pooli Chemicals. No address was given. The balance in the account on 30 September 1958 was $752.49. The largest amount taken out of the account was $161,739, which was drawn by Chew and deposited into his own Oversea Chinese Bank account. See *Straits Times* 17 Mar, 8 Apr 1959.

[12] *Straits Times* 5 Mar 1959; *Straits Budget* 11 Mar 1959. It was R Jumabhoy (Liberal Socialist Party) who informed the Legislature that Chew had paid $75,000 for a house at Wilkinson Road in February 1959, and that he had owned shares of tin mines in Ipoh. Francis Thomas, the Labour Front–SPA Minister for Communications and Works (1955–1959) also revealed that Chew had informed him when he received for the party US$100,000 in gold ($300,000) in 1957 (the SPA coalition had not been created at this time — the money Chew collected in 1957 was for the Labour Front). It was out of the $500,000 that Chew received in 1958 that $30,000 was taken to purchase a house at No. 12 Worthing Road, Serangoon Garden Estate. The money was given to Liu Yi Chih, the former owner of Ih Shih Press (defunct) to purchase the house. Thomas explained that although Chew had informed him of the $300,000 he collected in 1957, he kept

quiet about it because it would have "smashed" the government. And when it became clear to him that the Labour Front would not be cleaned up in 1958, he approached Lee Kuan Yew at the start of 1959 and revealed the $500,000 collected in 1958. And since the government had already been discredited in March 1959, there was also no point keeping quiet about the $300,000 (US$100,000 gold) collected in 1957. These monies were credited into Chew's personal bank account, and not the Labour Front's. See Straits Times 14 Mar 1959.

[13] Singapore Free Press 14 Mar 1959.

[14] Straits Times 14 Mar 1959. The SPA government had been discredited.

[15] Nevertheless, in the days leading up to the May 1959 Election, the CPIB continued to put up its regular elections notices, informing the public to contact the Bureau if they came across corrupt practices during the Election — and to call 27600 or send a letter to PO Box 2222. They could also visit the Bureau's office at the second level of the Supreme Court Building. See Straits Budget 13 May 1959.

[16] Straits Times 4 Mar 1959.

[17] Elias had submitted a bid to lease a bungalow at Adam Park from the City Council in February 1959. After some mix-up, during which he thought he had submitted the highest bid, his bid was not accepted, and another bidder's submission was accepted instead. Elias had said during the proceedings in February that he felt misled in the whole affair, having been told earlier that he had the highest bid. See Straits Times 22 Apr 1959. Lee Kuan Yew also pointed out that Elias had personally visited City Hall to enquire about his tender bid before the tender exercise was closed and awarded. Elias met with the Mayor. Lee declared this as "canvassing" which contravened the rules of tender submission to the government. See Straits Budget 29 Apr 1959. Furthermore, Elias had been a member of the previous City Council. The new Council led by PAP's Ong Eng Guan had reversed some of the former Council's decisions and had criticised the quality of the Murnane Reservoir (1956). The former Council had declared the reservoir a great achievement, but the new Council found substantial leaking and described the project as anything but outstanding. See Straits Budget 15 Apr 1959. The reservoir today is sited near the Bukit Timah and the Pan Island Expressways.

[18] Singapore Free Press 24 Aug 1959.

[19] Straits Times 28 Sep 1959; Straits Budget 7 Oct 1959.

[20] Straits Times 5 Mar 1959; Straits Budget 11 Mar 1959.

[21] Singapore Standard 26 May 1958; CPIB File 001 Director CPIB, Sardar Singh to Senior Attorney-General, 30 Jul 1959, p.5.

[22] CPIB File 001 Director CPIB, Deputy Chief Secretary to Commissioner of Police, 1 Mar 1957, copy to CPIB Director, 30 Jul 1959, p.6.

[23] Prior to 1958, the Bureau was placed directly under the Chief Secretary (formerly Colonial Secretary). A year before the 1959 polls, the CPIB came under the command structure of the Police Establishment, and the police force itself ultimately under the Governor, not the local government. In this arrangement, the Bureau came under the Attorney-General for investigations and the Commissioner of Police for Administration and Discipline. In any case, the Police, as well as the Bureau, were still colonial establishments. In the new regime, the Police came under the local government.

[24] Singapore Free Press 28 Jun 1960.

[25] Straits Times 6 Sep 1959. Sardar Singh was of the conviction that the sudden and wholesale change would not affect the efficiency of the Bureau because all the new uniformed men were also trained officers.

[26] Straits Times 28 Sep 1959; Straits Budget 23 Sep 1959.

[27] Straits Times 13 Oct 1959.

[28] Straits Times 31 Oct 1959.

[29] Singapore Free Press 18 Apr 1960; Straits Times 18 Jun 1960.

[30] Singapore Free Press 15 Dec 1960; Straits Times 16 Apr 1962.

[31] Straits Times 6 Jan, 7 Apr 1963.

[32] Straits Times 11 Sep 1963.

[33] Singapore Free Press 28 Jun 1960. The lower priority placed on anti-corruption measures

from the latter part of the 1950s was underscored by the placement of the Bureau within the Police Establishment; this essentially was an abandonment of its founding principle as an independent agency — independent of the Police. The police force was the government body with the largest number of corrupt officers (caught, dismissed and prosecuted). The CPIB was established for the very reason that the Police's ACB could not be trusted. Thus, returning the anti-corruption agency (CPIB) back into the Force was tantamount to subverting its very strength and reputation of being impartial.

[34] This was discussed in the previous chapter. There was no certainty that the Bureau would survive the constitutional changes even in the mid-1950s when limited self-government was granted. There was no guarantee that the elected local authorities would desire to retain the Bureau. Afterall, in the lead-up to the 1959 General Election, most political parties had already started their own "Complaints Bureau" to combat corrupt practices.

[35] *Straits Times* 21 Jul 1960.

[36] *Singapore Free Press* 28 Jun 1960; *Hansard, Singapore (Legislative Assembly Debates)* 13 Feb 1960.

[37] *Singapore Free Press* 28 Jun 1960.

[38] *Straits Times* 2, 21 Jul 1960.

[39] Although five new civilian officers were recruited, the Bureau's establishment did not actually expand by five. A few civilian investigators were dismissed the year before, and their positions had yet to be filled. See *Straits Times* 1 Jul 1960.

[40] For a 1958 advertisement for civilian investigator posts by the police force, see *Straits Times* 1 Dec 1958; 1961 advertisement for Special Investigator posts by the Ministry of Home Affairs, see *Straits Times* 12 Apr 1961; 1966 advertisement for Special Investigator posts by the Public Service Commission, see *Straits Times* 9 Dec 1966.

[41] *Singapore Free Press* 26 Sep 1960. CPIB's new office at the "White House" along Stamford Road was a true historical building built around 1912–1914. Erected as a school block extension of St Andrew's School, it was located within the grounds of the Anglican St Andrew's Mission. The School and all its Mission institutions had already moved out of the site prior to World War II. In the immediate post-war years, buildings on the site were occupied by the British Council and the St John's Ambulance Brigade. St Peter's Church (Chapel) was turned into the Brigade's Singapore Headquarters. By the mid-1950s, a number of government departments were located within the White House when they moved out of the Empress Place: the Registry of Marriages, the National Registration Office — Citizenship (i/c) and the Social Welfare Department's Advice Bureau, which counselled people who had missing loved ones (missing persons, presumed dead). See *Straits Times* 24 Sep, 2 Dec 1960.

[42] Before debating the Bill in the legislature, the Government first sought public feedback in early 1960; a Select Committee invited written representations in four languages. Copies of the Bill were also published and sold in public. The Bill was passed on 16 May 1960, and operationalised on 17 June 1960. See *Straits Times* 16, 17 Feb, 2 Apr, 17 May 1960; *Singapore Free Press* 26 Apr 1960; *Straits Budget* 25 May 1960.

[43] The Prevention of Corruption Ordinance (PCO) provided for the appointment of a Director and officers appointed by the Director — Senior Special Investigators and Special Investigators. The provisions of the new PCO also provided the staff of the Bureau more powers to carry out their tasks. The PCO 1960 further provided that all offences in the Ordinance to be seizable, and the CPIB was empowered to investigate bank accounts of any person who was suspected of having committed corruption. The maximum penalty for corruption was five years' jail or a $10,000 fine, or both. In certain cases, involving contracts with the British, Singapore Government and other government bodies, the maximum jail sentence was up to seven years. See *Singapore Free Press* 28 Jun, 29 Dec 1960; *Straits Times* 22 Jan 1960.

[44] There was the corruption case involving the post-war Food Control Inspectorate, implicating Chief Inspectors James McPherson and Claude William Roberts. McPherson had received thousands of dollars from eight Chinese merchants to bypass food control regulations (import and export). One of these merchants, Tan Kok Kheng, gave McPherson $14,000 to secure an export permit. The ACB, which was still in operation at this time, charged McPherson under the Prevention

of Corruption Ordinance (Section 3b, No. 41 of 1937). However, when the case was still pending, he was allowed to return to Britain while on medical leave. He did not return. As a result, the Colonial Office declared his "retirement" and the monies from his "corruption" activities, $26,800, was "treated" (confiscated) as "unclaimed property". The merchants were acquitted. At the same time, Roberts was caught helping several Chinese merchants to import rice from Siam. This was before McPherson left Singapore. McPherson was also implicated in the matter as he was with Roberts when the rice trucks were inspected. As the principal Chinese merchant involved had been acquitted and McPherson had already "retired" during the trial, Roberts was acquitted, even though the ACB had evidence he received money. Then there was the case of Mary Ng, the "femme fatale" of Singapore in 1956–1957. She was a realtor who had gone around claiming that she was connected to people who could help people. At the same time, she also joined clubs (e.g., Flying Club) to connect with helpful people. In 1956, when Liang San Han, a shopkeeper, asked her to connect with trial judge JM Devereux-Colebourn, she agreed but demanded $3,500. Liang gave her a lesser amount. She had claimed, in this instance, to be the judge's wife, showing a picture of her in the arms of the judge. In a separate case, Mary also offered to help Kok Min Yin, a jewel broker who was to appear before Devereux-Colebourn on opium charges. She collected $2,500 from Kok. Mary was caught, went to trial and was acquitted in September 1956 without having to call her defence. Kok was also acquitted by Devereux-Colebourn. In October 1956, Devereux-Colebourn was also allowed to retire and return to Britain. In mid-1957, the Attorney-General appealed against Mary's acquittal as the "Crown" had concrete evidence that Mary had indeed received a $1,000 cheque from Kok. In any case, what could be done? The judge in the middle of the affair had already retired and gone home. The CPIB had been the main agency investigating the Mary and Devereux-Colebourn case. See *Straits Budget* 10, 11 Oct 1956, 20 Jun 1957.

[45] The case of the great Ponggol Opium Heist comes to mind. Several CID inspectors had conspired to hijack an opium consignment that was smuggled into Singapore. Their intent was to hide their crime by prosecuting the smugglers for the original crime and to explain the disappearance of the opium loot by framing the smuggling crew of robbing their own opium boss. The inspectors arranged an elaborate web of false witnesses and fake account of events. All these were submitted to the Court when the smuggling crew stood trial. So, for many days, lawyers and prosecutors argued a fake trial till the defence lawyers peeled away all the false accusations. The smugglers were discharged (not amounting to an acquittal) but the inspectors were never prosecuted for the part they played in the fiasco. And all this played out in full view of the public. This was the case that "sparked" the birth of the CPIB.

[46] *Straits Times* 14 Feb 1960; *Hansard, Singapore (Legislative Assembly Debates)* 13 Feb 1960.

[47] *Straits Times* 14 Feb 1960.

[48] *Straits Times* 14 Feb 1960; *Singapore Free Press* 29 Dec 1960.

[49] *Straits Times* 16 Jun 1961.

[50] *Straits Budget* 25 Apr 1962.

[51] *Straits Times* 31 Jul 1987.

[52] When the men of the Bureau were placed in the Police Establishment in the 1950s, it was not surprising that they would fear for their own careers when the culprits they were pursuing were police officers, or senior police officers. Politicians in the 1950s pointed out correctly that junior officers (in the CPIB) were not in a position to question higher ranking officers (in the police force). The Bureau's civilian investigators then were also just contact staff. They could lose their jobs if no one backed their actions. It was in this context that many politicians mistrusted the impartiality of the CPIB then.

[53] *Straits Times* 17 Dec 1960. This echoes that famed maxim for democracy first uttered by Abraham Lincoln — "government of the people, by the people, for the people".

[54] *Straits Times* 17 Dec 1960.

[55] *Singapore Free Press* 16 May 1961. The Government also conducted courtesy classes for civil servants from time to time. Singapore's first (public) national courtesy campaign, launched in 1979, which had the slogan "Make Courtesy Our

Way of Life", was the administration's attempt to shape societal culture itself.

[56] *Straits Times* 30 Aug, 1 Sep 1961.

[57] *Straits Times* 30 Aug, 1, 2, 12 Sep 1961. One part of CCB staff responsibilities was to make on-the-spot checks on public servants.

[58] *Straits Times* 13 Jan, 1 Jun, 6 Jul, 26 Aug 1961, 2, 3 Jul 1962. It was touted as the bureau for grouses... "to assist in the eradication of discourtesy towards public, delay and petty bureaucratic attitudes".

[59] *Straits Times* 15 Jun 1962. The CCB had proven so effective at the start that the Government planned to "amalgamate the complaints bureaus of the other ministries" (for example, the bureaus of the Ministry of National Development and Ministry of Home Affairs) with the CCB. The CCB started in 1962 with the establishment of one Bureau Chief, two investigating officers (graduates) and a clerical staff of six. In 1963, the CCB dealt with 1,075 complaints, 666 walk-in cases, 404 by post and five by phone. See *Straits Times* 13 Feb, 15, 16 Jun 1962, 24 Feb 1965.

[60] Government expenditure during this nation-building phase had been significant; building housing, schools, social and communal infrastructures; creation of employment in healthcare, utilities and education services, and much more; this meant that there were jobs available and opportunity for the man on the ground to make a decent living. Of course, the caveat then was all these were on the condition that he kept the family size sustainable and lifestyle in check.

[61] *Straits Times* 26 Aug 1970.

[62] *New Nation* 31 May 1977; *Straits Times* 1 Jun 1977.

[63] *New Nation* 3 Nov 1977; *Straits Times* 5 Jun 1977. The value of transactions between the airline and these companies were worth $10,000,000; these officials got a certain percentage of the profits that ranged from $10,000 to $50,000 each.

[64] *Straits Times* 2 May 1979. In a separate case in 1978, a private clinic was rumoured to have been issuing medical certificates (MCs) too liberally. So, a CPIB officer acted as agent provocateur and went to see the doctor without having an actual illness.

He got his MC. On 13 July 1978, the CPIB sent its report on the doctor to the Singapore Medical Council. The doctor was suspended. See *Straits Times* 4 Nov 1979.

[65] As a case in point, in late 1959, Gian Hock Eng, a *Chap Ji Kee* organiser, offered to reward ASP DF Meyer, the officer-in-charge of the Gambling Suppression Branch, if Meyer helped some of his friends, who had been detained by the Police after a raid, to get a lesser charge. Meyer reported the matter to his superiors in the Criminal Investigation Department as well as to the CPIB. The Bureau then instructed Meyer to continue his liaison with Gian until the actual bribes were offered. It was during their final rendezvous that Gian offered $5,000 to $7,000 for each person that Meyer found to become "fixed" witnesses, and Meyer himself was given $2,000 as "coffee money". Gian was arrested. See *Straits Times* 30 Dec 1959.

[66] *Straits Times* 7, 10, 11 Nov 1961. This was exactly what happened in 1961 when a detective and constable posted to the Joo Chiat Police Station solicited gratification from a *Chap Ji Kee* runner they had caught. He offered the cops a $15 bribe to get out of his predicament, but the policemen demanded $300 instead. Desperate, the runner tried to borrow the money from his relatives. It was one of his relatives who contacted the CPIB over the matter. The Bureau subsequently set a trap for the officers. They were caught and sentenced to six months' jail for corruption. See *Straits Times* 7, 10, 11 Nov 1961. In another case that occurred in 1971, a *Chap Ji Kee* promoter, pretending to be an informer, thought he could make use of three policemen to detain a competitor. When the cops found betting slips worth about $30,000 on the man, instead of arresting the gamer, they demanded $10,000 from him. The amount was excessive, so the man asked his brother for help. He helped, by calling the CPIB. In the meantime, the gamer gave the policemen $400 as an initial payment. The CPIB arrested and prosecuted the officer. They were sentenced to 18 months' imprisonment. See *Straits Times* 15 Apr 1972.

[67] *Straits Times* 7, 10, 11 Nov 1961. It was around the latter part of the 1960s that 4D gaming rackets had also started getting more involved in the bribery of policemen. In 1968, a corrupt officer

was convicted for receiving $20 from a "self-confessed 4-digit lottery operator". See *Eastern Sun* 29 Feb 1968.

[68] *Straits Times* 22 Jan, 4 Mar 1970.

[69] *Straits Times* 28 May 1971, 23 Feb, 16 Mar 1974. In mid-1973, false accusations by six brothel keepers tied up more than 60 police officers. CPIB's Special Investigators were tied up for some time in the questioning; a handful were cleared instantly, some faced the possibility of departmental action and others continued to be investigated for other "irregularities" not related to the accusations. Of the group, two officers were eventually charged for "vice and graft". They were sacked.

[70] *Straits Times* 14 Oct 1975.

[71] A business owner whose shop was along North Bridge Road was fined $500 for offering a postal worker an *ang pow* on 3 February 1976. Around the same time, several other postmen delivering mail along South Bridge Road were also caught accepting *ang pows*; one of them had actually solicited the gift. See *Straits Times* 27, 31 Mar, 30 Jun 1976.

[72] In 1978, the CPIB arrested a postman for accepting an *ang pow* from a shop where he was delivering mail during the Chinese New Year period. He was detained as he left the shop. The shop owner was also taken to task for giving the red packet. She claimed that she did not know it was illegal to do so. The postman was fined $20 for accepting a $2 *ang pow*. He pleaded guilty. See *Straits Times* 12 Apr 1978.

[73] *New Nation* 27 Jan 1979; *Straits Times* 28 Jan 1979.

[74] Before the 1959 General Election, all employees of the City Council and the Rural Board were considered civil or public servants. When the PAP Government was formed and new government ministries and more statutory boards were created, the main government started to take over essential public services while the City Council retained the bulk of municipal services including the provision of water, gas and electricity. It was not until 1962 that a law was passed to integrate the City Council and Rural Board into the Central Government Administration. At the same time, the Public Utilities Bill was passed to create the Public Utilities Board (PUB) which would take over the provision of the Council's essential services when the Board became operational in 1963. Legally, when the Local Government Integration Ordinance came into force on 1 September 1963, the Council ceased to exist. However, the transference of essential services and Council staff to the government ministries and the PUB would stretch into 1964. See *Straits Times* 11 Jul, 3 Dec 1962, 3 May 1963, 7 Jun 1964.

[75] *Straits Times* 20 Apr 1965.

[76] *Straits Times* 6 Dec 1966.

[77] *Straits Times* 25 Mar 1964.

[78] *Straits Times* 3 Dec 1963.

[79] *Straits Times* 25 Jan 1964, 14 Oct, 5 Nov, 10 Dec 1970; *Eastern Sun* 26 Sep 1968, 27 Jun 1970; *Singapore Herald* 12 Sep 1970.

[80] *Singapore Herald* 10 Dec 1970.

[81] In the aftermath of the Bureau's clampdown on the corrupt traffic officers, the CPIB remained vigilant in keeping watch on traffic enforcement. By the end of March 1971, a total of 15,444 vehicles had been booked for excessive emissions over an eight-month period. The Government collected about $500,000 in fines. It was reported that recalcitrant car owners had found it cheaper to fix their vehicles than to continuously pay their fines. As a case in point, a motorist who had been booked four times for excessive smoky exhaust since 1970 had paid a total of $390. By April, a total of 32,680 motorists had been booked since the start of enforcement in 1970. See *Straits Times* 4 Mar, 20 Apr 1971, 13 Sep 1973; *New Nation* 31 Mar 1971. One reason for the better enforcement was the Registry of Vehicles starting their own enforcement squad in 1972 in light of the Traffic Police fiasco. Even though it had only 30 officers when its establishment permitted 80, they have shown again what just a few good men could achieve. See *Straits Times* 15 Oct, 23 Nov 1972; *New Nation* 10 Oct 1973.

[82] *Straits Times* 13 Feb 1971.

[83] *New Nation* 12, 13, 16, 17, 19 Feb, 3 Mar 1971; *Singapore Herald* 12 Feb 1971.

[84] *Straits Times* 13 Feb 1971.

[85] *Straits Times* 13 Feb 1971; *New Nation* 12 Feb 1971.

[86] *Straits Times* 13 Feb 1971. Over 20 members of the Mobile Squad were placed on the CPIB's initial blacklist. See *New Nation* 16 Feb 1971.

[87] *Singapore Herald* 13 Feb 1971.

[88] *New Nation* 17, 19 Feb, 3 Mar 1971. At the same time, 18 policemen were transferred to the Mobile Squad to strengthen the division after all the transfers out. The Bureau also continued screening the files at Traffic Police Headquarters to ensure that nothing had been missed.

[89] *Straits Times* 8, 10 Nov 1966.

[90] *Straits Times*, 2, 15 Sep, 12 Oct, 3 Nov 1967.

[91] *Straits Times* 26 Mar 1974.

[92] *Straits Times* 27 Oct 1976.

[93] *Straits Times* 14 Jan 1959. The matter was exposed by an unsolicited letter sent to the press. The CPIB was directed by the Police to look into the matter (the CPIB was still within the Police Establishment at this time).

[94] *Straits Times* 19 Feb 1959.

[95] *Singapore Free Press* 19 Jan 1962.

[96] *Straits Times* 26, 29 Oct, 14 Nov 1964; *Straits Budget* 4 Nov 1964. The seven-man Ethical Practices Committee appointed by the NTUC to enquire into the affair formulated the eight-point moral code for its 52 affiliated unions.

[97] *Straits Times* 3 Nov 1968.

[98] *Straits Times* 1 Jun, 10 Aug, 14 Sep 1962.

[99] *Straits Times* 10 Aug 1962.

[100] *Straits Times* 1 Jun 1962.

[101] *Straits Times* 14 Sep 1962. Loh joined the PAP's City Council in 1958. Mayor Ong Eng Guan himself appointed Loh as the Head of the Council's Public Complaints Bureau to fight corruption. Ong had described Loh to be a man of "courage, frankness and sense of proportion and honesty". Loh's father was a pork seller. Ong noted Loh's "courage to report without fear or favour friends, relatives or anyone in whatever occupation if they were alleged to be corrupt". Loh took over the helm of the Markets and Hawkers Department in February 1959. In 1962–1963, with the City Council discontinued, the Markets and Hawkers Department came under the purview of the Ministry of Health. The Ministry reorganised the department in early 1964. It was suggested then that a 11-men Hawkers and Markets Board would be set up to replace the department. However, by mid-1964, the Public Health Advisory Board was established instead, and the Markets and Hawkers Department was placed under the HDB. See *Straits Times* 5 Feb, 1 Jun, 1 Dec 1964.

[102] *New Nation* 9 Feb 1971; *Straits Times* 19 Dec 1970, 5 Jan 1971.

[103] *New Nation* 9 Feb 1971; *Straits Times* 19 Dec 1970, 5 Jan 1971.

[104] In the old days, Immigration, Registration and Customs authorities were separate government departments, even though they were present at all checkpoints.

[105] *Straits Times* 14 Jun, 27 Jun 1978.

[106] The PCO was amended in 1963 and 1966 to widen the powers of the CPIB. *Straits Times* 6 May 1963, 4 Mar, 22 Apr 1966 — Ordinance 6 of 1963, Prevention of Corruption (Amendment) Ordinance, 1963 and Act 10 of 1966, Prevention of Corruption (Amendment) Act, 1966.

[107] *Straits Times* 12 Jul 1968; *New Nation* 4 Jan 1972.

[108] *Straits Times* 12 May 1967.

[109] *Straits Times* 1 Nov 1963, 3 Jun 1964, 20 Feb 1976, 17 May 1978; *New Nation* 19 Feb 1976, 20 May 1978.

[110] *Straits Times* 12 Jul 1968.

[111] *Straits Times* 23 May 1965. Among the first people to use the term *incorruptible* to describe an aspect of Singapore was the Australian PM RG Menzies. He said in July 1959 that Lee Kuan Yew was an honest man, and that "people in the best position to judge assured me that Mr Lee was quite incorruptible and prepared to do a good job". See *Straits Times* 10 Jul 1959. Then in March 1960, S Rajaratnam, the Minister for Culture, reflected on the three fundamentals of democracy: dedicated and incorruptible leadership, self-disciplined people, and well-informed and critical public opinion. See *Straits Budget* 2 Mar 1960. A couple of months later, Lee Khoon Choy, the PAP Assemblyman for Bukit Panjang, reminded his branch members that "while working for

our aim, we must see too that our party remains the same efficient, disciplined and incorruptible organisation". See *Straits Times* 2 May 1960.

At the end of 1960, C Sharpe, the Assistant Comptroller of Customs, Federation, declared while in Singapore, "If we want an incorruptible Civil Service then we must be incorruptible ourselves. Honesty, like charity, starts at home." See *Singapore Free Press* 14 Dec 1960. In September 1965, an anonymous letter sent to the *Free Press* stated it was "Mr Lee's popularity among the people of Singapore, Malaysia, and elsewhere lies not in his mastery in the use of words, but in the Singapore Government's efficiency, effective and incorruptible administration. The record speaks for itself." See *Straits Times* 7 Sep 1965.

[112] *Straits Times* 25 Jan, 27 Jul 1969.

[113] *Straits Times* 14 Nov 1964. The Barisan Sosialis Assemblyman, Koo Young, feared that English expatriates may still be working for the "British colonialist".

[114] *New Nation* 4 Jan 1972.

[115] *Straits Times* 20 Feb 1976; *New Nation* 19 Feb 1976.

[116] *Straits Times* 9 Jun 1972; *New Nation* 4 Jan 1972. In 1972, the PCO was amended once more to allow for the creation of two new posts — the Deputy Director and Chief Special Investigator. See *Straits Times* 9 Jun 1972; Act 27 of 1972 — Prevention of Corruption (Amendment) Act 1972. In the 1972 promotion exercise, four posts of Senior Special Investigators were created. The post was equivalent to the Assistant Superintendent of Police. The post of Chief Special Investigator, equivalent to the rank of Deputy Superintendent of Police, was also created. Now, the Bureau's investigators drew the same pay as police inspectors. In 1979, the PSC promoted nine CPIB officers to their next rank. See *Straits Times* 20 Mar 1979.

[117] *New Nation* 18, 20 May, 9 Aug 1978, 20 Feb, 16 Aug, 29 May 1979; *Straits Times* 15, 17, 19, 24 May, 11 Sep 1978, 7 Feb, 30 May 1979. The first time a spate of resignations in the Bureau occurred was in 1972. It was said that the long hours at the Bureau had been the main cause of the departures in 1972. See *New Nation* 10 Feb 1972.

[118] *New Nation* 4 Jan 1972. CPIB Director, P Rajaratnam, explained, "Officers of the Bureau are required to work long and irregular hours because corruption does not occur only during office hours." See *Straits Times* 17 May 1978; *New Nation* 20 May 1978.

[119] *Straits Times* 19, 20, 23 Mar 1965.

[120] *Straits Times* 11 Jan 4 Nov 1966.

[121] *Straits Times* 4 Oct 1969.

[122] *Straits Times* 16, 31 Jul 1975.

[123] *Straits Times* 9 Jul 1975.

[124] *Straits Times* 20 Apr 1975.

[125] *Straits Times* 24 Jun 2015.

[126] *Today* 22, 23, Jan 2016; Phey resigned from his posts in the unions soon after his arrest at the beginning of December 1979. See *Straits Times* 4 Dec 1979.

[127] *AsiaOne* 28 Jun 2015.

[128] *Straits Times* 11 Dec 1979, 9, 25 Jan 1980; *Business Times* 9 Jan 1980; *Straits Times* 28 Jun 2015; *AsiaOne* 28 Jun 2015. Forward Supermarket, later renamed Savewell Supermarket, was a private chain which Phey helped set up. Under the Trade Unions Act, amended in 1977, Phey needed to obtain the Government's approval before he could use the union's funds to purchase shares in private companies. See *New Nation* 11 Dec 1979.

[129] *Straits Times* 22 Jan 2016.

[130] Interview with CPIB Director, 10 May 2022.

[131] *Straits Times* 1, 2 Sep 1965. Eventually, Lee still released the CIA man because there were bigger geopolitical concerns at stake; by 1961, Singapore was considering merger with Malaysia and the Government did not want to jeopardise this endeavour as Kuala Lumpur had a relationship with the Americans (merger talks had already commenced in 1961, although it only took place in 1963. See *Straits Times* 18 Sep 1961.). Also, the Government had been dealing with the Eisenhower Administration in 1960. By 1961, President Kennedy came into power and there was a new government in America. So, Lee simply dropped the whole matter.

[132] *Straits Times* 19 Nov 1966.

133 *Straits Times* 10 Nov 1966.

134 *Eastern Sun* 16 Dec 1966; *Straits Times* 28 Jan, 12 Apr 1967. When the workers' union found out about the impending reorganisation, they backed a strike by the workers, fearing that reforms might result in a reduction of their take-home pay. The Public Cleansing Department was particularly problematic for the Health Ministry. After the 1967 reorganisation, some aspects of the Ministry's cleaning responsibilities were tendered out to the private sector. However, this endeavour also encountered issues. In early 1968, the Ministry of Health suspected something was amiss when three winning bids over three months were all given up by the awarded tenderers. The contracts were for the cleaning of refuse and clearance of drains at catchment areas. So, the CPIB was brought in to investigate this "unusual and peculiar situation". See *Straits Times* 16 Mar 1968; *Eastern Sun* 15 Mar 1968.

135 *Straits Times* 20 May 1967; *Straits Budget* 7 Jun 1967.

136 The last of these seemed to have been conducted in 2014, for the Maritime Port Authority.

137 This Latin phrase comes from Juvenal's (Decimus Junius Juvenalis) Satires (Satire VI, 347–48).

138 *New Nation* 21 Jul 1971.

139 It was during the Lim Yew Hock government that the Government General Orders were introduced to cover a range of practices and conduct of civil servants. Specifically, General Orders 157 and 158 were issued to ensure government officers were not in the clutches of money lenders. While 157 specified the avoidance of bankruptcy, 158 covered guidelines relating to the taking of loans, indebtedness and prohibiting being a surety. Contravening these Orders could lead to departmental action that included disciplinary measures or dismissal. On the whole, both Orders were also formulated to deter gambling among civil servants. See *Straits Budget* 11 Jul 1957; *Straits Times* 6, 9 Jul 1957; *Singapore Free Press* 5 Jul 1957. The fact that the PAP Government found itself having to enforce these Orders (which presumes the declaration of personal finances, e.g., loans) after it came to power demonstrated how these Orders had not been enforced strictly during the previous administration. The Chew Swee Kee affair attested to just how serious the Lim Yew Hock government had been with regard to their General Orders.

140 *Straits Times* 24, 25, 26 Oct 1971. When the PAP Government came into power in 1959, it moved to rein in unregulated money lending activities with a new Money Lending Ordinance in 1959. It required all lenders to be licensed and operate within supervised guidelines. At that time, the Chettiars were charging rates of up to 48% annually. See *Singapore Free Press* 22 Jul, 10 Aug, 17, 22 Sep 1959; *Straits Times* 30 Aug, 24 Sep 1959.

141 There were two aspects to the General Orders that prohibited indebtedness and taking loans (GO 158) and bankruptcy (GO 157) among public servants. When the PAP Government pressed for the enforcement of these Orders, the public servants' union, the Amalgamated Union of Public Employees (AUPE), appealed for leeway. They requested that the Government suspend these Orders for two months (January to February 1961) in order that public servants may declare their liabilities during these two months without fear of disciplinary action. The AUPE enunciated the "untold miseries" of public servants. See *Straits Times* 29 Nov 1960. Meanwhile, the Singapore Government Administrative and Clerical Service Union (SGACSU) canvassed for the revision of GO 157 and GO 158 to remove dismissal as a measure allowable in the Orders and implement a less severe penalty instead. They argued that indebtedness was not a crime, and that many public servants might be deterred from making honest declarations, which would then place more of them under the clutches of moneylenders as they would continue to pay exorbitant interest. Since the Government's enforcement of the Orders, 200 public servants had already been dismissed. See *Straits Times* 24 Jun 1961; *Singapore Free Press* 14 Jul 1961. During the Government's "amnesty" exercise in 1961, when public servants were given the opportunity to declare their liabilities (from August to November), it was found that between "IOU chits" and "promissory notes", $400,000 were owed by public servants (who made declarations). Under General Orders, when they came into debt, they had three months to declare

the matter. See *Singapore Free Press* 24 Nov 1961. By 1962, with the Government's emphasis on "efficiency" (measure against corrupt practices) for all its 22,000 civil servants, the Government started the process of introducing new laws to require all public servants and assemblymen to declare their assets to the CPIB. *Singapore Free Press* 11 Jan 1962; *Straits Budget* 25 Apr 1962. The SGACSU continued to appeal for less severe penalties till 1964, when it merged with the AUPE, and from then, the AUPE took on the cause of the government employees. See *Straits Times* 8 Oct 1962, 22 Jan 1963, 6 Jun, 2 Oct 1964; *Eastern Sun* 6 Oct 1966.

[142] While the press announced that about 1,000 indebted civil servants were facing disciplinary action, including over 400 policemen, the Police Commissioner disputed these figures. Citing his own inquiry and the CPIB's review of the finance company's books, there were less than 60 officers in debt and some of them were indebted because they stood as surety for others. The CPIB somewhat concurred with the Commissioner. See *Straits Times* 24, 25, 26 Oct, 1 Nov 1971.

[143] *Straits Times* 11 Jan 1977.

[144] In 1969, customs and excise duties netted Singapore $239,000,000. See *Straits Times* 9 Mar 1970. This figure increased to $282,979,000 in 1970. See *Singapore Herald* 7 January 1971; *Straits Times* 7 Jan 1971. In 1971, custom revenue rose to $302,900,000. See *Straits Times* 23 Mar 1972. By 1972, excise revenue had increased to $358,000,000 (fiscal year), See *Straits Times* 20 Apr 1973, or $335,000,000 (calendar year), See *Straits Times* 30 Jul 1973. Revenue from excise duties was $420,200,000 in 1974, See *Straits Times* 16 Oct 1975.

[145] *New Nation* 29 Jan 1972.

[146] *New Nation* 3 Mar 1972.

[147] *New Nation* 19 May 1971. The CPIB was quick to realise that the smuggling of labourers was only the tip of the iceberg. The same network and routes were used to smuggle women and children into Singapore from Indonesia. This was already noted in the 1960s by the Indonesian authorities themselves — they had been using Tanjung Pinang in Riau as a launching pad for sending the women. See *Eastern Sun* 20 Aug 1967. However, little was achieved to end this illegal trade. In early 1972, the Indonesians sought Interpol's help with the matter. See *Straits Times* 29 Apr 1972. The Indonesians also requested help from the Singapore Police to deal with the "highly organised ring" which had been putting the women and children, mostly from Java, into night clubs in Singapore. The children were sent to foster families. See *New Nation* 1 May 1972. However, another report in the press stated that about a dozen Indonesian women were brought into Singapore by boat from Riau every month. They landed along the West Coast (Jurong) where the illegal women were sold by auction and picked up by buyers. The minimum price for these women was $1,500, while the attractive ones fetched up to $2,500. It was said that these women were kept as mistresses for six months to a year, and then sold to the brothels for prostitution. The women were tricked into coming here on the promise of jobs. They were given forged or stolen Singapore identity cards before they arrived. See *Straits Times* 2 May 1972. In September 1972, Malaysian businessman, Chen Voon Fee, was jailed a day and fined $8,000 for smuggling illegals into Singapore. He took five members of a family from Jakarta to Tanjong Pinang, over a period of eight months, from July 1968 to February 1969, and sent them to Changi Beach using fast speedboats. He charged each of them $1,250. Chen brought their servant girl to Singapore in July 1969. He brought the woman through Clifford Pier "bypassing immigration formalities" (bribery?). See *Straits Times* 13 Sep 1972.

[148] *Straits Times* 18 Apr 1972.

[149] In PM Lee Hsien Loong's speech at the 2016 Anti-Corruption Summit in London, he said that, "corruption is a scourge that can never be tolerated ... often corruption remains endemic, a cancer in the society", cited in Nicholas Lim Kah Hwee, "Singapore Experience in the Fight Against Corruption", Country Presentation Papers, United Nations Asia And Far East Institute, Eleventh Regional Seminar on Good Governance for Southeast Asian Countries, 17–19 October 2017, Hanoi, Vietnam, p.195, in https://www.unafei.or.jp/publications/pdf/GG11/23_GG11_CP_Singapore2.pdf.

[150] Since 1968, the CPIB had been probing a syndicate forging Singapore's passports. In that

year, a father and son (Ho Kin-man and Ho Chin-wa) were charged in a Hong Kong Court for possession of forged Singapore passports. The CPIB extradited the pair and Director Yoong flew to Hong Kong himself to escort the pair back. *Straits Times* 14 Jun 1969.

[151] *Straits Times* 20, 22 Sep 1972.

[152] *Straits Times* 2 Dec 1973.

[153] *New Nation* 6 Jan 1975.

[154] *Straits Times* 7 Apr 1976.

[155] *New Nation* 11 Sep 1973.

[156] *Straits Times* 1 Sep 1978.

[157] Singapore's airline began in 1937 as the Malayan Airways Limited (MAL). In 1963, when Singapore joined Malaysia, Malayan Airways was renamed Malaysian Airways. After Singapore separated from Malaysia in 1965, Singapore became co-owners of Malaysian Airways with Malaysia. In 1966, the airline was renamed Malaysia–Singapore Airlines (MSA). In January 1971, the decision was made for MSA to split. In January 1972, Singapore International Airlines was born. During the MSA phase of the airline's history, the Singapore Government had a representative on the airline's Board of Directors.

[158] *Straits Times* 6 Jan, 24 Jul 1969.

[159] *Straits Times* 25 Jul, 13, 16 Sep 1969, 14 Feb, 23, 25 Oct 1970.

[160] *Straits Times* 17 Jun 1969. As the Bureau had only about 15 Special Investigators at this time, the Bureau's administrative staff were likely to have participated in the raid as well.

[161] When the Singapore Government could not contact the Malaysian Minister for Transport before the raid, the Malaysian High Commissioner was informed instead. However, the Commissioner claimed that he had only been told of the raid four hours after the fact. See *Straits Times* 20 Jun 1969. The Singapore Government replied to the Malaysians that under the provisions of Singapore's 1960 PCO, the CPIB director had the right to seize documents related to an investigation. See *Straits Times* 18 Jun 1969.

[162] The airline's insurance payments amounted to millions annually. The CPIB conducted a second raid of MSA's office a day after. At the same time, it also raided the office of the Australian advertisement firm, Jackson Wain & Co. (Asia) Ltd at Hill Street, and left with documents relating to MSA's advertising contracts. Irregularities were found, but none involving Fernandez. See *Straits Times* 18, 19 Jun 1969.

[163] *Straits Times* 14 Sep 1969, 23, 25 Oct 1970.

[164] *Straits Times* 24, 27 Feb 1970.

[165] *Straits Times* 21 Oct 1970.

[166] *Straits Times* 7 Nov, 2 Dec 1970.

[167] *Straits Times* 16 Dec 1970.

[168] *Straits Times* 5 Dec 1970.

[169] *Straits Times* 16 Dec 1970

[170] *Straits Times* 15 Dec 1970.

[171] *Straits Times* 13 Jul 1971; *New Nation* 16 Jul 1971.

[172] *New Nation* 17 Jul 1971; *Straits Times* 17, 25 Jul 1971. Fernandez was charged only for the $5,000 gift he took from the firm. He was granted bail by the Singapore Court. His bail was set at $100,000, one of the highest in Singapore then. The Bank of Canton provided the banker's guarantee for his bail.

[173] *New Nation* 10 Sep 1971.

[174] *New Nation* 15 Sep 1971.

[175] Australian advertisement firm, Jackson Wain & Co. (Asia) Ltd at Hill Street, was raided by the CPIB during the second MSA raid. See *Straits Times* 18, 19 Jun 1969.

[176] *Straits Times* 30 Jul 1969. The Nation Defence Fund was started by the Malaysian Government in 1964 when Singapore was in Malaysia. It was started during the Confrontation with Indonesia. See *Straits Budget* 21 Oct 1964. After Independence, Singaporeans continued to donate to its own National Defence Fund, which by this time, went towards the development of the Singapore defence forces. See *Straits Times* 6, 9 Feb 1968.

[177] *Straits Times* 30 Jul 1969.

[178] *Straits Times* 30 Jul 1969.

[179] *Straits Times* 30 Jul 1969. During the course of the CPIB's investigation, canvassers had

continued to solicit money for advertisements in bogus souvenir magazine. One was arrested on 30 August 1969. See *Straits Times* 4 Feb 1970.

[180] *New Nation* 19 Nov 1975; *Straits Times* 20 Nov 1975.

[181] *New Nation* 26 Mar 1975. By early 1975, three of the 15 drug lords had already passed away, and the rest were still in detention at Queenstown Remand Prison, held under the Criminal Law Act (Temporary Provisions). It should be noted, though, that not all corrupt warders at Queenstown Remand Prison were linked to the drug lords interned at the facility. In late 1975, a warder colluded with a prisoner, who was serving a sentence for extortion, wrongful detention and impersonation, to get paid with the money that was taken off him at the prison when he was interned. The prison was holding $121.35 of his money. It was the warder who approached the prisoner with the scheme in late September 1975; in exchange for the money, the prisoner would receive special privileges that included soft drinks, cigarettes, and watching TV after restricted hours. The prison officer asked his cousin, a Cisco officer, to pretend to be the prisoner's cousin. He was to collect the money from the prison authority, giving the reason that he would send the money to the prisoner's wife in Malaysia. On 30 September 1975, the warder set the scheme in motion when he told the Chief Rehabilitation Officer at Queenstown Remand Prison that the prisoner's cousin was coming to take the money. The prison officer was subsequently imprisoned for four months and had to pay a penalty of $121.35. See *Straits Times* 4 Aug 1976. Yet, despite the clampdowns and prosecution of corrupt warders at Queenstown Remand Prison, more warders from that facility continued to be caught in the years following. In 1976, a warder obtained an interest free loan of $500 from a prisoner who was serving a nine-month prison sentence for theft. The warder was in financial difficulties and wanted a $500 loan which he could pay back in 10 monthly instalments. The money was to be given when the prisoner was released. The prisoner agreed, on the condition that he could be given cigarettes and send letters to his girlfriend. The CPIB received a complaint and investigated. The Bureau found that the warder had been showing favours to the prisoner for four months before he was caught. The officer was fined $200. See *Straits Times* 8 Oct 1976.

[182] *Straits Times* 16 Apr 1975.

[183] *Straits Times* 2 Aug 1977.

[184] *Straits Times* 24 Sep 1977.

[185] *Straits Times* 13, 15 Sep 1971; *New Nation* 13 Sep, 11 Oct, 5 Nov 1971, 8 Feb 1972. The exact weight of the haul was 991.9kg, see *Straits Times* 11 Apr 1972. However, another source said that 2,225 lbs (1,009 kg) were found, placing the value of the haul at $262,500. See *New Nation* 15 Nov 1972.

[186] *New Nation* 5 Sep 1974.

[187] *Straits Times* 24 Jun 1975.

[188] *Straits Times* 26 Aug, 24 Sep 1975. Every enforcement agency had their own budget for their reward schemes.

[189] *Straits Times* 18, 27 Nov, 18 Dec 1970.

[190] *Straits Times* 3 Feb 1971.

[191] *Straits Times* 25 Oct 1970.

[192] *Straits Times* 21 Sep 1971.

[193] *Straits Times* 13 Oct 1971; *New Nation* 12 Oct 1971.

[194] *New Nation* 22 Sep 1971.

[195] *New Nation* 20 Sep 1971, 27 Jan 1972.

[196] *New Nation* 7 Nov 1976.

[197] A bookmaker, or bookie, is one who accepts and pays off bets on sporting events, which included horse races. In Singapore, betting on races started as early as 1842 when the Singapore Sporting Club (renamed Turf Club in 1911) was established and races commenced; initially, most betting activities were in the form of wagers between gentlemen. Actually, people in Singapore had already been betting since the 1830s during annual yacht races. Such betting was not considered illegal. Eventually, public betting emerged with people playing the role of the bookie. By the 1880s, bookmaking was noted to have been going on "freely" during races. See *Singapore Daily Times* 26 Apr 1881. It was only in 1912 that a Betting Ordinance was promulgated to deal with public betting as a form of illegal gambling. See *Straits Times* 22 Jun 1912. One of the first prosecutions made under this law occurred in 1920 when two bookmakers were

arrested and spent 14 days in prison. See *Singapore Free Press* 18 May 1920. However, little more was done to suppress bookmaking activities because it mainly deprived the Turf Club of more revenue, and was not considered a serious public problem. In 1932, prosecution of bookmakers once again came under the spotlight when two men were caught bookmaking within the grounds of the Turf Club. It was considered a "test case" for the government in prosecuting bookmakers linked to the Turf Club. Up till this time, not everyone had considered all betting activities as gambling, especially when no "den" (shop) was involved. The "Crown" won, both men were fined, one for $100, the other $25. At this point, public betting on horses and bookmaking were already rife. See *Singapore Daily News* 16 Dec 1932; *Malaya Tribune* 16 Dec 1932; *Singapore Free Press* 16 Dec 1932. However, there was little evidence that bookmakers were involved in any connivance with public servants or fixing races. Still, there was little attention placed on bookmaking, probably because horse betting was still not an extensive problem. Most Chinese still preferred to frequent gaming tables, like *Chap Ji Kee*. In 1937, when the Police caught and charged two men for bookmaking on the grounds of St Andrew's Cathedral, they were only charged with loitering. See *Morning Tribune* 13 Jan 1937. Things changed after the Japanese Occupation. Following repairs and reopening of the Turf Club in November 1947, the betting on horses, officially at the Turf Club, increased exponentially. On opening day in 1947, $300,000 worth of bets was placed. Within a year, bookmaking had become a big business. It was estimated that illegal bookies took away from the Turf Club, and the government, $10,000,000 in tax revenue and deductions in 1948. During this period, one bookie revealed that bookies in Singapore and the Federation handled $50,000,000 annually. However, there were still not many bookies in Singapore at this time. The Police estimated that there were about 100 bookies operating on the island in 1948. See *Straits Times* 6, 9 Aug, 15, 17 Nov 1947, 28 Nov 1948. Still the government was concerned. It appointed a Betting Commission on 23 February 1949 to enquire if bookmaking and betting should be legalised to control the situation. The Commission submitted its report in September 1950; although it believed that there were malpractices relating to bookmaking activities in Singapore, there was still no proof that race tampering had occurred, although it admitted that there had been substantive bookmaking activities in 1950. As such, the Commission did not recommend amending the law to deal with the problem. See *Malaya Tribune* 22 Sep, 4 Oct 1950; *Straits Budget* 28 Sep 1950; *Singapore Free Press* 14 Jun 1951. The Commission, however, pointed out that a bookmaker's daily turnover (bets) could be around $1,000,000, and that most of activities were mainly conducted over the telephone. Hence, it suggested that the government could tap phone calls to get bookies' addresses and then the Police could raid their premises. *Straits Times* 5 May 1951.

[198] In fact, as early as January 1959, the CPIB uncovered a four-digit racket organised and patronised by civil servants at the government offices in Empress Place. See *Singapore Standard* 3 Feb 1959.

[199] *Singapore Free Press* 23 Nov 1957.

[200] *Singapore Free Press* 24, 27 Nov 1959. In fact, the clampdown on indebtedness amongst public servants started as soon as the 1957 General Orders were issued. More than 40 were dismissed, and seven of them for making false declarations. In 1958, the PSC investigated 74 cases and 53 of these were recommended for dismissal. See *Straits Times* 11 Jul, 27 Dec 1959; *Singapore Free Press* 26 Dec 1959. After the 1959 General Election, the new Government dismissed 20 government officers. See *Singapore Free Press* 19 Oct 1959. The new Government also introduced the Moneylenders Act in 1959 to control indebtedness arising from taking loans from moneylenders. See *Straits Times* 22 Aug 1959; *Singapore Free Press* 5 Sep 1959.

[201] *Singapore Free Press* 31 Dec 1959.

[202] *Straits Budget* 30 Mar 1960.

[203] *Straits Times* 6 Jun 1971; *New Nation* 19 May 1971.

[204] *Straits Times* 30 Jun 1971.

[205] *New Nation* 29 Jun 1971.

[206] *New Nation* 5 Jul 1971.

[207] *Straits Times* 15 Sep 1971.

[208] *New Nation* 12 Sep 1972.

[209] *Straits Times* 10 Dec 1972; *New Nation* 12 Sep 1972; 29 Jan, 7, 12 Nov 1973.

[210] *Straits Times* 4, 5 Dec 1973; *New Nation* 3 Dec 1973, 24 May 1974. In December 1973, Anthony arrested three of the club's officers for taking bribes. One was charged and sentenced to three months' jail. In May 1974, five Turf Club security officers were dismissed for accepting bribes from bookmakers; they received $30 to $100 each, every race day. One was charged in Court and fined $2,000.

[211] *New Nation* 3 Dec 1973; *New Nation* 25 Jun 1974.

[212] *Straits Times* 24 Jun, 9 Jul 1976.

[213] *New Nation* 9 Jul 1976; *Straits Times* 9 Jul 1976.

[214] *Straits Times* 3, 8, 9 Dec 1976, 16 Mar 1977. One of the officers charged, Detective Constable Wang Loke Yong, pleaded guilty to taking a total of $63 from Kee on five occasions, from April to June 1976. He was jailed for a year on each count, which ran concurrently, and he paid a $63 penalty. Wang originally faced 18 charges, but the prosecution only proceeded on five of them. See *Straits Times* 27 Feb 1977. Another officer, Detective Lim Hock Seng, who took bribes from bookmakers at Tampines, was arrested just three days before his retirement. He forfeited his $10,000 gratuity which he earned for 24 years of service. He also lost a $200 monthly pension. He originally faced 20 charges. As he pleaded guilty to three charges of accepting $15 bribes from Kee on three occasions, from May to June 1976, he was given three months' jail for each charge; the sentences ran consecutively. See *Straits Times* 16 Mar 1977.

[215] *Straits Times* 3 Dec 1976.

[216] *Straits Times* 14 Jul 1976.

[217] *Straits Times* 31 May 1977.

[218] *New Nation* 22 Sep 1971. In September 1971, the CPIB raided the offices of the Department to check if its staff had been on the payroll of the Indonesian businessman. See *New Nation* 20 Sep 1971. As a result, more than a dozen Telecommunications Department staff were suspended. Most of them were teleprinters, and two were supervisors. See *New Nation* 27 Jan 1972; *Straits Times* 28 Jan 1972. On 1 April 1972, the Telecommunications Department became a statutory body and was renamed the Telecommunication Authority of Singapore (TAS). See *Straits Times* 1 Apr 1972. In 1974, the Singapore Telephone Board (STB) was merged with TAS to form a larger Telecommunication Authority of Singapore (TAS). The new TAS was entirely responsible for both the internal and external telecommunications of Singapore. See https://www.nas.gov.sg/archivesonline/government_records/agency-details/33.

[219] *Straits Times* 21 Jun 1977. As a result of the raid, the CPIB found three persons engaged in bookmaking and illegal "10,000 character" lottery (four-digit) on site at the exchanges. See *Straits Times* 22 Jun 1977.

[220] There were many instances of corruption conspiracies by citizens: the medical certificate scandal among lower division government officers, the conspiracies of HDB clerks-of-works and the TAS' phone tapping (a network rerouting scandal that had no overarching mastermind). A bunch of employees simply decided to abuse their positions to create platforms with which they could make corrupt gains. One had to appreciate how organic their corruption network had been. It was during the trial of the TAS employees in late 1977 that we learnt just how extensive and varied their positions and roles were — four TAS employees were fined a total of $12,000; Sia Huan Boon, an assistant technician at the Main Distribution Frame, was fined $6,000 ($2,000 each on three charges); Lee Kim Hing, an artisan, working under Sia, listened to the transmissions and betting conversations was fined $2,000; two other technicians Ng Bak Thiah and Chua Hong Ling were fined $2,000 each; Lee Yak Whatt, a technician who tapped phone lines to obtain racing tips, and lost money as a result, was fined $1,500. See *Straits Times* 25 Oct, 29 Dec 1977.

[221] The CCB had closed at the end of May 1980 on account of the great reduction of complaints it received by this time. Most people were communicating directly with relevant Ministries or complaining to their own MPs. See *New Nation* 23 May 1980. It could also be said that the situation on the ground had greatly improved by 1980.

[222] *Straits Times* 25 Jan, 27 Jul 1969.

²²³ *Straits Times* 31 Jul 1987.

²²⁴ In the 1970s, the CCB continued to be an important pillar that supported good governance in Singapore. In 1970 alone, the CCB handled more than 28,000 public queries and 794 complaints against public servants; of these, eight received warnings, five received disciplinary action, one was dismissed, two retired and two resigned before investigations commenced. But more importantly, the CCB's investigation found that 65 complaints were unsubstantiated, thus clearing the names of these public servants. See *Straits Times* 23 Mar 1971. A number of these cases, if they had not been handled by the CCB, might have added to the basket of cases that the CPIB had to handle. In any case, from 1974, it became noticeable that more and more people were preferring to see their "MPs" with their complaints, or to write to directly to the relevant ministries and even to the press, rather than to report issues regarding public servants to the CCB, including matters of misconduct. This was mainly because the public was, by this time, more aware of their rights. Nevertheless, the CCB functioned as a third eye on civil servants. The falling complaints to the CCB reflected how bureaucratic rudeness and misconduct were being kept in check. From 1962 to 1975, the CCB investigated 9,887 cases. It paid surprise visits to government departments in civilian clothes to deter misconduct amongst public servants; between April 1974 and April 1975, it made a total 1,237 visits and inspections. See *New Nation* 26 Mar 1974, 11 Nov 1976. The CCB closed at the end of May 1980; it had been receiving fewer complaints. Nevertheless, the Ministry of Social Affairs took over its functions. See *New Nation* 23, 26 May 1980.

²²⁵ *New Nation* 4 Jan, 10 Feb 1972.

²²⁶ *New Nation* 4 Jan 1972. By 1978, the Bureau had three female officers. *Straits Times* 15 May 1978.

²²⁷ *Straits Times* 20 Feb 1976; *New Nation* 19 Feb 1976.

²²⁸ *Straits Times* 17 May, 11 Sep 1978; *New Nation* 20 May 1978, 20 Feb, 16 Aug 1979.

²²⁹ *Straits Times* 11 Sep 1978; *New Nation* 20 Feb 1979.

²³⁰ *New Nation* 12 Aug 1981.

²³¹ See *Business Times* 23 Mar 1991, 18 Sep 1999; *New Paper* 18 Sep 1999; *Straits Times* 18 Sep 1999.

²³² *Business Times* 20 Jun, 7 Aug 1984; *Singapore Monitor* 10 Jun 1984.

²³³ The Malaysia Cup, started as a soccer tournament in 1921. From 1921 to 1967, it was known as the Malaya Cup, named so because the trophy was donated by the British warship HMS Malaya.

²³⁴ *Straits Times* 12 Jun 1977; *New Nation* 12 Jun 1977.

²³⁵ *Straits Times* 21 Aug 1977.

²³⁶ *Straits Times* 4 Sep, 16 Oct 1982.

²³⁷ In 1986, the CPIB uncovered another bookies' racket involving the Merlion Cup. See *Straits Times*, 19 Apr, 29, 30 Aug 1986. In 2013, the CPIB investigated three Lebanese referees for match-fixing at the AFC Cup in Singapore. See *New Paper* 6 Apr 2013, "Kelong bust by CPIB: Referees caught with hookers". In October 2015, Singaporean Selvarajan s/o Letchuman was jailed 30 months for match-fixing in the game between Lions XII and Sarawak. He pleaded guilty.

²³⁸ Quoting Koh Boon Long, former national youth football team coach, Justin Ong, "Will Singapore ever be rid of '*kelong*' scourge?" *Yahoo News* 21 Feb 2013.

²³⁹ *Straits Times* 21 Jul 1981.

²⁴⁰ *Straits Times* 3 Jan 1981.

²⁴¹ *Straits Times* 18 Nov 1981.

²⁴² *Straits Times* 9 Aug 1981.

²⁴³ *Straits Times* 18 Dec 1982.

²⁴⁴ *Straits Times* 29 Jan 1989.

²⁴⁵ *Straits Times* 27 Mar 1987.

²⁴⁶ *Straits Times* 3 Jan 1988.

²⁴⁷ *Straits Times* 26 Jan 1987, "Teh Cheang Wan case: No way a minister can avoid investigations"; *Hansard, Singapore (Parliamentary Debates)* 26 Jan 1987.

²⁴⁸ Lee Kuan Yew, *From Third World to First: The Singapore Story: 1965–2000* (Singapore: Marshall Cavendish Editions, 2000), p.183.

Part Five

Vigilance & Readiness
1989–2010

By the 1990s, Singapore had already attained an international reputation of being the least corrupt nation in Asia. This was also the time the country enjoyed unmitigated economic success, becoming one of the four Asian Tigers of the decade: Singapore, Hong Kong, South Korea and Taiwan. While the first two had grown to become major financial centres, the latter two had developed into major manufacturing and technology hubs. The common traits which the four Tigers shared included their sharp "focus on exports, an educated populace, and high savings rates". It was also acknowledged that Singapore, in particular, owed its success to having been "one of the least corrupt nations in the world"; it had a "notoriously transparent regulatory environment" and had protected property rights, which provided "valuable commercial security to its private sector".[1]

It was also during the 1990s that the majority of Singaporeans became homeowners. More than 80% of the population had become Housing and Development Board (HDB) flat dwellers; of these, nine out of 10 owned their own flats.[2] This was a great leap from the 1950s and early 1960s when most working men resided in squatter housing. By this decade, having achieved socio-economic stability, Singaporeans enjoyed high employment, a generally clean city-state, low crime and a great sense of security. At the same time, social ills like gangsterism and deep-seated corruption in the bureaucracy had been kept under control. However, corrupt practices had not disappeared altogether. Singapore, and the Bureau, had to remain vigilant. Corruption amongst public servants and law enforcers could still rob the nation of its hard-earned wealth (and reserves), create inefficiencies and diminish public confidence in all state apparatus, which would then derail our nation-building endeavour.

Keeping vigilant in the late 1980s, the Government added another tool to its arsenal of measures against corrupt practices. It promulgated the Corruption (Confiscation of Benefits) Act in 1989 to work "in tandem" with the Prevention of Corruption Act (PCA) which, on its own, was not sufficiently adequate to deal with the confiscation and recovery of corrupt benefits.[3] The PCA allowed the Court to order, by way of a penalty, only on the sum equal to the amount or value of the gratification. The new Act, however, allowed the Court to confiscate the unexplained wealth and benefits that were derived from the corrupt acts. This was followed by the enactment of the Drug Trafficking (Confiscation of Benefits) Act in 1992. In 1999, it was renamed to the Corruption, Drug Trafficking and Other Serious Crimes (Confiscation of Benefits) Act (CDSA), and the Corruption (Confiscation of Benefits) Act was repealed in the same year. The CDSA would apply to corruption offences and has a wider scope from its original form, as it also includes provisions relating to foreign corruption offences and criminalises money laundering of proceeds from corruption and other serious offences.

While corruption amongst public officers persisted, the proportion of corruption cases in the private sector increased from the 1990s. The great wealth that flowed through the economy of the island had remained a constant source of temptation and corruption within the commercial sectors. However, the state's continual efforts in prevention and public outreach programmes, and certainly through the nation's education policies,[4] had also played a significant part in forging a national ethos that valued honesty and integrity. It was also during this period that the Bureau paid greater attention to collaboration and international cooperation in its anti-corruption efforts. Going into the new millennium, the Bureau prepared itself for the "future fight" against corrupt practices in the digital age.

The Bureau started getting ready for the challenges of the new millennium in the second half of the 1990s. While the Bureau spent the most part of the 1980s and early 1990s clearing up the remnants of rampant and deep-seated corruption that afflicted the public sector in the earlier decades, it was from the mid-1990s that the transformation of the Bureau's processes from within commenced; training, staff development, recruitment, investigation, public education, digitisation, computerisation, new investigation and forensic capabilities, and much more. In the mid-2000s, the CPIB took another significant step forward to meet the new challenges of the milieu when it ramped up its international engagements and cooperation with other anti-corruption bodies in the world. Preparation for new challenges in the horizon required the Bureau to build bridges and multiple forms of connections across borders.

In retrospect, the "success" against corrupt practices in these decades was not just a result of enforcement or preventive measures. Singapore, as a society, and as a nation, had already undergone a social transformation from the wild days — when *kopi* money was not only accepted, but also expected — into a nation that frowned upon public corruption and could boast of having a clean society and government.[5] In the larger scheme of things, the CPIB had to work hard to maintain the national status quo of a largely incorrupt society.

Chapter Twenty-One

Trends & Measures Towards the New Millennium

The much-improved socio-cultural environment in the 1990s had been the outcome of several decades of nation-building. Yet, there were still significant instances of corruption that were uncovered and prosecuted, not because the situation was still tenuous but because of increased vigilance and detection. Also, by this decade, Singaporeans were enjoying a degree of social stability and shared common social values, after years of government efforts to forge a set of national ethos and norms based on multiculturalism.[6] It was therefore not surprising that there had been less tolerance towards social ills like corrupt practices in the public sphere. Nevertheless, while the processes, prevention and enforcement had snuffed out most of the corrupt practices which afflicted the Public Service in earlier decades, and social attitudes had changed, there were still cases of corruption to be found within the public sphere at this time, albeit not as rampant as they had been in the decades before. The new trend from the 1990s, as far as corrupt practices were concerned, was the prosecution of more such cases in the private sector. Singapore's continual economic growth towards the new millennium was sustained by the progress achieved in the commercial and financial sectors. Therefore, it was no surprise that the draw of enormous illicit gratification, which this sphere was certainly capable of providing, would continue to fuel corruption. It was from this time that the Bureau's work and focus included more private sector cases. In fact, by the latter part of the 1990s, private sector corruption cases would outstrip instances of corrupt practices among public officers.

Private Sector

Corruption in the private sector is never simply a private matter. In 1997, the World Bank described how fraud and bribery in the private sphere could be "costly" for countries which did not keep them in check. It argued that "financial systems permeated with fraud can undermine savings and deter foreign investment" and that this might render "a country vulnerable to financial crises and macroeconomic instability".[7] The truth and relevance of this statement to Singapore's reality was most certainly understood and appreciated by the Singapore Government. In fact, Lee Kuan Yew himself articulated just how Singapore's reputation of having a good and clean government that followed the "rule of law" had been "a valuable economic asset" for the island state.[8] Private sector corruption could seriously affect economic development, undermine governance and dent confidence in the country.[9] In truth, a private sector with little corruption, or at least with such a reputation, was essentially an important aspect of Singapore's economic lifeline as the general socio-economic condition within the island state had a direct impact on "domestic" and "foreign" direct investments here.[10] In this context, even though the CPIB had been somewhat successful in keeping corruption in the public sector in check by the 1990s, there was still a lot more for the Bureau to do. Singapore had already achieved the reputation of being the least corrupt nation in Asia since the 1980s. From the 1990s, the annual survey reports of the Political and Economic Risk Consultancy (PERC) Limited, based in Hong Kong, were official recognition that Singapore was the least corrupt nation in Asia and that it was a "low risk" place for businesses.[11] Yet, there were still many cases of corrupt practices detected in the public and private spheres. There was still a risk that corruption in general would become rampant again. As such, the Bureau had to remain vigilant throughout the 1990s and into the new millennium.[12]

In the 1990s, corruption cases involving match-fixing were widely covered. This was one area of corruption that proved extremely difficult to eradicate. In the 1990s, there were several platforms in soccer that saw extreme and persistent "fixing": the Malaysia Cup, Malaysia League and the Singapore League (S-League). For the first competition, in April 1994, Thiru Rajamanickam, a former Fédération Internationale de Football Association (FIFA) referee, took a bribe from a bookmaker to arrange for the appointment of a "lenient" referee for the match between Singapore and Kelantan. He received eight months' jail and a fine of $1,000. He was also banned from all soccer activities for life and deregistered from the Football Association of Singapore's (FAS) approved list of referees.[13] A year later, Kannan s/o Kunjiraman, a former national team player, was convicted for conspiring with Rajendran R Kurusamy and Ong Kheng Hock to bribe David Lee, Singapore's national team goalkeeper, with $80,000 to let in a goal in a Malaysia Cup match.[14] It was also in 1994 that foreign players in the Singapore national team were caught up in match-fixing activities in the Malaysia League. Michal Vana and Abbas Saad, who were both in Singapore's 1994 Malaysia Cup winning team, were found guilty in 1995 for receiving bribes from one bookie, Kurusamy, to help fix separate matches refereed by Rajamanickam. Vana, Saad and Rajamanickam were all found guilty and convicted; Rajamanickam was jailed eight months while Abbas Saad was fined $50,000 and banned globally by FIFA. Vana jumped bail and fled from Singapore using another person's passport, a day before his trial. His $500,000 bail money was forfeited.[15]

The Singapore soccer scene was equally affected by match-fixing activities. Among some of the more well-known cases in the S-League was the 1997 involvement of two Balestier Central Football Club players, Manap Bin Hamat and Abdul Malek Mohammad, who fixed a game between their Club and the Tampines Rovers Football Club. In 2000, the CPIB investigated and prosecuted two foreign players in the league for conspiracy in fixing a match between their clubs: Mirko Jurilj of Sembawang Rangers

Football Club and Lutz Pfannenstiel, the goalkeeper of Geylang United Football Club. While Pfannenstiel accepted bribes amounting to $18,000, Jurilj took $22,000 from golf instructor Sivakumar Madasamy. Both players were sentenced to five months' jail each.

For years, the Football Association of Singapore (FAS) has maintained a zero-tolerance policy towards match-fixing. It has pledged to "permanently suspend any player or official who is convicted in a Court of law for football corruption offences".[16] The Association has also put in place an education and prevention system to combat match-fixing in Singapore. The FAS conducts briefings to all officials, players and staff before the start of every season. Measures have also been implemented for "officials and players to report immediately to their clubs or the CPIB should there be approach or attempts to manipulate results of the matches". In addition, the FAS has adopted random polygraph testing of players. The FAS' rules also forbid players and family members to place bets with the Singapore Pools for any FAS-sanctioned games.

In 2007, Wang Xin, the Team Manager for Liaoning Guangyuan Football Club, a China soccer team competing in the S-League, offered seven of his players $1,000–$2,000 each per game that they fixed. In all, six games were fixed. All seven players were charged and convicted to several months' imprisonment in 2008 (Operation Offside). As for Wang, soon after he was released on bail, he fled home to China.[17]

Entering the new millennium, among the more well-known corruption cases in the commercial sector were cases of bribery in multinational and local companies. The whole issue was turned on its head in 2010–2012 when senior executives of AEM-Evertech Holdings, a precision equipment company, were fined and jailed for bribing executives of other firms to purchase AEM's products between 2004 and 2005. The company had paid Siow Sing Heng, a manager of STS Shenzhen, $100,000 to select AEM's equipment, and more than $200,000 to executives of Seagate Technology International and Infineon Technologies Malaysia (Malacca) for their business. The company's Chief Executive Officer (CEO), Ang Seng Thor, confessed to his part in the wrongdoings in May 2007 when he came under investigation by the CPIB. Ang was initially fined $200,000 in 2010, but a year later, following the prosecution's appeal, he was jailed 12 weeks and fined $50,000. In 2012, the firm's Executive Chairman Tok Kian You was jailed 12 weeks and fined $60,000. It was said then that the AEM-Evertech case had set the precedence that "corruption in the public and private sector is treated with equal seriousness"; the giver and the receiver in private sector corruption cases could both receive jail time, not simply a fine.[18]

The AEM affair was an important case for the CPIB at this time because it "invoked extra-territorial provisions" of Singapore laws as the bribery occurred overseas. In this instance, it demonstrated that Singaporeans cannot escape the long arm of the law even if they committed bribery beyond our national borders.[19]

At this time, other bribery cases involving multinational corporations and local firms included Apple Inc. In 2010, the CPIB discovered that Apple Inc.'s Global Supply Manager, Paul Shin Devine, had taken bribes from Ang Kok Kiat and Chua Kim Guan, the Sales Director and Managing Director of Jin Li Mould Manufacturing Pte Ltd, respectively. From November 2006 to June 2009, both men had given up to US$387,600 to Devine for information about Apple launches to help them secure contracts. In December 2013, Chua was jailed for nine months while Ang was sentenced to 12 months' jail and fined S$281,985.51. As for Devine, he was already dealt with by the United States Federal Court for "wire fraud, conspiracy and money laundering" in 2011.[20]

In another case, Singapore-based Federal Hardware Engineering Company Pte Ltd was charged in 2004 for bribing Nakamura Tomohiro, a staff of Toyo Engineering Corporation (Japan), to award Federal Hardware contracts worth a total of US$247,088 in mid-2001. It was Nakamura who had asked for a commission to favour Federal Hardware in early 2001. Federal Hardware acceded and gave Nakamura US$17,500. In August 2004, the firm was charged under Section 6(b) of the PCA and fined

$60,000. It should be noted that the CPIB was able to pursue such cases, and the state prosecutors were able to apply charges to all these companies and individuals in their cross-border dealings, because of the "extra-territorial nature of the Prevention of Corruption Act, which allows charges to be filed against Singaporeans and Singapore firms, even for corrupt acts committed abroad".[21] Nonetheless, in the pursuit of such cross-border cases, the collaboration with and assistance from foreign authorities are also critical in bringing the perpetrators to justice.

It was important for the guardians preventing corrupt practices in Singapore's commercial firms to have the ability to pursue cross-border commercial cases. The corruption involving Citiraya Industries Ltd in 2004–2005 demonstrated just how the CPIB had this ability (Operation Cross Over). Citiraya, later renamed Centillion Environment & Recycling, was a large firm established in 1988 by Ng Teck Lee and his brother to recycle electronics waste. By 2002, when it became a listed company, it had a "presence" in 11 countries, from which it collected electronics waste for recycling. Everything fell apart for the company in early 2005 when police in Taiwan found, during raids, "scrapped chips belonging to one of Citiraya's US-based clients" in the premises of companies which had dealings with Ng. These computer chips were supposed to be crushed and recycled in Singapore. Instead, Citiraya "diverted them for sale overseas and the level of precious metal extracted from waste was falsely declared". In doing so, the company created 1,554 fictitious transactions in 2004. The fake sales were worth about $161,000,000. Large quantities of electronic chips from several other manufacturers were uncovered. The CPIB found that from 2003 to 2004, Ng and his brother diverted 62 containers of electronic scrap to customers in Hong Kong and Taiwan. Ng was highly successful in this scheme partly because he had employed extensive bribes along the entire chain that moved his scrap. Nevertheless, the CPIB was able to crack the case by leveraging "the pre-operations intelligence work" of its intelligence unit which established the network of people involved, and how the corruption and cheating offences were committed.[22]

In all, $1,820,000 of bribes had been paid. To hide his illicit gains from the sale of electronic chips, he opened two bank accounts in Hong Kong, which he used to purchase shares and properties. Eventually, when the walls came crumbling down, Ng absconded. Despite his absence, the CPIB continued its pursuit of the criminal proceeds (Operation Turn Over). In 2011, the Singapore Government seized $23,000,000 of Ng's assets under the provisions of the CDSA.[23] He could run, but he could never enjoy the fruits of all his ill-gotten gains. But more pertinently, the Citiraya case occurred at a time when the CPIB handled many private sector cases that "involved senior executives, CEOs and general managers in private companies". The successful prosecution of Citiraya sent a "signal" that "went out very clearly to the business community in Singapore that CPIB would not tolerate corruption in the business arena".[24]

In another case involving the commercial sector, Goh Peng Choy, a senior procurement executive with Advanced Material Engineering Pte Ltd (AME), obtained bribes from several contractors of AME to reveal the firm's confidential internal price list and to favour them in their bids. Goh was careful to accept only cash. After the CPIB investigated, it was discovered that he had a large stash of money for which he could not account for. In all, $385,000 cash was seized from Goh's safe while more were uncovered from his brother's residence and bank accounts. Goh was convicted for corruption and sentenced to 12 months' imprisonment in February 2014. He was ordered to pay a penalty of $372,923 and forfeited $12,077 to the state. He was also convicted to 10 months' imprisonment for money laundering offences. In the end, a total of $485,767.03 was recovered from the case, including the benefits derived from the bribes received between 2006 and 2009.[25]

Among the local private sector corrupt practices of the day, there were a number of "flavourful" and noteworthy cases which demonstrated business "acumen", but certainly not desperation. In July 2009, the CPIB received a tip-off about some "fishy business" occurring between a seafood supplier and the established head chefs of Singapore's most prestigious hotels and restaurants. Following its investigation (Operation Gourmet), the CPIB discovered how Tay Ee Tiong, the owner of Wealthy Seafood Product and Enterprise, approached up to 19 head chefs from 17 different "well-known Chinese restaurants and hotels in Singapore" and offered them personal "commissions" of 5% to 10% each on the value of their total purchases from Wealthy Seafood for their restaurants. From February 2006 to August 2009, Tay handed out bribes ranging from $232 to S$24,143 to each of the 19 chefs every few months. Over a period of three years, Tay paid out $992,404 in total. Mathematically, if the commission-bribes paid out were around 5% to 10% of their total transactions, Tay's turnover with these chefs would have been between $5,000,000 and $10,000,000! Nevertheless, not long after the CPIB started its investigation, Tay's business folded, and he was declared bankrupt in February 2010. In 2011, Tay had the book thrown at him; he was charged with 223 counts of corruption and received 18 months' jail time. In the aftermath, 18 chefs of the five-star hotels and restaurants involved were convicted of corruption. All the chefs convicted were ordered to surrender the entirety of the bribes received to the Government.[26]

While the emergence of a generally affluent middle-class Singapore in the 1990s saw the passing of an age when masses tended to accept small bribes to get around bureaucracies to secure jobs or obtain rations and licences, there arose new issues of the days that fed the appetite of those who were corruptible. The Wealthy Seafood affair hit at the very heart of Singapore's socio-economic success — food, good food, had become a want and desire of many, making it a lucrative industry up and down the "food" chain. When the trial judge meted out a deterrent sentence for Tay, his lawyer remarked that the "need for general deterrence is not significantly pressing" as "public interest was not compromised". To this, the trial judge replied that there was a "clear public interest in deterring such acts of corruption" as there was a need to ensure that the "interests of competitors and of the public are not harmed".[27] The fact of the matter was that

▶ Vigilance & Readiness

corruption was not only a matter of the abuse of official position for personal gain, or to seek special treatment from officials for personal gain by offering them personal rewards, it was also about dishonest practices that harmed individuals and social and corporate entities. The amounts that Tay and the chefs pocketed would certainly cost the hotels and restaurants part of their profits or revenue since the produce with better prices had not been procured. And with higher costs arising from "dearer" supplies, cooked food prices would have been raised to compensate narrowing margins. So, the consumers suffered, as they would have had to bear the cost of the hidden commissions. Moreover, the higher cost of business harmed the competitiveness of local industries. This case also educated the public that some customs or so-called norms in any industry are corrupt practices.

Another interesting corruption case surrounding food at this time that drew significant public interest was the one that occurred at IKEA's restaurant — an all-time popular dining place for many Singaporeans, known especially for its meatballs and chicken wings. When the CPIB investigated in 2009, it discovered that IKEA's Food Service Manager, Leng Kah Poh, had conspired with two others to provide IKEA with food supplies themselves. They marked up the prices of their goods and the trio shared the resulting profit. From January 2003 to July 2009, the conspirators amassed a profit of $6,900,000 just on their business with IKEA. One of Leng's partner, Lim Kim Seng, was the owner of the company that provided supplies to IKEA's restaurants in Singapore. It was Lim who introduced Leng to the third partner, Tee Fook Boon. The men put their plan together in 2002 to displace IKEA's raw ingredient supplier and for Tee to start a new business, AT35, from which Leng would procure the restaurants' future supplies. For his services, Leng was given part of AT35's profits. Sometime later, Lim set up another company, Food Royale Trading, which Leng then appointed to supply chilled and dried foods to IKEA. In seven years, from 2003 to 2009, the trio pocketed millions; Leng's share was $2,341,508, a third of the two companies' profits. By 2013, all three had been charged in Court. Lim was given 70 weeks' imprisonment while Tee was originally sentenced to 16 weeks' imprisonment and fined $180,000. Tee's jail sentence was later revised to 40 weeks. As for Leng, in July 2013, he was sentenced to 98 weeks' jail and given a penalty of $2,341,508, which was the proceeds of his corruption.[28]

The turn of the century also saw the Bureau handling an increasing number of cases of law breakers in the "private sphere" paying off or bribing others to take the rap for them. Those who accepted payment to shield the original culprits were deemed to have participated in corruption. Colloquially and popularly known as *Tua Pek Kong*,[29] this practice was syndicated and systematically organised in the 1990s. *Tua Pek Kong* cases included people involved in traffic accidents who paid others to take responsibility for the violation, or persons being investigated by the Police for criminal acts such as theft. There were also instances when drug addicts paid others to take responsibility for their actions when the authorities closed in on them. From 2001 to 2003, the CPIB even found a syndicate that supplied "fall guys" for hawkers who were found to have employed illegal labourers. These bribers had the means to pay for a "volunteer" to stand in, and there was no shortage of people, especially those unemployed or in debt, who were willing to take the money to become a *Tua Pek Kong*.[30] Although such scams were not exactly new to Singapore, they had become increasingly common and were detected because of greater vigilance of public officers during this period. Nevertheless, just like illegal bookmaking, *Tua Pek Kong* cases persisted.

In 2008, the CPIB investigated 21 *Tua Pek Kongs* involving illegal massage parlours (Operation Sleazy). Interestingly, one of the fall guys caught was not just a stand-in for the owner of the parlour at People's Park Centre in Chinatown when the shop was raided by the Police. He was, in fact, the frontman for the establishment and operations of the shop and the fall guy for the real owner when the shop was found to have gone afoul of the law. This fall guy was paid $1,000 per month to be the "front" for the parlour. He had no real work at the shop. He was being used to register an "aromatherapy" business and to find a shop space to rent for the business. The real boss was a woman from China who paid all the bills and managed all operations of the illegal massage parlour. He only visited the shop every fortnight to collect his "pay". It was only after the Police raided the shop in March 2007 and found seven women from China engaged in vices that he came forth to take responsibility. The Court fined him $2,500 for operating the illegal massage parlour but he chose the default of two weeks' jail time. The real boss could have paid the fine for him, but having chosen to go to jail, the boss gave him a "special bonus" of a few thousand dollars. However, when the CPIB discovered that he was really a *Tua Pek Kong* in June 2008, "he was jailed another two months and ordered to pay a penalty of $6,000 for accepting bribes". The real boss was also jailed two months for corruption.[31]

Using *Tua Pek Kongs* in the illegal massage parlour business in the latter part of the 2000s was a new phenomenon at that time (Operation Miscarriage). Till the 1990s, scapegoats were mainly used by entities that sold counterfeit luxury items and even in gambling dens and brothels. And when pirated video compact discs (VCDs) became popular with the masses, *Tua Pek Kongs* were also engaged to own VCD shops. It was only after the Government started clamping down on illegal massage parlours from mid-1996 that the trade started utilising scapegoats. This development paralleled the outcome of the Government's enforcement action against illegal foreign workers. Soon after, there was "a big demand for *Tua Pek Kongs*" to pose as their agents. This trend persisted through the 2010s.[32] During this period, the CPIB would continue to make it clear that it was "illegal to assume criminal liability for someone else", especially when monetary rewards were involved. For this offence, one could be jailed up to five years or fined up to $100,000.[33]

From 2007 to 2008, following the insertion of Sections 204A and 204B into the Penal Code, the Police are empowered to investigate cases involving obstruction and perversion of the course of justice, and the bribery of witnesses (which include *Tua Pek Kongs* unlawfully assuming criminal liability).[34] However, the CPIB continued to probe cases where vice syndicates bribe law enforcers for protection or for tipping off raids. It was common for illegal establishments, in particular massage parlours, to have had a policeman in their pockets who provided a tip-off of an impending raid. However, on occasions when this system of police protection failed because other agencies spearheaded the raid, for instance by the Immigration and Checkpoints Authority (ICA), then the parlour would "deploy" their *Tua Pek Kongs*, their safety nets.

Public Sector

Corruption in the public sector in the 1990s was not shaped by the socio-economic conditions of the time. There were far fewer cases of corrupt public officers disciplined or charged during this period compared to the preceding decades; almost all cases of public corruption that the CPIB dealt with had been the act of individuals who abused their position and authority as public officers rather than conspiratorial affairs involving a network of officers. Nevertheless, there were still corrupt public officers in the service who could spread the rot and threaten the success achieved by the nation thus far. Hence, the Bureau had to remain vigilant at all times. Going into the 2010s, the majority of the CPIB's corruption probes were from the private sector; from 2009 to 2013, only one in five corruption investigations had been of public officers. And "about two-thirds of the investigations involving public officers led to prosecution or disciplinary proceedings". Then Deputy Prime Minister Teo Chee Hean[35] noted that in total, during the period, cases involving public officers remained "low and quite stable".[36] At the same time, K Shanmugam, then Law and Foreign Minister,[37] also warned against complacency as there were still corrupt public officers, albeit far fewer than in the years before: "What we need to do is always be vigilant, be on top of it, and make sure these are the exceptions and they don't become the norm." DPM Teo was, nevertheless, optimistic that the nation was on the correct trajectory as far as corrupt practices were concerned. He noted that many of the graft probes "involving public officers were started after members of the public or fellow officers blew the whistle", which suggested that there existed "a strong culture in Singapore and in the Public Service which rejects corruption".[38]

There were only a couple of notable "syndicated" corruption cases at the beginning of the last decade of the twentieth century. Most of the graft cases investigated by the CPIB thereafter had been mainly of individual failings. In 1990, 14 corrupt immigration officers were charged for facilitating the illegal entry of Thai prostitutes and helping Malaysian visitors circumvent the 60/90-day visit restriction.[39] While this racket was not a big-money enterprise, it nevertheless gave the conspirators an additional source of income. The other notorious case was that of the infamous *Ah Long San*, whose real name was Chua Tiong Tiong. Chua was a well-known loan shark operating in the Geylang district. He was also the Managing Director of Tiong Tiong Building Materials and a shareholder of M KTV Karaoke Lounge on Geylang Road. He had already been convicted a couple of times in the 1980s for illegal moneylending, but he remained untouched most times because the people in the area generally feared his reprisal. Also, Chua had made friends with police officers who tipped him off on impending raids, mostly in exchange for gratifications in the form of entertainment. It was only in 1999 that the CPIB ended Chua's reign, detaining him and several police officers in a raid. The CPIB's investigation into Chua's activities and the police officers took several years.

The CPIB discovered that on some occasions, the corrupt police officers received money from Chua through his chauffeur, Lim Hock Ghee. When Chua was convicted and sentenced to 18-months' jail for bribery, he failed to appear in Court for the appeal and went into hiding. He was eventually rearrested in July 2001 and jailed for 10 years in October 2001.[40] As for the policemen involved, a number of them were fined or jailed, or both. The fines ranged from several hundred dollars to $8,000 each, while their jail time spanned from a few months to 33 months.[41]

Most of the other corruption cases involving public officers going into the new millennium were those lacking integrity and motivated mainly by personal greed to gratify themselves. Most of such cases reported or uncovered were handled by the CPIB with the cooperation of their parent departments and ministries. In November 1996, Station Inspector Ghulam Mustaffa Mahmood was sentenced to six months' jail and fined $5,000 for two counts of corruption. This was a most interesting case in the chronicles of both the Police and the CPIB because of the spectre of the crime that was committed as a result of the corrupt act. In June 1995, Lim Chwee Soon @ Ah Soon was remanded by the Police for robbery. Ah Soon's family approached a businessman, Roman Tan, to stand as his bailor. Tan agreed on the condition his fee for the assistance was to be 20% of the bail amount, which was $150,000. However, Tan had insufficient cash and needed to use his valuables as security for the bail. These included a few Rolex watches, a gold bar and some jewellery (all with receipts indicating their value). Nonetheless, when Tan presented his valuables to Ghulam, he was told that police guidelines did not allow such assets to be used in place of bail money because they were "non-secured items with subjective values". So, Tan offered Ghulam a total of $5,000 bribe if he could assist in the matter. Ghulam agreed but made it known that it could only be done when "a new and inexperienced officer was on-duty". This opportunity arose on 18 July 1995, and Ghulam instructed Tan to proceed with his valuables to bail Ah Soon. As expected, the officer consulted Ghulam who, accordingly, confirmed that she could verify the bail bond. The officer endorsed the bail form as a result, and following the approval, Ah Soon was released. On the same night, Ghulam met Tan to collect his bribe money.[42]

After Ah Soon missed his trial for the first robbery, he committed a more serious robbery in October 1995. This time, he used a firearm. Seven shots were fired in a jewellery shop, injuring the sales manager. He fled to Malaysia with four Rolex watches worth a total value of $75,000, but was arrested by the Malaysian authorities and extradited back to Singapore.

▶ Vigilance & Readiness

Ah Soon was convicted and was the first person to receive a death sentence under the new law imposing mandatory death sentence for using a firearm in the commission of a crime in Singapore.[43]

There were essentially two facets to this case: the bribery that led to Ah Soon's escape, and the subsequent armed robbery that followed. While the CPIB handled the first aspect, the Police dealt with the second. Through the investigations, pursuit and trial, the CPIB and the Singapore Police Force cooperated closely to ensure a successful conclusion of the matter.

In the late 1990s, the CPIB also worked with the Central Narcotics Bureau (CNB) on a case involving their officer, Corporal Yong Swee Fatt. He collected several thousands of dollars from a drug offender, Tan Chuan Hee, to shorten the latter's post-detention and release supervision period, as well as to settle his case of jumping bail in 1998. Yong also accepted paid "entertainment" from Tan. Yong was charged and convicted in 2003 for corruption. He was sentenced to a total of 27 months' imprisonment.[44]

The turn of the century also saw a number of cases involving human traffickers plying their trade through Singapore. This included three Singapore Airport Terminal Services (SATS) officers who were arrested and charged for taking bribes from a person running a human trafficking syndicate (Operation Exodus I). They needed the officers' help to facilitate their travel as they had no valid travel documents. Their ploy was discovered in November 2000 when two Pakistani asylum seekers, Abdul Wali Khan and Zia Uddin, were found travelling illegally with false travel documents while in transit at the Hong Kong International Airport via a Singapore Airlines flight from Singapore to San Francisco. The pair was aided by Madhavan s/o Rajagopal, who was a customer service officer with SATS. His main duty was to process the boarding passes for passengers in transit at Changi Airport's Terminal 1. Khan offered Madhavan $5,000 for every Pakistani he helped to smuggle to San Francisco. Madhavan then enlisted the help of Mohammad Ikhsan Bin Mohammad Zaini, a SATS Customer Services Supervisor, and promised him a sum of $4,500 if the scheme was successful. As Madhavan was unable to print fake boarding passes, Ikhsan sought the assistance of his wife, who was then working as a Customer Services Agent for SATS, to help print the passes. Madhavan also got Bhagat Singh s/o Dhola Singh, another SATS Customer Service Officer, to monitor the status of the two Pakistanis and to check from the computer system whether they had successfully taken off for San Francisco. On 10 April 2002, Ikhsan was sentenced to 12 months' imprisonment and ordered to pay a penalty of $4,500 for corruption while Bhagat was sentenced to 9 months' imprisonment and ordered to pay a penalty of $1,500 for corruption and offences under the Computer Misuse Act. In the course of the investigation, it was also found that Madhavan had assisted Khan to smuggle people to San Francisco on other occasions. On 10 October 2001, Madhavan was sentenced to 10 years' imprisonment and ordered to pay a penalty of $34,748. The sentence for Madhavan was one of the highest for a corruption offence and was meant to send a very strong message in the aftermath of 9/11 when security at the airport had been heightened. Madhavan's actions could not be tolerated as it had seriously compromised Singapore's security.[45]

In June 2001, Sergeant Cheong Kiong Heong, an auxiliary police with the Changi International Airport Services Pte Ltd (CIAS), was convicted for taking $9,000 bribes from a human smuggling syndicate to assist nine Chinese nationals who were leaving Singapore for America using other Singaporeans' passports. Cheong's job at CIAS was to ascertain the authenticity of travel documents for departing passengers. A Chinese National was arrested red-handed (Operation Exodus II) by CPIB officers when he attempted to board a Northwest Airline flight to America. Syndicate members who were present at Changi Airport were also arrested. Cheong was sentenced to 16 months' jail.[46]

Besides the uniformed and enforcement services, there was still a need for the Bureau to keep a look out for corrupt officers in the rest of the Public Service. Corruption amongst these public officers basically took the form of the abuse of their position and authority to provide illegal services for gratification from members of the public. Such corrupt practices, as had been in the decades before, could be found across all government bodies, albeit less pervasive from this period. Amongst the array of interesting cases surrounding the non-uniformed services was the 1992–1993 Singapore Telecom Pte Ltd corruption scandal. In December 1992, the Bureau received information that a Singapore Telecom artisan (skilled worker), Christopher Krishnan s/o Nadesan Packrisamy, had been tapping telephones illegally. The CPIB discovered that he had been collecting bribes from Joel Chan since 1991 to provide illegal phone taps to private investigation agencies. These agencies were charged $400 to $600 weekly for the service. Chan would bribe two to three Telecom staff to help him with the taps. In total, Christopher collected $300 from Chan over a period of time. In 1994, he received three months' jail for his part in the racket.[47]

Then there was the case of Sundara Moorthy Lankatharan, a Housing and Development Board (HDB) technician who was attached to the Safety Unit of the Structural Engineering Department from January 1991 to March 1995. He solicited a bribe from Tan Ah Lay, the Managing Director of a contract firm working on an HDB project. The bribe solicited was to be in the form of a $4,000 loan. A week after Tan rejected Sundara's request, Sundara announced that he would be inspecting Tan's worksite again. Fearing that he might fail the inspection, Tan agreed to the loan this time. Sundara was caught and sentenced to three months' jail and a fine of $4,000.[48] In another construction project, Peh Chew Seng, the Deputy Director of Projects and Development at Tan Tock Seng Hospital, rigged a tender for the construction of a four-storey office next to the hospital's main building in February 2009. After he secured an agreement with a tendering party to receive a commission for selecting the company, Peh instructed the project consultant to disqualify the lowest bids and select the company he had chosen. It was this instruction that exposed his "arrangement". Even though no money had actually changed hands, Peh was charged for soliciting bribes and jailed six weeks in September 2012.[49]

The reasons why there were still corrupt public officers in the 1980s and the 1990s were more because of wants and covetousness of individuals, a matter of greed, and less about circumstances of low wages, shortages and privation. It was also a growing trend that it was the public officer who initiated illegal gratifications rather than the general public; changing of social values and a much-improved standard of living fostered an environment where many in the public would know how to provide feedback or complaints to accomplish what they needed. However, the changing times did not alter the greed and debased dispositions of corrupt persons. This is why the Bureau is still very much needed even when Singapore had already become one of the least corrupt nations in the world.

Landmark and Public Interest Cases

Lee Kuan Yew explained in his memoirs, "It is difficult to live up to these good intentions unless the leaders are strong and determined enough to deal with all transgressors, and without exceptions... CPIB officers must be supported **without fear or favour** to enforce the rules."[50] In dealing with senior government officers, Lee added that "there is no way a Minister can avoid investigations and a trial if there is evidence to support one".[51] Essentially, Lee enunciated the importance of political will in the eradication of all forms of corruption.

Although there was no major corruption case in the 1990s and 2000s with the same magnitude as the Teh affair, there were still significant and landmark cases which had been of great public interest. Fundamentally these had been similar to every other corrupt public officer case which skimmed off some benefit from their place of employment or area of responsibility. There were also a number of larger-than-life cases that attracted great public attention. One such major case was the TT Durai and the National Kidney Foundation (NKF) debacle in the mid-2000s. Durai had been embroiled in controversy over malpractices involving NKF funds since the late 1990s when he sued individuals who suggested he had misused funds from the charity and spent lavishly. These accusations came to a head in 2005 when Durai sued Singapore Press Holdings (SPH) for defamation. Following explosive revelations in an audit report during his clash with SPH, in December 2005, the Commercial Affairs Department (CAD) and the CPIB took a closer look into the malpractices at the NKF. Durai was charged in April 2006 for deceiving the charity by approving invoice payments between December 2003 and January 2004 to two firms for fictitious services which were never performed; $20,000 to an interior design firm and $5,000 to an advertising firm. He was sentenced to three months' jail.[52]

The Bureau had received some information that there might have been corruption offences that occurred in the NKF. So, while the CAD and Ministry of Manpower (MOM) started to do their investigations, the CPIB was conducting covert intelligence gathering on Durai and the NKF. The CPIB eventually arrested Durai and investigated him for corruption offences. In the end, Durai was prosecuted for offences not associated with bribery per se, but offences under the PCA associated with falsifying documents. Along the way, the CPIB also uncovered various other associated offences against senior staff in the NKF. The NKF had an executive committee, and they were engaged in various irregular business dealings as well, such as corruption offences involving an NKF procurement staff, who was being bribed to award contracts to various suppliers, which the Bureau uncovered.[53] The NKF was a high-profile and well-supported organisation at that point in time. Durai was also a popular figure. Taking him to task, and cleaning up the NKF, required the Bureau's officers to have fortitude and tenacity, and the backing of the Government.

Another important public figure who fell from grace on account of corruption during this period was Glenn Knight, the Director of the Commercial Affairs Department (CAD). When the CPIB started investigating Knight in early 1991 (Operation IgNight), he was made to step down from the CAD. In May 1991, following two months of investigation, the CPIB arrested "Singapore's top white-collar crime buster". He was charged the next day with a bail set at $600,000. The charges were "related to" his investment "in the former Batam Island Country Club and on shipments of motor vehicles to the Indonesian island". Knight was trading second-hand cars through his car rental company in Batam. He also ran a healthcare centre and a sauna facility in Batam. In October 1991, he was convicted for an attempted cheating charge and for giving false information to secure a government car loan. He was sentenced to 3 months' jail, but upon appeal, was reduced to one day in jail and fined $17,000 in March 1992. Knight was also facing disciplinary hearings. He was terminated from the Public Service in March 1992, and the prestigious Public Administration Medal (Gold) awarded to him was revoked. In August 1994, he was also struck off the roll of advocates and solicitors. Then in 1998, Knight was charged with criminal breach of trust for misappropriating a total of $4,200 when he was still Director of the CAD in 1989 and 1990. He was eventually found guilty of misappropriation and sentenced to one day in jail and fined $10,000.[54]

The Knight and Durai cases were critical as far as public interest was concerned. These men were well-connected and had been custodians of the law and public monies. There was a need for the Government to demonstrate resolve and intolerance to corruption by anyone and in any form.

The 1990s also witnessed the corruption case involving the Public Utilities Board's (PUB) Deputy Chief Executive, Choy Hon Tim (Operation Dynamo). He had conspired with an acquaintance to provide services linked with the PUB, earning him the largest bribe amount in the Public Service in Singapore's history. When Choy was a PUB engineer in the 1970s, he had already benefitted from his relationship with Lee Peng Siong, a former PUB employee who had moved to the private sector. Back then, Choy facilitated Lee's "smooth laying of high-tension cables in his sub-contract works", and in return, Choy was given 20% of Lee's profits. This venture ended when Lee left the country. When he returned in 1983, both men renewed their cooperation. This time, Lee was a consultant advising international contractors bidding in the PUB's tenders. Choy provided Lee with "confidential and privileged information" on the tenders. This endeavour earned Lee $63,377,744. Choy was given $12,240,613 out of this sum as his share of the profits. Payments to Choy went directly to Choy's ex-wife. When the CPIB commenced investigations in 1994, Choy fled the country. He was brought back within a year and "charged for criminal conspiracy and accepting bribes totalling around $13,850,000". Choy was sentenced to 14 years' imprisonment.[55] What is interesting about Choy's infractions and eventual prosecution that spanned years was that it sent several messages to public officers who might have been contemplating lining their pockets at this time, and thinking that they were smart enough to get away with it, that most would be found out eventually, even if they were millionaires.

As a test of the integrity of the Bureau's men, their pursuit of corrupt public officers did not preclude those amongst its own ranks. In 1997, Chan Toh Kai, a Senior Special Investigator with the Bureau (while investigating a *Tua Pek Kong* case involving a businessman who hired someone to take responsibility for hiring foreign workers without valid work permits) tricked the man to pay $10,000 "to the Government" in order to be let off. Chan was sentenced to one year's imprisonment for cheating.[56]

Trajectory

The reduction in the number of corruption cases from the 1990s, as well as the marked shift from public sector corruption to more private sector cases, was due to several underlying factors. First, from the latter part of the 1980s, it was noted that the country's improving per capita income level had an inverse relation with the risk of doing business in Singapore. Therefore, with higher incomes and a more stable environment for businesses, instances of corruption had also decreased.[57] In 1995, Senior Minister Lee Kuan Yew would repeatedly stress that the "reputation for the rule of law" had been a "valuable economic asset" for Singapore. High wages for senior public servants, in particular "Judges and Ministers", would ensure that suitable men would be placed in the right positions in the Government.[58] It was the Government's stance that better wages would defeat corrupt practices in the country. And it was also contended that "political will" to bring about such changes was "the No. 1 weapon in fighting graft".[59] Having better wages for the junior public officers would also see an improvement in the corruption situation of the day. Unlike the 1970s, the public sector cases were not syndicated. At that time, the most difficult cases were called 'roadblock' where a few police officers, either uniformed or detectives, would gang up together, sometimes including ex-policemen and special constables, to conduct checks on a particular house, after which they would extort money from their targets. To the members of public, these were police officers, but when the Bureau conducted investigations and looked for their photographs, some could not be found as they were already retired. As a result, when the Bureau showed the victims photographs of those police officers suspected to have committed the raids, they often could not recognise or identify the suspects, as the photographs of those who actually did the roadblock were not available.[60] In the 2000s, such cases were seldom heard of probably because the organisation (police force) was vigilant, in addition to the higher salaries and better qualifications of the police officers.[61]

Over time, from 1990 to 2010, the total number of complaints received by the CPIB annually, of real corruption cases and those proven not to be so, had consistently hovered around 900.[62] However, an examination of the number of complaints that actually led to investigations had declined steadily from almost 1,000 in 1990 to just above 200 in 2010 — a fivefold decline.[63] Clearly, the number of corruption cases handled by the Bureau had declined significantly during this period, reflecting a much improved social environment at this time. Also, a breakdown of the nature of the cases from 1990 to 2010 showed a significant shift in the nature of corruption cases. In the early 1990s, corruption in the private and public sectors comprised approximately half the total number of cases each. By the latter half of the 1990s, about 60% of the total number of corruption cases handled by the Bureau had been private sector cases. In the first half of the 2000s, private sector cases rose to 66%, and in the latter half of that decade, private sector cases would rise to 77%.[64] Beyond doubt, the numbers illustrated that the Public Service had been "cleaned up", but corruption had not disappeared; there was still a need for the Bureau to remain vigilant during this period.

While the large-scale, grand corruption of the days of old involving syndicates might have by and large given way to the individual petty corruptors, and even though large amounts of monies could still be involved, there was a clear social transition by the new millennium. Corrupt practices amongst public officers were no longer a norm. In 2002, when addressing the increasing number of private sector corruption cases, the Bureau's Director opined, "CPIB has to a large extent, executed the Government's will. Propelled by a strong political will, CPIB helped to create a strong anti-corruption ethos and the accompanying odium attached to corruption. This, however, does not mean that we have completely eradicated corruption. No society ever will, given the fact that mankind is fallible, not infallible. By nature, man is acquisitive, almost covetous. While the majority in Singapore falls in line, there is always the offending few who will find it necessary to satiate either their greed or their needs."[65] Hence, the future would only bring new challenges which the Bureau had to be prepared to meet.

Chapter Twenty-Two

Being Ready

Going into the 2000s, the CPIB's leadership got the rank and file ready for future challenges by setting the tone and identifying the strategic directions for the whole Bureau; the CPIB would continue to improve the effectiveness of its operations through swift and sure, firm but fair action. It would be more proactive in its approach to combat corruption through intelligence gathering, staff training and innovation. To achieve these goals, the Bureau conceived two "frameworks". First, a quality framework, ISO Quality Management System to improve the Bureau's processes; Vision and Mission, and focusing on its Core Values

The accolades on quality and excellence achieved through the years.
Source: CPIB Archives.

as its foundation, and more. The second, a learning framework that gave due emphasis on training.[66] The Bureau's officers, prior to the 1990s, had undertaken all the investigation processes, including intelligence gathering. A dedicated Intelligence Unit was established within the Bureau in 1994. This enabled the Bureau to discover more information and investigate proactively rather than just wait for tip-offs. At the same time, the Bureau paid more attention on training its officers.[67] It further embarked on a business excellence journey.

Training and Staff Development

Since the 1960s, the Bureau's Special Investigators had to undergo basic police training at the Police Training School (Police Academy from 1969).[68] By the 1990s, the training at the Academy was considered insufficient for the needs of the Bureau's officers. This led to the Bureau's Director to change the training regime in 1996, and from then, the training of new officers was done in-house. It was from this point that Senior Special Investigators in the Bureau were called Corrupt Practices Investigation Officers (CPIOs). In 1998, the Bureau augmented its ranks by introducing the Corrupt Practices Investigation Assistant (CPIA) scheme for non-graduates. Both CPIOs and CPIAs were trained in-house (Corrupt Practices Investigation Course). The thrust of the CPIB staff training at this point was guided by its learning framework. This framework was the Bureau's main people development platform.[69] It has two salient aspects: the Training Road Map, which gave emphasis to teaching investigation and soft skills; and the use of the Learning Needs Analysis, which identified the specific learning gaps of each officer. It was this learning framework that helped the Bureau to attain its People Developer certification in 1999. A part of the CPIB's in-house training was on-the-job, which exposed trainees with real and practical experiences. The Director of CPIB in the 1990s shared his insights in choosing to embark on the in-house training endeavour:

"I knew for a fact that Police Academy does not equip our officers to be CPIO... you listen to people who have finished training, they don't even know the basic bible/gospel — the Prevention of Corruption Act.... People say, we are so small, how can you have your own training department...? We have a mentorship programme and after the course we have another mentorship programme. And it is structured in a sense that you have a checklist of things that during this one week, you must experience these things. If you have not, we have to arrange for you to experience them... you must have seen a trial in court; during this one week, you must have seen somebody interrogated or interviewing a case. So, it is structured. There is a checklist before you go for the course, and after you have gone for the course. Because if you don't have some idea of what interrogation is in real life, then you go to the course, you only hear theory, you cannot relate the two. You do not know exactly what it is like in real practice.... After the course, you go for mentorship again, then you can see for yourself. During the course, it is what I learnt in the classroom. After the course, I want to see whether it matches with what I learnt in the classroom."[70]

First in-house course for CPIOs, July 1996.
Source: CPIB Archives.

▶ Vigilance & Readiness

First in-house course for CPIAs, April 1998.
Source: CPIB Archives.

By the mid-2000s, the CPIB enhanced its in-house training to broaden its officers' horizon. The Bureau reached out to the Ministry of Home Affairs to have its officers sent to their senior leadership training programme. This was also done with other government agencies. Moreover, the Bureau started overseas training stints, which included courses organised by the Hong Kong Independent Commission Against Corruption (ICAC). There were "international workshops, conferences and seminars" that the CPIB officers attended. This way, CPIB officers were aware of the developments outside the CPIB and were able to "find new ideas, learn best practices and bring them back to improve CPIB operations".[71] Likewise, the CPIB also shared its expertise and knowledge with close foreign counterparts such as the Anti-Corruption Bureau (Brunei Darussalam) and Anti-Corruption Commission (Bhutan) when their officers attended the CPIB's in-house training course (Corrupt Practices Investigation Course).

Central to the Bureau's Training Road Map was the ethos of continuous learning. This was the only way in which the Bureau's officers could always be ready for future challenges. In the 1990s and 2000s, it was this mindset change that helped the CPIB adjust from a phase which relied solely upon confessions to one that is evidence-based. This need for the adjustment of the CPIB's learning framework in the 2000s was articulated by the then Director of the CPIB:

> *"Always encourage officers to have a learning mindset, because people who do anti-corruption investigation work can be expected to investigate cases in any sector or any industry.... We must also be capable of learning fast, given a new area, new industry, new forms of transaction ... then we are able to apply the investigative skills to investigate the matter at hand. So being adept at learning, and being lifelong learners capable of fitting in to different scenarios, is very important."*

Manpower and Staffing

Having adequate manpower and staff suitable for the projected needs of the CPIB in moving forward was another crucial aspect of being ready for the future. When Evan Yeo, the longest serving CPIB Director, retired in 1994, many of the Bureau's senior investigators were also within a year or two of reaching their retirement age. The new Director had to bring in new blood, and lots of them, as he had many positions to fill for all his new initiatives.[72] More headcount was requested from the Public Service Commission. This was granted. From 1995 to 1998, the CPIB recruited CPIOs and CPIAs in batches. Prior to this, the Bureau's investigation staff were known as Special Investigators or Senior Special Investigators (for graduates) and Assistant Special Investigators (for non-graduates). With the increased manpower, staff officers were also appointed from among the senior officers to assist the Director in administrative matters. The CPIAs' main role was to support investigation activities. The CPIAs were "trained to perform specialised tasks such as arresting and escorting accused persons and assisting in the seizure and examination of documents" and investigation work.[73] As part of the people development scheme at this time, the CPIAs could work hard and progress to become CPIOs one day. This was also the time the CPIB started tracking staff performance indicators.

Staff development during this period was also aided by the improvement of the Bureau's physical facilities. It was noted that when the CPIB moved out of its cramped Hill Street site to Cantonment Road in 1998, the availability of space alone fostered greater staff interaction, especially in social activities and sports. This was aided by the availability of funds received when the Bureau attained the ISO9000 certification (1997) and People Developer certification (1999). The CPIB was one of the first government agencies to attain these two and the Singapore Quality Class certification. The money was spent on organising staff gatherings.

The CPIB family gathering for a group photo at the Cantonment Road office.
Source: CPIB Archives.

The CPIB's office at Cantonment Road (March 1998 to 2004). Home to the CPIB for six years, most still remember this site as the CPIB office.
Source: CPIB Archives.

The CPIB's first Heritage Centre — the "CPIB Exhibition Room" at the Cantonment Road premise, 1998.
Source: CPIB Archives.

▶ Vigilance & Readiness

The CPIB flag, commissioned in 2004, has the colours of white and red, and the Bureau's logo emblazoned on it, signifying the Bureau's high standard of integrity, and its role as a state institution in keeping Singapore clean and corruption-free.
Source: CPIB Archives.

In 2002, the current CPIB logo was created to reflect the Bureau's development to meet the challenges of the modern era. "Swift and Sure" manifested the spirit and thrust of the Bureau at this time; working swiftly and with certainty of fairness. The first logo (1979) had embodied three values: Integrity, Impartiality and Efficiency. The second logo (1987) had espoused values of Uprightness, Resolve, Strength and Purity as signified by the symbols.
Source: CPIB Archives.

The CPIB moved into its current premises at Lengkok Bahru in 2004. This purpose-built building was certified an Eco-Office in 2012 and has retained this status since.
Source: CPIB Archives.

It was noted that the staff had slowly learnt to work hard and play hard. At Cantonment Road, they even played futsal. And when the Bureau moved to its present site at Lengkok Bahru in 2004, the staff were able to enjoy gatherings and celebrations at its rooftop garden, especially after a successful conclusion of a major operation.[74]

Staff recruitment from 2005 to 2010 was more focused on hiring people with the right aptitude for the job. Applicants went "through a three-stage recruitment process. Firstly, a pen and paper psychometric test, secondly, a case study, where applicants will be grouped together, and then given a case for discussion, and our officers can then observe them. And then finally, a panel interview based on structured interview format. So, that was an attempt by the Bureau to sieve out the best candidates for the CPIB."[75]

▶ Vigilance & Readiness

Proactive Approach

The Bureau's approach prior to the early 1990s had been mainly reactive. That is, it mainly acted on complaints and tip-offs.[76] And there were lots of these in the 1980s as Singaporeans no longer accepted corruption as a way of life and began to embrace the national ethos of a clean society. During this early period, the Bureau's main function was preventive. In 1967, Dr Goh Keng Swee conceptualised what could have been a measure of success for the Bureau when it was reported that he "disclosed in Parliament, the Corrupt Practices Investigation Bureau has ample reason to justify its existence. Its value is to be measured not simply by the number of irregularities it uncovers but by what does not happen because if its 'presence'."[77] Going into the 1980s, there was already a "zero-tolerance" stance against corruption in the Public Service within the Bureau, although not expounded widely. In 1981, just a year after Evan Yeo was appointed Director of CPIB, he told a new batch of civil servants that "if a public officer has accepted bribes, it is only a question of time before the CPIB catches up with him".[78] By the 1990s, much of what had happened decades earlier, i.e. corruption amongst public officers, was no longer rampant.[79] However, there were still corrupt activities, especially in the private sector. Hence, the Bureau still carried a heavy load, and the threat from corruption had to be dealt with resolutely.

It was clear that some decisive measures had to be taken. By the time Yeo retired in 1994, it could not be disputed that the Bureau was already considered highly successful. However, it remained inundated by hundreds of public corruption complaints. Not all of them were legitimate or valid, but almost all of them had to be given some attention. It took time, but the Bureau did eventually reduce the number of cases for investigations handled by the end of the 1990s. The new approach in the decade was to turn over cases swiftly and surely.[80] And of the cases handled, the Bureau made a conscious effort to quickly complete all opened cases.[81] Nevertheless, by the mid-2000s, the Bureau still handled many small-scale cases like the *Tua*

Pek Kong and marriage of convenience scams, although those without corruption elements were eventually passed on to other enforcement agencies.

This approach was accompanied by the proactive seeking out of real threats and was spearheaded by the establishment of the Bureau's Intelligence Unit in 1994. The unit was responsible for identifying and discovering a number of difficult cases in the decade.[82] The CPIB started actively seeking out corrupt activities in any industry prone to corrupt activities,[83] it no longer just waited for tip-offs. One significant contribution of the Intelligence Unit was the smashing of a match-fixing syndicate that involved well-known figures in Singapore's Malaysia Cup team, Abbas Saad and Michal Vana (Operation Offside).[84] It was during this period that the CPIB operations were given code names, making them less forgettable for the Bureau's officers. The Bureau's proactive checks on government agencies in the decade had also shown that corruption in many of these agencies was rare or no longer existed.

Checks and Balances — Who Guard the Guards?

One major step needed for the Bureau to be ready for the new millennium was the amendment of the law — Constitution of the Republic of Singapore (Amendment) Act 1991 — that enabled the Director of the CPIB to deal directly with the President on complaints of corruption against a Minister, should the Prime Minister withhold his consent. This legislative amendment was enacted in connection with the issue of the creation of an elected Presidency. There was a need to define the rights and role of the elected President. One of which is the role of the President, with the mandate of the people, to check government actions (in cases of corruption).[85] The very act of legislating this power of the elected President was itself a demonstration of how Singapore leaders had the political will to ensure that there are checks and balances in the Singapore system of governance. As far as the Bureau was concerned, in pushing the passage of this amendment, "Singapore's second Prime Minister, Mr Goh Chok Tong, also continued to display strong political will and cemented the clear realisation that CPIB's independence is critical.... The amendments in 1991 ... introduced necessary safeguards to the appointment of Director CPIB, and his ability to pursue investigations without any inhibitions. The Bureau continued to function without fear or favour, and several senior civil servants and influential businessmen were taken to task."[86]

The Constitution of the Republic of Singapore (Amendment) Act 1991 must be considered in the context of the Government's own checks and balances in the decade, as far as maintaining a clean government was concerned. Even though the Public Service was already well-known to be incorrupt by the 1990s, senior public officers continued to champion the strengthening of anti-corruption measures. In 1998, Lim Siong Guan, the Permanent Secretary, Prime Minister's Office (PMO) (1994–1998), advocated a National Integrity System to ensure that the Public Service remained corruption free.[87] In 2000, Eddie Teo, the Permanent Secretary, PMO (1998–2005), reiterated that we would still need the law to be tough and to be strictly enforced, we will have to trust that with adequate pay, a sense of responsibility and integrity (including a sense of shame), civil servants will be less inclined to succumb to temptation. "Given the Public Service ethos of service to the nation, dishonesty is also a betrayal of fellow Singaporeans."[88]

The strengthening of anti-corruption measures provided the CPIB with more power to deal with corruption cases. Legislatively, the Corruption, Drug Trafficking and other Serious Crimes (Confiscation of Benefits) Act (CDSA) was promulgated to provide for the "confiscation of benefits derived from, and to combat, corruption, drug dealing and other serious crimes." The CDSA gave the Government the power to confiscate the benefits of corrupt proceeds. While the PCA punishes the corruptor, the CDSA penalises offenders for laundering bribe money and it allows the authorities to confiscate the resulting benefits.

Chapter Twenty-Three

Standards, Capabilities & Engagements

The Bureau's beginnings in the 1950s was truly humble; it had no logo, crest, letterhead stationery and, for many years, no permanent leadership. Up till the 1990s, the only "standard" the Bureau had was etched on a wooden plaque that was hung in the Bureau's office: the CPIB's Code of Conduct. This was created during the directorship of Evan Yeo.[89] By the 2000s, the world had become far more complex and so was the fight against corruption: "the Integrated Resorts had opened and presented new areas of concern... The foreign population is high and we need to reach out to them. Singapore ratified the United Nations Convention against Corruption in November 2009... more Mutual Legal Assistance being sent to us. That's why we need to take stock...."[90] While Singapore was in a good place as far as international ranking on corruption-free nations was concerned, there was still a sense of urgency that the country must remain vigilant. And, to spearhead this measure, the Singapore Government had to demonstrate the political will to see through enforcement and reforms. In 1993, Goh Chok Tong, Singapore's Prime Minister from 1990 to 2004, declared, "I have every intention to make sure that Singapore remains corrupt-free. I will not let standards drop. And everybody should know that corruption in any form will not be tolerated. I expect all Ministers, all MPs and all public officers to set good examples for others to follow. All PAP MPs declare to me their family assets and all Ministers, including the Prime Minister, declare to the President their family assets... If there is any allegation against any MP or Minister of assets wrongfully or corruptly gained, the CPIB will investigate. If the MP concerned is unable to explain how he had acquired these assets, or why he had not declared them, he will be charged for corruption."[91]

Reorganisation, Enhancing Capabilities and Efficiency

Going into the new millennium, the Bureau underwent several rounds of reorganisation to improve its efficiency and effectiveness. In the early 1990s, the CPIB's organisational structure was composed of two main functional areas: Operations (which had four units) and Administration and Support Services (which comprised the Research Unit, Technical Unit [Transport, Operations, Photography sections], Computer Information System Unit [Systems, Registry] and Administration Unit).[92] In 1994, the Bureau underwent another reorganisation: the Bureau had two main departments, Operations (four teams) and the Specialist Support Division (Intelligence, Administration, Planning).[93] In the early 2000s, the Bureau was reorganised once more. It now had five main departments: Operations; Operations Support Services; Administration; Staff Support; and Prevention.[94] These changes were necessary to streamline the Bureau. The Bureau's establishment had increased significantly since the early years when it had no more than 15 executive staff, inclusive of the director.

It was important for the Bureau to keep pace with the challenges that each milieu presented. With limited manpower, the Bureau formed a Special Investigation Team (SIT) in 1996. It was renamed Special Investigation Branch (SIB) in 2010–2011. It pulled together the best CPIB officers to form a team to look into complex cases. After 2010, the SIB handled private sector and public sector investigations as two main areas of investigation. In terms of investigation support, while the use of the polygraph and having the support of the Centre for Forensic Science,

Health Sciences Authority for forensic work would seem to have given the Bureau a great boost,[95] the real capability enhancement for the decade came from the use of technology to aid the CPIB's processes.[96] In 2004, the CPIB established a computer forensic facility. It was "recognised that at that time, as technology become more and more prevalent, it was being misused for corruption offences". Hence, the Bureau invested in the enhancement of this capability. Officers were sent for training, and equipment bought to build up the computer forensic lab. To ensure that the Bureau had adequate support of its computer resources, the CPIB also increased the number of IT personnel to support the Bureau.[97] With all these enhancements in place, the Bureau then started its "investigation management system" as well as the "bail provision system" and "electronic reporting system".[98]

In order to understand the operating terrain and challenges in the private sector, the CPIB participated in platforms that allowed them to do so. One such platform they engaged in was Business Leaders' Series Talk, which provided them the opportunity to learn "what the business leaders and the business community were doing with regard to the measures that they can take to fight corruption".[99] The Bureau's mandate is wide and it could deal with cases in all sectors, be it in the property and construction industry, the marine industry, IT sector, banking sector, transport and services sector, etc. Moreover, the Bureau had received cases which involved corruption intertwined with other crimes, as well as malpractices and abuse. It alone could not solve some of these problems and needed to work with partner agencies. From the business perspective, as well as the law enforcement and regulatory perspectives, one could not just fight corruption and not touch fraud and malpractices; similarly, one could not just fight fraud and malpractices but ignore corruption. And where anti-corruption is concerned, there was a need to address the overall system of control that any business or company has."[100]

International Partnerships

At a time when many crimes were committed and corrupt activities had been transnational, there was never a greater need for the international community to work together. The Bureau did not have many overseas connections and cooperation prior to 2005, other than with the Association of Southeast Asian Nations (ASEAN) countries on occasions, and certainly with Hong Kong's Independent Commission Against Corruption (ICAC). In 2001, Singapore participated in the Anti-Corruption Action Plan for Asia and the Pacific held in Tokyo. Singapore was one of the 17 signatories of the event.[101] It was only after Singapore signed the United Nations Convention Against Corruption (UNCAC) in 2005 that the Bureau became more active in the international anti-corruption community and started representing Singapore at various international anti-corruption events.[102] Following the Convention, the Bureau organised its first Anti-Corruption Expertise (ACE) Workshop in August 2006, which saw 40 participants from 20 countries meeting in Singapore. Through this annual workshop, foreign anti-corruption agencies had a platform to learn from one another. The ACE Workshop also became an informal network in which these agencies collaborated.[103] This workshop eventually evolved into the Anti-Corruption Executive Programme, which is a four-week course.

In 2006, Singapore became a member of the Asian Development Bank (ADB)/Organisation for Economic Cooperation and Development (OECD) Anti-Corruption Initiative for Asia-Pacific, and a member of the Asia-Pacific Economic Cooperation (APEC) Anti-Corruption and Transparency Task Force. Singapore had also ratified the Treaty on Mutual Legal Assistance in Criminal Matters (MLAT), which was signed by 10 ASEAN member states. In 2013, the MLAT was ratified by all 10 ASEAN member states.

Partnership and Public Engagements

The Bureau's efforts to engage and work with other government bodies had always been a critical tool in its war against corrupt practices. The

Bureau could not operate alone and needed partners.[104] During this period, the CPIB was still producing review papers for various government bodies.

Besides the Bureau's "Government-to-Government" efforts, the CPIB also used its "prevention and outreach" programmes to engage external parties, including hosting "educational visits for students, local organisations and foreign delegates interested in Singapore's anti-corruption work". The CPIB conducted prevention talks for government agencies. Prevention through educational efforts reached a high point in the late 2000s with more than 10,000 people engaged annually from 2007 to 2010.[105] This public outreach approach was to be further broadened and espoused in the next decade.

As part of the CPIB's Corporate Social Responsibility efforts, we have been actively involved in community and charity work since 2002.
Source: CPIB Archives

Chapter Twenty-Four

In Retrospect

Fewer corruption cases did not mean there was no corruption in Singapore, even when Singapore was celebrated as one of the least corrupt nations in the world through the 1990s and 2000s. There was much data and real-life accounts to illustrate this truth. No matter how the people and Government of Singapore might try, for that matter anywhere else in the world, there would always be the basest people, and the best of us. Hence, vigilance by the Government, the Bureau and the people is the only option if we want to prevent any backsliding in the future. The CPIB will always have a place in Singapore society. It takes very little for our ugly side to show; the rush for groceries, for limited edition Hello Kitty toys, unending queues at Singapore Pools outlets, reckless outings and gatherings at the height of the pandemic... There is simply no guarantee that all of us will be on our best behaviour when the situation calls for it.

Occasionally, there are those few good men and women who become our exemplars demonstrating that change is possible. In fact, many in Singapore believe that our citizenry, by and large, are imbued with the national ethos and DNA that reject corrupt practices. Generally, this is true. Almost no one today offers *kopi* money unsolicited. And when we encounter a public officer demanding it, there is a likelihood that this person would be reported. So, few people dare to articulate a "squeeze", though some may still "go slow", hoping that the client gets the hint. In any case, by the 1990s, many Singaporeans have already embraced that ethos that makes us Singapore. There are many examples of honest public officers rejecting bribes and bribery practices in this decade.

It should also be remembered that the Bureau has never been just an enforcement agency. Since its inception, when circumstances permitted, the Bureau would work alongside other government agencies which may have been more than capable of cleaning their own houses. Even in the infamous 1999 *Ah Long San* case (Operation RZ), the Singapore Police Force (SPF) worked in tandem and in cooperation with the CPIB to clear out the bad hats. Of course, there was also a silver lining in the affair. The SPF itself realised that they also had to be vigilant from within. Following the *Ah Long San* case which resulted in a number of officers being charged for corruption, the police force altered its training course to include a focus on values and introduced annual ethics seminars.

This is tacit acknowledgement that enforcement was not enough. Values, too, had to change. Commissioner of Police Khoo Boon Hui summed this up succinctly in 2005: "Recruits are then put through integrity-based lessons during their basic training to build resilience to corruption. Such training continues throughout their career to ensure that our core values, including loyalty and integrity, are inculcated in each of our officers. Officers with a strong sense of loyalty take pride in being officers in the police force. With the interest of the Force at heart, officers with the right values not only have the will to resist corruption, they are also able to keep fellow officers in check against misdemeanours. Regular in-service training at front line units, which are more susceptible to corruption is conducted. Case studies of actual cases of police officers charged in court for criminal offences and corruption form part of our continuous integrity training programme."[106]

In later years, the SPF has adopted other anti-corruption measures to minimise the opportunities for corruption and to ensure that its officers resisted such opportunities. All officers in sensitive and vulnerable posts, such as investigators, field intelligence officers, and anti-vice and gambling suppression officers, were rotated every three years to reduce the opportunities for corruption. Those officers who failed to make an honest declaration of their unsecured debts were investigated or disciplined.[107]

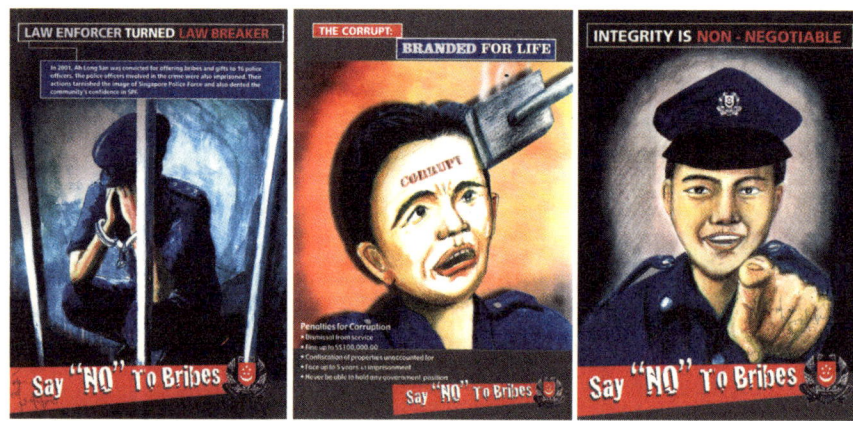

Anti-corruption posters produced by the SPF following the *Ah Long San* case.
Source: Singapore Police Force.

Endnotes

[1] It was noted in 1992 that Singapore was the only nation in "East Asia" that was not afflicted by corruption issues; it had "cracked down on graft, both official and private, by having a strong, honest political leadership, a tough anti-graft law and a vigilant Corrupt Practices Investigation Bureau". See *Straits Times* 8 Oct 1992. For Asian Tigers, see https://corporatefinanceinstitute.com/resources/knowledge/economics/four-asian-tigers/; https://www.investopedia.com/terms/f/four-asian-tigers.asp.

[2] https://www.gov.sg/article/evolution-of-public-housing-in-singapore; https://www.sutori.com/en/story/singapore-s-housing-history--5cZaAwi4cW9BfZqdcAUR2pvH.

[3] In 1995, the press identified the three strengths that aided Singapore's war on graft: the law against corruption (Prevention of Corruption Act), public vigilance (providing information on suspected corruption) and a scrupulous anti-corruption agency (CPIB). See *Straits Times* 8 Oct 1995. In 1989, Hong Kong-based Political Economic Risk Consultancy (PERC) Limited remarked that "Singapore's 'puritanical approach' (rule of law) to corruption made it the 'cleanest' country in Asia". See *Straits Times* 13 Dec 1989; *Straits Times Overseas Edition* 16 Dec 1989. In mid-1995, foreign investors, participating in a PERC survey, rated Singapore's legal system (that protected businesses) as top in the region. See *Straits Times* 22 Jul 1995; *Straits Times Weekly Overseas Edition* 29 Jul 1995. Soon after this, Lee Kuan Yew remarked that Singapore's reputation for rule of law was "a valuable economic asset". See *Straits Times Weekly Overseas Edition* 4 Nov 1995.

[4] In this decade, the Government gave emphasis to the teaching of shared values in schools through its Civics and Moral Education, and to some extent the Religious Education, and even National Education. They played a part in fostering a national identity, value system and, ultimately, a national ethos. Even the schools' Singapore Kindness Movement (1997) had been instrumental in forging better social values. Of course, public education to change anti-social behaviour had already started with popular campaigns that started in the 1970s and 1980s: the Courtesy Campaign, Anti-Littering Campaign, Anti-Spitting Campaign, etc. All these became part of the wider initiative to forge a gracious society ... that is, to change anti-social norms and the societal "tone" of the day, and this included corrupt practices.

[5] It was noted that "public education" and enforcing "heavy sanctions" had worked together to create "a society conditioned to be increasingly intolerant of" corrupt behaviour in general. See *Straits Times* 22 Jun 1998. PERC noted in 1988 that Japan and Singapore should be "rated the 'Mr Clean' of Asia". It noted that Hong Kong's "wild west environment... inevitably" invited "certain types of corruption". See *Business Times* 13 Dec 1988.

[6] National identity and multiculturalism were taught and experienced through housing, education (moral, civil and values), defence (National Service) and community development (grassroots) policies. In 1984, the Government introduced the concept of Total Defence, with Social Defence being one of its six core pillars. This thrust placed emphasis on "social cohesion among Singapore's diverse population through multiculturalism". In the 1990s, schools also reinforced these values through National Education. There was also an overt effort to forge these values though "national songs", like the oft sang *One People, One Nation, One Singapore* (composer: Jeremy Monteiro, lyricist: Jim Aitchison) became a regular tune at National Day parades after it was introduced in 1990. The introduction of such national songs eventually became more popular than traditional community folk songs (in all four national languages). It is noteworthy that Monteiro's song included the lines "Strangers when we first began, now we're Singaporean", "And when the time comes for the test, our vigilance will never rest, we'll be united, hand in hand". These lines, played over the radio, television and sang over and over again, became common "beliefs" of many Singaporeans. In 1990, People's Action Party (PAP) politician Dr Aline Wong spoke publicly about "multiple identities shared values". See *Business Times* 20 Jun 1990. In 1993, then Minister for Information and the Arts George Yeo enunciated the "principles that guide inter-tribal ties" (multiculturalism/multiracialism) which protected each community's cultural or ethnic traits. See *Straits Times* 12 Nov 1993. All these efforts, slowly but surely, created the framework

for Singaporean's shared identity and values. See Chong Chee Kin, "One People, One Nation, One Singapore: National Identity on Parade", Academic Exercise, Department of English Language & Literature, National University of Singapore, 1997; Lily Kong and Brenda Yeoh, "The Construction of National Identity through the Production of Ritual and Spectacle: An Analysis of National Day Parades in Singapore", *Political Geography*, 16, 31997213-39.

[7] "Helping Countries Combat Corruption: The Role of the World Bank", *Poverty Reduction and Economic Management*, The World Bank, September 1997, pp.11–12, http://www1.worldbank.org/publicsector/anticorrupt/corruptn/cor02.htm.

[8] *Straits Times Weekly Overseas Edition* 4 Nov 1995. By this time, Lee Kuan Yew had already stepped down as Prime Minister. He spoke as the nation's Senior Minister.

[9] Soh Kee Hean, "Effective Strategy to Combat Corruption", Address by CPIB Director, First Annual Conference & General Meeting of the International Association of Anti-Corruption Authorities, Beijing 23 October 2006.

[10] *Straits Times* 4 Jul 1999.

[11] *Business Times* 13 Nov 1990; *Straits Times* 9 Apr 1996, 3 Apr 1999; *Straits Times Weekly Overseas Edition* 13 Apr 1996, 11 Apr 1998, 11 Dec 1999; *Weekend East* 4 Apr 1997.

[12] In a 1992–1993 survey of 10 countries, PERC noted that corruption in Asia had "worsened". See *Business Times* 20 Apr 1993. Also, from 1996 to 2000, while Singapore retained its apex position in Asia as the most corruption-free nation, its position had slipped to seventh in the Transparency International Corruption Perceptions Index (TI-CPI) which surveyed all nations across the globe. In 1995, Singapore was third. See *Straits Times* 3 Jun 1996; *Straits Times Weekly Overseas Edition* 8 Jun 1996, 30 October 1999. The CPI was first published in 1995 by a Berlin-based German association, Transparency International. In fact, in 1997, it slipped further to ninth position before returning to seventh in the following years. Singapore's ranking in the CPI from 1995 to 2001 was as follows: 1995 (3), 1996 (7), 1997 (9), 1998–1999 (7), 2000 (6), 2001 (4), 2002–2006 (5), 2007–2008 (4), 2009 (3), 2010 (1), 2011–2013 (5), 2014 (6), 2015–2016 (7), 2017 (6), 2018 (3), 2019 (4), 2020 (3), 2021 (4). See Corruption Perceptions Index in https://www.transparency.org/en/cpi/1995. It is perhaps interesting to note that the CPI ranked Singapore as the most incorrupt nation in the world in 2010.

[13] CPIB case files; https://eresources.nlb.gov.sg/newspapers/Digitised/Article/newpaper19940813-1.2.3.2.

[14] CPIB case files; https://eresources.nlb.gov.sg/newspapers/Digitised/Page/newpaper19950316-1.1.6.

[15] *Straits Times Weekly Overseas Edition* 17 Jun, 20 Aug 1994; CPIB case files.

[16] https://www.fas.org.sg/fas-reply-to-queries-on-match-fixing.

[17] CPIB case files; *AsiaOne* 16 Jun 2012.

[18] https://www.cpib.gov.sg/files/news/2019.06.06_A%20cup%20of%20Kopi%20with%20the%20CPIB%20(1).pdf; https://www.elitigation.sg/gdviewer/s/2011_SGHC_134; *Straits Times* 15 Aug 2012; Homer E Moyer, *Getting the Deal Through — Anti-Corruption Regulation 2019*, 13th ed. (London: Law Business Research, 2019), p.103; https://www.lexology.com/library/detail.aspx?g=f42e3dd7-809e-4412-8530-19016ac1a271; CPIB case files.

[19] https://www.unafei.or.jp/publications/pdf/GG11/23_GG11_CP_Singapore2.pdf.

[20] CPIB case files; https://www.elitigation.sg/gdviewer/s/2011_SGHC_134.

[21] *Straits Times* 6 Jan 2018; CPIB case files.

[22] Oral history interview with Soh Kee Hean, former Director CPIB, 5 January 2021; CPIB case files.

[23] CPIB case files; https://isca.org.sg/ethics/resources/case-studies/major-local-accounting-scandals/local-case-8/; https://www.gmtresearch.com/citiraya-indust-cenr-sp/.

[24] Oral history interview with Soh Kee Hean, former Director CPIB, 5 January 2021; CPIB case files.

[25] CPIB case files; https://www.cpib.gov.sg/cases/pte_bros-cahoots.html.

[26] *Straits Times* 8 Jun, 29 Nov 2012, 29 Jan, 15 Feb, 12 Mar 2013; CPIB case files. Nearly all the chefs in cahoots with Tay were charged in Court in 2012 and 2013: Tan Ah Teng from Goodwood Park Hotel's Min Jiang Restaurant faced 20 charges for receiving over $190,000; Chik Ka Chung from Marriott Hotel's Wan Hao Chinese Restaurant faced 21 charges for receiving over $170,000; Yang Lai Fatt from Meritus Mandarin Hotel faced 15 charges for receiving nearly $130,000; Goh Wooi Cheat from Regent Hotel's Summer Palace faced 14 charges for receiving almost $160,000; Go Choon Heng from Hilton Hotel was fined $5,000 for receiving $4,496; Ng Wai Tong from Si Chuan Dou Hua Restaurant at Parkroyal Hotel was fined $6,000 for receiving $5,811; Tong Yu Chou from PFS was charged for receiving $74,355; Ong Tian Lock from Grand Hyatt Singapore was charged for receiving $36,900; Leung Wing Cheung from Holiday Inn Atrium was charged for receiving $28,796; Choo Soon Ling from Por Kee Eating House was charged for receiving $28,312; Leung Wing Hoi from Shangri-La Hotel was charged for receiving $82,288. Leung faced an additional 11 charges for conspiring with Tay to give $32,137 to Tsang Kang Hung, Shangri-La's executive chef, for his assistance to ensure the hotel continued to purchase supplies from Wealthy Seafood. During the trial of the chefs, KF Seetoh, a popular food critic in Singapore, lamented that "such transactions are not unheard of within the food industry. Suppliers started giving expensive hampers as appreciation in the past but 'upgraded' to ang pows."

[27] Sarah Ooi, *All for the Money: Bribery, Cheats, Swindles and Other Monetary Fraud in Singapore* (Singapore: Marshall Cavendish Editions, 2014), Chapter 11, Top Chefs.

[28] CPIB case files; *AsiaOne* 21 Sep 2013; *Today* 19 Sep 2013; *Straits Times* 20 Nov 2014. Upon appeal, the High Court acquitted Leng in September 2013. However, the Prosecution took the High Court's ruling to the Court of Appeal in November 2014 and had the original July 2013 sentencing by the District Court restored.

[29] *AsiaOne* 19 Nov 2008.

[30] CPIB case files.

[31] CPIB case files.

[32] *Straits Times* 19 Sep 1996, 21 Mar, 26 Oct 1997, 4 Jun, 4 Aug, 9 Oct 1999, 23 May, 29 Jun 2000, 28 Apr, 14 May 2004; *New Paper* 9 Oct 1999, 29 Jun, 11 Jul 2000; *Business Times* 18 Mar 1997, 9 Oct 1999; *Straits Times Weekly Overseas Edition* 1 Jul 2000; *Streats* 14 May 2004; *Today* 8 Jan, 28 Apr 2004; http://www.nas.gov.sg/archivesonline/audiovisual_records/record-details/47cfadc6-1164-11e3-83d5-0050568939ad; http://eresources.nlb.gov.sg/newspapers/Digitised/Article/today20040108-2.2.5.4.

[33] CPIB case files; *Straits Times* 19 Nov 2008.

[34] Penal Code (Amendment) Bill published in Bills Supplement on 18 Sep 2007 https://sso.agc.gov.sg/Bills-Supp/38-2007/Published/20070918?DocDate=20070918#pr40-.

[35] Teo Chee Hean is currently a Senior Minister and Coordinating Minister for National Security.

[36] *AsiaOne* 27 Jul 2013; Prime Minister's Office (PMO) Media Statement 2013: On Case of Misappropriation by CPIB Officer. In his opinion, "public institutions and public officers" were "held to the highest standards of integrity and conduct… it was vital to have in place systems and practices to ensure integrity in the Public Service."

[37] K Shanmugam is currently the Minister for Home Affairs and Minister for Law.

[38] *AsiaOne* 27 Jul 2013; Prime Minister's Office (PMO) Media Statement 2013: On Case of Misappropriation by CPIB Officer.

[39] CPIB case files.

[40] *The Journey: 60 Years of Fighting Corruption in Singapore* (Singapore: Corrupt Practices Investigation Bureau, 2012), pp.74-77; CPIB case files; *The New Paper* 28 Aug 2018; https://www.cpib.gov.sg/sites/cpibv2/files/2012.09.19.TNP_A%20shark's%20tale%20How%20Ah%20Long%20San%20rose%20to%20the%20top.pdf.

[41] CPIB case files.

[42] CPIB case files.

[43] https://deseret.com/1996/7/25/19256368/Singapore-gunman-gets-death-sentence.

44 CPIB case files; https://www.cpib.gov.sg/cases/public_corruption-addict.html.

45 CPIB case files.

46 CPIB case files.

47 CPIB case files; *Straits Times* 14 May 1994.

48 https://www.elitigation.sg/gd/s/2014_SGHC_166; https://www.cpib.gov.sg/cases/public_personal-interest-over-public-safety.html.

49 https://www.cpib.gov.sg/cases/pte_engineer-illegal-transaction.html; *Straits Times* 12 Sep 2013. "Corruption & Inducements — From a Legal Perspective", Institute of Singapore Chartered Accountants Ethics Seminar 13 April 2018 https://isca.org.sg/media/2239812/3-corruption-and-inducements-from-the-legal-perspective-by-hamidul-haq.pdf.

50 Lee Kuan Yew, in his 2000 memoirs, quoted in *Swift and Sure Action: Four Decades of Anti-Corruption Work* (Singapore: Corrupt Practices Investigation Bureau, 2003), p.42; Lee Kuan Yew, *From Third World to First: The Singapore Story: 1965–2000* (Singapore: Marshall Cavendish Editions, 2000), p.189.

51 Lee Kuan Yew in *Straits Times* 27 Jan 1987, quoted in *Swift and Sure Action: Four Decades of Anti-Corruption Work* (Singapore: Corrupt Practices Investigation Bureau, 2003), p.44. This was articulated during the Teh Cheang Wan affair.

52 CPIB case files; https://eresources.nlb.gov.sg/infopedia/articles/SIP_2013-07-01_120748.html.

53 Oral history interview with Soh Kee Hean, former Director CPIB, 5 January 2021.

54 CPIB case files; *New Paper* 23 Mar 1991; *Straits Times* 24, 26 Mar, 28, 30 May 1991.

55 CPIB case files.

56 https://www.acc.org.bt/?q=node/792; *Today* 25, 26 Jul 2013.

57 *Business Times* 11 Feb 1988; *Straits Times* 23, 24 Mar 1985. There was also a more concerted effort by the Government to place the right people in senior positions within the Government. Lau Yong Hin noted that by the 2000s, "Public officers" were adequately paid, commensurate with their job scope and in line with private sector earnings. There was then "less incentive for them to be involved in under table money. Corruption is a 'High Risk, Low Reward' activity." Oral history interview with Lau Yong Hin, retired CPIO, 14 Aug 2009.

58 *Straits Times Weekly Overseas Edition* 4 Nov 1995.

59 *Straits Times* 20 Jul 1997.

60 Oral history interview with Lau Yong Hin, retired CPIO, 14 Aug 2009.

61 Oral history interview with Lau Yong Hin, retired CPIO, 14 Aug 2009.

62 CPIB Annual Reports 1990 to 2010. Year and total number of complaints: 1990 (999), 1992 (949), 1994 (823), 1995 (956), 1997 (951), 1999 (1128), 2000 (991), 2002 (911), 2004 (844), 2005 (1046), 2007 (877), 2010 (876).

63 CPIB Annual Reports 1990 to 2010. Year and total number of cases from complaints received open for investigation: 1990 (980), 1992 (813), 1994 (575), 1995 (569),1997 (549), 1999 (734), 2000 (495), 2002 (371), 2004 (298), 2005 (428), 2008 (239), 2010 (206).

64 CPIB Annual Reports 1990 to 2010. Year and percentage of private sector cases in Singapore: 1990–1994 (51%), 1995–1999 (59%), 2000–2004 (66%), 2005–2010 (77%).

65 Address by Director Chua Cher Yak at the first International Independent Commission Against Corruption Forum in Seoul, November 2002.

66 *Swift and Sure Action: Four Decades of Anti-Corruption Work* (Singapore: Corrupt Practices Investigation Bureau, 2003), p.10.

67 *Swift and Sure Action: Four Decades of Anti-Corruption Work* (Singapore: Corrupt Practices Investigation Bureau, 2003), p.11.

68 The police training facility at Mount Pleasant Road was opened in 1929 as the Police Depot. It was renamed the Police Training School in 1945.

69 *Swift and Sure Action: Four Decades of Anti-Corruption Work* (Singapore: Corrupt Practices Investigation Bureau, 2003), p.16.

70 Oral history interview with Chua Cher Yak, former Director CPIB, 15 August 2017.

71 Oral history interview with Soh Kee Hean,

former Director CPIB, 5 January 2021.

[72] Oral history interview with Chua Cher Yak, former Director CPIB, 15 August 2017.

[73] https://www.cpib.gov.sg; "The Probe", September 2002.

[74] Oral history interview with Chua Cher Yak, former Director CPIB, 15 August 2017.

[75] Oral history interview with Soh Kee Hean, former Director CPIB, 5 January 2021.

[76] Notes from Ong Seng Hock, retired CPIO.

[77] *Straits Times* 20 Dec 1967.

[78] *Swift and Sure Action: Four Decades of Anti-Corruption Work* (Singapore: Corrupt Practices Investigation Bureau, 2003), p.28. Evan Yeo, 21 September 1981 at an induction course for Division I officers.

[79] Lee Kuan Yew himself declared in 2000, "We had established a climate of opinion which looked upon corruption in public office as a threat to society." See *Straits Times* 18 Sep 2000.

[80] *Swift and Sure Action: Four Decades of Anti-Corruption Work* (Singapore: Corrupt Practices Investigation Bureau, 2003), p.36.

[81] *Swift and Sure Action: Four Decades of Anti-Corruption Work* (Singapore: Corrupt Practices Investigation Bureau, 2003), pp.24–25.

[82] Notes from Ong Seng Hock, retired CPIO.

[83] Notes from Ong Seng Hock, retired CPIO.

[84] Notes from Ong Seng Hock, retired CPIO.

[85] *Parliamentary Debates* 7(2) vol 56, 4 Oct 1990, col 460–465.

[86] Oral history interview with Soh Kee Hean, former Director CPIB 5 January 2021; Welcome Address by Eric Tan, Director CPIB at the CPIB's 60th Anniversary Celebration, 18 Sep 2012, https://www.cpib.gov.sg/press-room/speeches/welcome-address-mr-eric-tan-director-cpib-cpibs-60th-anniversary-celebration.

[87] *Swift and Sure Action: Four Decades of Anti-Corruption Work* (Singapore: Corrupt Practices Investigation Bureau, 2003), p.72; CPIB Website: Speeches, 21 May 1998: Presentation by Mr Lim Siong Guan, Permanent Secretary, Prime Minister's Office Singapore at the Seminar on Hong Kong into 21st Century — Maintaining Integrity in the Civil Service.

[88] Speech, 31 Mar 2000: "Can the Civil Service Stay Honest and Succeed in the 21st Century?" Presentation on the Singapore Experience in Ethical Management in the Public Sector by Mr Eddie Teo, Permanent Secretary, Prime Minister's Office, Singapore, to the Ethical Leadership Forum 2000, Hong Kong.

[89] *Swift and Sure Action: Four Decades of Anti-Corruption Work* (Singapore: Corrupt Practices Investigation Bureau, 2003), p.9.

[90] Opening Address by Director Soh Kee Hean, Workplan Seminar 25 May 2010.

[91] Goh Chok Tong, declared in Parliament on 10 March 1993.

[92] CPIB Annual Report 1991.

[93] CPIB Annual Report 1994.

[94] Singapore Quality Award (SQA) Business Overview Document, 2001, p.2.

[95] CPIB adopted polygraph testing "as an investigative tool" in 1996. Among its varied uses, it was "administered on soccer players as a deterrence against match-fixing". As for in-house training, "the Bureau conducted its own basic training, customised to equip new officers with the basic survival skills to handle investigation of corruption offences".

[96] *Swift and Sure Action: Four Decades of Anti-Corruption Work* (Singapore: Corrupt Practices Investigation Bureau, 2003), p.86.

[97] Oral history interview with Soh Kee Hean, former Director CPIB, 5 January 2021.

[98] Oral history Interview with Soh Kee Hean, former Director CPIB, 5 January 2021.

[99] Oral history interview with Soh Kee Hean, former Director CPIB, 5 January 2021.

[100] Opening Address by Director Soh Kee Hean at Business Leaders' Series Talk, 9 July 2010, CPIB Auditorium.

[101] *Swift and Sure Action: Four Decades of Anti-Corruption Work* (Singapore: Corrupt Practices

Investigation Bureau, 2003), p.89.

[102] https://www.cpib.gov.sg; *The Probe*, September 2002.

[103] Closing address by Director Soh Kee Hean, 16 Oct 2008, 3rd ACE workshop; Notes from Ong Seng Hock, CPIB officer.

[104] Address by Director CPIB, 22 May 2008 Workplan Seminar.

[105] CPIB Annual Report 1990 to 2010.

[106] Jon Quah, "Preventing Police Corruption in Singapore: The Role of Recruitment, Training and Socialisation", *The Asia Pacific Journal of Public Administration*, Vol. 28, No. 1: 59–75.

[107] Jon Quah, "Preventing Police Corruption in Singapore: The Role of Recruitment, Training and Socialisation", *The Asia Pacific Journal of Public Administration*, Vol. 28, No. 1: 70.

Part Six

Metamorphosis & Roots
2010–2022

There are two narratives on the history and heritage of Singapore's CPIB etched in the pages of this book. The first chronicles the establishment and development of the institution. The second contextualises the development of the Bureau within the larger narrative of Singapore's nation-building story. It is when these two threads of the Bureau's development are interwoven that its rich tapestry can be seen and fully appreciated. This story of the CPIB is not only an account of its buildings, sites, cases, awards, accolades, statistics. It is also about the men and women who held the line against corrupt practices, and the pernicious effects of corruption, which threatened to "destroy" the fabric of Singapore society.[1] In this scheme of things, the Bureau occupies a unique place in Singapore's history as a guardian of the national ethos which formed the cornerstone that made Singapore a successful nation — a clean government and a society that "eschews corruption".[2] For more than half a century, the CPIB has been an integral part of Singapore's nation-building efforts, as its enforcement arm as well as the custodian of the laws promulgated to obstruct and punish corrupt practices.

After almost seven decades, the Bureau has become a bedrock of strength for the nation. Like Singapore's ubiquitous Angsana tree, the Bureau stands tall in public view, carrying the national advocacy for honesty and integrity in the Public Service as well as a country free of corruption. In this role, the Bureau aims to be a beacon for our countrymen, within and abroad, who occasionally need a guiding light when matters and perspectives become blurred. In the last decade, the Bureau has also gone well beyond its enforcement role by giving due attention to public education and engagement which assisted in the national endeavour of making Singapore "a clean and incorrupt country".[3] The leaders of the nation had learnt since the early days of Independence that fundamental changes had to occur at the societal level if our efforts to build a home and nation were to be successful; attitudes had to change and a national ethos had to be forged. While a country that was largely corruption-free had definitively been achieved by the 1990s, attested by the many international surveys and rankings which repeatedly singled out Singapore as the least corrupt nation in Asia, and among the top few in the world, there were still instances of corruption on the ground as well as high-profile cases. This underscores why Singapore, and specifically the CPIB, had to remain vigilant at all times. In this context the Bureau understood that it could not work in silos, and that enforcement of the rule of law alone could not keep Singapore free of corruption. There was still a necessity for the country to "continue to be imbued with the right values" that rejected graft in any form.[4] It was with this consideration in mind that the Bureau adapted and included the soft touches of public education in conjunction with its no-nonsense approach to corruption.

While the CPIB embraced the greater responsibilities of its mission, it has also encountered a uniquely Singapore situation in the last couple of decades. Singapore was already one of the cleanest countries in the world, what more was there to be done? Such was the enigmatic situation. Singapore had already achieved a status which made most nations of the world envious, but the prevailing cases of the day showed that a lot more had to be done. The Government has always been aware that the nation could ill afford to be complacent even when it basked in the success of having a low number of corruption cases and maintaining a "sound system" that kept such practices in the Public Service at bay.[5] Besides, entering the new millennium, the CPIB was still a lean outfit. The added responsibilities that required public outreach and educational initiatives, understandably, necessitated some level of adjustments on the part of the Bureau. During this period, the world was also changing at an accelerated pace; there was a need to adapt to the technological shifts occurring in the world, and within Singapore. The nature of business and commerce, and every aspect of transactions, had been transformed. These changes added new dimensions to the types of corrupt practices which required the Bureau to respond with corresponding reforms. More qualified and trained manpower were needed, but such changes took time to understand and take effect. It should also be appreciated that the impact of these structural changes of the milieu on an organisation that had to be constantly "on watch" would have been significant.[6] The men and women of the CPIB, not unlike the others in the private and public sectors who had to adapt to the times, were also stretched. Fortunately, having had many good years of corruption-busting successes, and having had more than just a few good men who cultivated a sense of esprit de corps in its ranks, the Bureau had roots deep enough to help the rank and file weather the storms of the day. The veracity of this truth was tested more than once in the past two decades.

Chapter Twenty-Five

Challenges in a Changing Time & Climate

Roots, Legacy and Values

Lee Kuan Yew declared that since its founding, the CPIB had been the nation's "graft-busting watchdog", and it had "helped raise Singapore's standing" in the world because it is this good standing that gives "confidence to investors".[7] This was essentially the Bureau's enduring legacy in Singapore's history — the overseer, protector and the bedrock holding up our solid reputation of being corruption-free. And within the Bureau, its pioneering warriors and long-serving staff have been the custodian of the tools and skills which the Bureau employed to undertake its duties. The four founding members who formed the original Special Investigation Team were Singapore's first "Incorruptibles". They were tasked to uncover the truth behind the conspiracies among corrupt law enforcers of the day who appropriated illegal contrabands from smugglers, and who, through trickery and betrayal, misdirected the Government's efforts to enforce the law. The first four, under-resourced, undermanned, and operating covertly in a unit which was not named, found the truth and even went beyond their call of duty to bring the original smugglers to justice. In many ways, they were not unlike the popularly depicted *The Untouchables* — four men co-opted by the American Treasury Department to form the Bureau of Prohibition which was tasked to stop corrupt officials and criminals smuggling illicit alcohol. Although the reality for our "Incorruptibles" was far less romanticised, there was still the uncanny parallel of four men facing extreme obstacles and succeeding against all odds. They carried out their duty with honour, and sacrifices were made. This is a legacy no one can take from the CPIB; at many junctures in history, the same mettle and tenacity of the Bureau's men and women would be tested time and again. This is a legacy that present-day CPIB officers will do well not to forget when things seem bad and when they have to dig deep to perform their duty. Bureau officers remind themselves of the reason they do their jobs: to stop corrupt practices in order to protect and sustain the nation's clean reputation, which is the pillar holding up Singapore's economic lifeline.[8]

The Bureau's success in fighting corruption has also become a part of the Singapore story. During the nation's "graft-ridden" past, up till the 1980s, when even a few corrupt officials could make a mockery of the rule of law, it was remarked, "corruption in Singapore was not a way of life but [it] remains a fact of life". However, this "fact of life", since then, "had become an exception".[9] The Bureau had played a significant role in this nation's social transformation. "Incorruptibility" was not only a much-valued national reputation which had to be protected, but it had also already become an ethos ingrained into the Singaporean psyche.[10] Undoubtedly, this outcome was the result of decades of hard work by CPIB officers, a legacy they must continue to sustain.[11] However, looking back in order to move forward was a tall order in the new millennium; new developments and challenges appeared over the horizon incessantly during this period. Be it the emergence of the knowledge-based economy or globalisation, or digital transformation, which included the computerisation of almost all aspects of life, the ways that business and commerce were conducted were undergoing tremendous changes. This also altered the way corrupt activities were manifested. For one, the world had become a smaller place, and businesses across borders had become far more common. It was not only the big corporations and businesses which had dealings beyond the borders, but also the many small and medium enterprises which aspired to succeed in an increasingly competitive environment.[12]

At the same time, many foreign companies were attracted to set up shop in Singapore.[13]

The new reality was that Singaporeans, who had already been imbued with the DNA of incorruptibility, were now increasingly doing business in places where people did not share the same ethos.[14] There was a real possibility that these Singaporeans, which included employees of government-linked companies, might choose to abandon their core values of integrity and honesty; to once again "grease" deals or "lubricate" their transactions. This has been a real challenge for the Singapore Government, and specifically for the CPIB. Social norms and values could change quickly if care was not taken to protect them. We could revert once more to a time when corruption was not only a fact of life, but a way of life. Nothing could be taken for granted, especially Singapore's good reputation. In a statement made at the recent June 2021 United Nations General Assembly Special Session on Corruption, Chan Chun Sing, the Minister for Education and Minister-in-charge of the Public Service, stressed that "although Singapore has had some success in combating corruption... there is no room for complacency". He pointed out that Singapore adopted a "four-pronged approach" in keeping vigilance against corruption: having a strong political will to fight corruption, having robust anti-corruption laws, having an effective and impartial Corrupt Practices Investigation Bureau and having a clean Public Service with "a strong ethos of serving" the people.[15]

Zero-Tolerance

Singapore has been fighting corruption in the country almost on a war-like footing since Independence. It was in the 1990s that it articulated its zero-tolerance stance towards any and all forms of corruption when the number of public officers caught for corrupt acts started showing signs that it was on the increase. In this instance, the CPIB took the lead in spearheading the Government's efforts to halt any possible resurgence of cases of public sector corruption[16] and to stop the return to "old practices".[17] In 2010, after more than a decade of resolve and hard work, Singapore climbed to the apex of the Transparency International Corruption Perceptions Index (TI-CPI) ranking to become one of the least corrupt nations in the world. Still, there were some corrupt practices which remained persistently difficult to eradicate till this day. One such activity is the fixing of soccer matches.

Like the illegal street hawkers of the days of old, enterprising vendors who had their entire stalls on wheels or wares on groundsheets, which could be quickly packed up and hence easily flee whenever the *mata* came, match-fixers were also equally agile in evading the authorities towards the end of the 2000s. The lure of immense profit was just too enticing to resist. In response, the CPIB doubled-down on its zero-tolerance messaging for match-fixing by articulating it each time the issue was reported by the press.

Just as the match-fixers had tentacles everywhere, the CPIB also became omnipresent in local and regional matches which led to scores of investigations and arrests: the Singapore Premier League, Malaysia Super League, Southeast Asian Games and all other soccer ties.[18] The fact that match-fixing would continue unabated was not an indication that the punishment was deficient nor that the Bureau's zero-tolerance stance had been weak or benign. Gambling, greed, covetousness and the promise of great wealth would tempt even high-ranking government officers to run the gauntlet to gain that pot of gold at the end of that illusive El Dorado rainbow. There is no level of deterrence, medication or education that can completely eradicate this addiction. The nation's Prime Minister has noted that "the problem of corruption will never disappear completely" and "from time to time, someone will succumb, out of weakness or greed".[19] So, what would a zero-tolerance policy achieve? Clearly, it is an ideal on which we could build our nation and not the ultimate goal which would never be wholly achieved. A corruption-free nation is our El Dorado. This, in essence, is the raison d'être for the Bureau's continual vigilance. The repeated corruption in soccer games or even within the Civil Service is not a sign of failure of the Government or the Bureau. It simply underscores the need for the rallying cry of zero-tolerance, lest this cancer returns and becomes fatal one day. The main match-fixing syndicate case in 2012 involved the bribery of a referee in a LionsXII's game.[20] No local players nor officials were implicated in this case. Suffice to say, in this light, the Bureau's zero-tolerance towards corruption is an indispensable and necessary policy that protects Singapore's way of life.

Corruption amongst public officers heading into the 2010s had been at an all-time low, at about 7.5% of total corruption investigations handled by the Bureau and prosecuted by the Government.[21] Nevertheless Peter Ong, Head of Singapore's Civil Service (2010–2017), declared that the Government would not be complacent, "every case is one too many", and that action against corrupt public officers will be taken, "no matter how senior he or she might be".[22] Zero-tolerance towards corruption includes integrity, one of the three core values of the Singapore Public Service.

Snapshot of Cases, Last Decade

An overview of the nature and number of cases that the CPIB dealt with in the last decade will show two divergent threads. First, unquestionably, there was the fall in the number of cases reported. Of those reported, few were big-money rackets of the old days, perhaps with the exception of the match-fixing syndicates. Between the 1990s and 2010s, about half of the Bureau's investigations involved *Tua Pek Kong* and marriage of convenience cases which were handed over to the Singapore Police Force (SPF) and Immigration and Checkpoints Authority (ICA), respectively, after 2007. From that point, the Bureau focused more on cases which involved bribery, while not excluding general misconduct cases. Nevertheless, with the general social environment greatly improved from the heydays of corrupt practices which stretched up till the 1970s and 1980s, the new millennium saw few large-scale corruption collusions, especially within the Public Service. It was from the 1990s that corruption in the public sector would see a steady decline and those in the private sector increase proportionally. However, on the whole, the trajectory of the total number of corruption cases had fallen significantly. By 2011, corruption cases investigated by the Bureau had fallen to 138, a seven-year low, and would remain in the region of 130 for most of the decade. Most of these cases were from the private sector.[23] By 2014, corruption complaints that led to investigations in Singapore had fallen to a 30-year low.[24]

Statistically, one could say that Singapore was in a good place in the 2010s. Most countries in the world would certainly be quite contented to have such low numbers, especially with regard to public sector corruption. The main body of public sector graft cases during the decade involved individuals who took bribes and had in some way committed criminal breach of trust as well. Although not as prevalent as in the decades earlier, there were still public officers who solicited or accepted gratification for their cooperation on a range of affairs; in 2010, a National Environment Agency (NEA) assistant manager was charged in Court for taking a $10,000 bribe to provide assistance to a gas company in securing contracts.[25] In 2013 and 2014, a number of immigration officers were charged for accepting bribes to facilitate the issuance of visit passes at the checkpoints,[26] a problem that recurs every now and then. In 2015, four Singapore Power Group technicians were charged with corruption for accepting bribes to "close one eye" during electrical inspections.[27] This is another perennial problem involving statutory staff carrying out compliance checks that required the CPIB's continual vigilance.

Similarly, corrupt practices in the private sector revealed nothing new, but often revolved around the corruption committed by individuals employed in major enterprises and industries which had deep pockets or handled large cash flows: construction, oil and gas, food and beverage, transport and logistics, information technology and more. As a case in point, at Changi Airport alone, the CPIB handled several corruption cases in the 2010s. In 2010, the CPIB uncovered a case involving an airport staff who received bribes from a contractor undertaking upgrading works at Changi Airport.[28] In another case, an airport staff received almost $44,000 in bribes, between 2008 and 2011, from a mechanical engineering firm for his assistance in rigging a quotation exercise in which the firm won the bid.[29] He was jailed 15 months.[30] In 2019, an employee of a Changi Airport unit was charged in Court for receiving bribes from an IT firm amounting to $215,237 on 98 occasions between 2015 and 2017. The money was a reward to the airport staff for helping the firm to secure service contracts with the airport.[31] It was not that Changi Airport had been a corruption magnet. Enterprises and businesses that required and procured extensive logistical and services support tended to draw many suppliers as they could and would pay. And amongst these companies, those which had been more desperate to secure the job, either for reasons of greed or need, may resort to bribery in order to gain an unfair advantage in their bids, or even as a means to rig the process.

In 2016, following an extensive investigation, the Bureau brought to Court the IT director of Schenker (Asia Pacific) for graft. He was charged for receiving bribes of an amount totalling about $238,000 between 2008 and 2011. The bribes were from a director of Asia Management Link and AML Managed Services in return for advancing business interest of the two firms with Schenker. Schenker is a global logistics and transportation service provider. In the course of the CPIB's investigation, the Schenker IT director was also discovered to have solicited additional bribes amounting to about $246,000 between 2011 and 2012.[32] Although such cases did not cause any loss of money for the Singapore public, if left unchecked to grow and fester and become a norm, the cases would have dealt a critical blow to Singapore's hard-earned reputation as a safe, clean and honest destination for business and investment.

All corrupt activities that had the potential to harm Singapore's clean reputation were given due attention by the Bureau. The Marina Bay Sands (MBS) Integrated Resorts, which opened in stages from 2010 to 2011, saw staff succumbing to corruption almost from the very start of the enterprise, not because it was a gambling hub, but because it used significant cash flows to operate its entertainment and hospitality facilities as well. In 2010, a dealer took bribes from a colleague, totalling $10,000, to "keep quiet" about the latter's collusion with a patron to cheat the casino at the wheel. In the end, the briber and the patron were jailed six months and 10 months, respectively, while the corrupt dealer who took the bribe received a staggering five years' jail sentence.[33] And before the dust on this case could settle, another MBS staff was taken to task for corruption. From 2012 to 2014, a senior manager of MBS accepted electronic gifts, entertainment and meals at high-end restaurants, worth thousands of dollars in total, from various vendors who were given jobs to set up event sites at MBS. He was fined and made to pay a penalty totalling more than $60,000 and also given a week's jail term. The CPIB seized his electronic gifts: an iPad and a high-end smartphone.[34]

In the past decade, there were many cases of corruption in the private sector which the CPIB had to handle. These incidents cut across different industries and businesses.[35] However, there was no sense of a real crisis, as in totality, the situation in recent years had been a great improvement from past decades. While these practices had to be resolutely dealt with because they had the potential to reverse the gains made if left unchecked, it was the high-profile cases involving individual senior public officers that truly affected the overall tone of the corruption situation in the country. Singapore's success in building a reputation of having a clean government has also made Singaporeans and their leaders less tolerant of such infractions. Even one dishonest senior public officer succumbing to corrupt ways is one too many. And in the 2010s, there were quite a few.

High-Profile Cases

The first high-profile case in the decade involved a deputy director of Singapore Land Authority's (SLA) Technology and Infrastructure Department, and his manager from the same department. Between 2008 and 2010, the pair awarded IT maintenance contracts through the government tender system to two companies which did not deliver any services. These maintenance services were never undertaken. In total, the SLA suffered a substantive loss; the men spent their ill-gotten gains on luxury cars, landed properties and financial securities instruments. In November 2011, the deputy director was sentenced to 22 years' jail, while the manager got 15 years. Following the discovery of the affair, the Ministry of Law "established an independent review panel chaired by a senior government official of another Ministry and comprising members from other Ministries. The Panel was tasked to identify how the irregularities could have taken place." The SLA tender system and internal processes were tightened and improved.[36]

In early 2012, an assistant director with the National Parks Board (NParks) procured a number of expensive bicycles. The cost for 26 bicycles was $57,200 ($2,200 per bicycle). The amount in itself had already caused some disquiet on the ground. It was later found out during an audit conducted by the Ministry of National Development (MND) that the NParks assistant director had purchased the bicycles from the shop of a friend, and that he and the shop owner had lied about their relationship and when they had first met. Both men became acquainted in October 2011 but told MND auditors that it was in March 2012, after the tender for the bicycles had closed. The MND then referred the matter to the CPIB in July 2012. The CPIB investigated and charged the NParks assistant director. In 2013, the Court fined the assistant director $5,000 but did not impose a jail sentence as the judge felt that only impropriety had been involved.[37]

At around the time when the NParks case was being investigated by the CPIB, one of the most sensational cases involving sex-for-contracts was slowly unfolding in the first half of 2012. It began with the Government's announcement that the chiefs of the Singapore Civil Defence Force (SCDF) and the Central Narcotics Bureau (CNB) had been suspended, arrested and released on bail, all within three days, and that the CPIB was investigating allegations of their "serious personal misconduct".[38] As few details were released at this point, rumours swirled in online forums that a mystery woman was involved and, erroneously, that both men were involved with the same woman.[39] The situation was so disconcerting at that time that it compelled Prime Minister (PM) Lee Hsien Loong, who was in Switzerland attending the annual World Economic Forum, to make a public statement to quell matters. He said, "Whoever he is, whichever position he occupies, we will pursue the matter and settle it one way or another."[40] It was not until early June 2012 when both men were charged in Court that the details were revealed and it was clarified that both cases were entirely unrelated. Nevertheless, both men were similarly charged for corruption involving sex-for-contracts.[41]

The charges against the Commissioner of the SCDF revolved around three women from three different companies which provided IT-related services. The Commissioner "obtained sexual gratification" from these women between 2010 and 2011 in exchange for contracts with the SCDF for their companies. The companies of two of these women were appointed vendors, while the third was in the process of bidding. In June 2013, the Commissioner was sentenced to six months' jail, and subsequently dismissed from the Public Service.[42] As for the director of the CNB, while he did not deny having had a sexual relationship with a woman who was the sales representative of the CNB's IT vendors, he denied that he was guilty of corruptly accepting sexual favours in return for awarding her company the CNB's IT contract. He was ultimately acquitted in February 2013. The trial judge had ruled that there was no question there had been a conflict of interest in the matter but "the presence of conflict does not automatically imply that there was corruption"; the woman involved had given contradictory accounts to the Court and the CPIB, and the director of the CNB had played no part in the IT procurement process in reviewing "potential vendors" and he had not intervened. Nevertheless, the former director was retired from the Public Service in January 2014, following the Public Service Commission's disciplinary proceedings. The decision was made in the interest of the public.[43] The trials of both the SCDF and

CNB chiefs had been sensational partly because of the saucy details revealed during the trial proceedings, but mainly because the whole country was watching. Would the Government be impartial and have the will to see through the application of the law when it is their "favourite sons" on the other end of the stick? But more pertinently, such high-profile cases affected the clean image of the nation and government. Unbeknownst to the CPIB, soon after the start of the trial of the SCDF and CNB chiefs in mid-2012, yet another high-profile case would also be brought to the docks for an even more egregious betrayal of the Bureau, and certainly of the Singapore public as well.

In September 2012, the Bureau discovered that Edwin Yeo, the assistant director and head of its Field Research and Technical Support Unit, had been pilfering from his workplace to cover his gambling losses.[44] As soon as Yeo's wrongdoing was suspected, he was suspended the day after, and an internal investigation commenced. To maintain impartiality, the Bureau reported Yeo to the CAD subsequently. Yeo was eventually jailed for 10 years for criminal breach of trust as a public officer and for forgery.[45] Right from the start, the matter had to be dealt with decisively and with complete transparency as the very reputation that had been drawing investors to our isles was at stake; American companies "regularly cite transparency and a lack of corruption as leading factors in their decision to invest here".[46] Months later, reflecting on the case, Singapore's Law Minister, K Shanmugam, said "it was human nature to be tempted, but that strong leadership had to be in place to ensure checks and balances are in place and that corruption does not spread like a 'cancer'... it was understandable for the public to be concerned about recent high-profile cases involving public servants... it was important that these cases were dealt with in a *transparent* way."[47]

For the Government, the case came at an inopportune time, close behind numerous high-profile cases involving senior government officers, some of which had yet to close. Certainly, public trust and confidence in the CPIB, and to some extent the Government, would have been affected. Accordingly, the Public Service Division introduced new Regulations regarding visits to casinos; all public officers had to declare their visits to local casinos if they had visited these places more than four times within a month, or if they had purchased an annual visit pass. It was mandatory that these declarations be made within seven days of their visit.[48]

Still, there were other high-profile public sector cases. In December 2012, the then Media Development Authority (MDA) uncovered irregularities and referred to the CPIB that one of its assistant directors might have been engaged in illicit activities. In 2014, the Bureau charged the man for corruption and forgery. He was responsible for the evaluation of MDA grant applications and the disbursement of grants. Between 2010 and 2012, as an inducement for facilitating the MDA grants, amounting to a total of $23,565. In 2014, he was jailed 14 months for corruption and had to pay a penalty of $18,000.[49]

The use of one's position of authority as a public officer to solicit "non-repayable loans" from persons and institutions that depended on his or her decisions for government jobs or grants as a means of corruptly attaining gratification is not new in the public and private sectors.[50] But it had become more prevalent amongst senior public officers — perhaps it offered the possibility of deniability, or that it would be harder to prove that it was an outright bribe, or the corrupt public officer might have believed that they could "pay back" their "loans" when their luck at the gaming tables or bets change for the better. Often, the hole they dug for themselves simply got deeper. In October 2018, the CPIB received a tip-off that a senior staff at the Land Transport Authority (LTA) had been doing just that. Following several months of investigation, the Bureau discovered that a deputy group director of the LTA had been obtaining loans from contractors and sub-contractors undertaking LTA projects. Amongst these companies were multinational firms working on the underground tunnels for Singapore's Mass Rapid Transit (MRT) stations. For this case, the Bureau had to employ extensive digital forensics and forensic accounting works which churned up incriminating phone messages, accounting documents and IOUs. The deputy group director was interrogated and he eventually admitted to having received gratifications totalling $1,240,000 from both contractors and sub-contractors from 2014 to 2019. He also confessed that he cheated 13 LTA colleagues a total of $726,500. He did not tell them that their loans were to be used to service his gambling habit and debts. The LTA deputy group director was charged in July 2020 with 36 offences (23 corruption charges and 13 cheating charges). In addition, six contractors, who gave him loans in return for favourable considerations, were also charged. The deputy group director ended up with a five-and-a-half years' jail sentence in 2021. During the trial, a psychologist diagnosed the man to have been afflicted with a "pathological gambling disorder".[51]

Despite the high-profile cases, the Government was not overly rattled. The nation's leaders remained focused on the real issues ahead. In early March 2012, then Deputy PM (DPM) Teo Chee Hean said, "Our zero-tolerance approach to corruption in the public and private sectors can only work if Singaporeans continue to be imbued with the right values and recognise that whilst corruption may be a fact of life, it is not our way of life in Singapore…. We also require good leadership by example at the top, as well as a population which rejects corruption and does not accept any form of corruption at all."[52] In short, we have to all work together, even in deterring corruption cases perpetuated by individuals in high government positions. There was a great need to include public engagement and education amongst all government agencies going forward, including the CPIB. Teo, while defending the efforts of the CPIB when the first of the high-profile cases surfaced, "outlined various outreach efforts by the CPIB in curbing corruption, including talks to government agencies, the business community and even schools".[53] At the same time, besides values education, the Government also reviewed a whole range of processes: gambling limits and restrictions, better procurement processes, review of financial processes, continual vigilance and more. If anything, these cases are simply a reminder that there is no room for complacency.

Brewing Storm

It was expected that organisations would have to undergo the process of change in order to keep in tune with the times, the technologies and innovations of the day, as well as to adapt to contemporary trends, which for the CPIB, included the nature of corruption in law and order. The spate of high-profile cases among civil servants from the 2010s, which also impacted the CPIB itself, was an indication that at some level, some changes had outpaced the Bureau, and perhaps even the Government. When the Edwin Yeo case surfaced, a sense of urgency awoke within the Government. The cancer which the Bureau was created to fight had afflicted the Bureau itself! Then DPM Teo Chee Hean, who was also the Minister-in-charge of the Civil Service, opined in July 2013, "This case is particularly serious because it involved a senior officer in the CPIB, which is entrusted with the mission of maintaining the integrity of the system... Public institutions and public officers are held to the highest standards of integrity and conduct. There must be strong enforcement when there is wrongdoing, weaknesses in processes must be tightened, and most importantly there must be good values."[54]

There was a storm brewing entering the twenty-first century. The changing times and global socio-economic climate brought new challenges for societies, economies, communities ... and for the CPIB, this meant that it had to adapt to dealing with new technologies and trends in the commission of crime and in crime fighting. Information technology (IT) was in the middle of everything. In the early 2000s, while many appreciated such conveniences, few understood the implications the facility had on the safety concerns (fraud) of such transactions, even if they knew about secure access and the use of passwords. It was not easy to apply similar safeguards for traditional transfers like requiring two signatories to sign a cheque on modern IT platforms for fund transfers. And things would become more complex in the years following, requiring constant reviews, adjustments and tightening up of processes by government bodies. In early 2015, it was reported that PM Lee Hsien Loong had said that there was a need for change in the fight against corruption; anti-graft efforts have to go beyond having a strong Bureau. Among other things, the authorities have to constantly review government procurement rules and use technology to detect wrongdoing in a faster-paced, more complex environment.[55]

While it was understood that regular reviews and changes were necessary and had been carried out, there was still a need to understand that the world was not just constantly evolving, but doing so in acceleration. Hence, changes had to be executed swiftly. Increasingly, the cases handled by the Bureau officers included IT aspects that required knowledge and skills to tackle. This was a challenge for the CPIB. Broadly covered under the overarching label of the "misuse of computer",[56] such cases emerged across multiple government agencies in the new millennium, and the Bureau had to build the capability for understanding and investigating such offences.

Closely linked to the challenges associated with the technological advances of the day was the emergence of more complex business models which operated with increasing velocity and higher volume of transactions. The nature of businesses, legitimate or otherwise, has grown in terms of sophistication, interdependence and complexity. The conduct of business has become more globalised, aided by technological advancement and the greater ease of mobility of people, money, goods and information across borders. In this environment, transactions had become increasingly difficult to track, making the detection and investigation of corruption cases a major challenge for enforcement agencies such as the CPIB. Just imagine what a simple mobile phone can do these days. Latching on to a virtual private network device also allows a person to operate covertly through online banking. Imagine, adding the use of cryptocurrency into this nexus of funds transfer, many criminal acts may remain undetected for a length of time. In this context, corruption cases have become more complicated as the nature of commercial, financial and business transactions has changed tremendously. And the pace of change is increasing.

The nature of business and commerce in Singapore had always had a global dimension. From the days of the Singapore entrepot and free port regime, Singapore companies had always been engaged in the import and export business. In modern times, this included services. Heading into the 1990s, homegrown companies were also encouraged to venture out of the country to search for opportunities and grow their businesses (cosmopolitans). Ultimately, this meant that the business dealings for private companies, and even government-linked companies (GLC), had become increasingly more transnational. To monitor the transactions occurring in this realm of commerce, the Bureau had to build capabilities and upskill its own people. Transnational corruption and foreign bribery have become new threats on the horizon. This transnational element is a complex situation; corrupt intent might be developed in one jurisdiction, while the actual act of corruption could be committed in another, and the corrupt proceeds concealed in a third country.

Another challenge that surfaced towards the new millennium was the cosmopolitan society arising from Singapore's open policy that added many more layers on the demographic front. While more Singaporeans were educated, and better educated, the populace was also more well-travelled and had become more cosmopolitan. The issue was not just multiculturalism; new citizens and visitors come from diverse societies that hold different social values and ethos, especially with regard to a corruption free government and society. There is still a need for conversation, education and a sharing of our national ideals.

Taken together, these exogenous challenges in the last decade required the Bureau to relook at how it could adapt to the changing times. The high-profile cases indicated that there existed loopholes and opportunities for corruption in the new age. Corruption in Singapore had become more sophisticated, interlinked and transnational. Changes were needed in order for the Bureau to remain relevant and effective.[57]

Chapter Twenty-Six

Metamorphosis

Building Strength and Standards

Prior to 2010, the CPIB's establishment comprised 92 posts, but the actual number of staff at the Bureau was far less due to resignations and vacancies not being filled fast enough. The Bureau's establishment was significantly increased, but the additional posts were only gradually filled. The increased manpower resources allowed the CPIB to better organise itself. The Bureau was reorganised into specialised functions such as finance and administration, human resources, planning, corporate communications, public education, international relations, among others. At the investigations and operations levels, branches specialising in financial investigations and private and public sectors investigations were created. Support sections such as Computer Forensics Unit and a Polygraph Unit were finally given full-time officers and professionals. Personnel with the requisite skillsets, experience and expertise were either recruited or seconded from other ministries to take up the newly minted positions in the various areas. On the whole, the 2010 changes allowed investigation officers to focus more on their core duties, which increased the effectiveness and efficiency of the Bureau. One area which needed greater attention at this time was financial investigations. The casino-resorts had just opened, and the Bureau knew that casino and gambling-related corruption might arise. In response, the Bureau also set up its Financial Investigation Branch (which evolved from the Financial Investigation Team (FIT)).

The leadership of the CPIB also strengthened its identity and ethos, by updating and articulating its core values. The core values since the

▶ Metamorphosis & Roots

1970s had been Integrity, Impartiality and Efficiency. Efficiency had been a uniquely CPIB value; in the old days, since the People's Action Party (PAP) first came into power, the government had been fighting inefficiency and corruption in public services. Back then, many corrupt public officers dealing with the public tended to go slow in order to pressure the people (who needed licences or ration cards to work or to eat) to give a little money. This was the "squeeze" of the day. Many a times, one could not tell if the public officer was simply "inefficient" or trying to "squeeze". It was so prevalent that the Government considered both to be the same. In fact, when the Central Complaints Bureau was still in operation in 1982, inefficiency was a failing that was seriously investigated. In modern-day clean Singapore, "efficiency" and "inefficiency" are no longer synonymous with dishonesty or being corrupt. So, some updating became necessary. On 28 April 2009, the new Vision, Mission and Core Values were officially launched.[58] These new statements reflected the Bureau's shared purpose and aspirations, as well as the qualities of its officers: Mission — to combat corruption through swift and sure, firm but fair action; Vision — to be a leading anti-corruption agency that upholds integrity and good governance towards achieving a corruption-free nation; Core Values — Integrity, Teamwork, Devotion to Duty.

In November 2011, the Bureau obtained re-certification of four business excellence standards (Singapore Quality Class, People Developer Standard, Innovation Class and Service Class) for a period of three years.[59] It underwent another renewal assessment in 2015 and managed to successfully renew its four certifications with higher scores obtained for all four standards.[60] On the whole, by strengthening the ethos and standards within the Bureau, the CPIB also started strengthening its esprit de corps within as well.

All these culminated in the CPIB's 60th Anniversary at the Istana in September 2012. For the staff, marking the event in this fashion was not only an affirmation of their work and commitment, but also a grand way to honour the former guardians and stewards of the Bureau. There were quite a few "firsts" for the CPIB that year, including the first CPIB Open House on 9 December 2012. The Bureau opened its doors for the first time to members of public, offering them a very rare glimpse behind the scenes of the Bureau. The event attracted about 500 visitors and also garnered a pledge from the Institute of Certified Public Accountants in Singapore (ICPAS) members to combat corruption and uphold the highest standards of integrity.

Prime Minister Lee Hsien Loong, Emeritus Senior Minister Goh Chok Tong and Founding Prime Minister Lee Kuan Yew at the CPIB's 60th Anniversary Commemorative Event at the Istana, 18 September 2012.
Source: CPIB Archives.

Prime Minister Lee Hsien Loong addressing staff and guests at the CPIB's 60th Anniversary Commemorative Event at the Istana, 18 September 2012.
Source: CPIB Archives.

Building Trust

By 2015, when most of the previous years' high-profile cases had been resolved and court sessions closed, the Government ramped up its anti-corruption fight — by building public trust through decisive measures. The Government announced at the start of 2015 that the Bureau's manpower would be increased by more than 20% and a new corruption reporting centre "for whistleblowers" would be set up to make the reporting of corruption easier.[61] The one-stop reporting centre, also a heritage centre, was eventually completed at the end of 2016. The Corruption Reporting & Heritage Centre (CRHC) was officially opened in June 2017 and it takes over the site, 247 Whitley Road, formerly the Whitley Neighbourhood Police Post.[62] The CRHC serves as a useful avenue for the Bureau to engage students and other local stakeholders on the ills of corruption. The Centre engages a broader audience as well, hosting its foreign counterparts and other delegates so that they can appreciate the CPIB's rich heritage and role in our nation's history. As a law enforcement agency of strong traditions, the importance of inculcating the right values in its officers cannot be overstated. The CRHC provides the environment where new CPIB recruits and younger officers, through sharing sessions by their seniors, are imbued with a sense of pride and mission in their work as well as a firm devotion to duty.

As another measure to regain public trust, the CPIB released its inaugural corruption statistics to the public. The CPIB's statistics show that between 2017 and 2021, the number of corruption reports received had been consistently low; the percentage of corruption-related reports registered for investigation had been on average around 32%. Of the 83 cases registered for investigation in 2021, 16 (19%) were from anonymous sources.[63] The Public Perception Survey (PPS) commissioned by the Bureau also affirmed the public trust in the national corruption control efforts and the CPIB's work in fighting corruption. In the PPS 2020, 94% of the

Artist's impression of the CRHC at 247 Whitley Road.
Source: CPIB Archives.

respondents rated the corruption control efforts in Singapore as good, very good or excellent. This was a 2% increase from 92% in 2018. Political determination to keep corruption under control, heavy punishment for corruption offences and effective anti-corruption laws were cited as the top three success factors that contributed to the low corruption rate in Singapore. It was noteworthy that the level of public trust in the CPIB and its work has improved, with close to 80% of respondents trusting the CPIB as an effective agency in the fight against corruption.

Building Character

The CPIB had been combating corruption in the public sector since the days of the first four Special Investigators. In fact, the pages of this chronicle are filled with accounts of corrupt officers whose actions constantly threatened to derail our nation-building project, and wreck Singapore's clean reputation as a safe venue for investors. A notable shift occurred in the 1990s when the number of private sector corruption cases outstripped those of the public sector. From 2017 to 2021, the percentage of private sector cases handled by the CPIB hovered between 86% and 92%. In 2021, of the 165 individuals prosecuted in Court for offences investigated by the CPIB, 93% (154) were private sector individuals. Only 7% (11) were public officers. This could be partly attributed to the success of the government's efforts to create a clean Public Service over the years. This status quo would improve further from that time till the present decade. In fact, in the last decade, there were a growing number of cases where public officers rejected bribes from the public.[64] In December 2017, the Bureau commended 18 persons "for acts against corruption". They included a policeman and a tester at a safety driving centre who refused a bribe.[65] While a group of people being publicly lauded by their own government for honesty might seem to be a uniquely Singapore phenomenon, the indications are that it was no hyperbole when Prime Minister (PM) Lee Hsien Loong said that "incorruptibility" had become "ingrained in [the] Singaporean psyche" in

2012.⁶⁶ The question, rather, is what happens when Singaporeans interact with peoples of other nations with different socialisations? A perusal of corrupt cases reported in the news in recent years involving bribery of public officers answers that question: In 2015, a Korean woman who was caught for solicitation attempted to bribe five policemen with $1,550. She ended up in Court for making the offer.[67] In May 2017, a Moldovan woman caught for vice activities in a hotel attempted to bribe three police officers to let her go. She was jailed for bribery.[68] In February 2017, a Chinese national tried to bribe a driving tester with $200 to pass the driving test. He was charged in Court.[69] In July 2017, on separate occasions, two foreigners, a Chinese national and a man from Kazakhstan, were arrested for trying to bribe policemen to release them after they were caught bookmaking at the Turf Club. Each were jailed four weeks. The former offered a $1,000 bribe while the latter, $2,150.[70] Clearly, there is something to be said about the Singapore character. While one may say that foreign nationals do not know better, or they do not believe public officers can be clean, there are also Singaporeans who still foolishly attempt to bribe enforcement officials today.

In recent years, Singapore has not been short of honest public officers. On 3 June 2014, Sergeant (SGT) Mohammad Khairudin Bin Rosli, a Primary Screening Officer with the Immigration and Checkpoints Authority (ICA) at Woodlands Checkpoint detected a female Vietnamese national who tried to perform a 'U-turn' via Malaysia. He alerted his Duty Officer and motioned for the woman to stand behind him in the booth. While waiting for an auxiliary officer to escort the woman to the Duty Office, the woman took out a stack of money from her bag, and offered Khairudin a bribe of $50 to grant her a Visit Pass into Singapore. Khairudin rejected the bribe and waited for an auxiliary officer to arrive. The case was subsequently referred by the ICA to the CPIB for further investigations, and the woman was sentenced to seven weeks' imprisonment for corruption on 17 July 2014.[71]

On 14 April 2016, two policemen were sent to Fortune Centre following a tip-off about an unlicensed massage establishment. When statements were being recorded, one of the women asked to speak with Assistant Superintendent of Police (ASP) Chan Wai Hoong privately. Chan refused and told her that she could say what she wanted in front of everyone present. She then tried to offer $10,000 to Chan to stop his investigations. Chan rejected the offer.[72] Then again in April 2017, Chan turned down another offer of money and gifts from another foreign national in exchange for her to be released from police custody. The two women were subsequently sentenced to four weeks' imprisonment each for their attempts to bribe Chan.

SGT Muhammad Sufi and SGT Sally Chua Wei Ting of the SPF were performing foot patrol on 9 October 2016, in the vicinity of Senja Road, when they noticed a red van surge forward before hitting a curb. The van was parked at the loading and unloading bays at Senja Road. Suspicious, Sufi and Chua made contact with the driver who smelt of alcohol. When asked for his identity card, the driver held out a $50 note towards the officers. Sufi and Chua informed him that they understood the action as an offer of a sum of $50 as a bribe. Both Sufi and Chua rejected the bribe and reported the matter to their superiors. The driver was charged and sent to jail for three weeks in 2017. He was also fined $2,100.[73]

Perhaps it is apt at this point to note that the emergence of a professional and honest Civil Service in Singapore, in no small part, had been due to a policy of paying decent and equitable wages to public officers. There has been less incentive to augment the pockets and a greater disincentive to risk one's own job and future.

Building Bridges

Amongst the more difficult aspects of the Bureau's work in modern times is dealing with the commission of corrupt acts by Singaporeans overseas. This affects the public and private sectors, as well as government-linked companies (GLCs). Some of these cases may also come under the umbrella of "high-profile" cases of the day.[74] Nevertheless, suffice to say, it did not matter if "high-profile" cases occurred within Singapore or offshore, as the potential damage to Singapore's reputation was just the same. Contextually, cases beyond our borders also underscore the importance of working with overseas authorities in resolving such crimes.

One offshore high-profile GLC corruption case involved senior executives of ST Marine (STM), the marine arm of ST Engineering, one of Singapore's largest companies. The CPIB started investigating the affairs of STM in 2011 when it came to light that the company had been giving commissions to the employees of client companies in return for ship-repair jobs since the early 2000s till 2011. In total, various payments amounting to $24,552,535 were made to the staff of these firms. These payments, and the falsifying of STM's accounts to camouflage them, were carried out with the full knowledge of STM's senior management. Between 2015 and 2017, six of STM's senior staff were convicted in Court and given custodial sentences.[75]

In another high-profile overseas GLC case, Keppel Offshore & Marine Limited (KOM) was discovered to have been paying bribes to officials from Petrobras, a Brazil state-owned enterprise, from 2001 and 2014, in exchange for rig-building contracts. Under a global resolution led by the United States Department of Justice (USDOJ) together with Brazil and Singapore, KOM entered into a deferred prosecution agreement (DPA) with USDOJ in December 2017. KOM had to pay a total fine amounting to US$422,216,980 to the US, Brazil and Singapore. The CPIB administered a conditional warning in lieu of prosecution which required KOM to remain crime-free for a period of 36 months, failing which it would be prosecuted for the said offences for which Keppel was served the warning. As part of the conditional warning, KOM has certified its Singapore operations under the ISO 37001 Anti-Bribery Management Systems Certification Programme since November 2018. Subsequently in November 2019, KOM also completed its ISO 37001 Anti-Bribery Management Systems certification for its global operations in the US,

Brazil, Middle East, China, the Philippines, India and Bulgaria. They completed the attainment of the ISO 37001 certification at all KOM operating entities in Singapore and globally.[76]

While these offshore crimes affected Singapore's reputation in the international community, they also brought to the fore the question of the extent of the CPIB's reach and ability to enforce the law. It is clear that in all overseas cases, it would be near impossible for the CPIB to get to the bottom of things without the cooperation of foreign governments and authorities. Some light was shed on the question in 2017 when the CPIB brought charges against a pair of siblings who conspired and accepted bribes from companies in Shanghai to secure contracts with Seagate (Singapore), the employer of one of the siblings. These contracts were awarded in 2006 and 2009. Between 2007 and 2010, the pair received a total of around CNY11,300,000. In January 2021, the siblings were sentenced to 50 months' and 41 months' jail terms, respectively. The sister also had to pay a penalty of $2,320,864.10. What is pertinent in this instance was that the CPIB was able to solve the case by working closely with the Shanghai City Zhabei District People's Procuratorate who provided invaluable assistance in the form of critical evidentiary records such as bank statements, and assistance in interviews and statement-taking.[77]

So, it is not surprising that the CPIB actively engages the international community to establish the networks that would help in its fight against corruption. In 2011, the CPIB set up a dedicated international relations branch which had the responsibility to manage the CPIB's involvement in a number of international anti-corruption platforms. In this decade, the Bureau has been involved in several new platforms including the Economic Crime Agencies Network (ECAN). Initiated by the New Zealand Serious Fraud Office (NZ SFO), ECAN is a formal network of law enforcement organisations from various countries involved primarily in the investigation and prosecution of economic crimes. The CPIB was elected as the ECAN Chair and hosted the second ECAN meeting in February 2014.[78] Another new international initiative is the International Anti-Corruption

Coordination Centre (IACCC) led by the UK. The IACCC brings together like-minded agencies from Australia (Australian Federal Police), Canada (Royal Canadian Mounted Police), New Zealand (Police and SFO), Singapore (CPIB), UK (National Crime Agency), US (Federal Bureau of Investigation (FBI) and Homeland Security Investigations) as well as Interpol into a single location to coordinate the global law enforcement response to allegations of grand corruption. A Memorandum of Understanding (MOU) was signed and the IACCC was operationalised in July 2017.[79] In 2018, the CPIB assumed Chairmanship of ASEAN Parties Against Corruption (ASEAN-PAC), a grouping of anti-corruption agencies from ASEAN countries.

Besides actively participating in international platforms, the CPIB accepts requests for study visits by foreign counterparts and other relevant authorities, organising training workshops and programmes, as well as taking up speaking invitations at regional and international events. One example of such a training workshop is the July 2019 session on "Proper Seizure of Cryptocurrency for Law Enforcement Agencies" and "Performing Open Source Intelligence Techniques" for anti-corruption agencies from ASEAN countries. In addition, the Bureau organised its 4th Anti-Corruption Executive (ACE) Programme in October 2019, which brought together 34 participants from 28 domestic and foreign agencies, including Anti-Corruption Bureau of Brunei Darussalam, NZ SFO, UK SFO and US FBI. Through seconding its officers to partners such as the Hong Kong Independent Commission Against Corruption (ICAC) and the UK SFO, the Bureau also learnt best practices in investigations and operational areas, as well as in prevention and community outreach.

The COVID-19 pandemic has not stopped the CPIB from being active on the international platforms. The Bureau represented Singapore at various international anti-corruption fora which were held virtually. These included regular meetings under the United Nations Convention Against Corruption (UNCAC), the United Nations Special Session of the General Assembly Against Corruption 2021 (UNGASS) and many more.[80] As far as the CPIB's

Members of the IACCC at their weekly meeting in London.
Source: CPIB Archives.

contributions to international capacity-building efforts is concerned, despite the pandemic, the CPIB continues to do so through digital means. For instance, when the Bureau participated in the Open-ended Intergovernmental Expert Meeting to enhance international cooperation under the UNCAC in November 2020, it participated via an online interface. The CPIB also hosted foreign visitors who wished to understand and learn about Singapore's experience in fighting corruption, owing to its status as one of the world's least corrupt nations.

All these networks established through international engagements have stood the Bureau in good stead as cooperation and partnerships are vital in tackling corruption and the flow of corrupt proceeds. While the CPIB strives to move as expeditiously as possible, not all aspects of the investigation are within its control, particularly in relation to the requests and applications made and filed in other jurisdictions. The current COVID-19 situation globally has also made cross-jurisdiction investigation efforts more challenging. The cooperation and assistance rendered by other jurisdictions play a key role in the progress of investigations. Aside from the Seagate case, the CPIB also received invaluable assistance and strong support from the Malaysian Anti-Corruption Commission (MACC) in arresting Siva Kumar S/O Ramachandran, who was on the run for more than 20 years for immigration offences he committed in Singapore in 1999. He had been involved in a conspiracy to bribe a CISCO officer to allow buses ferrying illegal immigrants to pass through the Woodlands Checkpoint from Malaysia into Singapore without immigration clearance.[81]

Operational cooperation with foreign authorities is by no means a one-way street. The CPIB is also committed towards assisting foreign authorities with their operational requests, as long as the Bureau is able to do so in accordance with our domestic framework and laws. In 2013, the CPIB worked closely with the USDOJ, US Defense Criminal Investigative Service and the US Naval Criminal Investigative Service on a joint investigation and to coordinate the complex operations in Singapore and the US into a case involving Singapore-based port services firm Glenn Defense Marine Asia (GDMA) which cheated the US Navy of US$35 million. The collaboration between the two agencies saw the successful prosecution of those involved in this case in the US and Singapore, including a Singaporean woman, a former lead contract specialist with the US Navy.[82] In another high-profile corruption case, this time involving Garuda Indonesia, the CPIB also assisted the Indonesia's Komisi Pemberantasan Korupsi (Corruption Eradication Commission) in securing evidence which led to the successful conviction of the former President Director of PT. Garuda Indonesia and the Beneficial Owner of Connaught International Pte. Ltd in May 2020. They were convicted and sentenced for corruption and money laundering offences.[83]

The CPIB's international engagement can be broadly described as having a three-pronged approach: an active participation in various international anti-corruption platforms; the provision of training and capacity-building assistance to foreign anti-corruption agencies; and operational cooperation with foreign counterparts to achieve positive investigation outcomes. Considering that the crime of corruption has become more transnational in nature, international cooperation and partnerships are ever more so important in fighting corruption.

Building Partnerships

The creation and maintenance of a corruption-free society is an ideal that cannot be achieved just "by rules alone";[83] it has to "go beyond having a strong bureau".[84] Hence, since the 1960s, the government has created "an ecosystem" of anti-corruption agencies, laws and protocols that aided in the creation of a home free of corrupt practices. It was never the intent that the CPIB would wage war on corruption alone. By the 1990s, with the ideal of a largely graft-free society having been achieved, and more instances of corruption occurring in the private sector, it became clear that a new anti-corruption "ecosystem" had to be considered. An important hallmark of the CPIB's transformation in the last decade is the close partnerships forged with the private and public sectors, media and the youths in the fight against corruption. The thrust of the CPIB's partnership initiative is also in line with the Singapore Together movement. The CPIB leverages strategic partnerships with broad segments of the community to draw ideas, tap on their expertise and co-create impactful solutions and initiatives to advance the CPIB's core capabilities, as well as bolster corruption prevention and outreach efforts. In the 2010s, one of the first partnerships the CPIB forged was with the ICPAS. The institute, which eventually became the Institute of Singapore Chartered Accountants (ISCA), would become an invaluable partner in the Bureau's fight against corruption.

Engaging the help of the private sector in combating corruption in that sphere has become the most logical next step. But the Bureau found that sometimes, the private sphere needed to be helped first. In 2016, in partnership with the Standards, Productivity and Innovation Board

Launch of SS ISO 37001:2016 Anti-Bribery Management Systems on 12 April 2017.
Source: CPIB Archives.

(SPRING Singapore) (now part of Enterprise Singapore), the CPIB acted as the National Convenor to lead a national working group comprising representatives from the trade associations, industry bodies and academia to develop the ISO 37001 on Anti-Bribery Management Systems. This is a new standard, launched on 15 October 2016, and was tailored to help businesses and companies implement an anti-bribery compliance programme. The CPIB–SPRING partnership also organised Singapore's first private sector seminar in April 2017 to launch the Singapore Standard (SS ISO 37001). Subsequently, the Bureau published a new guidebook, *PACT: A Practical Anti-Corruption Guide for Businesses in Singapore*, to help local business owners reduce the risk of corruption in their companies.[85]

The Anti-Corruption Partnership Network (ACPN) was also a result of this engagement strategy. Established in 2018 with the objective of promoting the proactive involvement of local companies in the anti-corruption movement, the network of 25 pioneering companies has now expanded to include selected associations and professional bodies. To date, it has 58 members. The Bureau continues to work closely with, and learn from, several members of the ACPN on their industry practices. This is important for the CPIB as it provides the Bureau the knowledge it needs to strengthen its investigative capabilities in the private sphere. This close collaboration with the private sector also ensured that the CPIB could provide preventive advice to the industry in question and put in place more robust anti-corruption measures. In the Bureau's opinion, there is a "need [for] our business sectors to take ownership and be effective when it comes to corruption prevention. We have to recognise that if we allow corruption to taint the way we conduct our businesses, Singapore's competitive edge and value proposition will slowly but surely be eroded."[86] In February 2021, the Bureau signed an MOU with ISCA, also an ACPN member, giving it access to the accountancy profession and the wider business community in its anti-corruption efforts. As part of outreach and corruption prevention efforts amongst the accounting profession, the CPIB and ISCA also co-created an e-learning module for ISCA members and professionals.

In another recent collaborative effort, the CPIB brought together a business association, the Container Depot and Logistics Association, and a Chinese media outlet, *Lianhe Zaobao*, to create content to educate forklift operators on corruption matters. This special feature story followed media coverage on several corruption cases involving forklift operators.[87] Other associations which the Bureau has collaborated with include the Football Association of Singapore, the Association of Property and Facility Managers, the Singapore Esports Association, among others.

On the school front, the CPIB has taken significant steps to collaborate with Institutes of Higher Learning in co-creating corruption prevention solutions. Over the past two years, the Bureau has worked closely with students of Nanyang Polytechnic (NYP) to co-create a series of novel digital resources which have been used to educate our youths on the importance

The Scouts playing with *Corruzione*, a web game which the CPIB co-created with students from Nanyang Polytechnic. *Corruzione* is an activity in the Anti-Corruption Badge Programme which the CPIB and the Singapore Scout Association have implemented via an MOU.
Source: CPIB Archives.

of being corruption-free. This initiative was undertaken in such a way that young people would find it fun and enjoy the experience. One of the resources was a web game *Corruzione*. The first to play the game were the cadets of the Singapore Scout Association. Following this, the Bureau worked with NYP to design an animated series for children aged nine and below to teach them the value of honesty. At the same time, the Bureau also embarked on the CPIB History Project which saw the creation of a joint team comprising students from Yale-NUS College and CPIB officers to conduct research on the Bureau's history and Singapore's journey in fighting corruption.

The CPIB also continues to work closely with other government agencies in its efforts to prevent corruption. For years, the Bureau had written review papers on public sector corruption cases (upon completion of investigations). These were used to inform government agencies of the loopholes in their processes and systems in order to help them improve their corporate governance and to manage, as well to prevent, the potential of corruption and fraud occurring in their backyard. This initiative eventually morphed into bilateral meetings and discussions with affected government agencies even when their corruption cases were at the investigation stage.

As far as collaboration within the public sector goes, the Bureau's engagement with the Civil Service College (CSC) to educate public officers in courses on the ills of corruption and their roles and responsibilities in reporting corruption has been most critical in helping to maintain a corruption-free Public Service. Together, the CPIB and CSC have developed learning resources for courses ranging from those for senior management to ground officers. The Bureau also delivered anti-corruption modules at platforms such as the CSC's Governance and Leadership Programme for public service leaders in 2020, and the Leaders in Enforcement Management Programme in 2021. These courses were created with the aim of providing public officers with a greater awareness of potential pitfalls and risk areas involving corruption and dishonesty.

One of the more important partnerships the CPIB has made in the last decade is with the Singapore media. Known for its mysterious and fearsome reputation, the CPIB has come a long way to working with the media. It had its first closed-door session with the media outlets on August 2012 when it was celebrating its 60th anniversary. For the first time, the media could engage the Director of CPIB on the Bureau's work, role and responsibilities, and could clarify why the Bureau could not share corruption cases of which investigations were still ongoing. They learnt about the Bureau's duty and responsibility, being fair even towards the persons and entities being investigated, and appreciated the Bureau's determination to leave no stones unturned to find the truth behind any case. The active engagement during this anniversary year saw the CPIB's debut documentary entitled *Corruption Crackdown: Inside the CPIB*, a collaboration with

Mediacorp for the first time. The documentary was broadcast on Channel News Asia on 15 October 2012. The Chinese version was shown on Channel 8 on 1 December 2012. It provided some rare insights into the CPIB and showcased some of the prominent cases handled by the Bureau. With the CPIB commemorating its 70th anniversary this year (2022), another collaboration with Mediacorp ensued. This time a 4-episode Chinese Documentary entitled *Abyss of Greed*, featuring cases throughout the 70 years of graft-busting.

Chapter Twenty-Seven

Planting for the Future

The story of Singapore's CPIB is anchored on the tale of one country's journey that took it through tumultuous times until a nation imbued with values of a good and incorrupt society was forged. There was a time during our nation-building journey when corrupt practices were rife. Back then, society was made up of sojourners and immigrants who had no collective identity and shared social values. All these started changing from the 1950s when the people of Singapore were on the cusp of becoming one nation, one people. But this metamorphosis of the Singapore nation was not an automatic or guaranteed outcome. Our pioneering generation had to struggle, as well as change their mindsets that accentuated their differences, in order that old residents could become a new community with common values. In this process, help was needed. The anti-social forces of the day had to be kept at bay while this burgeoning nation had the time and opportunity to grow. It was during this challenging time that the CPIB was started — planted in a land that was wild and overgrown with weeds and everything else that could strangle the hopes and aspirations of our new nation.

The story of the CPIB's own journey in the last 70 years is intertwined with the story of this land. The Bureau had struggled, standing shoulder to shoulder with the other arms of the Government, to clean up and to build what Singaporeans all enjoy today — One People, One Nation, One Singapore. So, we have arrived. However, events of the last decade have also shown us that Singapore's success in building this nation cannot be taken for granted; there are still fault lines, and there is always a possibility that the corruption cancer may still return and reverse all our gains. The CPIB, therefore, is required to remain vigilant at all times. The Bureau has to also adapt to the challenges that always appear over the future horizon. For the Bureau, it may have arrived at this point, but the journey and mission have not ended. The strong tree planted by the pioneers of the CPIB will have to continue growing for the future generation. While its deep roots will unquestionably help the Bureau withstand any storm that threatens itself, and the nation, there is still a need to grow stronger roots and new branches to add capabilities for the future. Today, the CPIB needs to prepare for tomorrow — to prepare our youth for the future and to prepare the men and women of the Bureau for challenges of the digital age.

Planting for the future in the last few years had taken on a new meaning for the Bureau; the importance of being digital-ready for the future was never more elucidating than during a global pandemic. The implementation of various "digital options" in the Bureau's work processes ensured minimal disruption of investigations, operations and other deliverables when social distancing became the order of the day. Amongst the digital platforms the CPIB introduced is the e-Reporting of Corruption Complaints. Members of the public could report corrupt activities or provide information through the Bureau's website. People accessing the portal are allowed to choose to remain anonymous if they wanted. And the system is still evolving. The Bureau also offers the public the use of an e-Bail platform where bailors and bailees are able to access bail extension services without having to go to the CPIB itself. This has already proven to save man-hours and allow the minimisation of contact during the Covid-19 pandemic. This system won the Exemplary Innovator Award in the annual Public Sector Transformation Award.

Within the Bureau, the adoption of the Digital Investigation Paper system has allowed the swift transferring of documents to the Attorney-General's Chambers (AGC) when Bureau officers complete their investigation papers. The facility, besides speeding up the submission of papers, also reduces the risk of missing documents in the Bureau's submission. It was realised in the last two years, when officers had to work from home, that the digital submission of papers had allowed the Bureau's work to continue without great disruption. The Bureau also has a new Command Centre equipped with an operations command system. It provides commanders with real-time operational information; this is important for operational commanders to make necessary decisions. In addition, the Bureau's Digital Forensics Analytics essentially provides the CPIB an intelligence review platform which "extracts, collates and contextualises" digital evidences across multiple digital devices. The Bureau's strength in this field has become an important capability; the CPIB's Digital Forensics Branch (formerly the Computer Forensics Unit), on a daily basis, "examines mobile devices, laptops, computers, cloud, and various multimedia devices including videos and audio enhancers that have been seized to extract evidence that can help the CPIB's investigation officers establish cases".[88] In recent years, the Bureau had leveraged on this capability to deal with the long and pervasive match-fixing problem afflicting Singapore. Of late, the modern bookmakers had started using encrypted data and communications in their mobile phones. While difficult to navigate and crack, the Bureau's forensic officers have the technical expertise to successfully extract information that led to the arrest of individuals involved in the football rackets. While technological advancements had enabled corrupt individuals to invent new means and processes to circumvent enforcement measures, law enforcement agencies like the CPIB have also been able to combat such new threats by using technology as well. The changing nature of crimes has been matched by innovation in forensic investigation.[89]

To meet future threats on this front, the CPIB is focusing on four "key forensic areas": mobile, computer, cloud and multimedia. The ability to handle these interfaces will help to solve crimes. For instance, "Cloud forensics" was introduced in 2018 when the Bureau noticed the increasing popularity of mega storage applications. On this technological front, the

Bureau "does not work alone". The CPIB also works with strategic partners like the Home Team Science and Technology Agency and Government Technology Agency to fight corruption in Singapore. Of course, the Bureau also cooperates with the private sector to combat graft. Using platforms such as the ACPN, the CPIB has been able to "tap on more helping hands across various sectors to curb corruption".[90]

The Bureau has also been giving due attention to prepare its staff to be "digital ready". It is important that the CPIB is able to "harness" the advantages of modern technology to enhance the Bureau's operational capabilities. The centrepiece of the CPIB's digitalisation effort involves formulating an ICT Digitalisation Blueprint for the Bureau, as well as commencement of intensive digitisation work. This started in December 2019, when all hardcopy documents were digitised and given indexing functions. This allows CPIB officers to act more swiftly in the course of their work. At the same time, the Bureau understands that it is not just about the tools. Emphasis and resources have been given to train staff on how to fully utilise the digital platforms at hand through self-learning and in-house training.[91]

While building capacity, capabilities and competency to meet future needs have been undoubtedly a core concern of the Bureau, the CPIB has not lost sight of the other aspects of fighting corruption in modern times. The continued fight for the "hearts and minds" will ensure that future generations share the values and ethos of the pioneering generations. Besides "software", the Bureau also had to focus on the "heartware" of the young adults and youths of the nation. The generation that built Singapore has already done its part in taking the country thus far, there is still a need to ensure that the next generation continues to be imbued with our national values. Hence, the next phase of the Bureau's public education thrust must focus on the education of both working adults and the school-going youth. This has already started in the last decade. One of the first initiatives in this direction was the launching of public exhibitions that showcased the work of the Bureau. Hitherto this initiative,

▶ Metamorphosis & Roots

Students enjoying themselves at the CPIB Exhibition
Declassified – Corruption Matters at the National Library in 2016.
Source: CPIB Archives.

the work of the CPIB had been shrouded in mystery. On 7 April 2016, the CPIB's *Declassified – Corruption Matters* Roving Exhibition was launched by Prime Minister (PM) Lee Hsien Loong. The interactive exhibition, which featured never-before-seen information on the Bureau's history and officers, attracted more than 15,000 visitors. More than 5,000 visitors at this event also made a pledge to stamp out corruption. The exhibition was circulated to three regional libraries and made its appearance in some Institutes of Higher Learning in 2017.

Focusing on the youth, the CPIB ramped up its public education platforms in places and spaces where youths congregate.[92] One of the first steps in this direction was the CPIB's first poster-slogan competition which culminated in the first public exhibition in 2013 for the Bureau at the National Library. Then came a video competition and the #IfILiveInDarkness short-story writing competition. The Bureau went on to venture into bolder endeavours in an effort to further connect with the youth. Four public education videos for four different target groups including students, featuring real-life cases through re-enactments, were produced. Through this media, several key messages such as "zero-tolerance towards corruption" and "no one is above law" are emphasised. Presently, these initiatives have evolved into web games, which provide the youth with additional interactive and sensory experiences that they can access anywhere, any time.

The Bureau then embarked on a series of new initiatives targeting younger Singaporeans. This included a collaboration with students of St Joseph's Institution (SJI) to develop a teaching kit for pre-schoolers. The result was a picture book *The Corrupted Chicken*. Copies of the book were distributed to childcare centres and preschools. The continued collaboration with SJI also resulted in another resource, the *Under the Table* board game. For teenagers, another book entitled *The Corruption Casebook: Stories from Under the Table* was developed specially for them. In addition, an Anti-Corruption Badge Programme was introduced to two uniformed groups in schools. Cadets (from the National Police Cadet Corps) were the first to proudly pin the anti-corruption badge on their uniform. The Singapore Scout Association was the next uniformed group to don the badge of honour.

In 2017, as part of the CPIB's outreach and engagement initiative, the Bureau introduced Kopi Lim, an online persona of a CPIB officer. Introduced as part of the CPIB's 65th anniversary, Kopi Lim was a social media initiative to reach out to youths and the community-at-large and educate them on the perils of corruption and on the CPIB's work in approachable and creative ways. Kopi Lim became an instant success on the CPIB's social media.

Interestingly, Kopi Lim's name was a play on the phrase *lim kopi*. In the old days, it was not a good thing to be invited to the CPIB to *lim kopi* (drink coffee in Hokkien). The cute online persona has become one of the most important outreach tools. Mainstream media carried the news about Kopi Lim when it first went viral on social media.

PROFILE

Age: 24 (in human years)

Gender: Male

Educational Institution: National Institute for Furry Friends

Likes: Anti-Corruption work, honey, fishing, swimming and reading with a cuppa

Dislikes: Vegetables, dishonest people and people who do not take responsibility for their own actions

Habits: Making sure my fur is always white

ABOUT ME

I am Kopi Lim. I love coffee, especially Kopi O Kosong because it is not sweet. I used to think I was going to be a barista when I grow up but it all changed when I heard about the work of the CPIB. I have seen for myself how corruption can have serious consequences for society and I want to make a change! I saw myself fighting corruption, and I believe I can do it because I am whiter than white. My friend Goldilocks said I am also very brave, so I think I have what it takes to stand strong and courageous against corruption. I will work hard with the rest of the CPIB officers to battle corruption swiftly and surely, without fear or favour!

ABOUT MY PERSONALITY

Kaypoh (Inquisitive)   Levelheaded
Organised   Innovative
Positive   Meticulous
Industrious

Curriculum Vitae of Kopi Lim, the CPIB's online persona when he was first introduced on the CPIB's official social media.
Source: CPIB Archives.

CPIB's online persona Kopi Lim sharing a photo shot with Parley (Parliament of Singapore's mascot) at a visit to the Parliament House.
Source: CPIB Archives.

Planting for the Future ◀

The men and women of the Bureau are fortunate that they are part of a rich legacy in the creation of the Singapore nation. This legacy, which anchors the Bureau, is also a resource from which they can draw knowledge and strength. The business community has remarked, "The future may bring fresh and heavier demands on the CPIB's resources and capabilities, but looking at what has been achieved by its team of officers, the signs are reassuring."[93] The CPIB must set the example for the man on the street, and the leaders of the Bureau must lead by example. Amidst the evolution and transformation with the tides of time, what remains unchanged, however, is the CPIB's commitment to its mission to combat corruption through swift and sure, firm but fair action. The Bureau has remained resolute and vigilant to keep corruption in Singapore low and under control. But it cannot do it alone and needs the helping hands of the community and especially the youths, who are the future. This future generation would have to shape and mould the **Place they call *Home***.

A commemorative artwork "A Clean Nation, A 70 Years Effort" by local artist 阿果 (Ah Guo) portraying a CPIB officer wiping away the gloom and darkness shrouding the sky as a metaphor for the CPIB's continuous fight against corruption.
Source: CPIB Archives.

435

▶ Metamorphosis & Roots

In 2016, CPIB was bestowed an artillery shell casing collected from the 21-gun salute fired by the 21st Battalion, Singapore Artillery during the State Funeral Procession of our founding Prime Minister Mr Lee Kuan Yew in recognition of the contribution that CPIB's work makes to Singapore's success. Mr Lee knew from the onset that Singapore's survival and progress is dependent on clean and incorruptible governance. He strengthened CPIB with necessary resources and legislative empowerment to carry out its duty in keeping Singapore corruption-free effectively and without fear or favour.
Source: CPIB Archives.

Prime Minister Lee Hsien Loong's well wishes to the CPIB
on its 70th Anniversary during his visit to the Bureau on 8 July 2022.
Source: CPIB Archives.

Endnotes

[1] *Today* 3 Aug 2010.

[2] *Today* 7 Jun 2017. Point made by PM Lee in 2017.

[3] *Straits Times* 19 Sep 2012. Noted in PM Lee's speech during the CPIB's 60th Anniversary celebrations.

[4] *Straits Times* 13 Aug 2013; *Today* 2 Mar 2012, 2nd ed. Point made by Teo Chee Hean in 2012.

[5] *Today* 27 Jul 2013. A point stressed by Peter Ong, Head of the Civil Service, in 2013.

[6] The Bureau remained constantly watchful because it could not be taken for granted that Singapore's "clean reputation" would be permanent and unchanging. See *Straits Times* 28 Sep 2012.

[7] *Straits Times* 19 Sep, 1 Oct 2012. Lee Kuan Yew's description of the CPIB during its 60th Anniversary celebrations in 2012.

[8] *Straits Times* 28 Sep 2012. Incorruptibility is one of the three pillars (values) of Singapore's Public Service; the others are Meritocracy and Impartiality. See *Straits Times* 28 Apr 2015. In other sources, the three governing principles of Singapore's Public Service are Meritocracy, Impartiality and Integrity. See https://www.psd.gov.sg/heartofpublicservice/our-institutions/building-a-public-service-ready-for-the-future/.

[9] *Straits Times* 17 Jan 2015. Noted in PM Lee's speech during the CPIB 60th Anniversary celebrations.

[10] *Straits Times* 19 Sep 2012.

[11] *Today* 7 Jun 2017. In 2017, PM Lee said that the nation had developed a system that rejected corruption, and it was imperative that we "keep it that way". PM Lee also reminded the public that everyone had a role in keeping the country corruption free. He pointed out that many successful CPIB investigations had been due to public tip-offs.

[12] At the heart of the issue of the Singapore identity and core values at this time was the debate on who was a "Heartlander or Cosmopolitan" in the country. In 1999, then PM Goh Chok Tong described heartlanders as being "the conservative majority in Singapore who live in public housing estates. They tend to be rooted in their cultures and traditions, respectful of authority and less vocal in their demands." As for the cosmopolitan, they "have an international outlook that enable them to work and be comfortable anywhere in the world". In this debate, the two groups were essentially different in their "socio-economic status, values, outlook and mobility". See Elaine Ho, "Negotiating belonging and perceptions of citizenship in a transnational world: Singapore, a cosmopolis?" *Social and Cultural Geography*, Vol. 7, No.3 (2006): 391; Stephan Ortmann, "Singapore: The Politics of Inventing National Identity", *Journal of Current Southeast Asian Affairs*, Vol. 28, No. 4 (1 Dec 2009): 23–46.

[13] *Business Times* 9 Aug 2019.

[14] Singapore's corruption-free culture was discussed, at times, with other "former British colonies" which had also gained their Independence in the post-war years. Unlike those who "made a mess of their countries" because of corruption, many of which were African nations, Singapore was considered very fortunate to have political leaders who steered the nation in the right direction. Among these leaders were Goh Keng Swee and Lim Kim San. Lim was the first Chairman of the Housing and Development Board, and he did this job pro bono. He was also touted as "the hands-on, no-nonsense slayer of corruption, inefficiency and mediocracy whose unsmiling attention, was the bane of businessmen trying to short-change the state". The main reason Singapore evolved differently from most new nations of the day was its leadership. See *Today* 17 May, 12 Jun 2010, 2nd ed.

[15] CPIB Press Release 2021: Special Session of the General Assembly on Challenges and Measures to Prevent and Combat Corruption and Strengthen International Cooperation.

[16] *Straits Times* 1 Jun 1999.

[17] *Straits Times* 3 Nov 1999.

[18] *Today* 4, 10 Jan, 5, 25 May 2012, 30 May, 10 Oct 2015; *Straits Times* 25 May 2012, 8 Feb 2014, 10 Jun 2017; *New Paper* 25, 30 May 2012, 10 Apr 2015.

[19] *Today* 14 Jan 2015. Remark by PM Lee made in 2015.

[20] *New Paper* 25, 30 May 2012; *Today* 9 Oct 2015.

[21] https://corruption.net/singaporegood-leadership-is-key-to-containing-corruption-says-dpm-teo/; *Straits Times* 2 Mar 2012; *Business Times* 2 Mar 2012; *Today* 2 Mar 2012, 2nd ed.

[22] *Today* 27 Jul 2013. In 2013, PM Lee declared that "we will never tolerate corruption", and that there will be "no let-up in fight against corruption." See *Today* 19 Sep 2012; *Straits Times* 19 Sep 2012. Half of the public servants caught for corrupt practices were from the "frontline enforcement units" and departments; Home Team, HDB, NEA, MOM, URA… involving the rank and file. Of these, 65% of those investigated took money for gratification, 12% took gifts, 6% accepted sexual favours and 5% took money and sex. Of those who took money, 40% of them took less than $1,000, while 18% more than $30,000. In 2012, the CPIB investigated 35 cases from the public sector and 144 from the private. Of all those investigated, 23% were university graduates, 29% had A-levels certification and diploma. The rest had O-levels certification and below. In terms of their infractions, among the public servants investigated, 53% were granted "unwarranted leniency", 21% provided services or information without authority and 15% provided favourable treatment in employment and opportunities. See *Today* 27 Jul 2013.

[23] *Straits Times* 16 Aug 2012.

[24] *Today* 3 Apr 2015, 8 Apr 2016; *New Paper* 3 Apr 2015, *Straits Times* 8 Apr 2016.

[25] *Today* 7 Apr 2010; CPIB case files.

[26] *Straits Times* 5 Sep 2013, 10 Jan 2014; CPIB Press Release 2013: Checkpoints Officer Charged with Corruption; CPIB Press Release 2014: Four Checkpoints Officers Charged with Corruption.

[27] *Today* 27 Nov 2015; CPIB case files.

[28] *Straits Times* 2 Sep 2010; CPIB case files.

[29] *Today* 11, 12 Mar 2015.

[30] *Today* 12 Mar 2015; *Straits Times* 28 Aug 2015.

[31] *Straits Times* 23 Dec 2019; CPIB Press Release 2019: Illicit Dealings Disclosed.

[32] *Today* 9 Sep 2016; *Straits Times* 8 Sep 2016, 9 Feb 2021.

[33] *Business Times* 6 Sep 2012; https://www.gamingzion.com/gambling/gambling-news/singaporean-money-wheel-dealer-gets-five-years-for-cheating/ – 13 Sep 2012, 4 Oct 2017; https://www.onlinecasinoselite.org/post/the-singaporean-criminal-laws-punish-3-cheating-gamblers – 1 Nov 2014; *AsiaOne* 5 Sep 2012.

[34] *Straits Times* 9, 10 Oct 2017, https://www.cpib.gov.sg/files/news/2017.10.10.ST_MBS%20manager%20jailed%20and%20fined%20over%20bribes,%20false%20overtime%20claim.pdf.

[35] For example, in the shipping and bunkering sector. See *Straits Times* 17 Apr 2014, 27 Mar 2015; *AsiaOne* 5 Sep 2012. In 2020, the CPIB even uncovered a scam involving more than $520,000 in bribes at NTUC FairPrice — for the supply of frozen fish by local companies. See *Channel News Asia* 6 May 2022.

[36] *Straits Times* 14 Oct 2010; *Today* 7 Aug 2013; https://www.mlaw.gov.sg/news/press-releases/singapore-land-authority-and-ministry-of-law-joint-press-release-on-fraud-case-in-singapore-land — 28 Sep 2010, 25 Nov 2012.

[37] *Business Times* 30 Aug 2013; *Straits Times* 11 Mar, 16 Apr, 10 Jun 2014; CPIB Press Release 2013: Case on NParks Brompton Bikes; *Today* 11 Jun 2014; *AsiaOne* 21 Nov 2014.

[38] CPIB Press Release 2012: Former CNB Chief Charged; CPIB Press Release 2012: Former SCDF Chief Charged; *Channel News Asia* 25 Jan 2012; *New Paper* 25 Jan 2012; *Tabla!* 27 Jan 2012.

[39] https://corruption.net/the-mystery-woman-involved-with-ex-scdf-cnb-chiefs/ – 27 Jan 2012.

[40] https://corruption.net/singapore-cpib-probe-into-scdf-and-cnb/ – 28 Jan 2012.

[41] *Straits Times* 6, 7 Jun 2012; *Today* 7 Jun 2012, 3rd ed; *Business Times* 7 Jun 2012.

[42] CPIB case files; https://corruption.net/singapore-ex-scdf-chiefs-trial-begins/; https://corruption.net/singapore-former-scdf-chief-faces-10-charges/; *Straits Times* 18 Mar 2013, 31 May 2013. https://corruption.net/singapore-peter-lims-trial/; https://www.cpib.gov.sg/cases/public_sex-contracts.

[43] *New Paper* 13 Jun 2012; *Straits Times* 25 Feb 2013; *Business Times* 13 Jun 2012; https://www.

cpib.gov.sg/press-room/press-releases/former-cnb-chief-charged; *Straits Times* 29 Jan 2014; *Yahoo! News* 14 Feb 2013.

[44] Edwin Yeo, who had been in the Bureau for 15 years, started to "steal" from the CPIB when he was in debt from gambling. Between 2008 and 2012, he lost $263,699 betting through Singapore Pools outlets, and within that time, from 2010 to 2011, he visited Singapore's two casinos 372 times, where he lost $478,583. At Marina Bays Sands alone, he lost $241,000. Accordingly, he used his position in the Bureau to misappropriate funds to cover his losses and debts. He was able to undertake a part of the heist by flouting government policy and instruction that a departmental bank account should have two signatories to authorise transactions. Yeo applied for the use of internet banking facilities which only "allowed online transactions to be carried out using a single internet banking token". Thus, from May to August 2012, with a free hand, he transferred $470,265 from the CPIB's account into his personal bank account. By this time, he had embezzled up to $1,760,000. The Bureau reported Yeo to the CAD in October 2012, a month after Yeo's illicit activities were first uncovered. Yeo was eventually jailed for 10 years for CBT as a public servant and for forgery. See *Today* 24 Jul 2013, 21 Feb 2014; *Straits Times* 21 Feb 2014. Six years earlier, another rogue CPIB officer, Chan Toh Kai, cheated a businessman of $7,000. Up to the time he was caught in 1997, Chan was considered to have been one of the Bureau's top investigators, winning commendations and promotions during his many years in the service. Yeo was a recipient of a commendation from the government as well. See *AsiaOne* 27 Jul 2013.

[45] *Straits Times* 24 Jul 2013.

[46] Stephanie Syptak-Ramnath, former Charge d' Affaires, US Embassy in Singapore, "Singapore's rule of law, zero tolerance for graft draws for foreign investors: US Diplomat", cited in *Business Times* 9 Aug 2019.

[47] *Today* 24 Jul 2013; *Straits Times* 21 Feb 2014; *Business Times* 25 Jul 2013.

[48] *Straits Times* 30 Sep 2013; *Today* 13 Aug 2013, 21 Feb 2014; *Business Times* 27 Jul, 13 Aug 2013.

[49] *Today* 17, 18 Jan 2014; *Straits Times* 8 Jul 2014.

[50] In 2002, the director of the Singapore History Museum was charged with two counts of corruption. He had taken two loans of $20,000 each from a vendor who was recommended to produce a 3D show for the Museum. He was jailed three months. *New Paper* 26 Oct 2002; *Straits Times* 13 Jul, 26 Oct 2002, 28 Mar 2003.

[51] *Today* 2, 3 Sep 2021; *Channel News Asia* 26 Aug 2021

[52] *Today* 2 Mar 2012, 2nd ed.

[53] https://corruption.net/singaporegood-leadership-is-key-to-containing-corruption-says-dpm-teo/.

[54] *AsiaOne* 24 July 2013.

[55] *Today* 14 Jan 2015.

[56] *Today* 5 Aug 2009, 4 Aug 2010 (Ministry of Manpower); *Straits Times* 18 Dec 2009 (police); *Straits Times* 8 Sep 2012 (Immigration and Checkpoints Authority).

[57] CPIB Annual Report 2010.

[58] CPIB Annual Report 2010.

[59] CPIB Annual Report 2011.

[60] CPIB Annual Report 2016.

[61] *Business Times* 14, 22 Jan 2015; *Straits Times* 14 Jan 2015; *New Paper* 14 Jan 2015; *Today* 16 Jan, 30 Mar 2015.

[62] *Straits Times* 23 Feb 2016; *Today* 14 Jan 2015; 23 Feb 2016, 24 Apr 2017.

[63] CPIB Annual Corruption Statistics 2021.

[64] Extracts from an interview with Mohamed Sa'at, Editor, *Berita Harian*.

[65] *Straits Times* 9 Dec 2017.

[66] *Straits Times* 19 Sep 2012.

[67] *New Paper* 4 Jul 2015; *Today* 12 May 2017.

[68] *Straits Times* 12 May 2017; *Today* 12 May 2017.

[69] *Today* 9 Jun 2017.

[70] *Today* 18 Jul 2017.

[71] CPIB case files; http://www.cpib.gov.sg/about-corruption/case-studies/public-sector/.

[72] *Today* 12 May 2017.

[73] *Straits Times* 30 Nov 2017.

[74] It is difficult to understand why such cases continue to occur when in this day and age, almost no one can hide their illicit activities forever, and when they are caught, the corrupt will certainly not be able to avoid the media spotlight. Yet, there are gung-ho characters who still engage in corrupt activities. Insights gleaned from an interview with Chua Chim Kang, Head and Chief Editor, News and Current Affairs Chinese, Mediacorp.

[75] *TNP* 5 Jun 2017; *Business Times* 12 Dec 2014, 11 Jun 2015, 14 Jan 2016; *Today* 12 Dec 2014; *Straits Times* 5 Jun 2017; https://maritime-executive.com/article/more-corruption-charges-for-st-marine-management.

[76] https://www.justice.gov/opa/press-release/file/1020711/download; *Straits Times* 24 Dec 2017. In a separate corruption case, a procurement officer of Keppel Shipyard, to which KOM had been affiliated, was charged with corruption that saw him taking $293,000 from various companies. He gave these companies business opportunities with the Shipyard. When the CPIB investigated, he was found to have assets worth $933,600 and $119,800 in his bank accounts. See *Today* 27 Sep 2017.

[77] *Today* 30 Jun 2017; *Straits Times* 30 Jun 2017; CPIB Press Release 2021: Custodial Sentence and Penalties for Committing Corruption Overseas.

[78] CPIB Annual Report, 2015. ECAN is the Economic Crimes Agency Network.

[79] CPIB Press Release 2017: CPIB and International Authorities Launched Multinational Centre in Fight Against Global Grand Corruption.

[80] CPIB Annual Report, 2020.

[81] CPIB Press Release 2021: Law Catches Up with Fugitive Who Spent Over 20 Years on the Run.

[82] *Straits Times* 6 Jun 2019; CPIB case files.

[83] https://www.kpk.go.id/en/news/press-releases/1687-international-cooperation-in-the-investigation-of-garuda-case.

[83] *Straits Times* 13 Aug 2013.

[84] *Today* 14 Jan 2015.

[85] www.cpib.gov.sg.

[86] Denis Tang, Director, Corrupt Practices Investigation Bureau, quoted in "Fighting Graft with Tech", *Business Times Weekend*, 1, 2 Feb 2020.

[87] CPIB case files.

[88] *Business Times* 1, 5 Feb 2020.

[89] *Business Times* 1, 5 Feb 2020.

[90] *Business Times* 1, 5 Feb 2020.

[91] CPIB Annual Report 2020.

[92] Extracts of an interview with Mohamed Sa'at, Editor, *Berita Harian*.

[93] "Why Singapore will not tolerate bribes of even 10 cents" in *Business Times*, 26 Apr 2019.

Afterword

Reflections from Our Youths

The CPIB has collaborated with a team of youths to research into the history of Singapore's and the Bureau's anti-corruption journey. They have added their thoughts and voices to Singapore's fight to purge corruption in our nation-building journey. They represent our future generations and future leaders. Their reflections provide a window into the perspectives of the youth of the nation; their hopes, aspirations, concerns and confidence going forward. Their commentaries about our past, our leadership and our future are of particular importance as they penned down their reflections. The CPIB Story would not be complete without them.

▶ Afterword

Singapore — If We Had Not Cleaned It Up
Tan Rui Min Tavis Hartanto
Yale-NUS College, Class of 2022

When considering this counterfactual, my initial response was that it seemed rather intuitive. After all, the Singapore I know and have lived to experience for the past 26 years of my life was one that had already been cleaned up. As a child, I was told to work hard and earn the right to be wherever I aimed to be. "You cannot buy people, not in Singapore," I would often hear, although never fully understanding how a person could be "bought" or "sold" per se. As I got older, I began to understand what "buying someone" meant, why it was a dangerous business, and most importantly, why "not in Singapore". It is almost inconceivable to conjure a Singapore laden with corruption today and if so, the most immediate and obvious conclusion one might come to is that we, as a country, would not be where we are today if it had not been cleaned up. After all, Singapore was built on a foundation free from corruption, and corrupt practices form deep crevices that must be filled or risk the foundation crumbling apart.

The idea of a corrupt Singapore feels so foreign. Even the word "corrupt" as an adjective to describe Singapore feels out of place and does not seem to roll off my tongue right. Yet, each time I stepped into the National Archives in London's beautiful Kew Gardens, I was confronted by hundreds if not thousands of documents dating back to the 1950s on Singapore. As I look back on the many hours spent in the National Archives, I realise I did not need to imagine a Singapore if we had not cleaned it up because the truth is, Singapore had not always been this clean.

The numerous files that laid open before me in Kew Gardens depicted a Singapore that would have been unrecognisable today. Imagine having to "tip" your postman daily to receive your mail or imagine buildings and construction sites passing inspections because the inspector was gifted a few bottles of whiskey. What this does to society is catastrophic. The social fabric that weaves us together begins to unravel when it lacks trust, and the seam that draws the boundary of what is acceptable comes apart when doubt and scepticism overshadow our daily interactions. How can we trust and rely on each other to build a nation when we cannot even trust our neighbours?

Corruption prides individualism over collectivism and undermines the social contract that we have with one another. At its core, corruption festers on greed, exploits desperation, and it often comes at the expense of others. Thus, to remain united as one people and one nation necessarily means that the systems and norms in place must guide outcomes that serve all equally and fairly. Otherwise, discord and disharmony will plague our society. Singapore had to be cleaned up, and so we did. Having studied Singapore's past, it is clear to me now that if we had not done so, society would have lacked trust in their government and each other. A fair and just system for governance would not have existed, the inequality gap would have widened, fissures would have deepened and Singapore would have become a dysfunctional society.

Moving forward, rather than contemplating what Singapore might look like if we had not cleaned it up, we should, instead, consider what Singapore might become if we allow corruption to creep back in. Singapore has come a long way since the 1950s, and I do not believe we will return to the state we were in pre-Independence. Even as new and innovative modes of corruption sprout now and then, they are nevertheless grounded in the same source of greed, individualism and, in some instances, desperation. Importantly, we must consider: for those with malicious intent, how do we continue to disincentivise and deter them from engaging in corrupt practices? And for those who feel like there is no other way, how can we ensure adequate support structures are available as an alternative?

The battle against corruption is a constant work in progress, but progress has, importantly, been made. If we allow corruption to fester and grow within our society today, we risk the progress we have painstakingly made over the past 70 years. To avoid this, it is crucial that we look out for one another, recognise the signs, offer our help to those in need and reserve our judgments. We are where we are today because we did it together, and we will chart our future in the same way — together. After all, our social fabric is only as strong and unyielding as we weave them to be.

▶ Afterword

How Far Have We Come?
Nur Hazeem Bin Abdul Nasser
Yale-NUS College, Class of 2022

In an age where trust between the government and its citizens is hard to come by, Singapore is an anomaly. In the 2021 Edelman Trust Barometer, Singapore ranked 5th where all institutions — government, media, non-government organisations (NGOs) and businesses — are seen as both competent and ethical. While citizens often debate on the direction of policies, very few can disagree that policies are implemented in a clean and professional manner. As Singapore celebrates her 57th birthday, her citizens enjoy a clean system of governance that adheres to the rule of law. Yet, this has never always been the case. Corruption today is a distant thought from many Singaporeans. A force that is amorphous and easily kept at bay by the system. However, the threat of corruption exists daily. It is an inimical and even intimate threat that directly relates to our own personal integrity. Corruption happens when professional and personal boundaries blur and the interests of self is prioritised over country and duty. Singapore is not immune to the sway of corruption, and our past reveals that.

Even in our early 1800s, corruption amongst public service officials was rife. Corruption was convenient because personal interests of officials could readily be satisfied with bribes to ensure crimes and vices continued. While it may be easy to say that strong legislation would deter corruption by increasing the cost to satisficing personal interests, post-Occupation Singapore illustrates that socio-economic conditions have to be stable for the integrity of our institutions to be upheld. Corruption was not just made convenient but helped some survive due to the poor socio-economic conditions caused by the Occupation. Wealth in the vice sectors helped keep some livelihoods afloat, which allowed vices to persist. While the upholding of integrity is always ideal, it must not be forgotten that external circumstances can force individuals into a bad hand. The loss of livelihood is an inimical threat that forces individuals into ethical quandaries.

Singapore has come a long way since the days of rampant poverty, soaring unemployment and disreputable institutions. The emphasis on securing good jobs for Singaporeans and keeping the economy afloat has safeguarded the livelihoods of many. Importantly, the strong stance against corruption has ensured trust in our institutions. This was made possible by clamping down on corruption in all segments of society. The investigations into former PAP Minister Tan Kia Gan, Minister of State for Environment Wee Toon Boon and Minister for National Development Teh Cheang Wan illustrate the unabashed need to crack down on corruption even if they are high-ranking officials. No matter how long ago the crime was committed, justice will be served. This was illustrated in the case of Phey Yew Kok who was charged in 1979 and would serve his time in 2015 after being on the run for 35 years. Even regardless of the amount, the conviction of a truck driver in 2018 for accepting $1 bribes reminds us of the scrupulousness of our system. The thoroughness of our institutions in clamping down corruption, namely the investigative work of the CPIB and legal prosecution of our Courts, has established a firm stance against the disregard of professional duties for personal satisfaction.

Ultimately, the implementation of strong anti-corruption policies could only be made possible if there was a collective will against corruption. Institutions can only go so far in clamping down corruption. Yet when the rest of the population collectively believes that a clean system is an ideal we want to achieve, a culture of honest work and trustworthiness can be fostered. The landscape for corrupt threats will be increasingly more complex. With emerging threats in cyberspace and numerous cross-border partnerships, the fight against corruption will be tougher. The fight is one that is not just a battleground for institutions but for all Singaporeans to keep a lookout for corrupt practices and nip corruption in the bud. As seen through our history, accountability and steadfastness in duty have to remain core tenets of being a Singaporean. The future is uncertain, but the values that we hold will remain constant. Singapore has done it before, and we can do it again.

▶ Afterword

What Would Be Necessary to Safeguard What We Have Achieved?
Tee Ming En Joshua
Yale-NUS College, Class of 2022

Over the past 70 years, the CPIB has been a pivotal player in Singapore's transformation from a den of unchecked, rampant corruption into a conglomeration of trustworthy modern institutions. There are many reasons — some might say, principles — attributable to the CPIB's success. These include its effective advocacy and implementation of regulatory safeguards, its sweeping investigative powers, its advancement of widespread public consciousness on the perils of corruption, and its willingness to adapt and evolve to changing circumstances. As we look back at 70 years of fighting corruption, I suspect that many of the policies that would continue the CPIB's legacy will draw from the same fundamental principles.

As an institution, the CPIB will need to maintain its independence and separation from the larger police force in Singapore to replicate its success. Many of the corruption cases that occurred in the 1950s and 1960s involved policemen who accepted bribes and negotiated with secret societies. The Anti-Corruption Branch (the predecessor of the CPIB) was intrinsically tied to the police force, which compromised its ability to objectively investigate corruption cases involving policemen. In the present day, the frequency of police corruption is low and the CPIB reports directly to the Prime Minister. These are good and necessary developments, but we cannot rest on our laurels. The CPIB must continuously strive to protect its integrity and maintain its independence. The Government must continue to uphold the CPIB's independence as sacrosanct, and Singapore's security forces must be open to, and even encouraging of, investigations concerning internal individuals suspected of corruption.

At the same time, the CPIB must continue to visualise its operations as part of a greater ecosystem of symbiotic institutions. Independence is important, but it does not mean isolation. To that extent, the CPIB can tap into the investments and efforts of different entities in order to empower its own activities. Firstly, it can enhance its connections with the different sectors that power Singapore's economy. Corruption takes many forms, many of them exclusive to specific industries. Constant dialogue with industry experts and an intimate awareness of an industry's operating protocols could go a long way towards combating corruption in an economy that is steadily diversifying and specialising, and could supplement advocacy efforts to educate about corruption regulations. Extensive research about the nature of corruption is also indispensable, and the CPIB's in-house researchers should continue to collaborate with academics and consultancies, whose data and experience might prove invaluable. The recent Singapore Standard ISO 37001 Anti-Bribery Management Systems is proof that such collaboration can be extremely productive. Instilling the importance of corruption in youth is also vital for the future. The CPIB has, of late, ramped up its outreach efforts towards students, with the Corruption Reporting & Heritage Centre at Whitley Road being open to school excursions. A healthy presence of anti-corruption sentiment in Singapore's social studies curriculum could reward Singapore with future vigilant citizens. Finally, international cooperation with other anti-corruption agencies can be bolstered. The CPIB is already a role model in the global anti-corruption sphere for its practices and success rate — Hong Kong famously modelled their own Independent Commission Against Corruption after the CPIB. Comparing notes with the CPIB's international counterparts could reveal novel anti-corruption strategies in an ever-changing economic landscape, and could also facilitate extraditions and investigations.

Of course, the CPIB must keep abreast of recent technological and economic developments to evaluate their utility in the fight against corruption. And many new ideas and systems do have the potential to destabilise the CPIB's capacity to counteract corruption. The advent of cryptocurrencies is one of them. Cryptocurrencies like Bitcoin and Ethereum, which utilise decentralised ledgers to denote ownership status, might prove difficult to trace to suspects of corruption through conventional methods. More research must be conducted to evaluate new mechanisms to minimise the risk that these new technologies pose to the CPIB's operations, and new legislation potentially conjured. The CPIB has always been nimble in promoting legislation that supports its needs, such as the Prevention of Corruption Act and the Corruption, Drug Trafficking and Other Serious Crimes (Confiscation of Benefits) Act. In this front, the CPIB must continue to be reactive and proactive.

The CPIB's operational policies have proven themselves to be remarkably effective over the past 70 years. The next few decades should not see grand revisions of these policies, but subtle changes and incremental revisions, as the CPIB's legacy puts it in good stead for the foreseeable future.

Good Singaporeans in Our Journey to Build a Corruption-Free Nation

Frances Pek Sze Hwee
Yale-NUS College, Class of 2022

The threat of corruption is ever-present. It is only through the effort of good Singaporeans that Singapore has one of the lowest levels of corruption in the world. The ongoing endeavour can be attributed to exemplary leadership that embodies a consistent stance against threats of corruption, tireless investigative work of the agencies involved and the combined effort of everyday people to curtail corruption.

Exemplary leadership is necessary to foster citizens' trust in their institutions and ensure incorruptibility. Many Singaporeans will attribute the tough stance against corruption to Singapore's founding father Prime Minister Lee Kuan Yew. In 1960, a CIA agent was discovered trying to pay for information on Singapore. This discovery led to an attempted cover-up with a US$3.3 million bribe to PM Lee. However, PM Lee resolutely rejected the bribe and when the US Ambassador to Malaysia and the State Department denied the incident, he threw a stern warning with formal evidence of the incident along with his famous words — "You do not buy and sell this Government." His iconic rejection of the CIA bribery reflected the steadfastness to deter and curtail any opportunity for corruption. Importantly, the incident sent a clear message to Singaporeans and the world that corruption was not tolerated even at the highest levels of office in Singapore. This tough stance towards corruption was further illustrated in the high-level proceedings of other senior level officials convicted of corruption charges. Yet, it is not sufficient for leaders to model the way. Investigators and prosecutors who administer justice and uncover the complex web of corruption trails have been critical in keeping the system clean.

Investigative work, especially into corrupt practices, is and will always be a messy matter. As I flipped through hundreds and hundreds of pages of case reports, statements and transcripts, I have gained a growing admiration for the tireless work that investigators push through. The thoroughness of

▶ Afterword

interviews and scrupulousness of accounting for every cent involved in corrupt transactions can only be credited to the dedication put into the work. Yet, investigation is not where the work ends. The prosecution has to read through these files and provide a case. With hours-long discussions and hearings, much effort is required to ensure justice is served.

The involvement of the community is also necessary to ensure that corruption is kept at bay. The efforts of everyday people are required to ensure that corruption never takes root in Singapore. For example, in 2013, Mr Abdul Wahab Bin Abdul Alim, a senior technician, was approached with bribes amounting to $300 to extend replaced cables without prior approval. Keeping to his principles, Mr Abdul Wahab rejected the bribes and reported the matter. It is these instances of exemplary integrity amongst citizens that ultimately drive the effort against corruption in Singapore. While senior leadership may set a steadfast example and investigative officers constantly work to keep corruption at bay, it is the efforts of individual citizens, of good Singaporeans, which ensure that Singapore remains clean and trustworthy. The collective integrity of a nation stems from individual efforts to be honest with ourselves.

Reflections from Our Youths ◀

A commemorative artwork "Garden With No Corruption" by local artist 阿果 (Ah Guo) depicting CPIB persona Kopi Lim and his colleagues stamping out corruption amidst a backdrop of generations of Singaporeans planting trees for a bright future. Also embedded in this artwork is the CPIB 70th Anniversary Logo which commemorates the milestone and embodies many more years of resolutely fighting corruption with the community.
Source: CPIB Archives.